T0342063

THE CENTRAL ASIAN ECONOMIES
IN THE TWENTY-FIRST CENTURY

The Central Asian Economies in the Twenty-First Century

Paving a New Silk Road

Richard Pomfret

PRINCETON UNIVERSITY PRESS
PRINCETON AND OXFORD

Published by Princeton University Press
41 William Street, Princeton, New Jersey 08540
6 Oxford Street, Woodstock, Oxfordshire OX20 1TR

press.princeton.edu

LCCN 2018938275
ISBN 978-0-691-18221-6

British Library Cataloging-in-Publication Data is available

Editorial: Hannah Paul
Production Editorial: Sara Lerner
Jacket Design: Layla MacRory
Jacket Credit: Turkmenistani president Berdimuhamedov and Kazakh president Nazarbayev
tighten the final bolts on the Turkmenistan-Kazakhstan rail link, May 2013 / *Railway Gazette*
Production: Jacquie Poirier
Publicity: Tayler Lord
Copyeditor: Brittany Micka-Foos

This book has been composed in Adobe Text Pro

Printed on acid-free paper. ∞

Printed in the United States of America

10 9 8 7 6 5 4 3 2 1

CONTENTS

PART I. THE BACKGROUND

PART II. THE NATIONAL ECONOMIES

IMAGES AND TABLES

Maps

Figures

Tables

PREFACE

The five Central Asian countries became independent with the dissolution of the Soviet Union on December 25, 1991, but remain little known outside the region. Initially, many questioned the ability of the countries, which had no previous history as nation states, to survive. A quarter century later there was no obvious threat to their survival as independent nation states—a much better record than that of the new independent states created in Eastern Europe in 1919. A less positive comparison is with the East Asian states that emerged from the Chinese revolution and the Korean War; twenty-five years later Taiwan and South Korea were flourishing newly industrialized economies.

This book analyzes the Central Asian countries' economic situation twenty-five years after independence and complements my earlier books written in the aftermath of independence (Pomfret, 1995) and after the transition from central planning had been essentially completed (Pomfret, 2006). The first book, written in 1993–94, analyzed the historical background of Soviet Central Asia, economic conditions at the time of the dissolution of the Union of Soviet Socialist Republics (USSR), and the creation of national economies in 1992–93. The second book analyzed the economic experience of the five Central Asian countries during the transition from central planning, emphasizing the diversity of policies and of types of market economy created in the five countries, and relating these national variations to economic performance and prospects.

In this book, the focus is on the twenty-first century. Two enduring questions of interest concern the types of economic systems adopted in the new independent states and their consequences, and the challenges of development for resource-rich countries. The five Central Asian countries offer a striking natural experiment on the first issue because the five countries, from similar initial conditions, adopted a wide range of strategies for the transition from central planning to more market-based economic systems. The transition was essentially complete by 1999, but identification of the longer-term and more important consequences of those decisions was overshadowed by the supercycle of world prices for key energy and mineral resources exported by some of the Central Asian countries.

The Central Asian countries are often considered as a group because of their shared geography, culture, and pre-1991 history. However, in the transition from central planning they followed very different paths. The 1999–2008 resource boom also created sharp cleavages, as the energy exporters (Kazakhstan and Turkmenistan) enjoyed huge increases in export revenues, while the poorer countries (Tajikistan and the Kyrgyz Republic) experienced massive labor emigration and became increasingly remittance-dependent. The years 2008–14 were a period of stasis, before the collapse of energy prices in 2014–16 signaled the unsustainability of the current situation. The book ends as the national governments contemplated responses to this challenge.

Amidst the dramatic economic changes, the political regimes, apart from in the Kyrgyz Republic, changed little over a quarter of a century. In all five countries, Soviet-era politicians established super-presidential regimes, seamlessly in four countries and after a bloody civil war in Tajikistan. The death of Turkmenistan's idiosyncratic first president in 2006 was followed by a smooth transition to a similarly all-powerful president. In the Kyrgyz Republic, presidents were overthrown after popular revolts in 2005 and 2010, and a parliamentary regime established. In Kazakhstan and Uzbekistan, the Soviet first secretaries continued to rule as national presidents. As this book was being written, the political landscape was changing; the death of Uzbekistan's first president in September 2016 signaled a potential generational shift in leadership and the October 2017 election in Kyrgyzstan was the first occasion on which an elected president was peacefully replaced by an elected successor.

The twenty-first century has witnessed major changes in the international context as the USA has come and gone from Afghanistan and closed its base in the Kyrgyz Republic, and as Chinese influence in Central Asia has grown. Fueled by the oil boom, Russia regained some lost influence; Russia has established the Eurasian Economic Union as a functioning customs union with Belarus and Kazakhstan since 2010, and with Armenia and the Kyrgyz Republic since 2015. However, events in Ukraine in 2014–15 raised concerns, especially in Kazakhstan, about Russian intentions towards regions with large Russian populations. The future uncertainty was highlighted in 2014–16 by the collapse of world oil prices, and associated drop in remittances from Central Asians working in Russia.

Long-term trends since independence include dramatic reductions in poverty in the twenty-first century, following sharply increasing poverty in the transition decade. Material living standards have increased, especially in Kazakhstan and more moderately in Uzbekistan, the Kyrgyz Republic, and Tajikistan. A key question after 2014–16 is how to maintain economic progress by becoming less dependent on a small number of primary product exports. The likely answer will be to integrate into the wider regional and global economy, but the extent to which this will be successful and how many Central Asian countries will join the process remain to be seen.

A window of opportunity for international integration may be opening in the late 2010s. China's One Belt One Road initiative, announced by President Xi Jinping during a visit to Central Asia and supported with funding from the Asian Infrastructure Investment Bank, promises to turn Central Asia from a landlocked to a land-linked region. The feasibility of Eurasian overland links has been demonstrated by commercial initiatives to provide rail services, especially since 2011, and regular daily service between Chongqing and Duisburg, weekly services on other EU-China routes, and many ad hoc services were in operation by 2018. The much-predicted new Silk Road is on the cusp of becoming a reality.

———

The five countries have, by geography, history, and culture, a shared heritage and are part of a common region. Part 1 emphasizes the heritage and especially the challenges all five countries faced upon becoming independent. Chapter 2 analyzes the transition from central planning, and chapter 3 the implications of resource abundance. The brief treatment of background conditions reflects their having been dealt with in my earlier books (and by others), and does not imply that they are unimportant; the Central Asian economies in the twenty-first century cannot be understood without knowledge of recent history and resource endowments. The natural resource base has changed little since independence, but assessment of the role of natural resources has changed with the resource boom (and possible bust) and its dramatic impact on labor migration and remittance flows.

The market-based economies established during the 1990s varied greatly, to the extent that each national economy must now be treated separately. The five countries' economies had become clearly differentiated by the turn of the century. Although legacies of the Soviet era remain strong, not least in the attitudes of many senior policymakers, the countries are transcending this heritage. The five chapters of part 2 examine each of the national economies in turn.

Geography and resource endowments matter not just for domestic development, but also because the Central Asian countries lie at the heart of the Eurasian landmass. For the new independent nations, the global economy (and their role in it) assumed an importance that was absent in the Soviet era, although at least until 2006 there was a process of regional economic disintegration. In the twenty-first century, the Central Asian economies face a choice between being landlocked and isolated or land-linked to emerging-economy neighbors and a vital link between the Far East and Far West of Eurasia. The five countries also have shared problems, notably involving water resources and perhaps security threats. Part 3 analyzes common and individual responses to the shared challenges.

———

The political, economic, and social changes in Central Asia during the period covered by this book were associated with a greater role for the national languages and many name changes. My general rule is to use forms familiar to English speakers (e.g., Bukhara, Samarkand, Tashkent, Kashgar), to avoid unnecessary use of local terms, and where there have been substantive changes to use the name in force at the time of the reference. The main internal divisions are referred to as *oblasts*, because Soviet administrative units are largely unchanged within countries and the Russian term remains understood even though it has been replaced by differing national terms.

The availability and reliability of data continue to improve, but unevenly, with data on the Kyrgyz Republic and Kazakhstan generally most plentiful and transparent. Independent research is also more abundant on these two countries, to a lesser extent on Tajikistan and Uzbekistan, and least of all on Turkmenistan. Nevertheless, important topics such as the narcotics trade or corruption can only be addressed with imperfect information.[1]

I continue to be grateful to the international agencies that have supported my Central Asian travel (the ADB, OECD, World Bank, UNDP, and UN-ESCAP). Although the Kyrgyz Republic since 2012 and Kazakhstan since 2014 no longer require visas for holders of many passports, including mine, such institutional support remains valuable. Without implicating them in the analysis or conclusions, thanks are also due to Central Asian academics, especially Roman Mogilevskii and Kanat Tikeleyev in the Kyrgyz Republic, Nozilakhon Mukhamedova in Uzbekistan, and Shigeo Katsu, Aktoty Aitzhanova, and Anara Makatova in Kazakhstan. As a Fellow of the Centre for Euro-Asian Studies at the University of Reading, I have benefited from intellectual support from the Centre's director Yelena Kalyuzhnova. Like its predecessors, this book has mainly been written at the University of Adelaide, and I appreciate the university's ongoing commitment to research. Since 2011, I have taught a course on the "Economies of Central Asia" at the SAIS Europe campus of the Johns Hopkins University, where I received stimulating comments from students and cheerful support from Gail Martin, John Williams, and Barbara Wiza (as well as the director, Mike Plummer).

1. The March 2015 issue of *Central Asian Survey* examines some of the issues with assessments of the extent of money laundering by "kleptocratic" regimes, a topic developed in greater depth by Cooley (2017).

ABBREVIATIONS

ADB Asian Development Bank

ADF Agricultural Development Fund (of Turkmenistan)

AFP Agriculture and Food Program (of Kazakhstan)

Agip KCO Agip Kazakhstan North Caspian Operating Company N.V.

AIDS acquired immune deficiency syndrome

AIIB Asian Infrastructure Investment Bank

AIOC Azerbaijan International Operating Company

APEC Asia-Pacific Economic Cooperation

ASYCUDA Automated System for Customs Data

ATC Agreement on Textiles and Clothing (from the WTO's Uruguay Round—to phase out the Multifiber Arrangement)

bcm billion cubic meters

BCP border crossing point

BEEPS Business Environment and Enterprise Survey (surveys conducted under the aegis of the EBRD)

BOMCA Border Management in Central Asia (program of the EU)

BOP balance of payments

BPD barrels per day

BRI Belt and Road Initiative (of China)

BTC Baku-Tbilsi-Ceyhan pipeline

CACO Central Asian Cooperation Organization

CADAP Central Asia Drug Action Programme (of the EU)

CAREC Central Asia Regional Economic Cooperation

CET common external tariff (of a customs union)

cif cost, insurance, freight—value of goods at the point of importation

CIS Commonwealth of Independent States

CMEA   Council for Mutual Economic Assistance (Comecon)

CNPC   China National Petroleum Corporation

COP21   21st Conference of the Parties to the United Nations Framework Convention on Climate Change, also known as the Paris Climate Conference, held from November 30 to December 12, 2015.

CPC   Caspian Pipeline Consortium

CPE   centrally planned economy

CPMM   Corridor Performance Measurement and Monitoring program (of CAREC)

CSTO   Collective Security Treaty Organization

DB   Doing Business (World Bank indicators)

DCFTA   Deep and Comprehensive Free Trade Area (with the EU)

EAEU   Eurasian Economic Union

EaP   Eastern Partnership program of the EU

EBRD   European Bank for Reconstruction and Development

ECE   United Nations Economic Commission for Europe

ECO   Economic Cooperation Organization

EITI   Extractive Industries Transparency Initiative

ES   (World Bank) Enterprise Surveys

ESCAP   United Nations Economic and Social Commission for Asia and the Pacific

EU   European Union

EurAsEc   The Eurasian Economic Community

FCC   Food Contract Corporation (of Kazakhstan)

FDI   foreign direct investment

fob   free on board (value of goods at the point of export)

GBAO   Gorno-Badakhshan autonomous oblast (eastern Tajikistan)

GDN   Global Development Network

GDP   gross domestic product

GNE   gross national expenditure

GNP   gross national product

GUAM   Georgia, Ukraine, Azerbaijan, and Moldova

GUUAM   GUAM during Uzbekistan's participation (1999–2002)

GVC   global value chain

GwH gigawatt hours

HBS Household Budget Survey (as inherited from the USSR)

HIV human immunodeficiency virus

ICG International Crisis Group

ICOR incremental capital-output ratio

ICT information and communication technology

ICWC Interstate Commission for Water Coordination

IFAS Interstate Fund for Saving the Aral Sea

IMF International Monetary Fund

IMU Islamic Movement of Uzbekistan

INOGATE **IN**terstate **O**il and **GA**s Transportation to Europe (EU program)

IPO initial public offering

IRP Islamic Renaissance Party (of Tajikistan)

ISI import-substituting industrialization

JETRO Japan External Trade Organization (government-related trade and investment promotion agency)

JICA Japan International Cooperation Agency (ODA)

KMG KazMunaiGas

KwH kilowatt hour

LNG liquefied natural gas

LSMS Living Standards Measurement Study

mbd million barrels per day

MW megawatt = one million (106) watts

NATO North Atlantic Treaty Organization

NDN Northern Distribution Network

NFRK National Fund of the Republic of Kazakhstan (SWF)

OBOR One Belt One Road (renamed the Belt and Road Initiative in 2017)

ODA official development assistance

OECD Organization for Economic Co-operation and Development

OKIOC Offshore Kazakhstan International Operating Co. (in 2001 renamed Agip KCO)

PPP purchasing power parity

PSA production sharing agreement

RRS Regions of Republican Subordination (central oblast in Tajikistan)

SCO Shanghai Cooperation Organization

SDGs Sustainable Development Goals

SME small and medium-sized enterprise

SOCAR State Oil Company of Azerbaijan Republic

SOFAZ State Oil Fund of Azerbaijan (SWF)

SPECA Special Programme for the Economies of Central Asia

SPS sanitary and phytosanitary measures

SWF sovereign wealth fund

TACIS (EU program of) Technical Assistance to the Commonwealth of Independent States

TAPI Turkmenistan-Afghanistan-Pakistan-India

TBT technical barriers to trade

tcm trillion cubic meters (natural gas)

TRACECA Transport Corridor Europe-Caucasus-Central Asia

UHVT ultra high voltage transmission (of electricity)

UNDP United Nations Development Programme

UNEP United Nations Environment Programme

UNHCR Office of the United Nations High Commission for Refugees

UNODC United Nations Office on Drugs and Crime

UNRCCA UN Regional Centre for Preventive Diplomacy in Central Asia

UPS United Power System of Central Asia

USSR Union of Soviet Socialist Republics

UTO United Tajik Opposition

VAT value-added tax

WCO World Customs Organization

WTO World Trade Organization

WUA water users association

$ all references to dollars are to US dollars

Since the end of the ruble zone the national currencies have been

Kazakhstan—tenge (since November 1993)

Kyrgyz Republic—som (since May 1993)

Tajikistan—Tajik ruble (May 1995—October 2000), somoni (since October 2000)

Turkmenistan—manat (November 1993—December 2008), new manat (since January 2009)

Uzbekistan—sum coupon (November 1993—June 1994), sum (since July 1994)

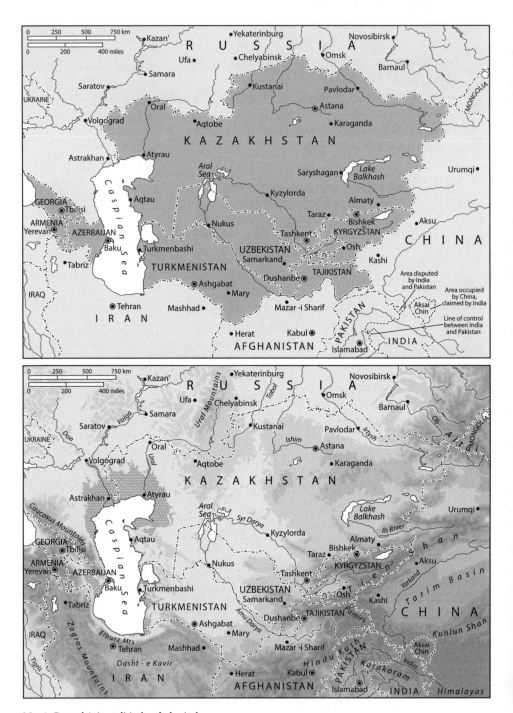

Map 1. Central Asia, political and physical

PART I

The Background

1

Introduction

RECONNECTING CENTRAL ASIA AS THE CROSSROADS OF EURASIA

For much of the last two millennia, Central Asia was a crossroads through which "silk roads" connected the major cities of Asia and Europe (Xian, Delhi, Baghdad, Damascus, Rome, Venice, etc.). At times between 900 and 1400, Merv (Mary), Bukhara, and Samarkand were among the world's largest cities and leading centers of learning. The empire of Tamerlaine (Emir Timur) covered much of Central and Western Asia around 1400, and it was from Central Asia in the 1500s that Babur established the Mughal Empire in South Asia. In the 1500s, however, Portuguese and Spanish sailors established new maritime routes between Europe and East Asia that supplanted overland routes. As the economic significance of Central Asia diminished, the region turned inwards and left the world stage.

The region continued to be divided between sedentary societies in the area defined by the two rivers that flow into the Aral Sea, the Amudarya and the Syrdarya, and nomadic people on the steppes to the north and the deserts to the west. Between 1688 and 1760, Russian influence gradually extended south, as various Kazakh groups sought protection against other nomads.[1] By the nineteenth century, the sedentary areas were ruled by the Emir of Bukhara and the Khans of Khiva and Kokand. In two decades starting in 1865, these territories and those of the Turkmen were brought into the Russian Empire.

---

1. Russian territory also expanded to include Siberia (1580–1640), the Caucasus (1785–1830), and the Far East (1850–65). Initial expeditions to conquer Central Asia failed, largely due to distance through inhospitable terrain.

The southern border of the Russian Empire was set in 1895, with Afghanistan as a buffer zone between the Russian and British Empires. Mountains to the east form a natural border with China, and the Kopet Dag range provides a less substantial natural border with Iran.

Russia administered the region as the province of Turkestan, ruled by a governor-general who reported directly to the tsar. In the half century after 1865, Central Asia was established as the major supplier of cotton to Russia's textile mills. The Russian government created some elements of a modern economy (notably railroads from the Caspian Sea to Tashkent and from Tashkent to Moscow), but investment in human capital was minimal as Asian and European populations were kept largely separate.

After the Bolshevik Revolution in 1917 and the ensuing civil war, Central Asia was incorporated into the Union of Soviet Socialist Republics (USSR). Central Asia became part of the centrally planned Soviet economy. Although the region was divided into five socialist republics that would become independent nations in 1991, the Soviet economy was planned as a single unit. After 1928, agriculture was collectivized, a process bitterly opposed and violently imposed in the pastoral regions. Little industrialization took place in Central Asia, apart from removal of factories in western USSR to Tashkent during the 1941–45 war with Germany. Central Asia's role in the Soviet economy was mainly as supplier of raw materials: the cotton sector expanded, and minerals and energy resources were developed. Major social development occurred, as basic needs were satisfied and education and healthcare became universally available.

In the 1920s and 1930s, the USSR was internationally isolated, forced to create "Socialism in One Country" rather than being in the anticipated vanguard of international communism. Even after 1945, Soviet allies and satellites in Eastern Europe were far away from Central Asia, and Asian countries that followed the Soviet model in the 1950s (the People's Republic of China, the Democratic People's Republic of Korea, and North Vietnam) were geographically disconnected from Central Asia after the Sino-Soviet split in 1960, when Central Asia's eastern border was sealed. In sum, both as part of the tsarist Russian Empire from the 1860s to 1917 and within the USSR from 1917 to 1991, Central Asia had minimal relations with outside countries.

The Soviet centrally planned economy was a coherent system that was difficult to change by piecemeal reform. Reform of central planning had begun in the late 1980s, but with little impact before the Soviet economic system began to unravel in 1991; the experiments with reform never took place in Central Asia.[2] The system was beginning to crumble in 1991 as some prices

---

2. Nove (1992) provides a concise economic history of the USSR. Ericson (1992) outlines the systemic nature of the Soviet planned economy, and its resilience in the face of partial reform.

were freed and inflation increased, but the real and sudden shock to the system occurred at the end of 1991 when Boris Yeltsin took Russia out of the USSR in December and freed virtually all prices in Russia at the start of 1992.

The five Central Asian countries became, somewhat unexpectedly, independent with the dissolution of the Soviet Union on December 25, 1991.[3] The Communist first secretary in each Soviet republic was transformed into president of a new country, whose status was quickly recognized as the five countries joined the United Nations in 1992. Nation-building and political consolidation of the leader's position were at the top of the agenda, but each country also had to establish a new economic system on the remnants of a centrally planned economy, with limited local capacity to replace central planning from Moscow.

1.1. Nation Building and Challenges of Transition from Central Planning

A striking feature of post-independence Central Asia has been the regional stability, reflected in the limited political evolution and the absence of interstate wars or secession. In 1992, there was considerable doubt about how long the five Central Asian countries would remain peacefully independent. In fact, there were no interstate wars in the region, and they have remained independent longer than the new states created after the dissolution of European empires in 1919.

In four of the countries, first secretaries appointed by Mikhail Gorbachev remained in power as presidents, and the national leaders retained much of the old political structure under new non-Communist names, even though they adopted diverse economic strategies.[4] The Kyrgyz Republic embraced

---

Pomfret (2002b) describes the collapse of central planning and the challenges of constructing a market economy. Åslund (2013) argues the benefits of rapid reform.

3. In 1990, the republics had made declarations of sovereignty, staking a claim over the resources on their territory. However, in the March 1991 referendum on the future of the Union, support for keeping the status quo was stronger in Central Asia than elsewhere in the USSR. When conservatives tried to oust Mikhail Gorbachev in August 1991, only the Kyrgyz republic's leader, Akayev, was quick to denounce the plotters; Kazakhstan's Nazarbayev more cautiously sided with Russian president Boris Yeltsin, while other Central Asian leaders welcomed the coup. After the coup's failure, the leaders made stronger declarations of independence on what are now public holidays: August 31 in Kyrgyzstan, September 1 in Uzbekistan, September 9 in Tajikistan, October 27 in Turkmenistan, and December 16 in Kazakhstan. However, the Soviet Union continued to exist until President Gorbachev resigned and the Soviet flag was lowered over the Kremlin for the final time on December 25.

4. Gleason (1997) and Luong (2002) analyze political development in the immediate post-independence period (1992–93). Roy (2000) reviews the post-independence political development, and Islamov (2001) and Gleason (2003) provide alternative accounts of the region's

advice from Western institutions and advocates of rapid change and, within limits, President Akayev fostered the emergence of the most liberal regime in the region.[5] Turkmenistan was the polar opposite; President Niyazov established a personality cult and minimized economic change. Kazakhstan in the early 1990s appeared to be accompanying the Kyrgyz Republic on a liberal path, but President Nazarbayev became more autocratic as the decade progressed and the economy became dominated by "oligarchs" who benefitted from privatization of state assets and controlled the media and the banks. Uzbekistan retained a tightly controlled political system, but without the personality cult of Turkmenistan; President Karimov's economic reforms were gradual and modest. Tajikistan was the only one of the five countries not to evolve peacefully from Soviet republic to independent state under unchanged leadership. The bloody civil war of 1992–97 dominated political developments and destroyed any vestiges of central planning; prices were freed, but without any serious and consistent economic strategy for establishing a market-based economy. By the end of the 1990s, President Rakhmonov had established a super-presidential political regime with many similarities to the rest of the region.

In all five countries, the political regimes were characterized by concentration of power in the executive branch that was in turn very personalized. Parliaments have been weak in all cases except the Kyrgyz Republic after 2010. Some writers (e.g., Cooley and Sharman, 2015) call the regimes kleptocracies rather than super-presidential, while Marat (2015) emphasizes that the twin motives of maintaining power and amassing wealth were often complementary.

During the 1990s, the Central Asian countries focused on nation-building and transition to market-based economies, the nature of which varied from country to country (Pomfret, 2006; Gleason, 2003). The new regimes had considerable discretion over the type of market-based economy to create, but also faced economic constraints.[6] Still using the ruble as a common currency, the Central Asian countries had no option other than to follow Russia's price liberalization, at least for tradable goods. With Russia and other newly inde-

---

economic development during the 1990s. Collins (2006) provides an insightful treatment of the wider political and social background, including analysis of the shift from strong support for continuation of the Union in the March 1991 Soviet referendum to independence before the year's end.

5. In May 1993, the country's official name was changed from the Republic of Kyrgyzstan to the Kyrgyz Republic. "Kyrgyzstan" continues to be widely used and the names will be used interchangeably in this book.

6. The blank page was comparable to the situation facing newly independent or modernizing governments in the late 1940s and 1950s, when leaders such as Nehru in India, Mao in China, Sukarno in Indonesia, Nasser in Egypt, and dozens of others in Asia and Africa created new national economic systems that would be difficult to change after flaws appeared in later decades.

pendent transit countries now charging for previously free transport services, many supply chains collapsed in 1992 and 1993.[7]

The five governments adopted diverse economic strategies, from the most reformist, Kyrgyzstan, to the least reformist, Turkmenistan's personalized autocracy. Given the shared geography, history, and cultural background of the five countries,[8] observers envisioned a natural experiment to test the efficacy of differing approaches to the transition from central planning and of the variety of market-based economic systems.[9] However, completion of the essentials of transition by the turn of the century coincided with the start of a super-cycle in world prices for resources, most importantly oil, that dominated economic performance in the early twenty-first century.

In 1992 cotton, energy products, and minerals dominated the Central Asian economy. The specific resource endowment varied among the new independent countries, as did the degree to which resources had been developed and the vintage of the inherited facilities. Being able to sell resources on world markets would yield benefits, but the actual impact depended on how easily resources could be transported to international markets and on world prices. All the governments faced the challenge of how to exploit their undeveloped natural resources, and whether and how to diversify the national economies beyond primary products.

Resource endowment was crucial for two main reasons. Firstly, it affected the choice of transition strategies. Cotton is easy to transport and in 1992–96 world prices were buoyant, so that revenues from cotton exports enabled the governments of Uzbekistan and Turkmenistan to postpone economic and political reforms. By contrast, the lack of any readily exportable resources contributed to Kyrgyzstan's decision to take the most radical reform path. Kazakhstan had abundant coal and minerals and potential oil wealth, but world energy prices stagnated after 1992; the government focused on signing agreements with foreign oil companies to explore for and to exploit oil and gas

7. Pomfret (1995) describes the economic background and the newly independent Central Asian countries' initial economic policies, which were dominated by reactions to the end of central planning and the collapse of the ruble zone in 1993.

8. Central Asia is a region defined by geography, history, and culture. The majority religion is Sunni Islam. In four countries, the national language is Turkic, while Tajik is related to Farsi (Persian); during the Soviet era, Russian was the common language throughout the region. Starr (2008) argues that the five countries are part of Greater Central Asia, and not a separate region. This is controversial, especially in Russia, which prefers to see Central Asia as part of a Eurasia that includes the non-Baltic former Soviet Union but not Afghanistan or other points south (Safranchuk, 2016).

9. There were, however, significant differences in administrative capacity. Uzbekistan inherited a better cadre of managers in Tashkent, the administrative capital of Soviet Central Asia, while Kazakhstan had a relatively large share of college graduates, so that the two large countries had greater potential for efficient economic management than the three smaller countries.

reserves—a process that distracted the government from early commitments to rapid reform and provided fertile ground for high-level corruption.

Secondly, although the transition from central planning was essentially completed by 1999, economic performance of the five countries over the next decade was dominated by their natural resource endowment rather than choice of transition strategy. As oil prices soared from under $20 a barrel to $140 before collapsing and partially recovering in 2008–9, Kazakhstan and Turkmenistan enjoyed energy-driven booms. Uzbekistan benefitted much less from the oil boom, while the Kyrgyz Republic and Tajikistan fell behind. The main impact on the last three countries was a rapid increase in labor migration to the booming Russian economy and the emergence of remittances as a dominant economic feature; by 2010 Tajikistan had the world's highest ratio of remittances to GDP and the Kyrgyz Republic had the third-highest ratio.

The early twenty-first century also saw changes in the external environment. Central Asian economic relations with China expanded rapidly in the first decade. In the second decade, the Russian-led Eurasian Economic Union became the first regional trading arrangement implemented in the former Soviet space, after two decades of regional disintegration. Starting in 2011 regular rail services were established between China and Europe via Central Asia, and in 2013 China announced its One Belt One Road project, which included strengthening the Eurasian landbridge with projects financed from the newly created Asian Infrastructure Investment Bank. China was also promoting the China-Pakistan Economic Corridor, which Central Asian countries could join via the Karakoram Highway to connect to South Asia without the risky passage through Afghanistan. In 2016, easing of Western sanctions indicated that Iran might finally be reintegrating into the global economy; the process was anticipated by India, which invested in facilities at Chabahar Port that was linked by sea with Mumbai and by rail through Iran to Turkmenistan and Uzbekistan or through the rail connection opened in December 2014 from Iran to Turkmenistan and Kazakhstan.

1.2. Outline of the Book

The next two chapters analyze the creation of a market economy and the impact of resource abundance from a region-wide perspective. Chapter 2 provides further background on the initial conditions and choice of development strategies, preliminary assessments of comparative economic performance, and a snapshot of social and economic conditions a decade after independence. The first decade was critical for the "transition" from central planning, because by the end of the decade the transition was essentially complete and "paths once taken are unlikely to be challenged and abandoned fast or frequently" (Wooden and Stefes, 2009, 249). Chapter 2 concludes with a statistical snapshot of the five economies in the twenty-first century. Chapter 3 analyzes the economic features of the region's key resource exports and the evolution of their world prices.

Part 2 describes the different national economies and analyzes the outcomes of the different transition strategies. Differences in the five countries' economic performance in the 1990s to some extent reflected policy choices, but after 2000 comparative performance became dominated by the global boom in oil prices. During the 1990s Kazakhstan's output performance was inferior to Uzbekistan's, but after the turn of the century Kazakhstan, as a significant oil producer with major new discoveries coming online, experienced an economic boom. For Turkmenistan, after 1999 the energy boom alleviated pressures to change poor economic policies. Both gradual-reforming Uzbekistan and rapid-reforming Kyrgyz Republic enjoyed less spectacular growth, and in the twenty-first century have clearly lower living standards than Kazakhstan. Tajikistan is even worse placed; the economy has recovered but slowly from a very deep trough, and Tajikistan now ranks among the world's poorest nations.

The Central Asian economies' in the twenty-first century do not operate in a vacuum. Chapter 9 analyzes alternative strategies, multilateral and regional, pursued by the Central Asian countries to integrate into a wider economic circle, emphasizing the shift from being part of the highly integrated Soviet economy to regional disintegration in the 1990s and early 2000s and then, after 2006, steps towards greater cooperation and integration. Chapter 10 examines bilateral relations with external economic powers and private foreign investors. Chapter 11 analyzes implications for Central Asia of new rail links between China and Europe, which foreshadow the region's return after half a millennium to being the central hub of Eurasia.

2

Creating Market-Based Economies

After December 1991, the new independent states had no alternative than to embark on the transition from central planning. Throughout Central Asia, the 1990s were a grim decade, with falling output and increased income inequality and poverty. The transitional recession was most moderate in Uzbekistan and most severe in Tajikistan, which suffered from civil war until 1997. Recovery began in the late 1990s, and in the first decade of the twenty-first century Central Asia was one of the fastest growing parts of the world economy, buoyed by a mixture of recovery from recession and soaring world prices for key energy and mineral exports. This chapter analyzes the first decade of independence and transition towards market-based economies, and it ends with a snapshot of the situation at the start of the twenty-first century.

2.1. Initial Conditions and Choice of Economic Policies

The Central Asian republics, together with Azerbaijan, were the poorest Soviet republics, with the largest proportion of households living below the poverty line. Over a third of individuals lived in households with a per capita expenditure inadequate for provisioning of basic needs (table 2.1). The World Bank estimated per capita output in 1990 between $1,130 and $1,690 for the four southernmost republics and $2,600 for the Kazakh republic. The relative values in table 2.1 are a reasonable guide to the ranking of Soviet republics by living standards, but the absolute dollar values must be treated with caution due to the insoluble problems of the Soviet Union's artificial relative prices.[1]

1. The World Bank estimates in table 2.1 place Kazakhstan's 1990 per capita GNP of $2,600 on a par with that of Hungary ($2,590) and somewhat lower than Iran's ($3,200), while the other four republics had per capita GNP comparable to that of Turkey ($1,370) or Thailand ($1,220);

TABLE 2.1. Initial Conditions: Republics of the USSR, 1989/90

	Population (million) mid-1990	Per capita GNP[a] (1990)	Gini coefficient (1989)	Poverty (% of population)[b] (1989)	Terms of trade[c]	Life expectancy (years)	Adult Literacy (percentage)
USSR	289.3	2870	0.289	11.1			
Kazakh	16.8	2600	0.289	15.5	+19	69	98
Kyrgyz	4.4	1570	0.287	32.9	+1	66	97
Tajik	5.3	1130	0.308	51.2	−7	69	97
Turkmen	3.7	1690	0.307	35.0	+50	66	98
Uzbek	20.5	1340	0.304	43.6	−3	69	99
Armenia	3.3	2380	0.259	14.3	−24	72	99
Azerbaijan	7.2	1640	0.328	33.6	−7	71	96
Georgia	5.5	2120	0.292	14.3	−21	73	95
Belarus	10.3	3110	0.238	3.3	−20	71	98
Moldova	4.4	2390	0.258	11.8	−38	69	99
Russia	148.3	3430	0.278	5.0	+79	69	99
Ukraine	51.9	2500	0.235	6.0	−18	70	99
Estonia	1.6	4170	0.299	1.9	−32	70	99
Latvia	2.7	3590	0.274	2.4	−24	69	99
Lithuania	3.7	3110	0.278	2.3	−31	71	98

Sources: Pomfret (2006, 4): columns 1–2, World Bank (1992, 3–4); columns 3–4, Atkinson and Micklewright (1992, table U13)—based on Goskomstat household survey data; column 5, Tarr (1994); columns 6–7, UNDP *Human Development Report 1992*.
Notes: (a) GNP per capita in US dollars computed by the World Bank's synthetic *Atlas* method; (b) poverty = individuals in households with gross per capita monthly income less than 75 rubles; (c) impact on terms of trade of moving to world prices, calculated at 105-sector level of aggregation using 1990 weights.

Inequality, as measured by Gini coefficients, did not differ much from the Soviet norm. However, the Central Asian republics had high social indicators (literacy, life expectancy) for their income levels.

The Central Asian republics' economic role in the USSR was as suppliers of primary products, mainly cotton, oil and natural gas, and minerals. The specific resource endowment varied from country to country. The Kazakh republic's higher living standards reflected a more diversified economy with grain exports and a variety of mineral and energy resources, and higher endowment of human capital (e.g., measured by the share of the population with university degrees). Central Asia was the most heavily rural part of the USSR, and Kazakhstan was the only Central Asian republic with over half of

figures for Iran, Hungary, Turkey, and Thailand from *1991 World Development Report*. Post-1991 experience suggested that the Central Asian republics were behind these comparators.

its population living in urban areas (Wegren, 1998, 164). The Uzbek republic's economy was dominated by cotton, as were neighboring parts of the other republics, although Tashkent was the largest and most industrialized metropolis in the region, and the fourth-largest city in the USSR. The Turkmen republic experienced a boom in natural gas production during the closing decade of the USSR. The mainly mountainous Kyrgyz and Tajik republics had fewer exploitable resources, and development of their hydroelectricity potential was hampered by opposition from downstream farms that relied on the water for irrigation.

With the dissolution of the Soviet Union, the new independent countries could sell their products on the world market, benefiting those countries whose goods had been undervalued by Soviet planners. Calculation of how much higher or lower the terms of trade of each Soviet republic would have been if they had traded their 1990 outputs at world prices rather than at the central planners' relative prices reveals the underpricing of energy and overpricing of manufactured goods in the Soviet economy (table 2.1). Kazakhstan and Turkmenistan (and Russia) as major exporters of oil and natural gas would have benefited substantially from replacing the artificial Soviet prices by world prices. The other Central Asian successor states would have gained sufficiently from improved prices for cotton and minerals and lower prices for manufactured goods to offset the higher price of energy imports. In practice, however, Uzbekistan benefited most quickly from the shift to world prices because it was able to reduce its dependence on imported fuel and because world cotton prices boomed during the first half of the 1990s, and cotton was relatively easy to export to new markets. Kazakhstan and Turkmenistan were unable to benefit immediately from access to the world market for their oil and gas exports because the dominant exit route was via the Russian pipeline network; moreover, world oil prices spent a decade below their 1990 peak.

As new independent states at the end of 1991, the Central Asian countries faced three major economic shocks: transition from central planning, dissolution of the Soviet Union, and hyperinflation. Dismantling the centrally planned economy created severe disorganization problems, which led to output decline everywhere in central and eastern Europe (Blanchard 1997). The dissolution of the Soviet Union added to these problems as supply links and demand sources were disrupted by new national borders. In Central Asia, the absence of any tradition of nationhood and the need to create new national institutions compounded the difficulties. Retaining the ruble as a common currency, in a vain attempt to maintain existing commercial links, fueled hyperinflation.

When Russia liberalized prices on January 2, 1992, the Central Asian countries had little option but to follow. With a common currency, attempts to maintain the old fixed prices while Russian prices increased rapidly would have led to a massive outflow of goods in return for paper rubles that were rapidly depreciating in value. Nevertheless, governments continued to regulate prices of necessities such as bread and of nontradables like urban transport fares. Already in this early decision, Kazakhstan and Kyrgyzstan showed greater willingness to free prices, while Uzbekistan and Turkmenistan retained more price controls.

In 1992 and 1993 all five countries experienced hyperinflation, with prices increasing by more than 50% per month, despite inflation being repressed by more extensive controlled prices in Uzbekistan and Turkmenistan. People continued to use cash due to its advantages over barter, but cash became increasingly inconvenient and hyperinflation obscured relative price signals, reducing the price system's efficiency as a resource-allocation mechanism. Hyperinflation also had immediate and large impacts on income distribution, as some speculators and traders benefited, while pensioners and others lost their life savings. In sum, although a common currency brings benefits from reduced transactions costs, these benefits were more than offset by costs arising from the inherent inflationary bias in the ruble zone (Pomfret, 2016).[2]

The currency became the dominant economic issue in 1993. Four of the countries introduced national currencies; the Kyrgyz Republic in May, and Turkmenistan, Kazakhstan, and Uzbekistan in November, while Tajikistan, torn by civil war, continued to use the Soviet ruble until May 1995.[3] A national currency was a prerequisite for gaining control over inflation and hence establishing a functioning market economy in which *relative* price changes could be observed and perform their allocative function. Although a national currency was a necessary condition for macroeconomic stability and effective economic reform, it was not a sufficient condition. Each of the five countries moved along a different reform path in the 1990s.

The Kyrgyz Republic was one of the most dynamic reformers among the former Soviet republics, and it received strong support from international

2. Although the Russian central bank controlled printing of banknotes, all fifteen successor states could issue ruble credits. The incentive was to create credits to pay for public spending because the issuer reaped all the benefits while the inflationary impact was spread across the whole ruble zone (Pomfret, 1996, 118–29). The IMF switched its position from support of the ruble zone to assisting creation of national currencies (Odling-Smee and Pastor, 2002; Pomfret, 2002c), although the switch was not smooth; the official IMF history talks of "something close to bureaucratic warfare over differing assessments of the viability of the ruble area" in mid-1992 (Boughton, 2012, 355). Russian reformers came to understand the free-rider problem, and in June 1993 issued new Russian banknotes and began pressuring other successor states to discontinue using the ruble (Åslund, 2013).

3. Tajikistan had de facto a separate currency after November 1993 because it was the only country still using the Soviet ruble, but the national authorities did not control the money supply. The Tajik ruble introduced in 1995 was replaced in 2000 by a more substantial national currency, the somoni.

institutions such as the International Monetary Fund (IMF) and World Bank. In July 1998, the Kyrgyz Republic became the first former Soviet republic to accede to the World Trade Organization (WTO). The Kyrgyz Republic became the first Central Asian country to curb hyperinflation, bringing the annual inflation rate below 50% in 1995. However, creating the institutions needed to support a functioning market economy was more arduous, and important markets (e.g., for labor, capital, and foreign exchange) did not function effectively in allocating resources. Manufacturing output fell substantially during the 1990s, and as unemployed urban workers returned to their family's village the share of agriculture in GDP increased. The only major growth pole was the Kumtor gold mine. These structural problems may reflect the initial backwardness of the economy, not just in income levels but also in human capital, which was exacerbated by substantial emigration.[4] The Kyrgyz reform impetus slowed after 1998 when the economy was hit by contagion from the Russian crisis and by a domestic banking crisis. Reforms were resumed in the twenty-first century.

Kazakhstan had a better base for creating a market economy, given its higher living standards and human capital endowments, and it too was initially viewed as one of the more reformist Soviet successor states. Kazakhstan moved quickly with price liberalization and enterprise reform, although macroeconomic control was attained more slowly than in the Kyrgyz Republic, with the annual inflation rate brought down below 50% in 1996. In the mid-1990s, however, the privatization process and policies towards energy and minerals rights were associated with widespread corruption and with a crony capitalism similar to that emerging in Russia in 1995–96.[5] Kazakhstan's economy remained closely tied to Russia's, and it was the hardest hit in Central Asia by the 1998 Russian crisis. However, following a large currency devaluation and, more importantly, upturn in world oil prices, Kazakhstan's economy grew rapidly after 1999.

Uzbekistan was often viewed as one of the least liberalized among economies in transition from central planning. To some extent, this reflected jaundiced views by the international financial institutions, with which Uzbekistan was on frosty terms, and a conflation of political and economic considerations. Although the political regime was authoritarian and illiberal, the economy was gradually reformed after independence. Macroeconomic control was achieved

---

4. After independence, both the Kyrgyz Republic and Kazakhstan experienced large net emigration, predominantly of ethnic Germans and Slavs, many of whom had above-average education and skill levels.

5. Two books on Kazakhstan by country specialists (Kalyuzhnova, 1998; Olcott, 2002, circulated earlier in draft) were both skeptical about the country's economic and political liberalization, in contrast to more upbeat assessments in earlier reports by international institutions and independent commentators (e.g., in the 1996 *World Development Report*).

more slowly than in the Kyrgyz Republic or Kazakhstan, with inflation only dropping below 50% in 1998. Price and enterprise reform proceeded slowly, but by 1996 practically all consumer prices had been liberalized and housing and small enterprises had been privatized. Cotton and wheat remained subject to state orders, and privatization of large and medium-sized enterprises proceeded at a glacial speed. Nevertheless, the government moved albeit cautiously to establish a market economy and provided good governance, at least by the low standards of the region, in managing infrastructure and maintaining social expenditures.[6] In 1998 the European Bank for Reconstruction and Development ranked Uzbekistan ahead of Kazakhstan in its annual index of cumulative progress towards establishing a market economy.[7] The government took a major step backwards in October 1996 when, in response to balance of payments problems following a decline in world cotton prices, draconian exchange controls were reintroduced. The consequence was a steadily widening gap between the official and the black-market exchange rate, leading to substantial resource misallocation. The negative effects of the exchange controls were slow to assert themselves, but they became gradually more onerous.

Turkmenistan was indisputably a slow reformer. The president established an extreme personality cult and adopted populist policies aimed at minimizing fundamental change. He promised the people a range of free utilities and other services, to be paid for by natural gas export revenues, although problems receiving payment for such exports undermined ability to maintain the promises. Several Commonwealth of Independent States (CIS) customers fell behind in payments for their gas and in 1997 Turkmenistan responded by cutting off deliveries with dramatic impact on GDP; deliveries were only resumed in 1999. National resources were frittered away on prestige projects such as a magnificent presidential palace and a new national airport, and a large debt was accumulated to fund import-substitution projects that were unlikely to ever generate (or save) foreign currency with which to repay the loans. Despite some promises of reform after the 1997 economic crisis, there was little

6. Corruption was pervasive in Uzbekistan, but appeared to be on a smaller scale than in other Central Asian countries—petty larceny rather than grand theft—and the government succeeded in creating a stable economic policy environment and providing physical infrastructure and law and order. The EBRD (*Transition Report 1999*), reporting the results of a survey of three thousand firms in twenty transition economies, found that almost half of the Uzbek firms bribed frequently (the third highest among the twenty countries), but when asked about the quality of governance under various headings Uzbekistan came out positively, ranking fourth behind Hungary, Slovenia, and Estonia, ahead of reform leaders like Poland and far ahead of Kazakhstan (fourteenth) and the Kyrgyz Republic (nineteenth); Tajikistan and Turkmenistan were not included in the survey, but would surely have ranked poorly on governance.

7. In *Transition Report 1998* (table 2.2.1), the unweighted average of the EBRD's eight indicators (on an ascending scale of 1–4) for the Central Asian countries was for Kazakhstan 2.1, the Kyrgyz Republic 2.9, Tajikistan 1.9, Turkmenistan 1.5, and Uzbekistan 2.3.

evidence of change, either economically or politically. Prices remained distorted, favoring import-substitution projects, especially in textiles and petrochemicals, and hurting farmers. After President Niyazov declared himself president for life, the EBRD took the unprecedented step of banning all public-sector loans to Turkmenistan, which underlined the increasing isolation of the country.

In Tajikistan, central planning was destroyed by civil war, rather than being reformed by a central government. A market economy emerged in the vacuum, but implementation of consistent economic policies was frustrated by the intermittent civil war. The economic disruption is captured in the huge decline in per capita output during the first half of the 1990s. Even after peace was negotiated in 1997, the political situation remained fragile, and the government's authority did not cover the entire national territory before the end of the century. The poor security situation discouraged investment, and lack of unified control also deterred economic activity because separate agencies sought to raise revenue by taxes and fees. The government was kept afloat in the early and mid-1990s by military loans from Russia, and after 1997 by aid from the multilateral financial institutions and from other donors. After 1997 legislation was liberal, but implementation poor.

The first decade after independence was important because the governments of the newly independent countries had a blank slate on which to write policies for establishing a market-based economy. The very different policies that they adopted will be described in greater detail in chapters 4–8. The Transition Indicators published annually by the EBRD provide summary measures of the extent to which countries have moved from a planned economy to a market-based economy (table 2.2). The indicators evaluate policies on a scale from 1 (no reform) to 4 (meeting standards of high-income market economies), with pluses and minuses represented by adding or subtracting 0.33.

The disaggregated transition indicators reflect that some reforms were easier than others. Small-scale privatization was easier than privatizing or restructuring large enterprises; in Central Asia land reform was especially contentious as commitments to privatization ran up against widely held beliefs that land was a common resource that should not be alienated. Price liberalization and related reforms of trade and foreign exchange systems were easier than creating efficient banks, nonbank financial intermediaries, or security markets. Legal reform and creation of regulatory systems requiring trained and experienced judges or regulators were most difficult of all.

By the overall EBRD Transition Index, which is a simple average of the nine disaggregated measures in table 2.2, at the end of the 1990s the five Central Asian countries were all among the bottom third of the twenty-seven countries covered by the EBRD. The Kyrgyz Republic and Kazakhstan, with scores just below 3, had made the most complete transition to a market econ-

TABLE 2.2. EBRD Transition Indicators, 1999 and 2009

		Large scale privatiza-tion	Small scale privatiza-tion	Enterprise restructur-ing	Price liberaliza-tion	Trade & forex system	Competition policy	Banking & interest rates	Securities markets & NBFIs	Overall infra-structure reform
Kazakhstan	1999	3.00	4.00	2.00	4.00	3.33	2.00	2.33	2.00	2.00
	2009	3.00	4.00	2.00	4.00	3.67	2.00	2.67	2.67	2.67
Kyrgyz Republic	1999	3.00	4.00	2.00	4.33	4.33	2.00	2.00	2.00	1.33
	2009	3.67	4.00	2.00	4.33	4.33	2.00	2.33	2.00	1.67
Tajikistan	1999	2.33	3.00	1.67	3.67	2.67	2.00	1.00	1.00	1.00
	2008	2.33	4.00	1.67	3.67	3.33	1.67	2.33	1.00	1.33
Turkmenistan	1999	1.67	2.00	1.67	2.67	1.00	1.00	1.00	1.00	1.00
	2009	1.00	2.33	1.00	2.67	2.00	1.00	1.00	1.00	1.00
Uzbekistan	1999	2.67	3.00	2.00	2.67	1.00	2.00	1.67	2.00	1.33
	2009	2.67	3.33	1.67	2.67	2.00	1.67	1.67	2.00	1.67

Source: European Bank for Reconstruction and Development, *Transition Report*, 2000 and 2010.

omy in Central Asia, while Tajikistan and Uzbekistan scored significantly lower with 2–2.5, and Turkmenistan was the least reformed of all twenty-seven transition economies with a score of less than 1.5.

In the first decade after independence, different forms of market-based economies were established in the five countries. After that, change became more difficult. The undemocratic governments may have seen little reason for further reform, but everywhere the systems created in the 1990s involved winners and losers, and the gainers would resist renewed change if that threatened to reduce their gains. In table 2.2, there is a substantial increase from what would have been universal scores of 1.00 in 1991 to the 1999 values, but little change over the next decade; in Turkmenistan and Uzbekistan there was even a slight retrogression on economic restructuring, as state-owned enterprises managed to push back some of the changes made in the 1990s.

2.2. Economic Performance in the Decade after Independence

All five Central Asian countries suffered a sharp drop in real output during the first half of the 1990s, whose impact on living standards was exacerbated by the cessation of intra-USSR transfers and by increased economic inequality. The initial decline in output is difficult to measure because of the problems of valuing Soviet-era output for which there was no demand after the end of central planning and because of quality changes and new products. Revaluation of energy products provided a boost to estimated GDP in Kazakhstan and Turkmenistan, which partly offset the decline in quantities. With these caveats in mind, we can relate changes in real GDP (table 2.3) to the initial conditions and policies described in the previous section.

Real GDP in the five countries followed different time paths. In Tajikistan, the disruption of civil war led to an exceptionally sharp fall in output in 1992, which continued until the 1996 ceasefire, when real output had fallen to two-fifths of its level at independence. Growth rates after 1997 reflected recovery from a low base, but by 1999 GDP was still less than half of its 1989 level.[8] The other countries' experience is more complex.

The Kyrgyz Republic saw real GDP decline by 45% between 1991 and 1995. This was due to the three shocks described in the previous section, whose impact was not softened by possession of readily tradable natural resources. The decision to adopt the most radical economic reforms in the region and

---

8. Growth rates may have been higher due to underestimation of GDP in the late 1990s, but they still represented only partial recovery from economic disaster. Amir and Berry (2013, annex 4.1) argue that there was substantial understatement of wages-in-kind, home production, and informal or illegal activities.

TABLE 2.3. Growth in Real GDP, 1989–99 (Percent)

	1989	1990	1991	1992	1993	1994	1995	1996	1997	1998	1999	1999; 1989 =100
Kazakhstan	0	0	−13	−3	−9	−13	−8	1	2	−2	2	63
Kyrgyz Republic	8	3	−5	−19	−16	−20	−5	7	10	2	4	63
Tajikistan	−3	−2	−7	−29	−11	−19	−13	−4	2	5	4	44
Turkmenistan	−7	2	−5	−5	−10	−17	−7	−7	−11	5	16	64
Uzbekistan	4	2	−1	−11	−2	−4	−1	2	3	4	4	94

Source: European Bank for Reconstruction and Development, *Transition Report Update*, April 2001, 15.
Note: Pomfret (2006, 107–22) discusses the conceptual problems associated with measuring GDP during the transition from central planning to a market-based economy.

the most rapid macroeconomic stabilization also exacerbated the severity of the post-independence recession. The theory of rapid reform, which has been to some extent vindicated by Polish experience, implies that after the pain the Kyrgyz Republic should have been best placed to grow. The Kyrgyz economy did indeed grow rapidly in 1996 and 1997, but much of the economic growth originated in one project, the Kumtor goldmine, which boosted real GDP during the investment stage in 1996–97 and added to real GDP after that. In 1998 economic growth was slower, due to the Russian economic crisis, domestic bank failures, and poor agricultural performance. The reform impetus slowed after 1998, when growth was anemic due to adverse weather conditions compared to those that abetted the bumper harvests of 1996 and 1997.

Kazakhstan's decline in real GDP in the first half of the 1990s was less than that of the Kyrgyz Republic, which may reflect the former's more abundant resources and perhaps its less radical reforms, but Kazakhstan did not enjoy the growth that the Kyrgyz Republic had in 1996–97. The Kazakhstan economy was buffeted by the Russian crisis in 1998, and real GDP was probably little different by the end of the century than it had been in 1995. The proximate causes of the disappointing medium-term performance by the potentially best-placed new independent state in Central Asia were exogenous developments such as commodity price trends, interminable delays in establishing new oil pipeline routes from the Caspian Basin to non-CIS markets, and the August 1998 Russian economic crisis. More fundamentally, the poor performance reflected a failure to truly reform the economy so that it could better weather such shocks, and central planning appeared to be being replaced by a rentier economy in which insiders lived off the resource rents rather than generating new output. There were, however, contra-indications, raising the question of whether President Nazarbayev was the biggest oligarch or the defender of the public interest against the ten megaholdings that controlled over four-fifths of the economy (a claim he made, for example, in the speech opening parliament on November 3, 2004). In 1997, the president articulated a *Kazakhstan 2030* strategy that foresaw a dynamic market-based economy. A positive feature in 1998–99 was that, despite widespread belief that Kazakhstan would default, the government continued to fulfill domestic and foreign debt service obligations Towards the end of 1999, the economic situation changed dramatically as world oil prices began to increase, and in 2000 a major new oil field was discovered.

Turkmenistan, which had abundant natural resources and enjoyed a decade of peace, had a similar outcome by 1999, albeit with a different time path. Turkmenistan's decline in real GDP was comparatively slow in 1992–93, accelerated in 1994–96, and went into collapse in 1997. Although growth accelerated in 1999 when gas exports were resumed and Turkmenistan benefited from rising energy prices in the early 2000s, there are questions about the reliability of Turkmenistan's economic data after the mid-1990s and it seems probable that, notwithstanding the high official growth rates, the economy still suffered from poor economic policies.[9]

Uzbekistan's economic performance posed the greatest puzzle among all former Soviet republics. The initial decline in real GDP was moderate, at least by the awful standards of the former Soviet Union in 1992–93. This could be ascribed to the avoidance of reform, but such stability proved short-lived in other nonreformers such as Belarus or Turkmenistan whose unreformed economies continued to stagnate or decline in the 1990s. Uzbekistan halted the decline in real GDP in the mid-1990s and even enjoyed modest economic growth during the second half of the decade. The relatively good performance between 1991 and 1996 was helped by buoyant world prices for Uzbekistan's two main exports, cotton and gold, although this appears to be only a partial explanation. Both commodities' prices fell substantially in the second half of the decade, but Uzbekistan's GDP grew steadily after 1995.

Two other macroeconomic aggregates (public budgets and international trade) shed further light on comparative performance. In the Soviet economy, planners accessed resources for infrastructure, social spending, and other public services directly from producers' turnover. With the end of central planning and lack of mechanism for levying income or sales taxes, the Central Asian countries suffered a drastic loss in public revenue, both absolutely and relative to the falling GDP. Uzbekistan and Turkmenistan could raise revenue relatively easily from cotton exports, and Kazakhstan to a lesser extent received

9. The reliability of data will be an issue throughout this book, but, apart from the war years in Tajikistan, the situation has clearly been worst in Turkmenistan. The figures quoted in this book are mostly from international institutions, and it is important to stress that, while these organizations adjust data for definitional consistency, the raw data come from national sources, and international organizations rarely correct undisclosed collection or reporting biases.

TABLE 2.4. Government Revenue (R) and Expenditure (E), as Percentage of GDP, 1995–2002

	1995		1996		1997		1998		1999		2000		2001		2002	
	R	E	R	E	R	E	R	E	R	E	R	E	R	E	R	E
Kazakhstan	22	26	17	20	17	19	18	25	18	22	22	22	22	22	22	21
Kyrgyz Republic	17	28	16	22	16	22	18	22	16	20	14	18	16	18	18	21
Tajikistan	10	17	12	18	15	19	11	14	12	15	12	13	14	13	18	na
Uzbekistan	30	33	34	36	30	32	31	33	29	31	28	29	26	28	26	28

Source: Pomfret (2006, 12), based on Asian Development Bank, *Key Indicators*, 2003.

Note: na = not available in the source. No data on Turkmenistan.

royalties on natural resources. By 1995, there was a big range between Tajikistan with public revenue at 10% of GDP and Uzbekistan with 30% in 1995 (table 2.4). An important issue for Tajikistan, the Kyrgyz Republic, and to a lesser extent Kazakhstan was to rebuild their tax-raising capacity in the late 1990s and early 2000s. Uzbekistan, by contrast, maintained public revenues and expenditures, which partly explains better aggregate performance over the 1990s.

For the two poorest countries, Tajikistan and the Kyrgyz Republic, government expenditures were not allowed to fall as far as public revenue. Faced with the dilemma of how to finance the budget deficit without inflation, the Kyrgyz Republic borrowed abroad to fund public spending. The consequence was a rapid build-up of external debt between 1992 and 1999, when the debt/GDP ratio passed 100% (Pomfret, 2006, 12).[10] Tajikistan ran smaller budget deficits and funded them with more inflationary finance than the Kyrgyz Republic, but it too had a debt/GDP ratio over 100% by 1999. The Kyrgyz Republic's borrowing was largely from international financial institutions such as the World Bank and IMF. Tajikistan's was mainly bilateral borrowing from Russia and, to a lesser extent, Uzbekistan for military purposes during the civil war.[11]

Before independence, the Central Asian countries had open economies with trade heavily concentrated within the USSR and to a lesser extent with Eastern Europe, but with no direct links to the global economy as all international trade went through the central trading offices in Moscow. In the 1990s a major redirection occurred as cotton and other primary products were increasingly sold on global markets. After the major shocks of the early 1990s, the Central Asian countries' trade recovered in 1994–97 and was gradually

10. The Central Asian countries' inherited external debt in 1992 was zero, because Russia assumed all external debts and assets of the Soviet Union.

11. In October 2004 President Putin agreed to write off $240 million of the $300 million owed to Russia in return for a permanent Russian base and control over Soviet-era antimissile facilities in Tajikistan.

TABLE 2.5. International Trade, 1993–2000 (Million US Dollars)

	1993	1994	1995	1996	1997	1998	1999	2000
EXPORTS								
Kazakhstan	1,107	3,227	5,256	5,926	6,497	5,511	5,598	9,876
Kyrgyz Republic	360	339	483	506	609	509	454	504
Tajikistan	350	492	749	772	803	597	689	770
Turkmenistan	561	1,163	1,881	1,693	751	594	1,187	2,505
Uzbekistan	693	1,991	2,718	2,620	2,896	2,310	1,963	2,132
IMPORTS								
Kazakhstan	1,704	3,285	3,807	4,247	4,302	4,373	3,686	5,048
Kyrgyz Republic	447	316	392	795	709	841	611	555
Tajikistan	532	545	810	668	750	711	663	671
Turkmenistan	586	904	1,364	1,313	1,228	1,007	1,476	1,788
Uzbekistan	918	2,455	3,030	4,854	4,538	2,931	2,481	2,067

Source: Pomfret (2006, 14), from IMF, *Direction of Trade Statistics*.

Note: Trade data for the 1990s must be treated with caution. In 1992 and 1993, when the region was using a common currency, trade within Central Asia and with important trading partners such as Russia and Ukraine was largely unmonitored. Even after the establishment of functioning national customs services, the coverage of official trade statistics remained far from complete; in Uzbekistan, gold output and exports were state secrets and, when restrictions were placed on retaining or accessing hard currency, exports were often under-invoiced and imports over-invoiced. Small-scale "shuttle" traders accounted for a large amount of imported consumer goods and other trade, but the recording of this trade was uneven; official estimates from Kazakhstan of shuttle trade accounting for a quarter of total imports in 1995, a third in 1996, and almost half in 1997 are based on heroic assumptions (Pomfret, 1999, 32n). Illegal trade was also important, with widespread smuggling and with much of the Afghanistan-originating drug trade passing through Central Asia.

redirected, with over half of trade outside the CIS by 1997. However, the ability to compete in international markets varied considerably; the growth in international trade during the 1990s was much less for the Kyrgyz Republic and Tajikistan than the other countries (table 2.5).

In both the Kyrgyz Republic and Tajikistan, trade per capita and total trade remained small in the 1990s. The relatively superior export performance of Kazakhstan and Uzbekistan was due in part to favorable energy and cotton prices, and their divergent experience after 1997 is partly explained by low world cotton prices between 1997 and 2001 and by booming oil prices after 1999. The value of Turkmenistan's exports in 1995–96 values is inflated by the inclusion of natural gas exports to CIS destinations that were not paid for (the invoice value was recorded as exports, while the accumulating payment arrears were recorded as foreign assets); recognizing that the bills would never be paid in full, Turkmenistan stopped supplying gas in March 1997. Turkmenistan's gas exports fell from about $1 billion in 1996 to $70 million in 1997 (Pomfret, 2001a, 158), coinciding with a poor cotton harvest and a fall in cotton exports from $332 million in 1996 to $84 million in 1997, after which export values (and GDP) collapsed until the gas flow was resumed in March 1999.

2.3. Distributional Consequences of Transition

In the transition from central planning to market-based economies, income inequality increased. Given the Central Asian countries' low initial incomes and declining average incomes during the first half of the 1990s, the outcome was high poverty rates. The data are less convincing than for real output, but in the most thorough attempt to assemble comparative data Milanovic (1998) found that in 1993–95 the Kyrgyz Republic had the highest poverty rate of any Eastern European or former Soviet economy.[12] Unemployment also increased although this too is difficult to measure due to the extensive informal sectors. More clear-cut was the decline in employment during the 1990s, especially in Kazakhstan, where the number employed fell from 6.5 million in 1990 to 4.3 million at the end of 1995, when registered unemployment was reported at 4% (Bauer et al., 1997, 3). Shifts in relative regional prosperity have also been best documented in Kazakhstan, where per capita income in Almaty jumped from 40% above the national average in 1994 to more than double the national average in 1998, while the share of national income in the coal-mining centers of Karaganda and Pavlodar fell sharply.[13] There was also a widely reported phenomenon of fifty to sixty "sick towns," mostly in Kazakhstan, which depended on a single large enterprise in the Soviet era.[14]

Average incomes fell and inequality increased throughout Central Asia during the 1990s. There were gainers as well as losers from the transition from Soviet central planning to more market-oriented national economies. Stories of profiteering and corruption were backed up by the presence of Mercedes and BMW cars on the streets of Almaty, Ashgabat, and other cities. Members of the old elite in the capital cities were the people best able to protect themselves against economic hardship and to benefit from new opportunities, while most employees of the state enterprises in heavy industries and of state farms lost their economic advantages.

Our best knowledge of the characteristics of gainers and losers during the 1990s comes from the Kyrgyz Republic, which has the best post-independence household survey data. Analysis of the 1993 household survey found that residence in the capital city and having tertiary education both significantly in-

12. The poverty rates given by Milanovic are difficult to compare across countries with different household surveys. Falkingham (1999) analyzes problems and pitfalls associated with Central Asian household survey data.

13. The petroleum-producing regions of Atyrau and Mangistau only increased their combined share of GDP from 9.0% to 9.5%, implying that although Kazakhstan's growth was fueled by the hydrocarbon sector the real beneficiaries were in the commercial capital rather than near the oil fields (Esentugelov, 2000, table 1). This pattern continued during the post-1999 oil boom.

14. Nurusheva (2017) provides a case study of Tekeli, which has been relatively successful in recovering from the shutdown in 1994 of the lead-zinc complex on which the Soviet town depended.

creased the probability of a household being above the poverty line, while nothing else had much of an effect. Given the very high poverty rate, this implies that a small group, presumably the old elite, had weathered the storm of the early 1990s better than anybody else.[15] More sophisticated analysis of the 1993 and 1996 surveys revealed more complex patterns of the determinants of household living standards, with large households suffering more than households without young children or pensioners. These results provide strong evidence of the decline in social protection offered by the state, especially the increased cost of raising children as benefits (such as kindergartens or school meals) previously provided by the state or the enterprise disappeared, and the erosion of the value of the generous Soviet-era pensions, although they still helped to protect pensioners in poor households. University graduates who were trained to think more broadly, even in the Soviet education system, were better able to respond to the extreme disequilibrium of the 1990s than narrowly trained specialists.[16] Many of these patterns appear to characterize the evolution of income distribution in the other Central Asian countries since independence (Anderson and Pomfret, 2003; Pomfret, 2006, 123–40).

Changes in the wealth distribution are likely to have been even more pronounced than changes in income distribution, although it is difficult to find data on wealth. Especially in Kazakhstan, privatization transferred valuable public assets to a small group, but everywhere there was a feeling that those in power could use their position to obtain rents that were transformed into cars and other consumer durables or invested abroad. Privatization of the housing stock with priority to current occupiers favored the old elite, which had the best housing and, especially in the capital cities, could benefit from a tiny market in good quality apartments to earn substantial rents from expatriates. For poor people, privatization of housing created new burdens on the household, which was now responsible for maintenance, and as provision of heating, hot water, and other utilities was gradually shifted to a user-pay system.[17]

15. Studies referred to in this paragraph are by Ackland and Falkingham (in Falkingham et al., 1997, 81–99) and by Anderson and Pomfret (2000). Multivariate analysis is desirable because variables such as ethnicity, location, education, and household size are connected. Simple cross-tabulations showing that, for example, Slav households fared better than Kyrgyz households may be confusing ethnicity with location, household size, or education because Slav households are more likely to be urban with a better-educated head and fewer children.

16. This is not to deny that within the broader university degree the subjects of specialization probably made a difference. People with training in English or computer skills were better able to find employment after the collapse of the planned economy.

17. Imputed income from subsidized housing played a major role in reducing inequality in the Soviet Union (Buckley and Gurenko, 1997). Many users of heating in Bishkek could not afford user fees set at any level, while outside the capital the underfunded heating system often failed, and this was associated with deteriorating health.

Social spending followed different national patterns. In the Kyrgyz Republic substantial foreign assistance enabled the government to maintain the share of public spending going to health and education, especially as donors encouraged investment in human capital, although the real amounts dropped with the decline in GDP.[18] In Kazakhstan, healthcare was one of the first casualties of independence, as the share of government spending going to health fell by about a third in 1992 and the percentage of GDP spent on health fell from 4% to 2% where it stayed in subsequent years (Brooks and Thant, 1998, 249). In Turkmenistan and Tajikistan social spending also declined as governments devoted public funds to pet projects in the one case and military spending in the other. Uzbekistan stands out as the exception where the government maintained domestically generated social spending (Pomfret and Anderson, 1997) and introduced innovative measures to target social assistance (Coudouel and Marnie, 1999), although there were growing complaints, especially after the educational reforms of the late 1990s, of falling standards.

The distributional effects of the national economic strategies adopted during the transition from central planning could be modified by individual responses and by social policy. The increased cost of children has been associated with a declining birth rate; in the Kyrgyz Republic, the crude birth rate was 32.0 per thousand population in 1985, 29.3 in 1990, and 27.5 in 1996. This will take decades to work its way through the workforce, and meanwhile the current generation of children will grow up with poorer education than their parents, and with a significant number of children outside family care.[19] Although emerging private health and education provision was in some respects more efficient than the old state monopoly, many people were excluded from these services by poverty.

The harsh economic conditions of the 1990s and unaccustomed inequalities left a lasting imprint.[20] After initial post-independence euphoria, suspicion of capitalism—and in some quarters nostalgia for the pre-1992 world of greater

18. There is also anecdotal evidence of regional disparities as the northern regions were treated better than the southern regions. Center for Preventive Action (1999, 180–81) quotes from a 1997 official report on Jalalabad oblast that "Since 1990, the education sector has had to cope with a severe cutback in financing. There have been virtually no allocations from the domestic budget for textbooks, school equipment or building maintenance. Teachers' salaries have fallen dramatically in real terms. Teacher morale and performance has been further undermined by the substantial delays in salary payments which are typically 2–4 months in arrears."

19. The increasing number of children outside the household system was a new phenomenon in post-independence Central Asia. Although orphanages existed in the USSR, they rarely catered to Central Asian children, who were taken care of within the extended family. The phenomenon of street children was not fully accepted, let alone accurately measured; one symptom was the increased number of children being held in detention centers on vagrancy charges (Bauer et al., 1998, 108).

20. This is not to deny the inequalities in the late-Soviet economy, but the Soviet elite was

economic certainties—grew and would remain a feature of the region in the twenty-first century despite rising living standards. Reduced and less equal human capital was a negative legacy of transition that will harm future growth prospects, and the emergence of an alienated under-class could challenge social stability. In the post-1999 oil boom, the latter feature was partly offset by the mass migration of the poorest young males from Tajikistan, Uzbekistan, and the Kyrgyz Republic to Russia, which created its own social problems.

2.4. The Situation in the Early 2000s

Table 2.6 provides a snapshot of social and economic conditions in the five Central Asian countries a decade after independence. The most striking feature is the much lower per capita output measured in current US dollars in all five countries, compared to the 1990 estimates reported in table 2.1. The energy-rich countries, Kazakhstan and Turkmenistan, just about remained middle-income countries, although Turkmenistan's data are unreliable. The Kyrgyz Republic, Uzbekistan, and Tajikistan had income levels comparable to some of the poorest countries in the world. Using purchasing power parity (PPP) measures rather than GDP measured with current prices and exchange rates gives a more positive picture with respect to income levels.[21]

The demographic data in table 2.6 bring out similarities and differences across the countries. The four southern states have higher birthrates, and hence younger populations than Kazakhstan. They are also more rural. These characteristics reflect Kazakhstan's more diversified and more developed economy, and its more "European" society, while the other four countries tend to be more traditionally Central Asian with a stronger hold of Islam and of the extended family. The relatively high birthrate is responsible for the rapid population growth in the region, although again Kazakhstan is the exception. Kazakhstan's population in 2002 was less than in 1990, due to the substantial emigration of non-Kazakhs and the increase in male mortality rates in the 1990s. Some of these patterns applied in the Kyrgyz Republic, but insufficiently to have a negative aggregate effect on the population. Tajikistan was affected by emigration, as well as by the civil war. Uzbekistan and Turkmenistan both experienced rapid population growth after independence.

Official development assistance went in almost equal measure to four of the Central Asian countries, with Turkmenistan as the exception. This trans-

---

generally careful to avoid ostentatious displays of wealth, while the nouveaux riches of the 1990s often preferred to flaunt it.

21. Pomfret (2006, 107–22) analyzes the issue of measuring economic well-being in greater detail. In capturing well-being, PPP is a valid corrective to the understatement of the current price GDP measures, but early PPP measures in Central Asia were not based on the detailed price data that we would normally expect if the measures were to be treated as reliable guides.

TABLE 2.6. Economic and Social Indicators, 2002

	Population	Population aged under 15	Urban population	Life expectancy at birth	GDP	GDP per capita	GDP per cap @ PPP	ODA	ODA per capita	Armed forces
	millions	percentage of total	percentage of total	years	$ billion	$	International dollars	$ million	$	thousands
Kazakhstan	15.5	26	56	66	24.6	1,656	5,870	188.3	12.2	60
Kyrgyz Republic	5.1	33	34	68	1.6	320	1,620	186.0	36.7	11
Tajikistan	6.2	37	25	69	1.2	193	980	168.4	27.2	6
Turkmenistan	4.8	35	45	67	7.7	1,601	4,300	40.5	8.5	18
Uzbekistan	25.7	35	37	70	7.9	314	1,670	189.4	7.4	52

Source: Pomfret (2006, 19), based on UNDP, Human Development Report 2004.

lates into much higher assistance per head of population for the two poor small countries, the Kyrgyz Republic and Tajikistan. Turkmenistan did not seek much in the way of international assistance, and the despotic nature of its regime did not encourage offers of ODA. Uzbekistan also asserted its independence, although it continued to maintain relations with the main multilateral agencies.

The GDP figures illustrate the shift in the balance of economic power in the region, especially after the post-1999 oil boom pulled Kazakhstan further and further ahead of the more populous Uzbekistan. At the time of independence, the Soviet successor states largely inherited assets on their territory at the time, which gave Uzbekistan the largest and best-equipped army in the region.[22] By 2002 Kazakhstan was able to support a larger army, and as the old Soviet equipment became obsolete it is likely that Kazakhstan's military was better equipped than that of Uzbekistan.

Measuring the extent to which the Central Asian countries have become market economies is inherently more difficult than measuring vital statistics or material well-being. Table 2.2 attempts to indicate the extent of reform in various areas. The Heritage Foundation assesses the degree of economic freedom on a scale from 1 (free) to 5 (unfree), based on fifty independent indicators related to freedom to trade, property rights, and so forth. The Central Asian countries were first included in 1998, when they all fell in the bottom group of "repressed" economies with scores of 4–5. By 2005 their scores had improved, but very slowly; from 4.0 to 3.29 for the Kyrgyz Republic, from 4.23 to 3.66 for Kazakhstan, from 4.30 to 4.00 for Tajikistan, from 4.68 to 4.10 for Uzbekistan, and from 4.50 to 4.36 for Turkmenistan (table 2.7). By Transparency International's Corruption Perceptions Index all five countries had high levels of corruption in 2004, with scores between 2 and 2.3 (on a scale from 1, most corrupt, to 10, least corrupt), which also suggests poorly operating market economies.

In sum, although the centrally planned economy had been largely displaced, the market-based economies that had been constructed offered very limited economic freedoms. In 2005, the Kyrgyz Republic and Kazakhstan both fell in the "mostly unfree" category (scores between 3 and 4), while the other three countries remained in the "repressed" category, ranking among the bottom 10% of all countries. By the Heritage Foundation Index only Zimbabwe, Libya, Myanmar, and North Korea offered less economic freedom than Turkmenistan. By the Corruption Perceptions Index only Azerbaijan, Para-

---

22. The Soviet Army's Turkestan Military Command was headquartered in Tashkent and large Soviet bases remained at Termez and Samarkand after the USSR's involvement in Afghanistan ended. Although Uzbekistan inherited a good part of the military equipment on its territory, some Russian officers refused to accept Uzbekistan's jurisdiction.

TABLE 2.7. Indicators of Economic Freedom and Corruption, 2004/5

	Heritage Foundation Index of Economic Freedom 2005 (n = 155)	Transparency International Corruption Perceptions Index 2004 (n = 145)
Kazakhstan	3.66 (130th)	2.2 (rank 122–128=)
Kyrgyz Republic	3.29 (97th)	2.2 (rank 122–128=)
Tajikistan	4.00 (144th)	2.3 (rank 114–121=)
Turkmenistan	4.36 (151st)	2.0 (rank 133–139=)
Uzbekistan	4.10 (147th)	2.0 (rank 133–139=)

Sources: Heritage Foundation, *2005 Index of Economic Freedom*, available at www.heritage. org and Corruption Perceptions Index available at www.transparency.org.
Note: Numbers in parentheses are the country's rank.

guay, Chad, Myanmar, Nigeria, Bangladesh, and Haiti had more corruption than Uzbekistan and Turkmenistan.

2.5. The Twenty-First Century

By the start of the twenty-first century, the transition to market-based economies was essentially complete. The expectation was that economic performance would be linked to the type of economy that had been created. In practice, however, the five economies' fortunes were dominated by the global resource boom that peaked in 2007–8 and only ended in 2014. This was especially true for the energy exporters Kazakhstan and Turkmenistan and to a lesser extent Uzbekistan, but the oil boom indirectly affected the Kyrgyz Republic, Tajikistan, and to a lesser extent Uzbekistan who all supplied labor to the booming Russian economy (table 2.8). Other commodities also enjoyed booms, with various minerals, especially copper (Uzbekistan) and gold (the Kyrgyz Republic), being crucial for individual countries, while Tajikistan benefitted from generally favorable aluminum prices. The next chapter examines the five countries' resource endowment, and the role of natural resources in their economic development, with focus on the differing characteristics and price history of the major commodity exports.

Part 2 covers the twenty-first century experience of each of the five countries, emphasizing their individual features. For all five countries, the transitional recession was in the past, and they all enjoyed continuous economic growth, albeit at varying rates (table 2.9). A beneficial consequence has been the virtual elimination of poverty at international benchmarks of under $2 a day, although some people are still poor (e.g., if a poverty line of $3 is used).[23]

23. Poverty rates are impossible to measure and compare with precision. National poverty lines differ, perhaps reflecting differing basic needs (e.g., due to climate). International compari-

TABLE 2.8. Economic and Social Indicators, 2015/16

	2015 population	2015 life expectancy at birth	2016a GDP	2016a GDP per capita	2015a GNI per cap @ PPP	2016 GNI per cap @ PPP	2015 external debt	2016 internet users	2016 Armed forces
	HDR	HDR	WDI	WDI	HDR	WDI	WDI	WDI	WDI
	millions	years	$ billion	$	International 2011 dollars	International 2011 dollars	$ million	per 100 people	thousands
Kazakhstan	17.6	69.6	133.7 (217.9)	8,710 (12,602)	22,093 (20,867)	22,910	13,624	54.9	71
Kyrgyz Republic	5.9	70.8	6.6 (7.4)	1,100 (1,269)	3,097 (3,044)	5,920	2,368	28.3	20
Tajikistan	8.5	69.6	7.0 (9.2)	1,110 (1,114)	2,601 (2,517)	3,500	1,700	17.5	16
Turkmenistan	5.4	65.7	36.2 (47.9)	6,670 (9,032)	14,026 (13,066)	16,060	247	12.2	37
Uzbekistan	29.9	69.4	67.2 (62.6)	2,220 (2,037)	5,748 (5,567)	6,240	3,795	43.6	68

Sources: UNDP, *Human Development Report 2016*; World Bank, *World Development Indicators* (accessed November 4, 2017).

Note: (a) 2014 in parentheses.

TABLE 2.9. Annual Growth in Real GDP, 2000–2017 (Percent)

	2000	2001	2002	2003	2004	2005	2006	2007	2008	2009	2010	2011	2012	2013	2014	2015	2016	2017e
Kazakhstan	9.8	13.5	9.8	9.3	9.6	9.7	10.7	8.9	3.3	1.2	7.3	7.5	5.0	6.0	4.3	1.2	1.1	3.3
Kyrgyz Republic	5.4	5.3	-0.0	7.0	7.0	-0.2	3.1	8.5	7.6	2.9	-0.5	6.0	-0.1	10.9	4.0	3.5	3.8	3.5
Tajikistan	8.3	10.2	9.1	10.2	10.6	6.7	7.0	7.8	7.9	3.9	6.5	7.4	7.5	7.4	6.7	6.0	6.9	4.5
Turkmenistan	18.6	20.4	15.8	17.1	14.7	13.0	11.0	11.1	14.7	6.1	9.2	14.7	11.1	10.2	10.3	6.5	6.2	6.5
Uzbekistan	3.8	4.2	4.0	4.2	7.4	7.0	7.5	9.5	9.0	8.1	8.5	8.3	8.2	8.0	8.1	8.0	7.8	6.0

Source: IMF, *World Economic Outlook*, October 2017 database (accessed 3 November 2017).

The picture is more complex with respect to inequality. Gini coefficients published by the World Bank suggest moderate levels of inequality, but these are often estimates based on extrapolation rather than on high-quality household surveys. The quality of household surveys varies considerably, but even the best omit some poor people (e.g., the homeless) and do not include the super-rich. Using a variety of other sources, Novokmet, Piketty, and Zveman (2017) found substantial inequality in Russia, defining inequality as the income share of the top 1%; similar exercises have not been done for Central Asia, but the outcome would likely be similar.

One reason for disagreement over inequality patterns is that "inequality" is often conceptualized in terms other than income.[24] The presence of expensive cars among widespread low income-levels can be a disturbing sign of wealth inequality. There are considerable rural-urban or other locational inequalities in Central Asia, and the situation does not appear to be changing. From the available data, gender inequality appears to be small in Central Asia, certainly in the sense of equal pay for equal work, but women receive lower wages on average, in part due to their relative concentration in low-wage occupations such as teaching or nursing. Nevertheless, the general impression, backed up by survey evidence, is that some deep-seated attitudes towards gender roles remain incompatible with gender equality, and there are clearly glass ceilings in both the private and public sectors.

Finally, a useful distinction is between equality of opportunity and equality of outcome. The Soviet system had a good record in establishing universal access to education and healthcare, and attitudes remain deeply supportive. Secondary school enrollments remain over 80%, which is well above global averages for the countries' income levels, and access to healthcare remains high in areas such as presence of skilled health staff at births or measles immunization. However, universal access has not been associated with universal high-quality healthcare or education. The rich are increasingly ensuring that their children go to good schools, whether public or private, but are not much concerned about the rest of the school system. Similarly, with healthcare, the rich have access to the best facilities (or receive treatment abroad). For poorer people, out-of-pocket payment for many health services can be a substantial burden. The outcome in both education and health is stratified systems that

---

sons must take into account differing price levels; PPP measures either involve a small selection of prices or years are connected by interpolation, both of which are approximations (but better than no attempt to adjust for PPP). The World Bank and the UNDP per capita income measures in table 2.8 illustrate the problem; World Bank data show Kyrgyz per capita incomes close to those of Tajikistan and well behind Uzbekistan, whereas UNDP data show Kyrgyz incomes similar to Uzbekistan and substantially higher than Tajikistan.

24. The assessments in this and the next two paragraphs are based on data assembled by Mogilevskii (2017).

TABLE 2.10. Inflation, Annual Change in Consumer Price Index, 2000–2017 (Percent)

	2000	2001	2002	2003	2004	2005	2006	2007
Kazakhstan	13.3	8.4	5.9	6.5	6.9	7.5	8.6	10. 8
Kyrgyz Republic	18.7	6.9	2.1	3. 1	4.1	4.3	5.6	10.2
Tajikistan	32.9	38.6	12.2	16.4	7.2	7.3	10.0	13.2
Turkmenistan	8.0	11.6	8.8	5.6	5.9	10.7	8.2	6.3
Uzbekistan	25.0	27.3	27.3	11.6	6.6	10.0	14.2	12.3

Source: IMF, *World Economic Outlook*, October 2017 database.

TABLE 2.11. Government Revenue and Expenditure, as Percent of GDP, 2000–2017

	2000	2001	2002	2003	2004	2005	2006	2007
REVENUE								
Kazakhstan	21.9	25.7	22.5	25.4	24.6	28.1	27.5	28.8
Kyrgyz Republic	19.6	21.4	23.7	23.4	24.2	25.8	27.4	31.2
Tajikistan	13.6	15.2	16.7	17.3	17.9	20.1	23.6	22.5
Turkmenistan	23.6	21.8	18.2	23.1	20.3	20.5	20.2	17.3
Uzbekistan	36.6	34.3	35.5	33.4	32.2	30.8	34.4	35.6
EXPENDITURE								
Kazakhstan	na	na	20.5	21.4	22.0	22.1	19.8	23.7
Kyrgyz Republic	30.3	28.1	29.6	28.6	29.1	29.6	30.1	31.8
Tajikistan	19.2	18.4	19.2	19.1	20.3	23.0	21.9	28.0
Turkmenistan	24.1	21.1	18.0	19.4	18.9	19.7	15.0	13.4
Uzbekistan	39.1	35.6	37.4	33.2	31.6	29.5	30.7	31.0

Source: IMF, *World Economic Outlook*, October 2017 database.
Note: na = not available.

give huge advantages to the children of rich parents and reduce social mobility.

Equality of outcome requires government intervention to transfer resources from the rich to the poor. Patterns of transfers established in the 1990s remain prevalent; pensions are relatively well maintained, while social support for households with small children remain inadequate. In general, social security and social insurance schemes have wide coverage, but with little targeting, so that adequacy in reducing inequality of outcomes is low.

With respect to macroeconomic policy, tables 2.10 and 2.11 indicate that Central Asian governments are doing a better job of maintaining monetary and fiscal balance in the twenty-first century. However, there are substantial variations, e.g., the low level of public spending reported by Turkmenistan.

Varieties of market economy have played a role in determining how the consequences of the resource boom filtered through to the population, and

TABLE 2.10. (*continued*)

2008	2009	2010	2011	2012	2013	2014	2015	2016	2017
17.1	7.3	7.1	8.3	5.1	5.8	6.7	6.7	14.6	7.3
24.5	6.8	8.0	16.6	2. 8	6.6	7.5	6.5	0.4	3.8
20.4	6.4	6.5	12.4	5.8	5.0	6.1	5.8	5.9	8.9
14.5	−2.7	4. 5	5.3	5.3	6.8	6.0	7.4	3.6	6.0
12.7	14.1	12.3	12.4	11.9	11.7	9.1	8.5	8.0	13.0

TABLE 2.11. (*continued*)

2008	2009	2010	2011	2012	2013	2014	2015	2016	2017
28.3	22.1	23.9	27.0	26.3	24.8	23.7	16.6	18.0	19.3
30.3	33.3	31.2	32.7	34.7	34.4	35.3	35.6	34.7	37.0
22.1	23.4	23.2	24.9	25.1	26.9	28.4	26.9	28.8	27.4
20.9	20.4	15.8	18.3	22.2	17.4	17.9	16.5	12.8	12.2
40.7	36.7	37.0	40.2	41.5	35.9	34.9	34.4	32.5	30.5
27.1	23.5	22.5	21.2	21.9	19.8	21.3	22.9	22.1	25.9
29.3	34.4	37.1	37.4	40.6	38.1	34.3	36.8	39.2	40.0
27.2	28.6	26.1	27.0	24.6	27.7	28.4	31.8	39.4	33.9
10.9	13.4	13.8	14.6	14.7	16.9	17.0	17.2	14.1	13.3
33.0	34.4	33.4	32.4	33.7	33.6	31.6	33.6	32.1	29.9

TABLE 2.12. Merchandise Trade as a Percentage of GDP, Selected Years, 1994–2016

	1994	2000	2004	2008	2013	2014	2016
Kazakhstan	32.0	75.7	76.2	81.7	57.6	54.8	46.4
Kyrgyz Republic	39.0	77.3	75.1	100.5	107.2	94.5	83.4
Tajikistan	76.9	169.7	101.4	90.7	62.4	61.7	57.5
Turkmenistan	141.1	147.8	105.1	91.0	65.8	58.0	49.8
Uzbekistan	40.0	40.1	63.8	70.1	45.1	43.4	32.0

Source: World Bank, *World Development Indicators* at http://data.worldbank.org/indicator/TG.VAL.TOTL.GD.ZS.

how the countries responded to reverses in global prices. All five countries have remained open to trade and investment flows (tables 2.12 and 2.13), although foreign investment has gone overwhelmingly to the oil and gas export-ers Kazakhstan and Turkmenistan. Variation in the ratio of trade to GDP re-flects degree of trade liberalization (greatest in the Kyrgyz Republic, least in

TABLE 2.13. Foreign Direct Investment

A. INWARD FOREIGN DIRECT INVESTMENT, 1992–2016 (MILLIONS OF US DOLLARS)

	1992	1993	1994	1995	1996	1997	1998	1999	2000	2001	2002
Kazakhstan	100	1,271	660	964	1,137	1,322	1,161	1,438	1,283	2,835	2,590
Kyrgyz Republic	0	10	38	96	47	83	109	44	−2	5	5
Tajikistan	9	9	12	10	18	18	30	7	24	9	36
Turkmenistan	0	79	103	233	108	108	62	125	131	170	276
Uzbekistan	9	48	73	−24	90	167	140	121	75	83	65

Source: UNCTAD, *World Investment Review*, various years.

B. STOCK OF FOREIGN DIRECT INVESTMENT, SELECTED YEARS, 2000–2016
(MILLIONS OF US DOLLARS)

	Inward Stock			Outward Stock	
	2000	2008	2016	2000	2012
Kazakhstan	10,078	59,035	129,773	16	20,731
Kyrgyz Republic	432	1,380	5,102	33	2
Tajikistan	136	1,081	2,399		
Turkmenistan	949	5,257	36,241		
Uzbekistan	689	2,888	8,957		

Source: UNCTAD, *World Investment Review 2017*, 229.
Note: For Tajikistan, Turkmenistan, and Uzbekistan, estimates of inward stock; no reported values for outward stock. Among "transition economies" in the source (i.e. not including EU members), Kazakhstan ranked second to Russia for inward stock of FDI in both years.

Uzbekistan and Turkmenistan), but also reflects the low GDP of the Kyrgyz Republic and Tajikistan (and hence highest trade/GDP ratios).

A new phenomenon in the twenty-first century, associated with the oil boom, has been the large labor flows from the three poorer Central Asian countries to Russia and, to a much lesser extent, to Kazakhstan. The flow started earlier from Tajikistan, as people escaped the civil war and dire economic conditions of the 1990s, but the number of migrants increased rapidly as the oil boom stimulated demand in Russia for unskilled workers on construction sites and elsewhere (table 2.14). The number of migrants and size of remittances were largest for Uzbekistan, but the ratio of remittances to GDP was highest for Tajikistan and the Kyrgyz Republic.[25] By the early 2010s, for

25. As with the migration numbers, remittances estimates are approximate. The World Bank migration and remittances team provides the best series that is consistent over time. The volatility in 2014–15 meant that whereas Tajikistan (42%) and the Kyrgyz Republic (30%) had the world's highest remittances/GDP ratios in 2014, they had been overtaken in 2015 by Nepal (32%) and

2003	2004	2005	2006	2007	2008	2009	2010	2011	2012	2013	2014	2015	2016
2,092	4,157	1,971	6,278	11,119	14,322	13,243	11,551	13,973	13,337	10,321	8,406	4,012	9,069
46	175	43	182	208	377	189	438	694	293	626	248	1,142	467
32	272	14	190	398	815	131	155	227	262	168	408	545	434
226	354	418	731	856	1,277	4,553	3,632	3,391	3,130	3,528	3,830	4,398	4,522
83	177	192	174	705	711	842	1,636	1,635	563	629	632	65	67

the poorest three countries remittance flows dwarfed foreign investment or development aid (table 2.15).

Measures of the ease of doing business (table 2.16) and of economic freedom and corruption have improved slightly in the twenty-first century (compare tables 2.7 and 2.17), with Kazakhstan giving the best impression on all of these indicators. Economic and political liberalization has helped the Kyrgyz Republic to score well on most of these measures, but the country suffered from poor institutions despite generally good economic policies and potentially favorable political developments.[26] The legacy of administrative capability may be important in enabling Uzbekistan to fare better than might have been expected given the political regime, policy missteps, and increasingly apparent corruption in high places. Tajikistan is frequently considered to be a potential failed state, while Turkmenistan remains difficult to fathom given its closed system.

The early twenty-first century saw much improved economic conditions compared to the 1990s, in the exceptionally favorable external conditions of the global commodity boom. The fall in world trade in 2009 imposed a temporary setback (table 2.9), but economic recovery was rapid, apart from the Kyrgyz Republic, which experienced political unrest and ethnic strife in 2010. A more severe external shock came in 2014, when oil and other commodity prices fell, and then did not recover. The magnitude of the shock is illustrated by the collapse in GDP between 2014 and 2016 (table 2.8); from $218 billion to $134 billion in Kazakhstan and from $48 billion to $36 billion in Turkmenistan, and by smaller amounts in the Kyrgyz Republic and Tajikistan (but probably with more drastic effect given those countries' income levels). The

---

Liberia (31%), who were followed by Tajikistan (29%), Tonga (27%), and the Kyrgyz Republic (26%), according to rankings from World Bank (2016b, 14).

26. Poor institutions are reflected in the poor scores for corruption, contract enforcement, paying taxes, and getting electricity.

TABLE 2.14. Remittances, 2006–17 (Million US Dollars)

		2006	2007	2008	2009	2010	2011	2012	2013	2014	2015	2016	2017e
Kazakhstan	inward	84	143	126	198	226	180	178	207	229	194	275	297
	outward	2,958	4,212	3,462	2,934	3,006	3,409	3,809	3,804	3,550	3,116	2,395	na
Kyrgyz Republic	inward	473	704	1,223	982	1,266	1,709	2,031	2,278	2,243	1,688	1,995	2,541
	outward	68	90	101	107	168	228	286	390	454	363	378	na
Tajikistan	inward	1,019	1,691	2,544	1,748	2,306	3,060	3,626	4,219	3,384	2,259	1,867	2,031
	outward	395	184	199	124	231	201	263	240	304	165	87	na
Turkmenistan	inward	14	30	50	34	35	35	37	40	30	16	9	10
Uzbekistan	inward	898	1,693	3,007	2,071	2,858	4,276	5,693	6,689	5,828	3,062	2,479	2,695

Source: World Bank (2016b, 244), and World Bank Migration and Remittances database (accessed November 3, 2017).

Note: For Turkmenistan and Uzbekistan only inward remittances are reported in the source. The cost of sending remittance has fallen substantially since the early 2000s, as efficient electronic transfer displaced more basic methods of physically remitting cash; this may have caused underestimation in earlier years and led to better coverage in later years.

TABLE 2.15. Major International Financial Inflows, 2012 (Billion US Dollars)

	FDI	Remittances	ODA
Kazakhstan	15.117	–3,764	0.130
Kyrgyz Republic	0.372	2.308	0.473
Tajikistan	0.198	3.362	0.394
Turkmenistan	3.159	0.037	0.038
Uzbekistan	1.094	5.693	0.255

Source: ADBI (2014, 85), based on World Bank and OECD data.

Note: Remittance data for the first three countries differ slightly from World Bank data in table 2.14; remittance data for Turkmenistan and Uzbekistan are not given in the ADBI source and are taken from table 2.14.

TABLE 2.16. Ease of Doing Business, June 2015 and June 2016

Economy	Overall Rank	Starting a Business	Construction Permits	Getting Electricity	Registering Property	Getting Credit	Protecting Minority Investors	Paying Taxes	Trading Across Borders	Enforcing Contracts	Resolving Insolvency
Kazakhstan	35 (41)	45 (21)	22 (92)	75 (71)	18 (19)	75 (70)	3 (25)	60 (18)	119 (122)	9 (9)	32 (47)
Kyrgyz Republic	75 (67)	30 (35)	32 (20)	163 (160)	8 (6)	32 (28)	42 (36)	148 (138)	79 (83)	141 (137)	130 (126)
Tajikistan	128 (132)	85 (57)	162 (152)	173 (177)	97 (102)	118 (109)	27 (29)	140 (172)	144 (132)	54 (54)	144 (147)
Uzbekistan	87 (87)	25 (42)	147 (151)	83 (112)	75 (87)	44 (42)	70 (88)	138 (115)	165 (159)	38 (32)	77 (75)

Source: World Bank at www.doingbusiness.org.

Notes: Rank out of 190 countries in ten areas; overall rank based on unweighted average of scores in the ten areas. Number in parentheses is June 2015 ranking out of 189 countries. Turkmenistan not included.

TABLE 2.17. Indicators of Economic Freedom and Corruption, 2016/17

	Heritage Foundation Index of Economic Freedom 2017	Transparency International Corruption Perceptions Index 2016
Kazakhstan	69.0 (42nd)	29 (rank 131=)
Kyrgyz Republic	61.1 (89th)	28 (rank 136=)
Tajikistan	58.2 (109th)	25 (rank 151=)
Turkmenistan	47.4 (170th)	22 (rank 154=)
Uzbekistan	52.3 (148th)	21 (rank 156=)

Sources: Heritage Foundation, 2017 Index of Economic Freedom, available at www.heritage.org; and Transparency International Corruption Perceptions Index available at www.transparency.org (both accessed on November 3, 2017).

Note: Both indicators are on a scale from 0 to 100 (most free/least corrupt); numbers in parentheses are the country's rank. The Heritage Foundation ranked 181 countries and Transparency International 176 countries.

reduction was less dramatic in domestic-currency terms, as captured in the PPP estimates in table 2.8. Nevertheless, the sustained economic growth since the end of the 1990s appeared under threat, and by 2016 all governments were recognizing the need to diversify their economies from narrow focus on commodity exports or from labor exports to oil-exporting neighbors.

3

The Role of Natural Resources

Central Asia's post-independence economic history can be explained in large degree by the region's resource endowments and by variations in the world price of the main primary product exports. The inherited legacy was partly a consequence of each republic's natural resource endowment, e.g., Uzbekistan had a larger cadre of administrators because the cotton sector's irrigation system required central control and efficient local management, while Kazakhstan had a larger proportion of people with higher education qualifications due to the mining engineers in its coal and mineral operations. Uzbekistan's good economic performance during 1992–96 coincided with buoyant cotton prices, and after 1996 this economic boost was absent. Kazakhstan's fortunes revolved around world oil prices, which were stagnant during the 1990s, and its untapped reserves, which led to proliferation of new contracts even before oil prices began to rise in 1999. Turkmenistan's idiosyncratic path was fueled by cotton and natural gas rents, while the Kyrgyz Republic and Tajikistan struggled because they had few readily exploitable and exportable natural resources.

Although economic policymaking during the 1990s was dominated by challenges associated with the dissolution of the Soviet Union and collapse of central planning mechanisms, the newly independent countries made decisions about how to exploit their natural resources in the post-Soviet environment. The implications of these decisions were highlighted in the first decade of the twenty-first century as prices of oil and gas and some minerals increased rapidly.

The impact of the commodity boom varied. Kazakhstan and Turkmenistan were the major beneficiaries due to their oil and gas reserves; the net barter terms of trade, i.e. the ratio of export unit values to import unit values, more than doubled for Turkmenistan and Kazakhstan between 2000 and 2008.[1] A sharp decline in energy prices in the second half of 2008 was largely reversed in 2009–10, but another large decline in 2014 appeared to signal the definitive end of the energy boom. With a different resource endowment, less abundant gas but valuable deposits of gold, copper, and other minerals, Uzbekistan benefitted from a 2000–2010 terms of trade increase of around 50%. Copper prices followed a roughly similar time-path to energy prices, but gold prices rose steadily from under $400 per ounce in 2003 to over $1,700 in 2011, before falling in 2013. The Kyrgyz Republic's terms of trade were roughly constant over the decade 2000–2010, and Tajikistan's terms of trade deteriorated, especially after 2006, due to increased energy imports. The boom in oil and gas prices mainly impacted the last two countries through the increased demand for labor in Russia.

This chapter analyzes the characteristics of the natural resources that are important for Central Asia. At independence, cotton was the most important commodity export from Central Asia, but cotton did not share in the commodity boom, never repeating the 1995 peak price of over a dollar per pound.[2] In the twenty-first century, cotton has been displaced by oil and gas and minerals. All the governments have shown concern about ongoing dependence on primary product exports, whose importance increased after independence despite plans for economic diversification. The first section reviews the resource curse literature that highlights why primary product dependence may be harmful. The remaining sections analyze features of the main primary products.

3.1. Is Natural Resource Abundance a Curse?

Coincidentally in the early 1990s as the Central Asian countries became independent, a debate raged about the paradox that resource abundance could be bad for a country. Some countries whose export revenues increased greatly during the 1973–81 commodity boom subsequently experienced negative long-run growth. In cross-country regressions, Sachs and Warner (1995) found a negative relationship between resource abundance and economic growth. Contributions after Sachs and Warner refined the debate, establishing that the relationship is conditional (on variables proxying for institutions) and that the negative relationship is stronger for point-sourced resources such as

1. Numbers in this paragraph are from Mogilevskii (2012a, 11), based on World Bank data.

2. The Cotlook A Index recorded a brief peak over $2 in early 2011, but this price does not seem to have been paid for any Central Asian cotton; the end of year value of the Index was ninety-seven cents.

oil and minerals.[3] The conditional nature of the resource curse is apparent from the success of some resource-abundant economies, such as Botswana or Australia or Malaysia. Among oil producers, where there have been many disappointing outcomes in the decades since the oil price increases of the 1970s, there are also cases of the oil revenues being used to create equitably distributed high incomes and future growth prospects, as in Norway or Alberta.

Identification of transmission mechanisms from resource abundance to poor economic growth has focused on three links: through relative prices and structural change, through volatility, and through rent-seeking and distortion of institutions. These can be viewed as price and real productive sector links, public finance links, and political economy links.

An increase in resource-intensive exports will be associated with a decline in output of other traded goods, primarily because exchange rate appreciation will make other traded goods less internationally competitive. If the latter have desirable externalities or there are costs to reversing their decline when the resource revenues dry up, then there is a negative effect on long-run growth (the Dutch Disease).[4] A second potentially deleterious price effect arises if the resource sector uses foreign expertise plus domestic capital and unskilled labor; a resource boom pushes down the price of domestic skilled labor relative to the price of unskilled labor, i.e. resource abundance reduces the incentive to invest in human capital. The empirical magnitude of both of these effects is debated, but in most cases they do not appear to be large.

Natural resources typically have more volatile prices in world markets than other goods and services. This can negatively impact growth if the earnings are invested in domestic projects whose marginal return is low, e.g., because the sudden increase in available funds is not matched by a comparable increase in good projects needing finance, or if the earnings are used for consumption that is costly to reverse.[5] If the bust following a boom requires cuts in domestic absorption that fall on those least capable of protecting themselves, then volatility can increase poverty directly as well as indirectly via slower growth.

---

3. Frankel (2010), van der Ploeg (2011), Pomfret (2012, n1), and Venables (2016) survey the resource curse literature.

4. The phenomenon is named after the 1959 Netherlands' gas boom, which did not kill the Dutch economy or the nongas sector, mainly because the government used the boom revenues to invest in infrastructure and education.

5. The negative effects of volatility are emphasized in the case studies in Gelb (1988) and in the survey by Frankel (2010). With 1962–2011 data for eighty-four resource-rich countries, Coutinho et al. (2013) found that a 1% increase in output growth was associated with a 2.5% increase in public consumption expenditure, creating entitlements that people are loath to lose. Using increased government revenues for public investment rather than public consumption is likely to be more beneficial in the long run, but abundant revenues may reduce the impetus for careful cost-benefit analysis and *ex post* project evaluation, leading to wasteful expenditure.

Volatility can be addressed by investing some of the boom-period revenues in diversified assets as in Norway's oil fund or Alberta's Heritage Fund, which can be drawn upon as the resource runs out or when boom turns to bust.

The impact of resource abundance on rent-seeking and on institutions depends upon the nature of the resource and on preexisting institutions. Economic historians have traced the links between the nature of resource endowments and institutional development. Agriculture suited to production on the family farm is associated with human capital formation, democracy, and other institutional features amenable to inclusive economic development, while resources such as minerals or plantation agriculture have been associated with less democratic political systems and less favorable institutional development. The impact of a resource boom on inequality depends upon the nature of the resource; "point-sourced" resources such as oil or mining have rents that may be relatively easily grabbed by a few, while more diffused resources such as rice or wheat are less suited to rent-seeking. However, institutions developed before the resource boom may be resilient; resource abundance has been a blessing not just for democratic oil-rich countries, provinces, or states such as Norway, Alberta, and Alaska, which already had high-incomes before their oil rents, but also middle–income countries such as Malaysia or low-income countries such as Botswana. The less happy outcomes are where resource abundance has led to despotic and corrupt political and institutional set-ups that inhibit development and impoverish the majority of people, or when competition for rents has led to civil war.

An alternative framework is to recognize the potential bounty from resource abundance, but to realize the bounty a country must surmount several hurdles (Pomfret, 2012; Venables, 2016). First, the resources need to be found and exploited, and for many mineral and energy resources this requires specialized skills not possessed by domestic companies. Foregoing significant external participation can constrain output and lead to missed opportunities (as happened in Turkmenistan and Mongolia in the 1990s and early 2000s), but attracting foreign investors may create institutional problems, such as opportunities for corruption. Second, when the resources are sold, revenues need to be divided. Resource rents typically accrue to the state, but individuals may try to capture rents and excessive competition for rents can lead to a tragedy of the anticommons (i.e. too little output, because inadequate returns are left for the producer) or to state capture by a narrow elite, in both cases institutional degradation is the result. Recontracting to decrease the share of rents accruing to foreign partners will reduce a country's attractiveness to future foreign investors. Third, once rents have accrued to the state, it is natural to want to increase public spending, but a too procyclical fiscal stance is undesirable. Having an easy source of public revenue may be associated with poor public policy and lack of accountability, as the government does not need to seek public approval (e.g., through the parliament) for its spending policies; both the size and composition of current public spending may be inappropriate for long-run economic development. By the third stage the issues are more general development issues; the current consensus on development is that public expenditures should focus on improving soft and hard infrastructure and on investment in human capital. Resource-rich countries may have an advantage in the third stage because they have more public revenues to spend, but they must overcome the first two hurdles, and then aim for efficient use of the revenues.

The resource curse debate was important in alerting resource-rich countries to potential dangers. One common reaction during the post-1998 resource boom, in contrast to the 1973–81 commodity boom, was for resource-rich countries to set up sovereign wealth funds (SWFs) to manage the windfall revenues.[6] SWFs may sterilize part of the resource export revenues (holding foreign assets will reduce Dutch Disease effects), smooth the earnings flow across cycles, save for future generations or unanticipated national emergencies, and increase transparency over how resource rents are used.

The degree of SWF independence and the role of the government in directing its activities vary. The Central Asian SWFs include the extreme of non-transparency in Turkmenistan under President Niyazov, where the fund was off-budget and under the president's personal control. The National Fund of the Republic of Kazakhstan (NFRK) has been more transparent but with mixed motives (stabilization, intergenerational transfer, and national development); after 2007, when the NFRK was accessed to counter the country's financial crisis, bailed-out companies became subsidiaries of the state-holding company Samruk-Kazyna, blurring the distinction between the SWF as a holder of financial assets and as an investor in, and creator of, state-owned enterprises.

Resources are not destiny. There are choices to be made, which determine whether resources are a boon or a curse. Initial policy choices may lead to adverse institutional developments, but these institutions in turn may be changed. Failing to take advantage of resource abundance may be a missed opportunity, because the value of resources in the ground is constantly changing and what is valuable today may be obsolete in the future, a "stranded asset." Resource exploitation is, however, only the first step towards a resource boon. Failure to pursue good policies can often produce a resource curse, as the cross-country evidence shows. The formerly centrally planned economies

---

6. A common definition is that SWFs are government-owned funds that operate in private financial markets (e.g., in Revenue Watch Institute, 2011, 10). Not all SWFs are in resource-rich countries, and different lists vary. Carpantier and Vermeulen (2014) report that twenty-two of thirty-seven SWFs in 2010 had been established after 1998.

may have been especially prone to such an outcome due to their inexperience with policymaking in market-based economies and the absence of strong economic institutions, but the malleability of institutions can also be an advantage as adverse institutional consequences of initial decisions can be corrected.[7]

All the resource curse arguments are potentially relevant to Central Asia. The Dutch Disease is generally viewed as the weakest transmission mechanism in practice, and is dismissed by many observers of Central Asia, but the limited extent to which the countries have diversified their economies is striking. Volatility varies according to commodity and country; Turkmenistan's use of resource rents for prestige projects and a personality cult, generous social benefits, pervasive security forces, and investment in import-substituting industries is unlikely to be sustainable, and in the post-2014 environment appears profligate. Resource abundance may have contributed to delayed (or canceled) economic reform in the main cotton exporters in 1992–95 and hurt investment in education in the poorer countries. Institutional degradation is the greatest threat, and the outcome may be country-specific. These issues will be taken up in the chapters on the individual countries.

3.2. Oil and Natural Gas

During the Soviet era, Central Asian oil resources were underdeveloped relative to the established oil-producing areas of Azerbaijan and the newer oil fields in Siberia. In part, this was due to the technical difficulties of exploring and exploiting the offshore fields in the Caspian Basin, and even onshore fields posed problems; the Uzen onshore field in Kazakhstan was discovered in 1961, but poor outcomes by 1981 dissuaded Soviet planners from further Central Asian projects.[8] Natural gas production had a long history in Uzbekistan, but the old gas fields were becoming exhausted. In the final decade of the Soviet Union, large investments were made in Turkmenistan's natural gas; at independence, Turkmenistan was the only Central Asian country producing more than 1% of the world's oil or gas output (table 3.1).

After independence, the approaches to the oil and gas sectors differed among the three countries with the largest potential reserves. Kazakhstan, like

7. Esanov et al. (2001) argued that resource abundance was particularly harmful in the Soviet successor states because it allowed reform to be postponed and encouraged rent-seeking behavior in a context of weak institutional development. Brunnschweiler (2009) reached the opposite conclusion; among former Soviet and Eastern European countries in transition, oil had a positive impact on growth between 1990 and 2006. Alexeev and Conrad (2011) found that, across a range of indicators, resource-rich transition economies performed neither better nor worse than other transition economies.

8. The CIA (1982) argued that Soviet planners erred in pushing for too rapid development at Uzen when the geology and high paraffin content were poorly understood. Initial errors were followed by inappropriate remedial action, including purchase of expensive Western equipment that did not resolve the problems.

TABLE 3.1. Oil and Gas Production and Reserves

OIL PRODUCTION AND CONSUMPTION (THOUSAND BARRELS PER DAY)	1994		2006		2016	
	prod^n	cons^n	prod^n	cons^n	prod^n	cons^n
Kazakhstan 485 (421)	446	248	1,579	196	1,672	265
Turkmenistan 142 (96)	87	60	187	112	261	135
Uzbekistan 55 (232)	124	158	114	146	55	56
World production	67,0	82,519	92,150			

OIL, PROVED RESERVES (END OF YEAR, BILLION BARRELS)	1996	2006	2016
Kazakhstan	5.3	9.0	30.0
Turkmenistan	0.5	0.6	0.6
Uzbekistan	0.6	0.6	0.6
World	1,148.8	1,388.3	1,691.5

GAS PRODUCTION (BILLION CUBIC METERS)	1994		2006		2016	
	prod^n	cons^n	prod^n	cons^n	prod^n	cons^n
Kazakhstan 4.9 (8.4)	4.1	10.0	12.0	5.7	17.9	13.3
Turkmenistan 75.3 (8.4)	32.3	9.9	26.6	15.0	60.1	29.5
Uzbekistan 31.3 (31.9)	42.7	40.1	46.2	43.4	56.5	51.3
World production	2,077.1	2,711.3	3,212.9			

GAS, PROVED RESERVES (END OF YEAR, TRILLION CUBIC METERS)	1994	2006	2016
Kazakhstan	na	1.3	1.0
Turkmenistan	na	2.3	17.5
Uzbekistan	na	1.2	1.1
World	119.1	156.5	186.6

Source: British Petroleum, *Statistical Review of World Energy,* 2015 and 2017.

Notes: Numbers in column 1 are production and consumption, in parentheses, in 1985 (the earliest year reported for Soviet republics); na = not available in the source.

Azerbaijan, offered a direct role for foreign firms in stimulating the energy sector, while Uzbekistan and Turkmenistan chose to maintain state control and minimize the role of foreign companies. Jones Luong and Weinthal (2001; 2010) argue that this split reflects that Uzbekistan and Turkmenistan had substantial alternative sources of export revenue from cotton and their leaders faced less contestation over rents than the leadership in Kazakhstan. While it is true that Presidents Karimov and Niyazov ruled over more ethnically homogeneous countries and could perhaps take a longer time horizon than President Nazarbayev, who faced potential secessionist threats in the Russian-dominated areas of Kazakhstan, the physical nature of the resources also mattered.

Exploration and exploitation of Kazakhstan's onshore and offshore oil fields would have been difficult without the participation of major energy companies. The Tengiz onshore project had already been signed with Chevron in the final years of the Soviet Union, and offshore prospecting was even more technically challenging. Kazakhstan negotiated production sharing agreements (PSAs) that sped up exploitation of its oil reserves and helped in securing finance for new pipelines, but raised controversy over the PSAs' terms. Whether Kazakhstan could have negotiated better deals or retained more substantial ownership shares is a question that will be addressed in chapter 4, but there was no alternative to a direct role for foreign firms if Kazakhstan wanted to exploit its oil and gas resources quickly.

Turkmenistan's gas fields had been recently developed, and retention of state control over natural gas production reflected the fact that a passive position was sufficient to ensure that revenues flowed into the government's coffers with minimum effort. Turkmenistan could have turned to foreign energy companies to better manage output and to explore for offshore gas fields, but the demand side was the binding constraint on achieving higher revenues from gas sales.[9] Markets for Turkmenistan's gas were dictated by the direction of pipelines, and the resulting bilateral monopoly; Turkmenistan's main customers in Ukraine and the Caucasus were dependent on Turkmenistan's gas, but Turkmenistan was dependent on the customers paying their bills. Without new pipelines, the government saw little incentive to expand production in the 1990s, and Turkmenistan slipped from being the world's sixth-largest natural gas producer in 1993 to twelfth in 2003. The situation would only change with the pipeline to China that came into service in 2009.

The expansion of oil and gas production in Uzbekistan was more limited and less problematic than energy development in either Kazakhstan or Turkmenistan. Expertise was sufficient to develop the oil and gas fields, and most of production during the 1990s was for domestic consumption as Uzbekistan became energy self-sufficient in both oil and gas. Exports started to grow after the turn of the century. Uzbekistan shipped 2.5 billion cubic meters (bcm) of gas to Russia in 2002, and a May 2004 agreement with Gazprom envisaged rapid expansion of sales to Russia, starting with 7.7 bcm in 2004. In June 2004 LUKoil signed a billion-dollar PSA to develop Uzbekistan's southern gas fields. Nevertheless, for both oil and gas, Uzbekistan's export potential was limited

9. Development of Turkmenistan's gas resources had encountered substantial technical problems, associated with high pressure and sulfur content, and lack of expertise in addressing these problems may have hindered further expansion after independence. Turkmenistan did enlist oil majors in exploring its share of the Caspian Sea, but they withdrew, in part because of difficulties in dealing with the regime, but also, and fundamentally, because they were not finding oil. Exxon-Mobil pulled out of Turkmenistan in 2002, citing disappointing drilling results as the reason, and Shell cut back its operations in 2003 due to poor prospects.

by poor pipeline connectivity, until after 2009 when Uzbekistan could access the Turkmenistan-China pipeline to export gas to China.

The fortunes of oil producers are hostage to world prices. In March 1998 when the world price hovered just above $10 per barrel, landlocked Central Asia with transport costs to deep-sea ports in excess of $10 did not look an attractive region for production.[10] Even after the Caspian Pipeline Consortium (CPC) pipeline opened in 2001 and reduced the cost of transporting Kazakhstan's oil, it cost $6.5 per barrel to transport oil from Tengiz to Novorossiysk and another $2 to Rotterdam. Transport costs from the second-largest producing oil field, Kumkol, averaged around $12 per barrel (Raballand and Esen, 2007). After the world price of oil reached $30 in 2001 and edged up above $50 in 2004, Central Asia became a much more attractive source of oil, and construction of the Baku-Ceyhan pipeline and a pipeline across Kazakhstan to China increased transport options and ended dependence on transiting Russia.

Natural gas is more dependent on pipelines than oil, which has feasible second-best transportation alternatives such as rail or trans-Caspian shipping. Gas suppliers and buyers have typically only been willing to construct a pipeline after agreement has been reached on both quantities and prices and long-term contracts have been signed. Thus, gas is less sensitive to price changes than oil. Nevertheless, the strength of demand for natural gas is influenced by the price of alternative energy. The price for Russian gas exports to the European Union is set by a formula that includes the price of oil, and hence increased rapidly after 2000. This became an increasing source of conflict between Turkmenistan and Russia in the 2000s, because Russia profited from the widening gap between what it paid to import Central Asian gas and what it received for gas exports to the EU.

Much international interest in economic events in Central Asia during the 2000s focused on the high politics of pipelines, which will be discussed in section 10.1. The economics of pipelines is complicated by the large initial cost and anticipated long life, over which the potential returns could be limited by the world price of oil or gas. Since 2000, falling shipping costs for liquefied natural gas (LNG) have increased the attractiveness of offshore gas fields and reduced the attractiveness of overland delivery from landlocked countries such as Turkmenistan (Denison, 2012).[11] Fortunately for Central Asia several oil pipelines were built during the 1998–2007 oil boom and the gas pipeline

10. In 1999, major oil companies like Shell and BP Amoco were operating on the assumption that the world oil price for the next five years would average $10. *The Economist* ("Cheap Oil," March 6, 1999) thought this was overoptimistic and that, due to new technologies and the availability of substitutes for oil, a more realistic projection was of prices between $5 and $10 per barrel.

11. In contrast to Denison's "Game Over" scenario, Yafimava (2015) contends that dramatic

from Turkmenistan to China was completed in 2009, eliminating Turkmenistan's dependence on delivering gas to Russia. However, future pipeline construction is unpredictable.[12]

3.3. Minerals

Before independence, Kazakhstan's economy was centered on minerals rather than on hydrocarbons. The coal miners in Karaganda were the elite workers, who suffered the biggest reversal of economic fortunes after 1991. Coal output declined from 130 million tons in 1991 to 58.5 million tons in 1999, and net exports fell by two-thirds in the first half of the 1990s, before plummeting further in 1998 as Russian demand collapsed. Domestic coal consumption in Kazakhstan fell from 86 million tons to 36 million tons during the 1990s, and continues falling in the twenty-first century as the country seeks to reduce carbon emissions. Kazakhstan has the world's largest uranium deposits and extensive sources of chromium, copper, gold, iron, lead, manganese, and zinc.

Other Central Asian countries were believed to have rich mineral resources, but few were exploited in the Soviet era. In the 1990s, gold production in Uzbekistan was around eighty tons a year, and the country's second-largest export after cotton. Tajikistan's nonferrous metal sector was dominated by aluminum, which reflected abundant hydroelectric power and not mineral wealth.

The most dramatic new mineral project after independence was the Kyrgyz Republic's Kumtor goldmine. The government moved quickly to reach a production sharing agreement with Cameco of Canada. The PSA was successful in bringing in appropriate foreign expertise and ensuring rapid exploitation of the resource, just in time for the boom in gold prices. However, the government has been repeatedly accused of giving too favorable terms to the foreign firm, and this has been a disruptive political issue in the country (chapter 7.3). Kazakhstan has also sought foreign partners to exploit its mineral wealth, but the assignation of property rights has been complex and progress slow.

Political conflicts are an almost inevitable counterpart to PSAs. The typical PSA allows the foreign company to recoup most of its upfront costs before the revenues are divided between the host and the company. The fairness of a PSA is difficult to assess due to the inherent uncertainties of mining, and a better-informed foreign partner may hide knowledge of the project's real costs.

---

changes are unlikely because setting up a network to distribute imported LNG across Europe, and especially to some eastern EU members, will take many years.

12. Security is also an issue. Proposed pipelines to South Asia have made no progress due to concerns about crossing Afghanistan.

The timing of exploitation matters. In the first decade of the twenty-first century the relative price of oil and gas and of copper and gold increased dramatically. Being able to take advantage of those favorable price trends gave resource-rich countries greater opportunity to create physical or human capital. Despite allegations of corruption, concerns that the foreigners were taking the country's resources, and environmental setbacks, the Kumtor mine began production and was generating about a sixth of Kyrgyz GDP in the early 2000s. This contribution was highlighted in 2002, when production suffered technical disruption and GDP growth dropped to zero. A striking contrast is Mongolia, whose government prevaricated over the terms under which its resources would be exploited, discouraging major mining companies.[13] Delay in exploitation may be even worse if country-specific resources become less valuable due to technical change (as, for example, happened to guano-exporting countries when superphosphate fertilizers were developed). Turkmenistan may face this scenario for its gas; if LNG or shale gas drive down prices and make new pipelines from Central Asia uneconomic, its gas will be a "stranded" resource. If resources are not extracted, then there is no domestic resource boom.

If the resources are produced, how this is done may make a difference. Luong and Weinthal (2010) laud the Uzbek/Turkmen approach of domestic ownership and control, but this can smother pressures for economic reform and become associated with stagnant output. Corrupt allocation of exploitation rights to favored partners may also have negative consequences, although the jury is still out on the long-run impact of institutional degradation in Kazakhstan in the 1990s, when granting of exploration rights and reapportioning of shares in consortia were associated with massive corruption; for Tengiz, the lead operator was technically competent, but this is less clear for the troubled Kashagan offshore megafield.[14] Similarly in the Kyrgyz Republic, the

13. Even when one of the world's largest copper and gold deposits was confirmed at Oyu Tolgoi, exploitation was delayed by a decade due to negotiations over contracts and amendments to the mining and taxation laws. Thus, Mongolia left its copper and gold in the ground during the boom, because it had not created conditions for exploitation of its mineral resources.

14. The Kashagan PSA was signed in 1997 with Eni as the lead operator. Repeated delays and cost increases led some of the consortium partners to sell out, while Italian prime ministers Prodi and Berlusconi flew to Astana to negotiate terms for maintaining Eni's position (Nurmakov, 2010, 29–32). In November 2010, Kazakhstan's financial police reported that Eni was under investigation for overrepresenting costs at Kashagan, which meant that the company had "avoided taxation and stolen state property" (reported in *Financial Times* (London), November 20, 2010). The government may, however, have been overreacting to unanticipated, but legitimate, delays and cost increases due to the harsh geological and climatic conditions. The costly misspecification of pipes that ended the first attempt to go online in 2013 (chapter 4) appears to have been more clearly Eni's responsibility.

initial deal with Cameco, for all its shortcomings, was with a major producer, whereas the more convoluted negotiations in the 2000s over other goldfields have been with companies of lesser standing.[15] The best outcomes are when a government keen to do business makes a deal with a good foreign partner, but haste may lead to poor bargaining over distribution of the spoils.

Sharing the rents is typically the most controversial part of a PSA. Host governments are understandably concerned about the extent to which revenue from national resources accrues to foreigners. Preserving the rents for the host country can, however, lead to a resource curse when the government becomes addicted to the grasping hand (as in the treatment of cotton in Uzbekistan and Turkmenistan) or when internecine conflict among the elite challenges social cohesion (as in the Kyrgyz Republic). Kazakhstan's resource nationalism in the 2000s involved increased shareholdings for the state-owned energy company KazMunaiGas (KMG) even when it contributed little, creating a poorer national environment for future foreign investment.

Sharing the rents equitably is difficult. Foreign participation is necessary when only foreign firms have the required technical expertise, skilled labor, and financial resources to explore and exploit the resources. The firms need to recoup their costs and make a normal profit, as well as self-insure for projects that prove barren. Moreover, there is a time-inconsistency problem; the foreign firm becomes more expendable once production is under way, so the foreign firm will insist on front-loading its share to reduce the costs of possible expropriation. PSAs are typically structured to reflect this time inconsistency, but with asymmetric information and transfer pricing the foreign firm may present the accounts to exaggerate the time taken for cost recovery. Many services and other inputs are intrafirm transactions with no market price, fueling the suspicion that foreign firms are using transfer-pricing to shift accounting costs to the PSA project. If the state fails to specify environmental or work-safety obligations or to hold the partner responsible for other negative externalities, then the partner will not be obligated to spend money on these. Because many energy or mining PSAs cover long-life projects, conditions will change, but the host may be tied to a contract under which changes can be challenged through arbitration that focuses on the narrow contractual arrangements without concern for social or other politically sensitive matters; ignoring an arbitration decision risks serious loss of future foreign investment.

Sharing the rents is controversial because changing the shares is perceived to be a zero-sum game, but there are long-term implications. The host nation should leave the foreign firm with a reasonable return on its physical and

---

15. Doolot and Heathershaw (2015) paint a negative picture of gold mining concessions in the Kyrgyz Republic.

knowledge capital, recognizing that investment in natural resources is a risky business. If the government pushes too hard, as in Mongolia, there will be no resource exploitation; PSAs worked better in Azerbaijan and Kazakhstan than in the Kyrgyz Republic, because the size of the oil price increase after 1998 led to massive windfall gains to the host countries even if they had not managed to maximize their share of the rents. Nevertheless, after about half a decade, the governments of both Azerbaijan and Kazakhstan tried to shift the shares in their favor by increasing the national oil companies' participation, with some success but at the risk of discouraging future foreign investment. If domestic companies are part of the exploiting consortium, then more revenues accrue domestically. The trade-off is that the domestic energy or mining companies often do not have much to contribute to the consortium; absence of technology and skills is the principal reason for involving foreign companies.

The possibility that the rents may be siphoned off in the negotiating stage or through a nontransparent state entity highlights the potential for rent-seeking rather than productive behavior, and hence for institutional degradation. Rents from the Kumtor goldmine were a source of internecine conflicts among the elite and of popular criticism of Kyrgyz presidents and their families in the first decade of the twenty-first century. Since 2010, competition over resource rents has shifted from the presidential palace to the Kyrgyz parliament, and the challenge will be to forge a political system in which governments are held accountable for public spending.[16] In Tajikistan, the Talco aluminum smelter was a major prize in the civil war, and a source of revenue for (and conflict within) the elite after the ceasefire; the main battleground, however, has been London law courts, rather than domestic regime change (chapter 8). Such conflicts have been less obvious in the oil and gas producing countries, perhaps because the size of the post-1998 boom allowed regimes to

16. Extractive Industries Transparency Initiative (EITI) commitments can provide a signal of transparency, although EITI endorsement does not reduce corruption if the government makes no implementation effort. Ölcer (2009) found that, in the six years after the EITI launch in 2002, countries endorsing EITI principles performed worse than the global average on measures such as the World Bank Governance Indicators or Transparency International's Corruption Perception Index. In April 2008, the World Bank proposed a new initiative (EITI++) focusing on the generation, management, and distribution of revenues, rather than just on the relationship between companies and governments as in the EITI. Both Kazakhstan and the Kyrgyz Republic made early commitments, but they took years to obtain validation—Kyrgyz Republic in March 2011 and Kazakhstan in October 2013. Tajikistan became an EITI candidate in 2013. Subsequently, Kazakhstan appeared to move to greater transparency, being praised as the first country to publish 2014 data on use of oil revenues (https://eiti.org/news/kazakhstan-takes-lead-timely-eiti-reporting). In March 2017, the Kyrgyz Republic and Tajikistan were suspended for making inadequate progress in the area of civil society reform, and were required to implement corrective actions before September 2018 in order to be reinstated as EITI members in good standing.

buy support or pay for repression.[17] Succession crises could be a catalyst for internecine conflicts over rents in the autocratic countries, but this did not happen in Turkmenistan in 2006 or Uzbekistan in 2016.

Once resources are being exploited governments face the question of how to use the revenues. As oil prices began to rise after 1998 and then soared after 2003, revenues in Kazakhstan far exceeded domestic absorption capacity, and the government created a sovereign wealth fund, the NFRK, to manage the windfall.[18] A major issue has been making a credible commitment to avoid short-term plundering of the fund's assets. Surges in social spending may be associated with diminishing returns and waste.[19] Kazakhstan has placed more emphasis on diversification of the economy and on human capital formation, but in the 2008–9 stimulus package withdrawals from the NFRK supported delinquent banks and funded inefficient diversification.

Reliance on resource revenues rather than taxes reduces the need for governments to seek popular support for spending, which fosters undemocratic systems and a lack of checks on executive power. This is most clearly apparent in Turkmenistan where the country's cotton and gas rents were largely spent on prestige projects in support of a personality cult or disappeared into foreign bank accounts. Populist measures to provide free or low-cost basic needs were provided at the government's pleasure, and residents had virtually no property rights (e.g., if the government chose to bulldoze their houses to make way for a new statue) or security of supply of power, heating, or plumbed water. In the absence of financial markets or real opportunity cost prices, the limited attempts at increasing productive capacity or diversification of the economy were grossly inefficient; textile mills and clothing factories to process Turkmen cotton had negative value-added at world prices (Pomfret, 2006, 94–95). Economic management has been better in Uzbekistan, but resource rent addiction fed an autocratic regime. This contributed to the disastrous decision to strengthen foreign exchange controls in 1996, and to the difficulties that the government had in unraveling the system based on economic controls rather than on individual decisions taken in a market framework.

17. In Turkmenistan, rents are simply placed in off-budget accounts under presidential control. When the first president died in 2006, a Deutsche Bank account in Frankfurt under his control contained over three billion dollars.

18. Kalyuzhnova and Kaser (2006) and Kalyuzhnova (2008) provide assessments of the oil funds of Azerbaijan, Kazakhstan, and Turkmenistan. The NFRK was established by presidential decree rather than by legislation that passed through parliament, leaving it subject to presidential discretion.

19. Esanov (2009) finds diminishing efficiency of expenditures as spending on health, education, and social policy increased in resource-rich former Soviet republics. Najman et al. (2008), using household surveys, conclude that the substantial decline in poverty rates in Kazakhstan during the oil boom was almost entirely due to direct impacts through the labor market, and that redistribution by the government played no discernible role.

Governments of fossil-fuel- and mineral-rich countries must decide how and how fast to exploit their natural resources, how to share the revenues between companies and the state, and how to use the state's revenues. These are interconnected. If the desired "how to exploit" is unacceptable to any company with the technology to exploit the resource, then the other questions become irrelevant. If the terms are too attractive to a private-sector partner, then the country may achieve rapid exploitation, but not have revenues to spend—or a stable government. Moreover, this is not a one-shot game: either side may try to recontract, leaving the other to accept, renegotiate, or give up on the deal. In a bilateral monopoly situation, the government may win a battle over division of the spoils, but deter future investors concerned about the credibility of government commitments.

3.4. Agriculture and Pastoralism

Central Asia has a large and varied agricultural and pastoral sector. In the southern part of Central Asia, the area watered by the two great rivers that flow into the Aral Sea, the Syrdarya and Amudarya, contains fertile oases. Under Russian tsarist and Soviet leadership, the cultivated area was increased, largely as irrigated cotton fields. Between 1960 and 1985 the irrigated area expanded from 4.6 to 8 million hectares and annual water use for irrigation increased from 56 bcm to 106 bcm, leading to the desiccation of the Aral Sea with large environmental costs that will be analyzed in section 9.4. The ecology of the northern steppes and the mountain regions of the southeast is different; the main Soviet-era innovation was the Virgin Lands campaign begun in the late 1950s by Khrushchev, which brought large areas of northern Kazakhstan under wheat, cultivated largely by Russian farmers.

In all the former Soviet Union, the initial stages of transition from central planning saw prices of agricultural outputs fall relative to the price of inputs. This led to a fall in output that was exacerbated by the disorganization that followed the end of central planning and dissolution of the USSR. Eventually, with institutional reform and appropriate relative prices agricultural output began to increase, so that the time-path of output followed a J-curve, although there was no reason to expect that the new equilibrium would involve a higher or a lower level of agricultural output than under central planning (Rozelle and Swinnen, 2004). The output mix in agriculture could be expected to change with the shift from planning to market-based economies, although the mix was also determined, especially in Uzbekistan and Turkmenistan, by government policies to promote grain self-sufficiency and to regulate cotton output.

In Central Asia, where most of the population was rural, a priority in large-scale restructuring was reform of the Soviet-era collective and state farms.

However, agrarian reform was among the slowest areas of enterprise restructuring, and had made the least progress by the end of the 1990s. Each country legislated land reforms early and often, reflecting evolving attitudes towards private ownership of land and about the desirable structure of production and farm size distribution; in few areas of the economy did implementation vary so dramatically. Even within countries, there could be substantial variation in the speed and nature of change, often determined by regional variations in type of farming, but sometimes depending on the local administration or power of former collective farm mangers aiming to retain their influence. Delays in implementation were often associated with a power vacuum in which asset-stripping in the collective farms was rampant. Local governments or individuals seized hold-up points in the agricultural supply chain, not just the cotton gins described in the next section, but also for tobacco, sugar, and oil processing. The variation in land reform and agrarian policies at the national level will be addressed in the country chapters.

Land reform in all but the pastoral areas and northern Kazakhstan is intimately linked to water, and there is widespread resistance to market-determined pricing of water.[20] Without water pricing and with unclear property rights, the profligate use of irrigation water inherited from the Soviet era has continued, and the maintenance of irrigation systems has deteriorated.[21]

Institutional reforms have had, at best, mixed success. In Uzbekistan, the introduction of Water Consumer Associations after 2003 was top-down, with variation in implementation across regions, and led to discontent.[22] The Kyrgyz Republic and Kazakhstan decentralized maintenance to farmers, who could not afford it. Collapse of monitoring led to piercing of irrigation channels to withdraw water illegally, especially in upstream areas. Downstream farmers became caught in a vicious circle, as diminished water flows increase the cost of maintaining irrigation facilities due to the greater accumulation of silt in irrigation channels. Pumped systems are often out of commission due

20. O'Hara (2000) analyzes the history of water management in Central Asia over the last eight millennia. Abdullaev and Rakhmatullaev (2015) cover the transformation since the Middle Ages.

21. Even in the Soviet era maintenance was neglected. According to reports summarized in World Bank (2002, vol.1, 5n), about half of the irrigation systems of Uzbekistan, Kazakhstan, and the Kyrgyz Republic were already in need of capital repairs in the early 1990s. The ICG (2014) highlights the poor maintenance of crucial upstream facilities, i.e. the Toktogul Dam and reservoir that controls the Syr Darya water flow and the silting of the Nurek Dam on an important Amu Darya tributary.

22. See Sehring (2002) and Veldwisch and Mollinga (2013). Regional case studies include Djanibekov et al. (2013) on Khorezm and Zinzani (2015) on Samarkand. Suspicion of top-down arrangements may reflect Uzbek citizens' experience of *mahallahs*, which were decentralized institutions for improving social welfare in the 1990s but became integrated into the government system as instruments for social control (Sievers, 2002).

to unavailability of parts. Given the difficulty of farm-level response to degradation of the irrigation systems and increased salinization, the principal consequence has been substantial declines in agricultural yields and rural incomes.

On the international level, water poses the most serious intra-Central Asia problems, because of conflict over water use and unwillingness to recognize a basis for agreement. Soviet planners in Moscow allocated water in the Aral Sea Basin, giving priority to release of water from the reservoirs in spring for irrigation, and guaranteeing that the upstream countries would receive gas, coal, and oil for their winter energy needs. After independence, the Central Asian countries continued to more or less accept the pre-1992 allocation. In February 1992, the five countries' ministers of water resources affirmed the existing structure of allocation (the Almaty Agreement). Water allocations in the Syrdarya Basin are 50.5% of the actual flow to Uzbekistan, 42.0% to Kazakhstan, 7.0% to Tajikistan, and 0.5% to the Kyrgyz Republic, and in the Amudarya Basin 42.3% to Turkmenistan, 42.3% to Uzbekistan, 15.2% to Tajikistan, and 0.3% to the Kyrgyz Republic. The arrangement was under stress by the end of 1990s due to excess demand and disagreement over priorities that pitted upstream against downstream countries, and the outcome was less and less water reaching the Aral Sea.

Many national measures, notably more efficient water allocation and use, could improve the situation (Khasanova, 2014; ICG, 2014), but incentives are weak as long as water is under- or unpriced for the most important users. Since 97% of the fresh water is consumed by irrigated agriculture (Punkari et al., 2014, 11), there will be severe shortages unless progress is made in areas such as reducing water demand, increasing efficiency of water use in agriculture, and recycling irrigation water. At a regional level, the main issues to be settled are the balance between water use by upstream and downstream nations and sharing of the cost of maintaining reservoirs and other facilities that affect the flow but are disproportionately in upstream countries and maintained (or not) at their expense.

3.5. Cotton

Cotton is by far the most important crop in Central Asia. The timing of the incorporation of the area south of the steppe into the Russian Empire in the 1860s partly reflected fears of a cotton famine due to the American Civil War.[23]

23. The Russian conquest of Central Asia is the subject of a special issue of *Central Asian Survey* 33(2), 2014. Morrison (2014) downplays the importance of cotton in the conquest, arguing that the conquest had begun in the 1840s and the 1853–56 Crimean War delayed the capture of Tashkent.

The importance of finding locations with a climate suitable for cotton production reflected the value of the crop since the industrial revolution, when cotton textiles became the world's major manufactured good, a feature that gave cotton the nickname "white gold" (Beckert, 2014). Features of cotton production are the crop's thirst for water, and the high seasonal demand for labor during harvesting; mechanization of cotton picking is only profitable with high labor costs, and tends to damage the crop, so that hand-picking has better quality results. Before being baled and shipped to the spinning mills, raw cotton must be ginned to separate the lint from the seeds.

The cotton economy expanded during the tsarist and Soviet eras, and especially rapidly after 1945. Major irrigation projects, of which the Karakum Canal in southern Turkmenistan was the largest and most environmentally disastrous, brought large new areas into cotton production at the cost of reducing the Aral Sea, the world's fifth-largest lake in 1960, to a couple of ponds in the 2000s. Mechanization of cotton harvesting was a propaganda coup in the 1960s aimed at showing the Third World how modernization was occurring in the poorest part of the USSR, although in fact conscripted student or child labor picked much of the harvest. Most of the cotton output in the Soviet era went to cotton mills in the Russian republic, while cotton sold on world markets went through centralized foreign trade agencies, with little benefit to the growers.[24]

According to data from the International Cotton Advisory Committee, in 1990 Uzbekistan was the world's second-largest cotton exporter (397,000 tons) and Tajikistan the fourth largest (200,000 tons). Cotton was also a significant export for Turkmenistan and was regionally important for the southern part of the Kyrgyz Republic and for South Kazakhstan. In 1988, of the 3,133 hectares sown with cotton in Soviet Central Asia, 2,017 were in the Uzbek republic, 636 in the Turkmen republic, 320 in the Tajik republic, 128 in Kazakhstan, and 32 in the Kyrgyz republic (Lewis, 1992, 144).

After independence, a major windfall to the southern republics was that they now controlled cotton sales. Cotton was readily sold through international brokers, such as Paul Reinhart in Winterthur, Switzerland, or Cargill in Liverpool, England, and its portability and high value to weight ratio meant that it could be transported by rail or air. World prices more than doubled between 1992 and 1995, benefitting especially Uzbekistan and Turkmenistan because Tajikistan was devastated by civil war. Uzbekistan increased its cotton

24. The Uzbek republic, however, benefited by more than it was supposed to as the local leadership masterminded an overstatement of cotton output that directed billions of extra rubles into the republic. The Uzbek leadership was one of the first targets of Mikhail Gorbachev's anticorruption campaign, although long-term leader Sharif Rashidov avoided punishment by his timely death in 1986. After independence Rashidov was treated as a national hero in Uzbekistan, and one of Tashkent's main streets was renamed in his honor.

supplies to the world market, reaching a peak of nine hundred thousand tons exported in 1998 and in 1999. The ability to realize export revenues immediately allowed Uzbekistan and Turkmenistan to avoid the public finance difficulties experienced by other former Soviet republics.

Cotton production has the characteristics of a point-sourced resource, even though cotton is grown across large areas without obvious economies of scale. Raw cotton must be ginned, a process that removes cotton fiber from the seeds and cleans out other impurities, reducing the weight by about two-thirds. Because baled cotton after ginning has far lower transport costs than raw cotton before ginning, farmers tend to deliver their cotton to the nearest gin, and accept the price paid at that point. The gins' local monopsony power facilitates rent extraction by the gin-owners or the state.

The governments of both Uzbekistan and Turkmenistan use state-marketing monopolies to regulate the price paid to the farmers. The gap between the procurement price and the world price, minus ginning and other costs, is the main source of transfers from agriculture to the state budget. In the mid-1990s, transfers out of agriculture, primarily from cotton, were large, amounting to 11–15% of GDP in Turkmenistan and 8–10% of GDP in Uzbekistan (Pomfret, 2006, table 7.6). Both governments became addicted to resource rents. They were unconcerned by failure to implement a tax system suited to a market-based economy, or by incentive problems and difficulties controlling quality associated with state-marketing.

Outcomes were similar, but not identical. In Uzbekistan, the state played a positive function in maintaining irrigation channels and ensuring input supply so that long-run cotton output remained roughly constant, whereas in Turkmenistan these functions were not performed well even though virtually all cropland in Turkmenistan is irrigated.[25] The explanation is partly in terms of initial conditions; Tashkent was the center of Soviet Central Asia with greater administrative capacity (and the Ministry of Water Resources employed more people than any other ministry in the Uzbek Soviet Republic), but Turkmenistan lacked such a legacy of competent administration.

The downturn of world cotton prices, which had dropped more than a third by October 1996 when Uzbekistan was starting to sell that year's harvest, provided the backdrop to panic over the balance of payments that led to the hurried introduction of exchange controls. Worse was to follow as the world price of cotton bottomed out in October 2001. Two years later it had doubled, but it then fell by over a quarter in the 2004–5 harvest season. The volatility

---

25. During the 1990s the budget for maintaining the Karakum Canal, the core of the irrigation system in southern Turkmenistan, fell from $3.2 million to $20,000 and the personnel employed in maintenance fell from 1,700 in 1987 to 640 in 1999. By 2001, the World Bank estimated that 97% of the irrigated land in Turkmenistan was affected by salinization, a problem that had been avoided in irrigated agriculture in the area since prehistoric times (O'Hara and Hannan, 1999).

largely affected government revenues in Uzbekistan and Turkmenistan, because the state order systems insulated farmers from world price movements. In 2002 Uzbekistan was still the world's second-biggest cotton exporter (with 717,000 tons), but the government was concerned that world prices seemed to be in secular decline; the nominal price was lower in January 2002 than in January 1952 or January 1992.[26] These worries contributed to Uzbekistan's decision in 2003/4 to undertake economic reforms aimed at economic diversification.

Tajikistan and Turkmenistan had had cotton harvests of over a million tons in the Soviet era, but they were producing only a fifth of that in the 2004/5 harvest (table 3.2a), in large part because of poor maintenance of irrigation canals. Poor management and sale to domestic textile mills reduced Turkmenistan's cotton exports to the point that they were lower than Kazakhstan's. Cotton production in Tajikistan was disrupted by civil war until 1997, after which the government gave substantial power to a foreign cotton agent, and the sector went through a nontransparent evolution during the 2000s (Kassam, 2011). Tajikistan had slipped to the ninth-largest cotton exporter with 147,000 tons in 2002. Over the next decade there was some recovery in Central Asian cotton output and exports, but less than in other major producers, so that Uzbekistan slipped to the fifth-biggest exporter and Tajikistan to sixteenth biggest (table 3.2b). Turkmenistan's data are suspicious; reported exports were exactly one thousand bales (or 218 metric tons) in 2012/3 and several succeeding years.

Domestic conditions in Central Asian cotton producers have varied considerably since independence, and are more difficult to document than world market conditions. In contrast to the state procurement systems for cotton in Turkmenistan and Uzbekistan, the Kyrgyz Republic eliminated state procurement in 1992 and Kazakhstan and Tajikistan did so in the mid-1990s. Petrick et al. (2017) argue that Kazakhstan's laissez-faire cotton restructuring of the 1990s fostered good performance, reflected in the 2004/5 output levels compared to the much larger, by hectares sown, cotton sectors of Tajikistan, Turk-

---

26. The nominal price comparison is sensitive to the choice of dates, but it is indisputable that in real terms (e.g., relative to the price of manufactures) cotton prices declined substantially over the second half of the twentieth century. Part of the decline was due to tastes and technology, as artificial fibers challenged cotton and as genetically modified cotton raised the productivity of cotton producers in the USA, Australia, and China; part reflected policy decisions in the USA and the EU who provided huge subsidies to cotton producers in the 1980s. Estimates of the effects of removing these production and export subsidies went as high as a 71% increase in world cotton prices (using 2001/2 as the base year), and a 6% increase in the volume of Uzbekistan's cotton exports (Baffes, 2004, 18–19), which would increase Uzbekistan's GDP by around five percentage points (Pomfret, 2005a). Cotton prices were also depressed by rich countries' polices towards imports of textiles and clothing; the worst of these arrangements were phased out as part of the 1994 Uruguay Round agreement, but the back-loaded process was only completed in 2004.

TABLE 3.2A. Cotton Output, 2004/5 Season and 2012/13 Season

	2004/5 season (thousand tons)		2012/13 season (thousand tons)	
	Production	Exports	Production	Exports
Kazakhstan	142	114	147	76
Kyrgyz Republic	48	44	31	22
Tajikistan	174	131	194	142
Turkmenistan	207	87	555	218
Uzbekistan	1,089	740	1,307	697
World Total	25,412	7,247	52,801	10,174

TABLE 3.2B. Cotton Output and Exports, 2014/15 Season

	2014/15 season (thousand 480-pound bales)	
	Production	Exports
Kazakhstan	200	130 (27th)
Kyrgyz Republic	40	40 (37th)
Tajikistan	335	325 (16th)
Turkmenistan	1,300	1,000 (8th)
Uzbekistan	3,700 (6th)	2,300 (5th)

Source: United States Department of Agriculture, Foreign Agricultural Service at
http://apps.fas.usda.gov/psdonline/circulars/cotton.pdf.
Note: World rank is in parentheses.

menistan, and Uzbekistan (table 3.2a). However, after cartelization in 2004 and introduction of new government regulations in 2007, cotton output, exports, and acreage all declined in Kazakhstan.

Different organizational structures led to substantial differences in farmgate prices. In the 1997 harvest season, the average border parity price for Central Asian cotton (i.e. the world price minus transport costs) of $404 per ton was not far from the prices received by farmers in the Kyrgyz Republic, Tajikistan, and Kazakhstan, but it was substantially above the prices received by farmers in Turkmenistan or Uzbekistan (table 3.3). By 2003 large gaps had emerged between farmgate prices in Kazakhstan and the Kyrgyz Republic and lower prices in Tajikistan, as the hold of a few members of the Tajik elite over the cotton gins tightened. The difference between the farmgate price and the border parity price accrues as government revenue in Uzbekistan and Turkmenistan, and as monopoly profits in Tajikistan.[27]

27. Markowitz (2013) argues that both Uzbekistan and Tajikistan have suffered a resource curse as cotton rent extraction led to institutional degradation, but the symptoms differed. In Uzbekistan, the relatively even geographical dispersion of cotton farming across provinces al-

TABLE 3.3. Cotton Price Received by Farmers, 1997 and 2003 (US Dollars)

	Kazakhstan	Kyrgyz Republic	Tajikistan	Turkmenistan	Uzbekistan
1997	349	394	388	240 (188)	242 (105)
2003	550	450	165	na	200

Sources: Goletti and Chabot (2000, 55); Swinnen, Sadler, and Vandeplas (2006).
Notes: Numbers in parentheses at parallel exchange rate; na = not available in the source.

The state marketing system in Uzbekistan and Turkmenistan provided an incentive for an overvalued official exchange rate, which would make the gap between farmgate and border parity prices less transparent.[28] In Uzbekistan, the procurement price at the black-market exchange rate was about a quarter of the border parity price in 1997 (table 3.3), and the burden of the overvalued exchange rate, represented by the gap between domestic and world prices, increased in the remainder of the 1990s. Turkmenistan's black-market premium only became substantial in 1998 so the effect of forex controls is not so great in table 3.3, but it became a major source of price distortion after 1997.

In Uzbekistan's more regulated system, farmers receive subsidized inputs and appear to benefit from more reliable supply of seed and fertilizers and better-managed irrigation than farmers in the Kyrgyz Republic or in Tajikistan. Farmers in Turkmenistan and Uzbekistan also benefit from advanced interest-free partial payments, although it is unclear how promptly these and the final payments were made available and how free farmers are to use monies credited to their bank accounts. Detailed information is scarce and dated.[29]

Based on a 2013 workshop of Uzbek and Kazakh cotton farmers, Shtaltovna and Hornidge estimated costs and revenues in each country (table 3.4).

---

lowed the central government to retain control over a corrupt system. In Tajikistan, the concentration of cotton wealth (around Khujand and in the southwest) led to conflict between these regions and poorer regions, leading to a fractious state in which the central government has little control over parts of the country where local elites, lacking resource rents, rely on the narcotics trade.

28. Krueger, Schiff, and Valdes (1988) found that overvalued exchange rates imposed a more serious burden on farmers in eighteen developing countries than did trade barriers or other direct taxes.

29. Goletti and Chabot (2000) provided data on differences in fertilizer prices, and reported that all five countries' cotton sectors were wasteful of water, relative to cotton growers elsewhere; in 1996–98, kilograms of seed cotton produced per thousand cubic meters of water used were 309 in Kazakhstan, 230 in the Kyrgyz Republic, 125 in Tajikistan, 256 in Turkmenistan, and 273 in Uzbekistan, which were all much lower than in other cotton-producing countries, e.g., 462 in Syria, 487 in California, 610 in Australia, and 1,027 in Greece. Although these numbers, and others reported in the text, are old, anecdotal evidence suggests that the cotton sector has not fundamentally changed in the opening decades of the twenty-first century.

TABLE 3.4. Revenues, Costs, and Gross Margin per Hectare of Cotton Farmers in Uzbekistan and Kazakhstan, 2013

Uzbekistan		Kazakhstan	
REVENUES			
Yield (tons/ha)	2.6	Yield (tons/ha)	2.9
Price (USD/ton)	409	Price (USD/ton)	432
		Subsidy	118.8
Revenue per hectare	**1,063.4**	**Revenue per hectare**	**1,371.6**
EXPENSES			
Harrowing	19	Harrowing	32.4
Plowing	87	Plowing	54.0
Rental/use of cultivator	152	Rental/use of cultivator	40.5
Sowing	19	Sowing	10.8
Seeds	38	Seeds	16.2
Cutting	57	Cutting	54.0
Fertilizers	143	Fertilizers	67.5
Defoliation	19	Defoliation	37.8
Weeding & plant protection	111	Weeding & plant protection	67.5
Hand harvesting	182	Hand harvesting	290.0
Transportation	29	Transportation	37.8
Other mechanical works	48	Other mechanical works	70.2
Income tax	33	Taxes	14.0
Pension fund	15		
Social insurance	33	Irrigation	8.1
Land tax	40		
Road fund	18		
School fund	6.5		
Other labor costs	130		
Meeting attendance	10		
Bank charges	25		
Costs per hectare	**1,214.5**	**Costs per hectare**	**800.8**
Gross margin	**−151.1**	**Gross margin**	**570.8**

Source: Shtaltovna and Hornidge (2014, 29).

Notes: Prices in USD calculated at the official exchange rate; in Uzbekistan at the unofficial rate the US dollar was worth about 30% more sum.

They found little difference in the price received by farmers (at least if calculated at the official exchange rate in Uzbekistan), but that farmers in Uzbekistan had much higher costs, apart from for irrigation. Shtaltovna and Hornidge (2014, 28) conclude that Uzbek farmers continue to accept the state procurement system and produce at a loss because cotton growers who help the local governor to meet output targets are rewarded by favors such as permission to operate other businesses or preferred access to non-cotton-related subsidies.

Full costing of the net benefits of cotton production is complicated by lack of information about harvesting techniques. Given relative factor scarcities it seems unlikely that mechanization of cotton picking has ever been efficient in labor-abundant Central Asia (Pomfret, 2002a), and the share of the cotton harvest picked by machine has declined substantially since independence as farms are unwilling to purchase new machines and even appear to let existing machines stay idle to avoid the running costs. The estimates in table 3.4 indicate that hand-picking dominates. In Turkmenistan, Uzbekistan, and Tajikistan the Soviet-era practice of forced labor was continued to varying degrees (ICG, 2005, 18–25; Keller, 2015); despite official bans on child labor, children as young as nine have been required to pick cotton. Apart from the negative impact on their education, the children are exposed to various health risks from being required to spray pesticides or from only having access to insanitary water. Progress toward ending the practice in Uzbekistan is discussed in chapter 5.

3.6. Hydroelectricity

The large dams on the two main Central Asian river systems, the Amudarya and Syrdarya, were constructed in the Soviet era primarily to regulate the flow of water to irrigate the downstream cottonfields during the spring and summer growing season. Hydroelectricity was generated, but it was of secondary importance (apart from in the South Tajik aluminum complex), and the two upstream countries, Tajikistan and the Kyrgyz Republic, were compensated by shipments of gas from Uzbekistan and coal from Kazakhstan to cover their winter heating needs. In the twenty-first century, as downstream countries demanded higher prices for their gas and oil while expecting the same flows of water, the upstream countries looked to generate their own power by hydroelectric projects.

A key characteristic of renewable energy sources such as hydro, wind, or solar is that, unlike fossil fuels such as coal, oil, and gas, they can only be transported as electricity. The Soviet Union did not have a single electricity grid; coal-based power stations in Aktobe (Aktyubinsk) and Uralsk in northern Kazakhstan supplied electricity to Siberia as well as locally, but not to the rest of Kazakhstan. The United Power System of Central Asia (UPS) was developed in the 1960s with installed generating capacity of about 25,000 megawatts (MW), of which just under two-thirds was thermal power stations and just over a third hydropower; the largest hydropower stations are Nurek in Tajikistan (3,000 MW capacity) and Toktogul in the Kyrgyz Republic (1,200 MW capacity). Of the total UPS power, 51% was generated in Uzbekistan, 15%

in Tajikistan, 14% in the Kyrgyz Republic, 11% in Turkmenistan, and 9% in southern Kazakhstan (Biddison, 2002, 7). The UPS operated as an integrated power pool, whose main transmission lines covered southern Kazakhstan, the other four Central Asian countries, and part of Afghanistan; Afghanistan's own electricity supply is tiny, with installed generating capacity of less than 500 MW.

The UPS and other electricity facilities, built with equipment from the USSR and Eastern Europe, were poorly maintained after 1991; estimated actual working capacity of the UPS power stations in the 1990s was less than 19,000 MW (Biddison, 2002, 7). During the 1990s, the Central Asian countries generally ignored the problems (e.g., increasing difficulty in obtaining parts, poor design for metering usage, and generally antiquated control and monitoring systems), or rather exacerbated the problems by charging less than cost-recovery prices for electricity. Thus, while electricity tariffs in 2008 were between $0.11 and $0.23 per kilowatt hour (KwH) among the Eastern European countries that joined the EU, they were $0.05 or lower in the Central Asian countries; Kazakhstan was the best of the worst with tariffs equivalent to 5.3 US cents (Carvalho, 2015, 6). Cheap electricity is, of course, politically popular, and any tariff increases would be politically explosive in a poverty-stricken country like Tajikistan, but with tariffs of $0.01 per KwH for residential users, the Tajik system was hopelessly underfunded and the consequence was frequent black-outs.

As general economic conditions improved in the twenty-first century, steps were taken to improve the electricity supply system either at the national level or through foreign investment. However, the outcomes have been uneven, with Tajikistan left in a precarious position since 2009 when Uzbekistan withdrew from the regional grid; Fields et al. (2013, xiii) estimated that after 2009 approximately 70% of the Tajik people suffered from extensive shortages of electricity during the winter.[30] Kazakhstan began experimenting with private-public partnerships or divesting its electricity companies by auction, but with limited success. Nevertheless, generation assets remain old, technical losses are high, and billing, collections, and payments are poor (Waters, 2015, 88).

Because the sector is politically sensitive, the problem is hidden by capital consumption, poor service, underpricing of electricity, and lack of enforcement of payment (especially from state-owned enterprises). These so-called "quasi-fiscal deficits" amount to a drain on the state budget, and often transfer the problem, e.g., by sustaining unproductive state enterprises or by hampering small enterprises' activities through unpredictable blackouts (Saavalainen

---

30. Fields et al. (2013, 3–4 and appendix B) summarize the complex history of the regional grid, from which countries have exited and rejoined.

and ten Berge, 2006). The dire situation is reflected in the low EBRD scores for infrastructure reform (table 2.2): on electricity, the EBRD gave Kazakhstan a score of 3+ in 2010, but the other countries all received 2+ (Kyrgyz Republic and Uzbekistan), 2 (Tajikistan), or 1 (Turkmenistan). Since then Kazakhstan has made some progress in unbundling and privatizing parts of the electricity sector and increasing investment, which is related to a transition to cleaner energy sources (section 11.2).[31]

The basic principles of the Soviet water arrangements have been maintained in annual agreements, but the upstream countries have been tempted to use the water to generate more power in winter, causing the downstream countries to complain about the inadequate flow of water in the spring when it is needed for irrigation. The two distinct but related issues are seasonality and the size of the flow. Seasonality leads to conflict between use for hydroelectricity in winter when demand is highest in the upstream countries and release in spring and summer for irrigation in downstream countries. New hydro projects have been strongly opposed by downstream countries, and the Tajikistan-Uzbekistan relationship became especially tense in the twenty-first century. An implicit incentive for the Kyrgyz Republic and Tajikistan to accede to the Eurasian Economic Union is to obtain more concrete military guarantees from Russia in case Uzbekistan escalates the water conflicts.

Water from the river system is already fully utilized, to the extent of having destroyed the Aral Sea. As facilities deteriorate the situation is getting worse, spilling over into declining quality and in some places reduced availability of water for households. Longer-term prospects are even worse, if Afghanistan's economy recovers and if climate change predictions prove accurate. Demand for water will continue to increase with population growth, and especially if peace in Afghanistan leads to farmers in northern Afghanistan taking their historical share of Amudarya water.[32] In the longer term, there is a threat of lower supply due to climate change over the twenty-first century reducing the volume of mountain glaciers, whose melt contributes a significant part of the flow (38% of the Amudarya and 11% of the Sirdarya flow, according to Punkari et al., 2014, 11), and whose predicted melt will accelerate. Punkari et al. (2014) predict an average increase in annual mean temperature of about three degrees Celsius by 2050, with some variation in incidence and consequences; parts of

31. If Central Asia does establish a modern transmission system to transport electricity produced from renewables, it could benefit from major technical advances such as ultra-high-voltage transmission and smart systems that can reduce costs and adjust demand and supply to meet short-term fluctuations, as well as strengthening billing procedures.

32. Afghanistan's portion of the basin is primarily along its border with Tajikistan, before the water reaches Uzbekistan or Turkmenistan. Of the Amudarya's average annual flow of 63 cubic kilometers (km^3), about 19 km^3 is generated in Afghanistan.

Kazakhstan may gain from global warming, while the major losers will be Turkmenistan, Uzbekistan, and western Kazakhstan.[33]

3.7. Conclusions

The country chapters in this book emphasize policy choices and their consequences, but short- and medium-term outcomes were strongly influenced by external forces as the countries entered world markets after the dissolution of the USSR. Swings in world prices of cotton and oil, for example, had unsynchronized effects on the two largest Central Asian countries. Uzbekistan's relatively good performance in 1990–95 was helped by buoyant world cotton prices, but in 1996–2009 Uzbekistan faced substantially lower world cotton prices. Meanwhile, Kazakhstan struggled through the 1990s, but then rode an oil boom between 1999 and 2014.

The long-run relationship between resource abundance and economic performance is harder to assess. Resource booms create the potential for investment in physical and human capital and in infrastructure to promote long-run economic growth, but global evidence indicates that resource abundance can be a curse. The extensive resource curse literature in the late 1990s and early 2000s influenced some policymakers and their economic advisers, e.g., it was understood that steps needed to be taken to avoid a curse outcome associated with Dutch Disease or excessively procyclical fiscal policy.

Resource curse outcomes are not inevitable, but resource-abundant countries do face significant obstacles if they want to avoid such an outcome. Maximizing exploitation in an efficient and timely fashion may require some degree of surrender of local control; a PSA needs to be carefully drafted. Once the resources are being exploited and revenues are flowing, the host government needs to ensure that it receives a fair share of revenues, in which it may be hampered by asymmetric information. Thirdly, the revenues must be used efficiently, both in the present and future. Turkmenistan in the 1990s stalled at the first hurdle, while the Kyrgyz Republic in the 2000s became bogged down at the second hurdle. Kazakhstan reached the third hurdle, and has made good efforts to use resource revenues effectively, indicating that "institutions" are not unchangeable; the evolution from a state apparently mired in oil-related corruption in the 1990s to present-day Kazakhstan provides an example of how flexible a transition economy could be.

---

33. The World Bank (based on Fay et al., 2009) ranks Tajikistan as most vulnerable to climate change among all countries of Europe and Central Asia, in part due to its low adaptive capacity, and the Kyrgyz Republic the third most vulnerable. Lioubimtseva and Hennebry (2012) predict net gains to Kazakhstan from global warming.

The Kyrgyz Republic and Tajikistan suffer from a paucity of readily exploitable natural resources and their isolated location. Attempts to increase hydroelectricity generation bring them into conflict with downstream countries. The issue has brought together the leaders of Uzbekistan and Kazakhstan, who in meetings regularly affirm the need to involve downstream countries in any dam construction or reservoir decisions. Tensions between Tajikistan and Uzbekistan may have eased since the death of President Karimov, and in 2017 Tajikistan pushed ahead with construction of the Rogun Dam (chapter 8). Expansion of renewable energy sources such as hydropower and wind and solar energy, which cannot be transported like fossil fuels, will require upgrading of Central Asia's decrepit electricity generation and transmission system.

PART II

The National Economies

4

Kazakhstan

Kazakhstan is on the borderlands of Central Asia, with southern areas typical of Central Asia and northern areas more closely resembling neighboring regions of Russia (and heavily populated by Russian speakers), and sparsely populated arid land in the middle. Russia was welcomed into the Kazakh steppes in alliances with differing nomadic groups, in contrast to the forcible incorporation of the rest of Central Asia into the Russian Empire. Soviet documents frequently referred to the region as Kazakhstan and Central Asia. At independence, Kazakhstan had higher incomes, less poverty, more human capital, and apparently better economic prospects than its southern neighbors. In the twenty-first century, Kazakhstan has been distinguished by massive oil exports.

Kazakhstan's national economic history divides sharply between 1991–98 and the years since 1999. The first period, dominated by nation-building, saw traumatic economic adjustment to the shocks of the early 1990s, and a large unanticipated decline in living standards. As the country started to recover from the economic nadir in 1997 it was hit by the 1998 Russian crisis, and only in 1999 did sustained economic growth begin. However, when growth did begin, stimulated by policy decisions such as a large currency devaluation and sustained by rising oil prices, Kazakhstan enjoyed a decade during which it was one of the fastest growing economies in the world.

The boom was interrupted by a banking crisis in 2007–8, whose impact was exacerbated by the collapse in the price of oil in the second half of 2008. The government responded in 2009 by bailing out the troubled banks as part of a stabilization package, which relative to GDP was one of the world's largest stimulus packages. The economy recovered, thanks also to the rebound in oil prices, initiating a period of consolidation amidst uncertainty about world energy prices. In 2014, oil prices again fell drastically, and this time there was no quick rebound. Despite the setbacks, Kazakhstan remains far richer than its southern neighbors.

The first two sections of this chapter trace out the path from the dismal 1990s through the 1999–2007 oil boom. Section 4.3 covers the agriculture sector, which accounts for the largest share of employment, and section 4.4 examines the health, education, and other social sectors. The fifth section analyzes the 2007–8 banking crisis, which interrupted the boom and whose resolution led to increasing roles for the state holding company Samruk-Kazyna and other parastatals between 2009 and 2014, and a diminished role for private banks. Many observers identified the outcome as resource nationalism, similar to developments in Russia, and backtracking from the reforming intent of the 1990s. In 2014–16, however, the government appeared to be reasserting a commitment to market-led development that had been embodied in visions such as the *2030 Strategy* of 1997 and restated in 2012 in the Kazakhstan 2050 strategy as a path to becoming one of the world's thirty leading economies (section 4.6).[1] In sum, the balance between strong leadership of a developmental state and a less centralized market-driven economy remains uncertain.

4.1. The Dismal 1990s

In the initial years following independence, the policy focus was on nation-building, the transition from central planning, and securing foreign participation in developing the country's rich energy reserves (Cohen, 2008, 17–63). As elsewhere in Central Asia, Kazakhstan's economy was hit by three shocks—the end of central planning, the dissolution of the Soviet Union, and hyperinflation—causing massive economic disruption that lasted until 1996–97. Additionally, given the unique situation in which the titular nationality was not in the majority, Kazakhstan's leadership faced mass emigration from urban areas of people with German or Slav backgrounds, and real prospects of secession or internal conflict in the northern Russian-dominated part of the country. Among the consequences for economic policy were President Nazarbayev's attempts to maintain close economic relations with Russia, and the decision to relocate the national capital in 1997 from Almaty in the southeast to the center-north of the country, adjacent to the main regions of ethnic Russians.[2]

1. I do not address political issues although they were the first two priorities in the strategy. Nation-building, national security, and political stability have been achieved by President Nazarbayev despite some inauspicious initial conditions.

2. Kazakhstan was the last Soviet republic to formally declare its independence in 1991 and in 1992–94 its president was the most assiduous in trying to construct a viable successor organiza-

The 1990s were dismal years of severe and unforeseen hardship. This could not be explained by war as in most of the CIS economic disasters, and with its high initial income and human capital and abundant natural resources Kazakhstan might have been expected to do much better. The most plausible explanation is in terms of disorganization—a theory of transitional recession popularized by Olivier Blanchard (1997) and applied to Kazakhstan by de Broeck and Kostial (1998). Kazakhstan's government moved quickly towards price liberalization in January 1992, but it failed to follow up with the institutions required for a well-functioning market economy. Thus, the functioning, albeit inefficiently, coordinating mechanisms of central planning were followed by a coordinating void.

Physical disintegration was exacerbated because, among the Soviet republics, Kazakhstan was one of the most tightly integrated into the Union economy. Kazakhstan's mineral wealth was associated with single-enterprise towns dependent on production chains involving suppliers, smelters, and end-users elsewhere in the Soviet Union, usually in Russia. The fledgling oil industry in western Kazakhstan relied on Russian pipelines, but Kazakhstan's own major refineries in Pavlodar in the northeast and Shymkent in the south were linked by pipeline to Siberian oil fields.

The privatization of large enterprises in 1995–96 added to the short-term confusion. The long-run implications are less certain. Providing clearer ownership rights may have facilitated restructuring of large enterprises, but Hoff and Stiglitz (2004) argue that the disregard for legality or fairness in Kazakhstan-style privatization had long-run negative consequences for the emergence of the rule of law. Pastoralists, faced with the privatization of farms plus unclear property rights to grazing, look back to the 1990s and early 2000s as "the period of chaos" (Kerven et al., 2016).

Kazakhstan experienced high emigration during the 1990s (table 4.1), as its population fell from over seventeen million at the time of independence to less than fifteen million a decade later. In the final Soviet census in 1989, the population consisted of roughly two-fifths Kazakhs, two-fifths Russians, and one-fifth other ethnic groups. The Russians, who had been the largest group in the republic a decade earlier, were concentrated in the capital city, Almaty, and in northern and eastern regions bordering the Russian Federation. Among the "other" groups were large contingents of ethnic Germans and Koreans who had been shipped to Kazakhstan by Stalin who feared their potential to be a fifth-column supporting invaders from the west and east. Most of the Germans took advantage of German citizenship laws to emigrate to Germany in the early 1990s. Together with Russian emigration, both of which contained

---

tion to the USSR. The city that would be the new capital went through a series of name changes from the pre-independence Tselinograd to Akmola to Astana.

TABLE 4.1. Kazakhstan: Immigration and Emigration, 1991–2003 (Thousands)

	1991	1992	1993	1994	1995	1996	1997	1998	1999	2000	2001	2002	2003
Immigration	171	162	111	70	71	54	38	41	41	57	54	58	65
Emigration	228	327	333	481	310	229	299	144	165	156	142	120	74

Source: International Organization for Migration data.

a disproportionate number of the country's well-educated and skilled people, this constituted a substantial brain drain in the early post-independence years.[3]

About one million Russians and seven hundred thousand Germans left Kazakhstan during the 1990s (Kolstø, 2004, 170). The exodus slowed substantially with the Russian crisis in 1998, but until 2002 annual emigration remained over one hundred thousand; it only began to drop substantially with the post-2000 oil boom. After 2003 Kazakhstan became a country of net immigration, although the numbers are complicated by the fact that many immigrants were undocumented temporary workers attracted by booming construction in the major cities and by higher wages for farm and other workers than in neighboring Uzbekistan or Kyrgyzstan.

Emigration complicates comparison of Kazakhstan's economic performance because output comparisons across transition countries are usually by total output rather than per capita GDP, so that Kazakhstan's relative performance may look worse than it would if output per head were the criteria. In addition, the biases of all GDP estimates for transition economies probably overstate the extent of the initial recession. Other indicators of well-being reinforce the impression that Kazakhstan did not perform as poorly as the GDP estimates suggest, and that this gap between estimates and reality was bigger for Kazakhstan than for neighboring CIS countries (Pomfret, 2003c). Nevertheless, whatever its absolute or relative magnitude, Kazakhstan's output performance in the 1990s was well below potential.

The institutional environment deteriorated from a promising pluralism in 1993–94 to crony capitalism in 1995–96, largely due to competition over resource rents. In 1992 Kazakhstan followed Russia's price liberalization and path of rapid reform, but during 1993 President Nazarbayev encountered strenuous opposition from the parliament over the pace of reform.[4] The con-

3. There were smaller flows of Ukrainians, Belorussians, and Tartars to other parts of the Commonwealth of Independent States, and of Jews to Israel (Becker et al., 2005, 108). The emigration was partly offset by immigration of Kazakhs (*oralmans*) from the former USSR and Mongolia; the UNDP (*Human Development Report Kazakhstan 2000*, 6) estimated the number of repatriations over the 1990s to be 260,000, while Marat (2016, 539) reports estimates of roughly one million *oralmans* moving to Kazakhstan between 1991 and 2013.

4. Blackmon (2011, 52–58) argues that initial opposition to reform in the Supreme Soviet

flict between president and parliament was resolved when President Nazarbayev ruled by presidential decree between March and December 1995. A new constitution adopted by referendum and other changes consolidated presidential power and reduced that of the legislature.

Despite statements to the contrary, economic reform was put largely on hold after 1995. The WTO application lodged in 1996 was allowed to languish, unlike that of the Kyrgyz Republic. Trade reform commitments included in 1998 programs supported by the IMF's Extended Fund Facility were not implemented, although Kazakhstan did maintain its commitment to current account convertibility, unlike Uzbekistan and Turkmenistan. Financial reform moved forward slowly, and foreign investment was associated with shady dealings surrounding large oil and gas production sharing agreements. The large-scale privatization process (described in Pomfret, 2006, 44–50) was widely identified with burgeoning corruption and deteriorating standards of governance. Kazakhstan came to be seen less as one of the reformist CIS counties and more as an example of a corrupt Soviet successor state; in 1996 Kazakhstan ranked below neighboring Uzbekistan, a self-styled gradual reformer, on the EBRD's transition index. The 1999 referendum, which allowed President Nazarbayev to stand for another seven-year term, and the ensuing election were blatantly rigged.[5]

In contrast to the gloomy picture of institutional degradation and at the low point of the transitional recession, President Nazarbayev set out a positive vision of the country's future in his 1997 document *Kazakhstan 2030*. The 2030 strategy highlighted seven long-term priorities: (1) national security, (2) political stability, (3) economic growth based on an open-market economy with high levels of foreign investment and domestic savings, (4) health, education, and well-being of Kazakhstani citizens, (5) oil and gas exports, (6) transport and communications infrastructure, and (7) a professional state. On the third priority, the "strategy of healthy economic growth rests on a strong market economy . . . [and] limited interference of the state in the economy," although there is some ambivalence in the emphasis on the need for the state to be strong in support of the market economy. Although the strategy envisaged a leading role for oil and gas exports, the boom in export earnings over the next decade exceeded any expectations and provided a far more favorable financial environment than could have been hoped for in 1997.

Just as Kazakhstan was pulling out of the transitional recession in 1996–98, the economy was hit by the August 1998 Russian crisis. Although the Russian

---

arose from powerful men defending their vested interests, while in the more democratically based parliament after the March 1994 election opposition to rapid reform reflected concerns about the impact on vulnerable members of society.

5. See Kolstø (2004, 170) on the 1999 election. In 2007 a pliant parliament voted to exempt President Nazarbayev from term limits.

crisis was an exogenous negative shock, Kazakhstan's susceptibility to contagion reflected to some extent the failure to create a vibrant market economy that could withstand such a shock. The government responded with a large devaluation, which helped to kick-start the economy in 1999 and 2000.

4.2. The Boom Years, 1999–2007

Following an upturn in oil output, proven oil reserves, and world oil prices, Kazakhstan entered a boom period in the early twenty-first century. In May 2000, the government paid off its debts to the IMF ahead of schedule, as a signal of the health and financial strength of the economy. From 2000 until 2007 Kazakhstan experienced rapid economic growth (table 2.3), led by a boom in foreign trade fueled by oil exports. In 2000, the government established the National Fund to counter the volatility of oil and mineral prices and to save for the country's future economic and social development. The extraordinary boom continued as oil prices increased until 2007, raising the question for Kazakhstan's economic future of whether oil would turn out to be a curse or a blessing. A "curse" outcome could arise if the corruption and rent-seeking of the 1990s had become so deeply ingrained that growth outside oil extraction was prevented, or if volatility due to oil price fluctuations led to poor macroeconomic management. On the other hand, booming oil revenues freed Kazakhstan from financial constraints to realize the *Kazakhstan 2030* vision and improve the physical and institutional infrastructure, so that living standards could be raised and economic growth could become self-sustaining.

During the 1990s the oil and gas sectors stimulated expectations, but with stagnant output (table 4.2) and flat world prices they made little contribution to improving current economic well-being before 1999. Kazakhstan assumed the state's share in the TengizChevron joint venture, but Russia claimed rights to part of the oil and controlled the only existing pipeline, about whose access no commitment had been made in the original agreement. The ownership status of Tengiz was only resolved, together with some easing of the pipeline problems, when Russian shareholder participation was agreed. At the same time, bargaining over adjustments to ownership shares led to recurrent charges of corrupt practices, inevitably labeled Kazakhgate.[6] Pipelines were

---

6. A Mobil vice president was jailed for not declaring a bonus on his income tax form, but otherwise the lengthy legal proceedings did not lead to imprisonment. Senior Kazakhstan officials were included in the indictment, e.g., as KO1 and KO2, but were neither named nor punished. Chevron was reportedly unhappy at Mobil's buying into Tengiz, but in 1997 Chevron itself sold a 5% stake in the joint venture to LUKoil. Delays in the late 1990s and early 2000s in agreeing upon new investment in Tengiz were related to the increased number of principals and Chevron's wariness of its partners.

TABLE 4.2. Kazakhstan's Oil and Gas Production, 1985–2016

	1985	1986	1987	1988	1989	1990	1991
Oil production (tbpd)	485	503	523	545	556	571	589
Natural gas production (bcm)	4.9	5.2	5.7	6.4	6.1	6.4	7.1

	1992	1993	1994	1995	1996	1997	1998
Oil production (tbpd)	569	507	446	450	493	557	558
Natural gas production (bcm)	7.3	6.1	4.1	5.3	3.9	5.7	4.6

	1999	2000	2001	2002	2003	2004	2005
Oil production (tbpd)	656	740	841	993	1,081	1,248	1,294
Natural gas production (bcm)	6.2	7.7	8.6	8.5	11.1	12.3	12.7

	2006	2007	2008	2009	2010	2011	2012
Oil production (tbpd)	1,370	1,415	1,485	1,609	1,676	1,684	1,664
Natural gas production (bcm)	13.4	13.8	16.1	16.5	17.6	17.3	17.2

	2013	2014	2015	2016			
Oil production (tbpd)	1,737	1,710	1,695	1,672			
Natural gas production (bcm)	18.4	18.7	19.0	19.9			

Source: British Petroleum, *Statistical Review of World Energy,* 2015 and 2017.
Notes: tbpd = thousand barrels per day—one barrel holds 159 liters (converting this to metric tons depends on the grade of oil, e.g., with specific gravity of 0.88 there are just over seven barrels of oil in a metric ton); bcm = billion cubic meters.

controlled by the Russian state-run oil pipeline monopoly Trasneft, which discriminated against Kazakh oil by artificially high assessments of technical losses, arbitrary long route allocations, and other discriminatory pricing practices, including absence of a quality bank that would recognize the higher quality of Tengiz oil; the net effect was that transit tariffs for Kazakhstan's crude were typically double those for Russian crude.[7] Prospecting for new reserves under the potentially oil-rich North Caspian was delayed by disagreements over delimitation of national territories and by domestic wrangles over selling exploration rights to foreign firms possessing the technology to explore the offshore fields.

The turnaround in 2000 was highlighted by rising oil prices and discovery of the Kashagan offshore field—the largest oil field outside the Middle East, but with difficult exploitation conditions.[8] World oil prices surged in 1999 and

7. IMF estimates reported in Pomfret (2006, 51). The Kumkol fields in central Kazakhstan suffered from even higher transport costs, estimated by the IMF at $12 per barrel (Raballand and Esen, 2007), which left little profit at 1990s world oil prices.
8. The technical difficulties associated with offshore production, such as the effects of cor-

2000 from around $10 per barrel to over $30, and oil production from Tengiz and the smaller oil fields increased by a third and oil exports by almost half between 1998 and 2000; the value of oil exports increased from $1,650 million in 1998 to $4,429 million in 2000 (Pomfret, 2006, 42). Higher oil prices and larger quantities increased the benefits from constructing new pipelines, so that after 2001 the transit situation became more favorable to Kazakhstan. In sum, around the turn of the century Kazakhstan's oil sector experienced a "perfect storm" of increased output and investment, lower transport costs, and rapidly rising world prices.[9]

The combination of increased output and rapidly rising world prices was fortuitous, but lower transport costs were in part endogenous. Pipelines involve a large initial fixed cost, which was less justifiable with the 1990s prices and quantities, but larger and larger pipeline projects became attractive after 2000. The opening in autumn 2001 of the first privately owned and commercially operated pipeline, the Caspian Pipeline Consortium (CPC), provided an alternative route through Russia, which cut transport costs from Tengiz in half. Other producers in Kazakhstan also benefited from the CPC, e.g., in 2003 a 450 km pipeline was completed to link the Aktobe oil field, operated by the Chinese National Petroleum Company, to the CPC.

Russia's pipeline power was definitively undermined by pipeline links with Turkey and China that increased Kazakhstan's options. The 1,760 km Baku-Ceyhan pipeline became operational in 2005 with an eventual capacity of one million barrels of oil per day. The pipeline mainly serves Azerbaijan, but Kazakhstan's Caspian oil can be shipped across the Caspian from Aktau to Baku; the most efficient delivery, by pipeline under the Caspian Sea, is hampered by lack of agreement among the five littoral countries over demarcation of the sea. Construction of a 988 km pipeline from Atasu in central Kazakhstan to the Chinese border began in September 2004 with an initial capacity of two hundred thousand barrels per day (bpd) upon completion at the end of 2005— compared to twenty to thirty thousand bpd reaching the Chinese border by

---

rosive and poisonous hydrogen sulfide (H_2S) gas from the seabed, and the extreme climate were underestimated, and the Kashagan field has cost well over its projected budget with repeated delays moving production a decade behind the original estimated date of 2006. Production started in 2013, but was halted after less than a month due to pipeline problems; the two 95 km pipelines to the onshore processing facility had to be replaced by carbon steel pipes lined with corrosion-resistant material, for which the subcontract cost $1.8 billion. Production resumed in late 2016.

9. To appreciate the magnitude of the unexpected windfall after the late 1990s, see the survey by Ruseckas (1998), who in 1997 placed Kazakhstan's total oil reserves at ten billion barrels and saw $18 per barrel as a reasonable, but perhaps optimistic, estimate of world price over the life of the reserves. When the National Fund was established, it was expected that revenues would be placed there whenever the world price of oil exceeded $19. By 2014 Kazakhstan's proven reserves were thirty billion barrels (table 3.4), and since 2000 the world price has never fallen close to $19.

rail before 2004—and further pipeline links between Kazakhstan's oil fields and the Chinese border were completed in 2009.

Kazakhstan is primarily an oil, rather than gas, producer (table 3.4), but since 2006 gas production has been increasing faster than oil production (table 4.2). The largest gas and gas condensate field is Karachaganak developed by British Gas, Agip, ChevronTexaco, and LUKoil in west Kazakhstan, with estimated reserves of 1,000 bcm of gas and 2.6 billion barrels of oil. Until the early 2000s gas exports were sold to Gazprom in Orenberg at well below Russian, and even further below European, market prices. After 2001, the Russian company took a less aggressively monopsonistic position and a 2002 agreement to create a joint venture, Kazrosgaz, with Gazprom led to more attractive prices for Kazakhstan's gas exports and access to Western European markets.[10] Kazakhstan also benefited from construction of the Turkmenistan-China gas pipeline in 2006–9, from which Kazakhstan receives royalties and the option to export its own gas through the pipeline.[11]

To take advantage of the increasing revenues from the resources boom, the NFRK was established in 2000 with revenues to come from the nine largest petroleum companies and the three largest mining companies (Tsalik and Ebel, 2003; Kalyuzhnova and Nygaard, 2011). Originally designed to receive oil rents when the world oil price exceeded $19 per barrel, the NFRK grew rapidly as the price rose to $140 in 2007. The investment strategy foresaw a mix of stabilization activities (with 25% of assets in liquid short-term instruments) and saving for the future (with 75% of assets in bonds and high-rated stocks). In 2008–9 the NFRK provided the funding for the stimulus package to address the country's financial crisis (see section 4.4).

Oil and gas production and prospects are heavily concentrated in three projects: Tengiz, Kashagan, and Karachaganak, with estimated oil reserves of 9.0, 15.0, and 2.6 billion barrels of oil (and Karachaganak is mainly valuable for its gas and condensates). In 2002, the government established the state oil company KazMunaiGas (KMG) to gain a larger share of revenues than was contracted to the state in the original production sharing agreements. By becoming a shareholder KMG took part of the early revenues, while the government's revenues only become substantial after the shareholders have recouped the upfront costs. KMG took a 10–20% shareholding in the three biggest oil and gas projects, and a larger share in the less high-profile fields with reserves under one billion barrels. Foreign investors acquiesced in diluting their shares

10. Kazakhstan had some bargaining power because Gazprom's pipeline services for gas from Turkmenistan and Uzbekistan relied on transit rights through Kazakhstan.

11. In October 2017 China agreed to import 5 bcm of gas from Kazakhstan over the coming year. Shortly before this, Kazakhstan reached an agreement to transport gas from western Kazakhstan to South Kazakhstan via Uzbekistan.

to include the national company, perhaps assuaged by the dramatically increasing energy prices between 2003 and 2008.[12]

In 2008, the government announced that it would not sign any new PSAs, and future projects would be developed by KMG or as joint ventures between KMG and a partner selected by KMG.[13] In 2010 local content requirements were increased. To further the state's benefits from the oil boom, the government invested in refineries and port terminals in Romania and Georgia and created the Almaty Regional Financial Centre. The increased public involvement was a form of resource nationalism, but less virulent than the policies being pursued in Russia.

The government reacted to the boom by accumulating money in the NFRK, which combined prudent management with structural weaknesses, i.e. lack of transparency and presidential control that was not subject to public scrutiny (Kalyuzhnova, 2011). The combination of public prudence and sound macroeconomic policies may have contributed to private profligacy, as people overborrowed to fuel an excessive consumption boom, most obviously in real estate (Esanov and Kuralbayeva, 2011). A consequence was a financial crisis when the oil revenues suddenly fell in 2008, and NFRK nontransparency permitted controversial disbursements from the NFRK in 2008–9. However, during the oil boom there was little complaint as oil revenues flowed into the public accounts.

The government quickly began to look for ways to use the increased revenues to promote the country's economic development as set out in the *Strategy 2030*. This must be placed in a context of official liberalism tempered by a shift towards ad hoc interventionism.[14] The government established new institutions for development: in May 2001, the Development Bank of Kazakhstan (now owned by Samruk-Kazyna), and in May 2003 the Investment Fund of Kazakhstan (part of the Ministry of Industry and New Technologies since 2012) and the National Innovation Fund (reorganized as the National Agency for Technological Development in 2012). The billion-dollar *2003–5 Agricul-*

12. The most contentious was Karachaganak. The original partners took the government to arbitration over its plan to involve KMG, but in 2010 they reached agreement on the price to be paid by KMG for a 10% share.

13. The partners have included firms from India and South Korea, rather than the oil and gas majors that run the major projects. On KMG, see Olcott (2007a) and Kennedy and Nurmakov (2010), and on local content requirements, Kalyuzhnova et al. (2016).

14. Distinction between paper plans and aspirations and implementation and actual outcomes is also relevant to the 1990s. The privatization process, on paper a radical and equitable voucher-based system, turned into a distorted distribution of public resources such that a few people gained control over the country's most valuable assets. Kazakhstan's trade policy after mid-1996, when export duties were removed and the average tariff on imports fell to 12%, was liberal on paper, but ad hoc impositions made actual trade policy unpredictable, e.g., in response to the 1998 crisis Kazakhstan suddenly raised duties on intra-Central Asian trade.

ture and Food Program and the *Innovative Industrial Development Strategy for the Years 2003–15* signaled a more proactive approach in using public policy to promote economic development. The 2004 launch of the *Diversification of Kazakhstan's Economy through Cluster Development in Non-Extraction Sectors* project indicated that the development strategy would be achieved by promoting clusters, based on the ideas of Michael Porter.

Three new institutions, the "Samruk" state-holding company, the "Kazyna" sustainable development fund, and the Regional Financial Centre, Almaty, were established in 2006 to promote President Nazarbayev's goal of transforming Kazakhstan into one of the "50 most competitive, dynamically developing countries in the world" within a decade.[15] In February 2007, the government announced a new *Program of 30 Corporate Leaders in Kazakhstan*, intended to complement the clusters approach by identifying enterprises that would be internationally competitive drivers of development. Samruk, Kazyna, and the state-owned holding company KazAgro were to be the vehicles for identifying and supporting the Leaders, supposedly on the model of Temasek in Singapore and Khazanah in Malaysia.

The drawback of the top-down approach to development is that policy-makers rarely replicate the discovery process under which clusters emerge in a market economy. The choice of clusters in 2004–5 and of projects in 2007, e.g., large-scale dairy cattle investments and a project to promote organic fish production, reflected policymakers' priors about the desirability of processing Kazakhstan's primary products in activities such as agribusiness, textiles, and metallurgy or about upstream and downstream investment in the energy sector rather than following any scientific approach (Wandel, 2010). Other untested priors included belief in scale economies and distrust of transnational corporations.[16] Agriculture was an early and substantial beneficiary of

15. The Samruk holding company had been established in January 2006 as an active shareholder in KMG, Kazakhstan Temir Zholy state railways, KazakhTelekom, KEGOC electricity company, and KazPost with the prospect of adding other large companies (Olcott, 2007; Kennedy and Nurmakov, 2010). Creation of the Kazyna Fund for sustainable development, established in April 2006 to improve management in areas of industrial and innovative development, was linked to a perceived need to streamline the institutions associated with industrial policy. Kazyna's initial capital exceeded $1 billion, and seven clusters were identified that would form the core of competitive economic strength: tourism, metallurgy, textiles, construction, agriculture and food processing, oil and gas machinery, and logistics and transportation (Zabortseva, 2009).

16. The Background section of the 2001 *Strategic Plan of Development of the Republic of Kazakhstan till 2010* stated that "The major factor in development is the globalization of the world economy" dominated by transnational corporations, which "are in fact the national companies of the developed countries." To withstand the TNCs and the power of the developed countries hosting these TNCs, Kazakhstan's domestic companies must "have a scale commensurate with the scale of the national economy . . . [and] the state must not withdraw from controlling them and regulating their activities."

increased assistance in part because policymakers identified the agricultural sector as a major part of Kazakhstan's culture.

4.3. Agriculture

Traditional Kazakh lifestyle centered on livestock, and after the Virgin Lands program Kazakhstan became a major wheat and barley producer. In the Soviet economy, Kazakhstan exported grains, meat, and fruit and vegetables, as well as cotton and wool. During the 1990s the farm sector was in deep crisis (Gray, 2000). Between 1992 and 1995 input prices were liberalized while important output prices remained controlled, leading to farm losses and resort to barter. Most farms became indebted and the problem was exacerbated by drought conditions in much of the country during the 1996–98 seasons.

Overall, policy towards agriculture in the 1990s was one of neglect, as the government addressed other priorities. Relative price movements and reduction of subsidies changed farmers' situation from one in which they mostly benefited from public policies under central planning to a situation where the net impact was close to zero.[17] Some farmers faced locally monopsonistic buyers for their outputs (e.g., cotton gins, dairies, grain merchants, or flour mills), and high trade costs often led to shortened value chains, i.e. exchanging products with neighbors or selling at the local market. Partial land reform, under which the large farms were in principle broken up and farmers obtained ninety-nine-year leases to the land, was unsuccessful in changing incentives, as many farms remained essentially unrestructured in practice. The sector was characterized by continuing power of former state-farm managers and of local authorities, and by the Soviet-era phenomenon of household plots producing a large share of output, especially of milk and meat and of fruit and vegetables.

Output of all agricultural products fell substantially after 1990. The trend is difficult to determine due to volatility and generally poor climatic conditions during the 1990s, but average output was 50% lower in 1996–2000 than in 1987–91 (Pomfret, 2013, table 1). Grain production in 1998 was 6.5 million tons compared to 30 million tons in 1992, and the number of cattle fell from nine million to less than four million over the same period (Pomfret, 2006, 55–56). Large-scale livestock farming almost disappeared as animal stocks became concentrated on the small household plots, and meat, milk, and eggs became essentially nontraded goods. In addition to the disorganization and shift in the relative price of inputs to outputs, this was an adjustment to the policy of the previous two decades that had encouraged meat production and

---

17. Subsidies for agriculture declined from 10–12% of GDP before 1991 to 2–3% in 1993, and between 1995 and 1999 subsides for agriculture were negligible. For details and estimates of producer support, see OECD (2013) and Petrick and Pomfret (2018).

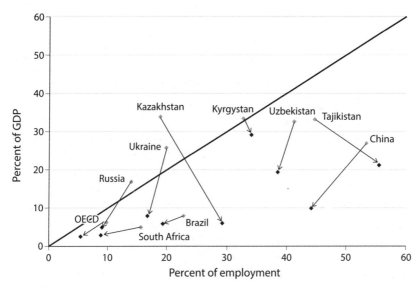

4.1. Changes in agriculture's shares of GDP and employment in two decades after 1990. Source: OECD (2013).

consumption to a level that was far higher than in other countries with similar income levels.[18]

Meanwhile, the rural share of the population increased as people who lost urban jobs returned to their ancestral village where subsistence living was relatively easier, or they used their dachas to become self-sufficient. This pattern, which contrasts to the usual time-path of falling rural shares in output and employment, was still visible in 2010 (figure 4.1).

Policymakers saw the decline of agricultural output as a problem, both because they believe that Kazakhstan has a strong comparative advantage in many farm products and because of social issues associated with a large population with rural connections. Reversal of the price squeeze began in 1999, when the government introduced a price support system for wheat and then extended it to other goods. However, price support was an inefficient response leading to accumulated grain stocks. Land reform continued to be ambivalent as a 2001 decree reduced the length of leases to forty-nine years and sent mixed signals about subleasing. Overall, despite the policy neglect

18. Pastoralism on arid rangelands was especially hard hit. In Soviet times, sinking of deeper wells with powerful mechanical pumps had permitted increased size of herds organized in large collective farms. In the 1990s neither the wells nor the pumps were maintained; any metal was stolen and sold for scrap. When the decline was reversed in the 2000s, it was to much lower levels, e.g., in the area surveyed by Kerven et al. (2016) the livestock population in 2012–14 was only 20% of that of the late 1980s.

of agriculture, there had been significant price and enterprise reform in the 1990s that created a more market-based agricultural sector, although the effectiveness of the changes was dubious as output languished and many producers were deeply indebted.

The turning point in agricultural policy dates from the *aul* (village) program initiated in 2001, or more definitively the billion-dollar 2003–5 Agriculture and Food Program (AFP) announced in 2002. The driving force was the oil boom, which provided revenues for public support, as well as arousing concerns about lack of economic diversification. The Ministry of Agriculture's budget increased from 26 billion tenge in 2001 to 81 billion tenge in 2005, and its share of the total central budget went from 2.5% to 6.5%. The AFP provided general services support to agriculture aimed at improving infrastructure and product quality. Input subsidies (e.g., on fertilizers, fuel, and seeds) and price support schemes aimed to stimulate output; price support was provided through increased funds for the Food Contract Corporation (FCC), which purchased 1.5 million tons or 20% of the 2002 grain harvest, and for a parastatal created in 2001 to provide producer support for the livestock sector.

The livestock sector's situation improved dramatically as the government took steps to reverse the decline in quality that accompanied the disintegration of large production units in the sector, e.g., sponsoring the import of breeding cattle from North America to live on model farms that would be privatized once established. The nominal rate of assistance to livestock producers went from minus 15% in 2000 to plus 31% in 2004 (Pomfret, 2008). Wheat producers in the early 2000s had negative market price support, i.e. farm-gate prices were below a reference (border) price, although the price gap was due mainly to high trade costs rather than lack of public support. Conditions in the market-based cotton sector were far better than in neighboring Uzbekistan, and trade costs lower than for wheat farmers due to the more concentrated location of farmers in the south.

Evaluation of the AFP in 2006–7 pointed to institutional weaknesses.[19] Implementation of the subsidy programs for grain and livestock producers was plagued by discrimination and inefficiency. Fuel subsidies encouraged corruption as farmers requested more gasoline than they needed and sold the surplus for profit. Fertilizer subsides were paid only to domestic suppliers, acting in a similar trade-distorting way to local-content requirements and perhaps discouraging innovations, such as drip irrigation, that work better with high-quality fertilizers that had to be imported. The emphasis on scale economies in livestock farming reflected Soviet-era preconceptions, rather than evidence

19. In, for example, the 2006 report, *Kazakhstan—Agricultural Policy Assessment*, by the Joint Economic Research Program of the World Bank and the Government of Kazakhstan in collaboration with USAID and FAO, and the 2009 World Bank report, *Kazakhstan: Public Expenditure and Institutional Review for the Agricultural Sector*.

from Eastern Europe where many small farmers could be efficient suppliers of dairy products with appropriate institutional arrangements along the supply chain.[20] Centralized policymaking was often insensitive to the local variations inherent in agriculture.[21]

With growing evidence of a financial market bubble, associated distrust of market mechanisms, and increased economic nationalism in the oil and gas sector, the reaction was to reorganize rather than reform institutions. The national strategy associated with creation in 2008 of the state holding company Samruk-Kazyna (see chapter 4.6) was mirrored in the agricultural sector in 2007–8 with the consolidation of policy-related institutions, first under the aegis of the Ministry of Agriculture and then under the KazAgro holding company, which had been established in December 2006 to amalgamate seven institutions providing support to agriculture. The Ministry of Agriculture's budget continued to increase, to 139 billion tenge in 2008, of which some 45% went to KazAgro. In the 2008–9 crisis program, KazAgro received 120 billion tenge; the KazAgro budget was dominated by price support and financing (92% of the budget in 2011), while a separate entity, KazAgro Innovation, was responsible for promoting technical change.

In sum, the level and composition of Ministry of Agriculture spending changed dramatically after the turn of the century. The share of subsidies increased from 6% in 2001 to 24% in 2008 and 39% in 2009, and the majority went to area (i.e. per hectare) subsidies. In the same period, the share of spending on infrastructure fell from 16% to 5% and on crop and livestock services from 19% to 17%.

Meanwhile, land reform took a major step forward when the 2003 Land Code allowed private ownership with full property rights. Previous land reforms asserted state ownership of land and use rights that were gradually reduced from lifetime rights to forty-nine-year leases at minimal rents. The government's caution about deciding whether land belonged to the state or

---

20. The bias against small farmers was also evident in the cotton law developed in 2005 and adopted in 2007 despite considerable opposition from cotton farmers (Petrick et al., 2017, 440). Combined with other centralizing policies in the 2007 law that crowded out private funding and provided inconsistent incentives, this led to a declining area under cotton and output of cotton despite positive world price trends after 2008.

21. For example, the recovery of transhumance in the arid rangelands has been evolutionary, rather than planned. Policy played a role, as options for land access became clearer after 2003, but the entrepreneurial herders often operated in grey areas of property rights, and were more concerned about relative market prices than about state support (Kerven et al., 2016). Dynamic pastoralists have rehabilitated wells using imported pumps from China, Russia, or Ukraine, occupied rangelands and pastures more distant from villages, and expanded their herds, typically to sheep rather than goats—goats were more popular in the transition due to their low maintenance and easy breeding, but in the more commercialized setting of the 2010s sheep fetch higher prices.

whether to embrace private ownership of land and hesitancy about restructuring large agricultural enterprises, equating size with efficiency, has had long-term consequences. Some large farms were consolidated and will be difficult to break up even if the state wishes to. Perhaps more importantly, many small properties for which people have forty-nine-year leases at minimal rent are unused, but the owner prefers to keep the asset and pay the rent.[22] The net effect is that a land market has been very slow to develop since 2003, and ambitious, efficient farmers looking to expand their holdings have limited opportunities to do so.

The reforms led to an increase in the number of individual farms, but the process was slow and subsectors remain dominated by large enterprises run by the former state farm managers (grain) and by household plots (meat, milk, and eggs). The number of farms increased from 5,000 in 1990 to 161,962 in 2006, of which 4,919 were corporate farms (average size 12,000 hectares) and 156,978 family farms (average size 248 hectares); the remaining sixty-five state farms are all experimental stations. In 2002 corporate farms accounted for 63% and family farms 36% of agricultural land use, but by 2006 these shares were almost equal (51% and 48%).[23] There is, however, large variance between the northern wheat-growing regions where family farms accounted for only 30% of land and southern and southeastern Kazakhstan where family farms accounted for about 70% of land use. There is also a correlation with output mix; in 2006, agricultural enterprises produced about two-thirds of grain output while family farms produced 95% of cotton, 70% of sugar beet, and 64% of sunflowers. The five million household plots produced 91% of milk, 83% of meat, 79% of potatoes, 74% of fruits, and 64% of vegetables.

A new state planning system was adopted in 2009. Agriculture was a priority development area for the decade to 2020, with the Ministry of Agriculture focusing on eight subsectors (fruit and vegetables, grain, meat, milk, oil crops, poultry, sugar, and wool), which have priority over other products such as honey or cotton. After October 2009, these subsectors received priority loans from KazAgro, and larger subsidies or lower interest rates on loans/leasing. Regions were responsible for implementation, but central control ensured coherence. Evaluation of policies was primarily in terms of quantitative targets, mostly for output, with little concern for allocative efficiency (could the

22. Kerven et al. (2016, 111) mention that only one of the ninety-seven pastoralists interviewed in 2012–14 had converted land into ownership; for others "the low rental costs made land purchase relatively unattractive." I heard similar explanations of low take-up of ownership in the northern wheatbelt.

23. A group of some fifteen very large grain holdings had also emerged by the mid-2000s, e.g., Ivolga-Holdings controlled about a million hectares of farmland and owned eleven elevators in Kazakhstan (as well as 140,000 hectares and ten elevators in Russia) and accounted for five hundred to seven hundred thousand tons of grain exports from Kazakhstan per year (Wandel, 2009).

resources have been better used?) or productivity (could better techniques have been adopted?). Socioeconomic and environmental concerns were referred to, but do not appear to have a high priority in practice.

Agricultural policy is almost entirely supply-side oriented. The FCC buys grain, but it does little to help farmers to increase the unit value of their sales by creating international awareness of Kazakhstani quality standards or by improving supply chains. The 2010 customs union with Russia and Belarus reinforced this pattern with, for example, quantitative targets for supply of beef from Kazakhstan to Russia. Some goals are poorly articulated or inconsistent. Although reference is made to public good provision, the share of funds devoted to infrastructure has fallen. Food security is defined by a minimum level of domestic supply (80% for each food product), rather than in terms of households' ability to obtain food (allowing for substitution from goods with increasing prices). Too many agricultural subsidies were WTO-incompatible, delaying the WTO accession process. In providing subsidized credit, KazAgro works with the commercial banks, but by directing credit to specific producers it is crowding out independent commercial loans; because government loans are at predetermined interest rates, this may be reducing the prospects of financing for riskier but potentially high-return projects.

Implementation is bureaucratic, and policies are poorly coordinated. Farmers complain of difficulty in knowing what support is available and how to obtain it. Even when subsidies or other support are provided they are often delayed, e.g., arriving after the farmer has purchased inputs for sowing and fertilizing, and apparently transparent rules on subsidy scales appear to be discretionary when applied at the local level. Division of responsibilities among government ministries is not accompanied by coordination. The Ministry of Education finances fundamental research, but the Ministry of Agriculture funds applied research. Implementation is largely by regional administrations that can augment schemes with their own funds, leading to regional inequities and cross-regional inefficiencies. To facilitate consolidation of farms in order to realize scale economies, the Ministry of Employment is responsible for providing alternative jobs for self-employed farmers, e.g., by providing microcredit or relocating people from regions with poorer economic prospects. Land improvement is financed by the Ministry of Ecology. The list goes on.

Agriculture remains an important sector of Kazakhstan's economy. When the oil boom began, it was the first and most important beneficiary of additional state funding to promote economic diversification. Increased support was a desirable antidote to the neglect of the 1990s, but the government was impatient for quick results. Increased subsidies were only partially successful as output increased but with some adverse side effects, and in the targeted livestock sector household production continued to dominate. The impact of poor policy design was exacerbated by a process of land reform in which early missteps were only slowly overcome in the twenty-first century. The formula of effective price signals and responses in an appropriate institutional setting takes time to get right in the naturally fragmented and often conservative rural economy, and Kazakhstan is no exception. The government's instinctive reaction to slow progress, in the wider context of the 2008 national economic crisis, was to turn to more interventionist policies that were unlikely to be effective. The positive sign is that the government continues to debate policies openly and interact with institutions such as the World Bank, OECD, and FAO that can call on extensive international experience and skilled specialists.

4.4. The Social Sectors

Kazakhstan inherited the Soviet system of universal social assistance programs, including generous pensions. In the early and mid-1990s as GDP fell and the government's tax-raising capability was low, many programs were characterized by lengthy payment arrears, and assistance was poorly targeted. By 1997 the social programs accounted for 10% of GDP and almost four-fifths of government expenditures. By 2002, as GDP recovered, government spending on social assistance programs had shrunk to 5.4% of GDP, or a quarter of total government expenditures, and over four-fifths of this spending went to pensions.

Kazakhstan's was the first former Soviet republic to introduce a privately funded pension program. Although harsh on the current cohort of pensioners, the January 1998 reform, whose principal pillar was a system of mandatory savings, was intended to benefit future generations. A residual public system was retained for workers who had accumulated years of service, but the net cost of the residual system was forecast to decline to less than 2% of GDP by 2016 The new pension system boosted development of the financial sector; by 2002 pension fund assets amounted to $1.4 billion, which was at 6% of GNP—a larger share than in any other transition economy (compare 4.5% in Hungary, 3.5% in Poland, and 0.8% in Bulgaria), although much lower than Chile's 54% (Chan-Lau, 2004, 18). Private pension fund assets grew rapidly and amounted to 12% of GDP in 2012.

As the oil boom gathered momentum, the social sectors, like agriculture, benefited from increases in public spending. Kazakhstan's social protection system's main components since 2002 are the social assistance program and other allowances, housing benefits, and the pension system. In January 2002, the government introduced the state-targeted social assistance program, which provides means-tested assistance to individuals and families living below the poverty line in each oblast; the targeted social assistance was successful in reaching the poorest people, and according to the World Bank's 2002 poverty assessment it halved the poverty headcount from what it would have been without the program. The government announced a substantial increase in funding for social assistance programs over the 2002–7 period, and the poverty rate declined rapidly during the 2000s. Housing benefits, intended to benefit the poor through allowances to assist with utility bills and household maintenance, were less successful, and had a poor targeting record in terms of helping the most needy. Other social assistance measures—such as insurance against death, disability, and other life events—were consolidated, e.g., by a law on Mandatory Social Insurance, which became effective in January 2005. These measures are not targeted, although because benefits are unrelated to previous income they tend to be progressive, as lump-sum payments are relatively more beneficial to poor recipients.

Expenditure on education and health dropped substantially during the 1990s. Expenditure on education from the public budget was equal to 3–4% of GDP in every year from 1994 to 2003, which signified a sharp drop in total expenditures before GDP started to grow after 1999. As elsewhere in Central Asia, the decline in preschool places was especially pronounced. Private education institutions emerged, especially offering vocational training and tertiary education. These developments at the start and the end of the educational process increased inequality of access. Similar changes occurred in the health sector, where public expenditures were around 2% of GDP, but the private health sector expanded. The grey area between free and paid medical services was associated with a high level of unofficial payments to medical workers.

As the economy recovered, spending on education increased after 2000. The *Balapan* program aimed to increase the number covered by early childhood education, while preschool training was made mandatory and now covers 95% of the age group. The *Bolashak* program, which had been launched in 1993 and provided generous assistance for outstanding students to study overseas, received increased funding; numbers soared from under a hundred in every year from 1995 to 2004 to 1,796 in 2005 and by 2012 the *Bolashak* program had financed over 8,000 students. By that time, it was becoming accepted that the long-term solution was to build up the domestic tertiary sector, and the process was set in motion with the well-funded Nazarbayev University, intended to become a world-class center of higher education in Astana that other state universities would eventually scale up to match.[24] There are also some highly visible foreign-funded universities, such as KIMEP, the Kazakh-British Technical University and others in Almaty, and

24. Literal scaling up is unlikely given the generous funding for Nazarbayev University. The exercise is being repeated at the secondary school level, where Nazarbayev Intellectual Schools are attended by twenty thousand pupils (2–3% of the total) but receive over 20% of school funding. These are elite institutions with rigorously meritocratic admission (and students not keeping up must leave) and strict ethical integrity.

the multicampus Aga Khan Foundation's University of Central Asia in the Kyrgyz Republic, Tajikistan, and Kazakhstan

In sum, during the 1990s, despite the social traumas of the transition from central planning, the government's stance on social issues was quite weak. Expenditures were allowed to fall substantially, and only in the area of pensions, where burgeoning costs and accumulating arrears required action, did the government take action. Around the turn of the century the government's attitude to social policies became more proactive; in the first half-decade of the 2000s the social protection system was redesigned in generally desirable ways, and after 2002 more funds were allocated to these programs. Revenues from the oil boom were directed specifically to preschool and tertiary education. Nevertheless, while access to education and healthcare remains universal and spending has increased, concerns about quality remain.

4.5. The 2007–8 Banking Crisis, Resource Nationalism, and Samruk-Kazyna

The banking sector was considered a success of Kazakhstan's economic transition, and in the early 2000s Kazakhstan's banks were thought to be the most efficient in the CIS. During the 1998 Russian crisis, Kazakh banks expanded into the Kyrgyz Republic, where over 70% of the assets of the banking sector were Kazakh-owned by 2007, and later they moved into Tajikistan. Especially after the economic boom began at the turn of the century, Kazakhstan's financial sector development far outstripped that in other Central Asian countries; the insurance and mortgage markets flourished, and real estate markets were active, especially in the cities of Almaty, Astana, and Atyrau. In 2004, the government announced its intention to bring Kazakhstan's banking legislation in line with that of the EU, and by 2007 the government felt comfortable enough to allow foreign banks to do business. In the first substantial foreign investment in the banking sector, UniCredit of Italy paid $2.1 billion in November 2007 for a 91.8% stake in ATF Bank, Kazakhstan's fifth-largest bank. This was followed in March 2008 by Korea's Kookmin Bank paying $630 million for a 30% share in BCC, Kazakhstan's sixth-largest bank. In lower profile deals, Russia's Sberbank acquired Teksaka Bank and Israel's Hapoalim Bank bought Demir Bank.

After the 1999 devaluation, the central bank reverted in May 1999 to a de facto exchange-rate anchor; although there had been fluctuations, the exchange rate in February 2006 was 130 tenge/$, the same as at the end of May 1999, despite strong pressures for currency appreciation as oil exports mushroomed. With the expectation that there was little exchange rate risk, banks made profits by borrowing in international markets at lower interest rates than they could charge eager borrowers at home. By 2006 Kazakhstan's banks were raising large amounts of capital abroad, where the cost of capital was less than the double-digit interest rates that they could charge borrowers at home. In the first half of 2007 medium- and long-term debt-creating capital inflows more than doubled, largely due to external borrowing by the banking sector. The potential problem was that banks borrowed in international markets at shorter maturities to those on their loan portfolios.

Signs of a financial bubble emerged in 2007, when banks started to compete in making deposits more attractive. At the same time, they increased the interest rates on loans, which by the start of 2008 had reached about 20%, double the rates of two years' earlier. In November 2007, the government provided support of around $4 billion, targeted at construction projects in danger of being abandoned half-finished, and the central bank raised the official refinancing rate, which had been unchanged at 9% since July 2006, to 11%. The value of the banks' external debt peaked at €31 billion at end of 2007 (Barisitz and Lahnsteiner, 2010). International rating agencies began to reassess Kazakhstan banks' creditworthiness in late 2007, when Standard and Poor's downgraded Kazakhstan's sovereign debt to BBB–.

The bursting of the real estate bubble, collapse of world oil prices in late 2008, and devaluation of the tenge in February 2009 cut domestic demand, liquidity, and solvency, and the share of nonperforming loans soared from 7% at the end of 2008 to 38% a year later (Barisitz and Lahnsteiner, 2010). As the number of nonperforming loans increased, foreign investors repatriated their loans before the Kazakh banks went bankrupt. Under any circumstances external lenders would have reacted by repatriating their funds, but in the post-Lehman context the capital outflow was exacerbated by liquidity crises in the world's major financial markets. The rush to withdraw money from the Kazakh banks made fears of their collapse self-fulfilling.

The government's response in 2009 was an anticrisis package, estimated to amount to $16 billion or 15% of GDP (Jandosov, Sabyrova, and Mogilevsky, 2010), mainly funded from the NFRK and channeled through Samruk-Kazyna, Kazagro, and the central bank. In 2009 Samruk-Kazyna reported that it had received 1,087.5 billion tenge from the NFRK, of which 486 billion was used to stabilize the financial sector, 360 billion for the real estate market, 120 billion for small and medium-sized enterprise development, and 121.5 billion for implementation of innovative industrial and infrastructure projects.[25] At the same time, 120 billion tenge were allocated to KazAgro, all of which had been used by the end of 2009. The central bank meanwhile loosened monetary policy by cutting the refinancing rate and by easing reserve requirements.

25. *IMF Staff Report*, June 19, 2009.

Central bank governor Marchenko estimated that the total amount spent in 2008 and 2009 to shore up the banking sector was around €13 billion (Barisitz and Lahnsteiner, 2010, 69n). A new tax code introduced on January 1, 2009, which included cuts in corporate income tax from 30% to 20% and in the value-added tax from 13% to 12%, added a standard fiscal policy stimulus.

About two-thirds of the anticrisis package was channeled to support the financial sector. In February 2009 Samruk-Kazyna acquired an equity stake of 75% in BTA (the largest credit institution), and in May 2009 it took a 20.9% share in Halyk (the country's second-largest bank) and a 21.2% stake in Kazkommertsbank (the third largest). In January 2010, the government purchased all shares in Alliance Bank (the fourth largest), giving a 67% stake to Samruk-Kazyna and the remainder to the bank's creditors. In sum, two of the country's four largest banks (BTA and Alliance) had been nationalized (majority state ownership) and two others recapitalized; together they accounted for two-thirds of banking sector assets.[26]

In addition to acquiring equity in the four largest banks, Samruk-Kazyna deposited cash in the banking system and provided support to construction projects, mortgages, small and medium-sized enterprises, and farm lending. In sum, the domestic banking crisis, coinciding with a global economic crisis and downturn in world trade in 2008–9, was the catalyst for a stimulus package that involved bringing a large part of the economy into a single state holding company whose component businesses came to account for half of GDP.[27]

Kazakhstan's stimulus package was, relative to GDP, perhaps the world's biggest. Revenues from the post-1999 resource boom were used to increase the state's involvement in the economy, reinforcing a pattern that could be traced to the 2003–5 Agriculture and Food Program and the clusters policy of promoting industrial development. After the crisis, Samruk-Kazyna and KazAgro were designated as the main instruments for implementing a new

26. The two nationalized banks defaulted on their foreign liabilities and initiated debt-restructuring negotiations. A large loan from Kazkommertsbank provided temporary help for BTA, but in 2014, BTA was shut down, after costing the government $9 billion for its unsuccessful rehabilitation (Kapparov, 2016, 3). A state-run distressed asset management company (the Problem Loans Fund), set up to act as a "bad bank," bought BTA assets and in 2017 took over Kazkommertsbank's bad loans as it too was declared failed, and sold to Halyk Bank (Reuters, *UPDATE 1-Kazakhstan Announces $7.5 Bln Bailout of Top Lender Kazkommertsbank,* March 16, 2017, at https://www.reuters.com/article/kazkommertsbank-ma-halyk-bank/update-1-kazakhstan-announces-7–5-bln-bailout-of-top-lender-kazkommertsbank-idUSL5N1GS4NK). See also section 10.7 on Kazkommertsbank's links to Meridian Capital.

27. OECD (2013, 5) reported Samruk-Kazyna's share of GDP at 57% in 2010, and ICG (2013, 9) stated that "By 2013, Samruk-Kazyna owned assets worth $103 billion accounting for just over half of GDP."

industrial policy for 2010–14.[28] Combined with the increased activity of KMG, itself part of Samruk-Kazyna, several observers saw a pattern of rising resource nationalism, similar to that occurring in Russia (Domjan and Stone, 2010; Kennedy and Nurmakov, 2010; Kalyuzhnova and Nygaard, 2009 and 2011). Institutionally, the major change was the creation of the huge state-owned entities, Samruk-Kazyna and KazAgro, whose influence rivaled that of the line ministries responsible for policy implementation.[29]

4.6. Kazakhstan 2050

Kazakhstan at independence had a promising future in terms of strong fundamentals as a middle-income country well endowed with human capital and abundant natural resources. In the short term, however, the country faced formidable difficulties associated with nation-building and ethnic diversity. Policy errors in the 1990s such as the flawed privatization of large enterprises and corrupt process of allocating oil and mineral exploitation rights hindered establishment of a well-functioning market economy and threatened to leave the country with a form of crony capitalism inimical to equitable growth. The oil boom of the twenty-first century provided a golden opportunity to overcome the errors and missed opportunities of the 1990s. Kazakhstan became the richest country in the region in the decade after 2000. The oil revenues were beyond anybody's dreams in the 1990s, but would they be used to promote long-term economic development and growth with equity or would they enrich a self-perpetuating elite who can prevent any political or institutional reform that will challenge their control of the revenue stream?

Under President Nazarbayev there has been a concerted effort to improve the functioning of the economy so that it can be numbered among the top fifty economies in the world by 2050. A particular challenge is the nature of the professional state—the seventh priority in *Kazakhstan 2030*. The technical competence of the public sector, in terms of understanding and implementing polices for a market-based economy, has increased substantially since independence. However, the practice of medium-term plans fitting into the long-term strategy and of annual targets driving actual policy implementation may

28. The State Program on the Accelerated Industrial-Innovation Development of the Republic of Kazakhstan 2010–14 highlighted seven sectors: agriculture, construction and construction materials, oil and gas, metal products, chemicals and pharmaceuticals, energy, and transport and communications infrastructure.

29. In 2013, with the creation of Baiterek as a parastatal for research and technical development (Kazyna's old role), the status quo before the amalgamation of Samruk and Kazyna was reinstated.

be counterproductive. The highly centralized nature of the state means that presidential pronouncements drive the annual plans as administrators try to divine precisely what the president intended in his annual state of the union speech. This process has often led to medium-term goals, let alone the long-term strategy, being forgotten. One manifestation has been the frequent shifts in industrial policy. While it is obviously desirable to identify policy errors and correct them, too frequent policy shifts do not provide a good environment in which markets can flourish.

The tension between long-term goals and short-term implementation continued into the *Kazakhstan 2050* blueprint articulated by President Nazarbayev in 2013 (Aitzhanova et al., 2014). In many respects, it continues the vision of *Strategy 2030*, but short-term adjustment followed the collapse of oil prices in 2014–15. In August 2015, following depreciation of the tenge, monetary policy shifted to a floating exchange rate.

The pattern in 2015–16 appeared to be a shift to more market-friendly policies (World Bank, 2016a), encapsulated in the May 2015 launch of a new institutional reform program *One Hundred Steps, A Modern State for All*. The shift was evident in the new monetary policy, reduction in transfers from the NFRK to finance state-owned enterprises, and tax reform beginning with merging of the tax and customs codes. In November 2015, Kazakhstan joined the WTO. Also in November, the president announced the $9 billion *Nurly Zhol* (Bright Path) program of infrastructure development to modernize roads, railways, ports, IT infrastructure, and other services. There was an explicit link to trade and export diversification as the *Nurly Zhol* program was frequently connected to China's One Belt One Road program, and as Kazakhstan adjusted to WTO membership.

The collapse of oil prices also provided a trigger for Kazakhstan to reconsider its future as an energy exporter. Kazakhstan ratified the 2015 Paris Agreement on Climate Change, and adopted *Future Energy* as the theme of Expo 2017 in Astana. Kazakhstan has abundant wind and solar energy potential, although current levels of generation are tiny, and taking advantage of the potential will require upgrading of electricity transmission lines (Kalyuzhnova and Pomfret, eds., 2018). Kazakhstan has some of the largest uranium deposits in the world and is the world's largest uranium producer, but Kazakhstan's only nuclear power plant, a BN-350 nuclear reactor at Mangyshlak, was decommissioned in 2001.[30]

30. On uranium output see World Nuclear Association, *World Uranium Mining Production*. Kazatomprom formed joint ventures for uranium enrichment in 2006 and bought a stake in reactor manufacturer Westinghouse from Toshiba in 2007 (Domjan and Stone, 2010, 56–58). Although plans have long existed to build additional nuclear power plants, there has been little progress, in part out of respect for a long antinuclear tradition dating from protests against nuclear testing in Kazakhstan during the Soviet era.

4.7. Conclusions

Kazakhstan has been on an economic roller coaster since independence. Dissolution of the USSR and the depth of the transitional recession were totally unexpected. Policymaking in the 1990s seemed rather aimless despite the visionary *Strategy 2030*. The high-level corruption surrounding the privatization process and award of energy contracts conjured up images of a resource curse. However, after 1998 Kazakhstan experienced one of the world's biggest decade-long booms, leading to rapidly improving living standards and diminished poverty rates.

Despite worries about institutional degradation and poor governance, Kazakhstan's government clearly got the big decisions facing a resource-rich country right.[31] For all the negative issues surrounding energy contracts, production sharing agreements ensured that Tengiz and Karachaganak came onstream in time to benefit from the rise in oil and gas prices, and that Kashagan was discovered and billions invested in the offshore field. The PSAs provided the government with revenues to fund ambitious economic and social policies as well as stockpiling a large sovereign welfare fund. Revising the distribution of revenues during the boom was done by inserting KMG in the consortia without, so far, deterring future investors in Kazakhstan. Finally, and this may be where the jury is still out, the government made good use of the revenues in improving social programs and spending on education and infrastructure, although some microeconomic policies (e.g., on agriculture or cluster formation) may have been unproductive. Investments in infrastructure included road improvements (notably upgrading a 2,700 km highway across northern Kazakhstan from Khorgos on the Chinese border to Aqtobe near the Russian border), high-speed trains between Almaty and Astana (and an Almaty-Tashkent line inaugurated in 2017), a rail link to Turkmenistan and Iran, port upgrading on the Caspian, and improved air service with Astana and Almaty as twin hubs.

When oil prices collapsed in 2008 and Kazakhstan faced a banking crisis, the government acted purposefully, using NFRK funds to finance a large bailout and stimulus package that helped to stabilize the economy. The negative side to the package was its support for more dirigiste development policies, most notably in the creation of megaparastatals, Samruk-Kazyna and KazAgro. There have been some signs of pullback from this path, such as the People's IPO Program, but these have been slow to progress.[32]

---

31. Concerns about high-level corruption continue to be raised (e.g., the report on the large minerals company Kazakhmys by Global Witness, 2010), as do rifts in the elite such as the alleged murder of two bankers by the president's former son-in-law Rakhat Aliyev, who died in custody in Austria.

32. The People's IPO Program was launched in 2011 to privatize Samruk-Kazyna subsidiaries

A second major challenge was the steep decline in world oil prices in mid-2014 from prices just over $100, which had been the norm since 2011, to under $50 at year's end.[33] The decline continued in 2015, convincing policymakers that the oil boom was truly over. The government had to revise its budget estimates and start thinking of a world in which fossil fuels would be replaced by renewables—a situation highlighted by preparation for EXPO 2017 in Astana and the December 2015 climate conference in Paris.

For Kazakhstan, this challenge coincided with the crisis in Ukraine, which led to questioning of the country's relationship with Russia. Like Ukraine, Kazakhstan had decommissioned its nuclear arsenal in return for guarantees of territorial integrity that seemed nugatory after Russia's absorption of Crimea in March 2014. On the economic front Kazakhstan had to assess its membership in the customs union with Russia, which transformed into the potentially more substantial Eurasian Economic Union in 2015. This will be analyzed in chapter 9, along with the impact of Kazakhstan's WTO accession in 2015 and other aspects of the country's external economic relations.

---

and to provide opportunities for citizens to own shares of some of the country's biggest enterprises. However, the first shares were only offered in 2014, for the pipeline maintenance company KazTransOil and for the electricity distributor KEGOC.

33. There was also a challenge in December 2011 of oil workers in Mangistau protesting against poor working conditions in Zhanaozen and Shepte, and being subject to brutal policing that left at least nineteen miners dead. The government dealt effectively with the issue to stifle further dissent while punishing some of the officials responsible for poor workplace relations (Marat, 2016).

5

Uzbekistan

Uzbekistan is the most populous of the Central Asian countries, and in both the tsarist and the Soviet eras Tashkent was the metropolitan center of the Central Asian region. At independence Uzbekistan inherited important assets, including the best civil aircraft fleet, the military command (and significant military equipment), and the best administrative capacity in Central Asia. During the 1990s some observers saw a struggle for regional hegemony between Uzbekistan and Kazakhstan, but in the twenty-first century Kazakhstan clearly became the leading economy with both the largest GDP and income per head. By other benchmarks, Uzbekistan's economic performance has been good; for example, estimates of real living standards indicate that the Uzbek republic lagged the Kyrgyz republic in 1990 (table 2.1), had caught up by 2002 (table 2.6), and had moved ahead of the Kyrgyz Republic by 2014 (table 2.8).

Uzbekistan's transition strategy has been explicitly gradual. During the 1990s, Uzbekistan was the most successful of all Soviet successor states in terms of limiting the fall in output, and in the early 2000s it became the first former Soviet republic to regain its pre-independence level of GDP. The government's focus during the 1990s was on cementing presidential power and on creation of a national economy, e.g., by minimizing dependence on transport corridors through other countries.[1] The government sought to diversify the economy through import substitution, most notably in wheat, cars, and a domestic textiles industry to add value to its major primary product, cotton.

1. Several new railway lines improved domestic connections. The two largest cities, Tashkent and Samarkand, were linked by a completely domestic road; the Soviet road passed through Kazakhstan and was subject to frequent disruption after the two countries became independent. An improved highway through the Kamchik Pass, connecting the populous Fergana Valley to the rest of Uzbekistan, removed the need to transit the easier route through Khujand in Tajikistan.

At independence Uzbekistan Airways' slogan claimed that Tashkent was the Crossroads of Asia, but the inward-looking strategy negated pretensions to be a regional hub.

Uzbekistan was fortunate that world cotton prices increased substantially after independence, providing the resources to maintain public services, and when cotton prices fell in 1996 the government overreacted by introducing foreign exchange controls. A new phase of Uzbekistan's economic development dates from the termination of forex controls at the end of 2003. Although the need for reform was recognized, implementation was slow and incomplete. At the same time, Uzbekistan benefitted from the global resource boom that accelerated after 2003 by exporting gas, gold, copper, and other minerals, and Uzbek workers could also find jobs in the booming economies of Russia and Kazakhstan. With prudent macroeconomic policies and a closed financial sector that sheltered the economy from the 2007–10 financial crises in the USA and Europe (and Kazakhstan) and from the 2008–9 downturn in world trade, Uzbekistan enjoyed a decade of economic growth.[2]

Analysis of Uzbekistan's economic progress under President Karimov is tinged by ideological battles. While the paradox between what are regarded as poor policies and evidence of good economic performance remains difficult to reconcile for many outside observers (e.g., Ruziev et al., 2007, and many reports by multilateral institutions), for others Uzbekistan is an example of rejection of "neoliberal" economic ideology and successful implementation of "heterodox" policies (e.g., Popov, 2013; Cornia, 2014). Many writers find it hard to grant any credit to a repressive regime for achieving economic progress—e.g., Olcott (2007b) in a contribution to a book on "the worst of the worst" repressive regimes described Uzbekistan as a decaying dictatorship— or to see beyond reprehensible practices such as the use of torture against dissidents or of child labor to harvest cotton.

5.1. The Uzbek Paradox, 1991–96

Uzbekistan's performance during the 1990s was seen by many observers as a paradox, because it contradicted the conventional wisdom that a rapid transition from central planning was desirable.[3] As President Karimov continually stressed, Uzbekistan's strategy was one of gradualism. Gradualism did not

2. The official statistics, reported by the World Bank and other agencies, show GDP growth of 7–9% per year. Bogolov (2016) questions the official data and argues that the good performance is a mirage, and that large-scale emigration and the size of the informal economy are indicators of poor performance.

3. Uzbekistan's performance was also paradoxical insofar as it was an outlier in cross-country growth studies (e.g., Berg et al., 1999), which typically underpredicted Uzbekistan's growth in the 1990s (Olimov and Fayzullaev, 2011, 6).

mean no change, and Uzbekistan's transition was more progressive than that of Belarus or Turkmenistan, two countries with which Uzbekistan was often lumped together as the slowest reformers among the former centrally planned economies. The hallmark of Uzbekistan's economic policies was cautious recognition that economic change is inevitable, and a commitment to gradual reform in order to minimize negative or disruptive consequences of change.

Caution was reflected in macroeconomic policy. After independence, Uzbekistan's leadership was suspicious of the Big Bang approach to price liberalization and monetary stabilization pursued by Poland in 1990 and associated with Russia in 1992, and the government's reluctance to embark on macroeconomic stabilization brought Uzbekistan into conflict with the IMF. However, once the government had become convinced of the costs of inflation and the merits of orthodox counterinflation policies, it embarked in January 1994 on a macrostabilization path that followed IMF blueprints fairly closely.

The national currency was introduced in July 1994 and supported by reductions in the growth rate of money supply over the next three years. Price controls were reduced and food rationing abolished, so that open inflation reached a peak in 1994 before declining to below 50% per year in 1997 or 1998 (depending on the data source). Foreign trade was liberalized and exchange restrictions relaxed. The fiscal deficit was cut from 10.4% of GDP in 1993, to 6.1% in 1994, and 4.1% in 1995. The tax system was reformed and collection improved, while expenditure on supporting state enterprises and on consumer subsidies was reduced. There was some unnecessary hardship due to the monetary confusion before July 1994 and the extended inflationary period in the mid-1990s, but the country's economic development suffered little irremediable damage.[4]

Caution on price reform delayed the spread of market forces. Especially in 1992–94, significant parts of the economy remained characterized by shortages and queues rather than by market-clearing prices. Nevertheless, there were benefits, both in reducing the disruptive effects of sudden price liberalization on supply chains, which explains some of Uzbekistan's relatively shallow output decline during the first half of the 1990s, and in protecting people from sudden real income loss. The benefits were, of course, not sustainable as subsidies blew out the government budget, and the main consumption subsidies were abolished or reduced after 1995. By the end of the 1990s the major remaining price controls were on cotton, interest rates, and foreign exchange.

4. The government seemed to be caught unawares by the rapid collapse of the ruble zone in November 1993 and issued a sum coupon, which looked unimpressive and was explicitly temporary. Confiscatory elements of both the exchange of rubles for sum coupons and of sum coupons for sum in July 1994 and the nonconvertibility of the sum all undermined confidence in the currency and made monetary policy less effective.

In 1992, the government moved quickly to privatize housing and small businesses, which picked up on traditions of home ownership rights and of the bazaar. However, large-scale privatization and agrarian reform were limited. Land reform illustrated the tension between maintaining control and creating a vibrant farm sector; the 1998 amendment to the land code reaffirmed that land is state property, at the same time as it tried to create new categories of "private" farmers. Control over natural resource rents, e.g., through state marketing of cotton exports, was an important source of government revenue. Financial sector reform was limited by the same forces that stifled privatization; commercial banking was legalized, and there were over thirty banks by 1998, but the state-owned National Bank of Uzbekistan accounted for over 70% of loans (Akimov, 2001).[5]

Uzbekistan benefited from good governance in the economic sphere, at least by a narrow definition of economic management and by the generally low standards of the CIS. Although some revenue was frittered away on wasteful public investment in industrial projects, the government did well in maintaining health and education expenditure and in providing a social safety net (Pomfret and Anderson, 1997).[6] The government acted innovatively and effectively in decentralized targeting social assistance through local *mahallahs* (Coudouel and Marnie, 1999). Public building improved the cityscape in Tashkent and other towns, without the grandiose aspirations of the Presidential Palace in Turkmenistan or the new capital in Kazakhstan. Transportation and other public services continued to function. Loosening of restrictions on small-scale activities and rising disposable income in the late 1990s, at least in urban areas, saw a revival of eating and drinking out, which recalled a past cultural heritage and raised the quality of life for many. In the 1990s, President Karimov appeared to enjoy a degree of popularity for maintaining relative stability with social justice.

Corruption was endemic, but widely accepted, with little perception that it created *nouveaux riches* comparable to in other CIS counties. Survey evidence (cited in chapter 2) and anecdotal evidence suggested that corruption in Uzbekistan was universal petty theft rather than the grand larceny of Ka-

5. The Republic Stock Exchange Tashkent, the country's only stock exchange, opened in January 1994, but few shares traded. The bond market was even slower to start, with the first treasury bills issued in March 1996.

6. In 1998, when government expenditures amounted to 34.5% of GDP, 45.3% of these expenditures were allocated to health, education, and other social policies (*Uzbek Economic Trends*, January–March 2000, 89–90). Measures of inequality and poverty are even more dubious than the output measures of the 1990s, but the evidence points to a relatively good performance by Uzbekistan. The Uzbek republic's poverty rate in 1989 was the second highest in the USSR, exceeded only by that of the Tajik republic (table 2.1), but by the mid-1990s, according to the IMF (*World Economic Outlook*, May 1998, table 23, based on estimates by Branko Milanovic), Uzbekistan's poverty rate was the second lowest of the eight listed CIS countries.

zakhstan or Russia. The potential rents from cotton and gold are large, but the ostentatious cotton magnates from tsarist times (and the Brezhnev era) had not yet reappeared on the same scale in 1990s Uzbekistan.

During the mid-1990s Uzbekistan emerged as a paradox among CIS countries. Economic reform lagged that in the Baltics, Russia, or even the neighboring Kyrgyz Republic, but the cumulative decline in GDP between 1989 and 1996 was the lowest among all former Soviet republics. Taube and Zettelmeyer (1998) examined the relative importance of various potential explanations of the "Uzbek Puzzle" and, although measurement errors and favorable initial conditions played a part, their impact was dismissed as small in magnitude, and good policy and public investment were left as the major explanatory factors. Zettelmeyer (1998) also mentioned the role of cotton as a readily exportable product and the achievement of energy self-sufficiency in 1995.

The resource endowment was fundamental to the balance of payments, the public-sector budget, and investment. Buoyant export earnings from cotton and gold contributed directly to GDP and were a major source of government revenue. Gas and oil production, leading to close to energy self-sufficiency, helped to ensure that Uzbekistan did not suffer from the shift from Soviet to world prices for primary products. The government kept tight control over the mining, energy, and cotton sectors. State control was associated with better (relative to neighboring countries), although still far from good, administration of the irrigation network on which agriculture depends.

Resource rents siphoned from agriculture by a state order system that gave farmers a small fraction of the world price amounted to as much as a twelfth of GDP in 1996 (see chapter 3.5). The government used the revenue to maintain public spending on education and healthcare better than in other CIS countries. Public investment contributed to GDP, although the attempt to pick winners had mixed results. Achieving oil self-sufficiency and increasing gas exports were significant achievements, especially when world energy prices boomed after 1998. Other import-substituting projects, such as the large chemical and petrochemical projects in the desert, are difficult to assess with the limited available data. The heavily subsidized cotton textile mills were socially wasteful, even though they survived through distorted prices (Golub and Kestelman, 2015). The government increased food self-sufficiency by using state orders for the two main crops to reallocate land from cotton to wheat, even though the foreign exchange savings from an additional hectare under wheat amounted to $500 less than the foreign exchange earnings from a hectare under cotton (Spechler et al., 2004, 180).[7] The import-substituting

---

7. Apart from increased food self-sufficiency, a further benefit is that wheat is less energy- and water-intensive than cotton. However, the price for these benefits, paid in foregone export revenues from cotton, is high.

nature of these projects illustrates the inward-looking development strategy, even though Uzbekistan was an open economy by measures such as the export/GDP ratio.

Foreign direct investment into Uzbekistan was modest in total, but included some high-profile projects. Apart from Newmont Mining's involvement in gold production, practically all the foreign investment was in import substitutes such as Mercedes Benz in trucks, BAT in cigarettes, Coca-Cola in soft drinks, and Daewoo in cars. Daewoo decided in the early 1990s to make Uzbekistan its base for Central Asian operations, investing $100 million in a car factory that started production in 1995 and $45 million in consumer electronics and textile joint ventures. The Daewoo car plant, in language familiar from Beijing Jeep in China or Proton Saga in Malaysia in the 1980s, was claimed to be a base for exporting to the region but its two cars and a minibus were sold only in domestic markets during the 1990s.[8] Car production increased from 82 in 1994 to 25,358 in 1996, 64,908 in 1997, 54,456 in 1998, and 58,800 in 1999, but then stagnated as the Daewoo parent company went bankrupt.

Economic success was accompanied by greater confidence in international relations. In the early years of independence President Karimov represented himself as a bulwark against Islamic fundamentalism, and continued to work with Russia in the Tajikistan conflict as well as in trying to maintain economic ties from the Soviet era (Bohr, 1998). After a brief period of economic nationalism tinged with isolationism in late 1993, Karimov started to exert a more positive leadership role in Central Asia during 1994 and then on the world stage. Relations with the USA warmed considerably as Karimov took opportunities to denounce Iran and vote with the USA at the United Nations, and in July 1996 Presidents Clinton and Karimov met in Washington.

5.2. The Reintroduction of Exchange Controls, 1996–2003

Up until the summer of 1996, relations between Uzbekistan and the IMF and World Bank had been thawing. Uzbekistan was still seen as a slow reformer, but there were signs of improvement. In particular, Uzbekistan was committed to liberalizing its foreign exchange regime and establishing convertibility for current account transactions. In autumn 1996, however, the government reneged on this commitment by reintroducing draconian exchange controls.

8. Within Uzbekistan, the ubiquitous Daewoo cars were a conspicuous sign of higher living standards during the second half of the 1990s, and the symbolism was egalitarian; the little Tico (which cost not much over $1,000 at black-market exchange rates in 1999) was less opulent and exclusive than the imported Mercedes and BMWs, which appeared in Kazakhstan and to a lesser extent in Turkmenistan and the Kyrgyz Republic.

The exchange controls appear to have been a drastic reaction to balance of payments pressures, triggered by a drop in the world price of cotton, rather than part of a considered strategy. The impact on the balance of payments was exacerbated by a poor cotton harvest, increased prices for imported wheat, and lower world price for gold (Blackmon, 2011, 36). Resort to controls to deal with an adverse external shock was symptomatic of the delayed structural reforms, which made the economy less flexible, and may also have reflected the mindset of a leadership still suspicious of market mechanisms. The exchange controls were strongly criticized by the IMF, which suspended a conditional loan negotiated in December 1995, but the Uzbekistan government took pride in asserting its independence by defending the policy.

By 1999 officials were worrying about a growing external imbalance, which was not fully reflected in official statistics. The gap between the official exchange rate and the black-market rate widened from 100% in autumn 1998 to 300% a year later. Negative external developments, such as declining cotton and gold prices and the 1998 Russian crisis, contributed, but the major problem was the import substitution strategy exacerbated by the foreign exchange policy. Production for export was discouraged by policies directing capital to import-competing projects and skewing relative producer prices in favor of such activities. Voluntary exports through official channels became less and less attractive, while the large black-market premium encouraged rent-seeking activities. The controls encouraged smuggling, both of imports and exports, and enforcement of import restrictions and exchange controls diverted resources from productive use. Capital was allocated mainly by government directive; the outcome was declining productivity of capital.[9]

Apart from the continued misuse of public resources by directing credit and foreign exchange to specific enterprises, the government continued to spend relatively wisely by maintaining health and education spending and extending the social support delivered via the *mahallahs*. Nevertheless, wise use of GDP is not a substitute for misuse of productive investment in promoting future economic growth. From 1997 to 2002 Uzbekistan's GDP grew at 3–5% per year, against a background of minimal economic reform and increasing political repression. Although that would have been a respectable growth performance in the earlier transition period, it looked less positive when compared to other transition economies emerging from their transitional recessions in the late 1990s.

Uzbekistan's economic malaise could be traced to the exchange controls that muffled price signals and added a significant level of regulation to stifle

9. By 1999, official estimates of the incremental capital-output ratio (i.e. the units of additional capital required to increase the output stream by one unit) were around 6 and the IMF estimate was 8.3, compared to ICORs for well-functioning economies of 3–4.

entrepreneurial initiative in the traded goods sectors. The negative effects of state procurements for cotton and wheat became more pronounced over time, as production patterns were distorted and farmers sought unofficial marketing channels.[10] The government was in principle committed to rolling back the state order system, but revenue dependence led it to resort to subterfuges. For example, although the percentage of wheat and cotton subject to state order was reduced to 30% in the late 1990s, the percentage was calculated on exaggerated expected harvests, and state orders ended up applying to 90% of the actual 2002 cotton harvest (EBRD, *Transition Report 2003*).

More fundamentally, Uzbekistan's experience illustrated the dynamic dangers of gradual reform. As the economy's performance lagged and popular support waned, the government became more reliant on regional and sectoral elites to deliver stability (and repression) and on controls to generate the rents that kept its clients in line.[11] Border closure measures, justified by the need to keep out terrorists, increased the cost of cross-border trade, at the same time as stricter controls in Uzbekistan increased the incentives for arbitragers to import goods from the more open markets of the Kyrgyz Republic or Kazakhstan.

The need to retain control over the rents from the cotton sector meant that the biggest gap between claims of establishing a market economy and the reality of public policy was in land reform. The large collective farms from the Soviet era were renamed *shirkat*, but their operation changed little as the staff and management were appointed by the regional government and remained an integral part of the power structure. Individual members of the *shirkat* had little incentive to work hard or to innovate and productivity remained low (ICG, 2005, 3), apart from the time spent on the small plot of irrigated land that households could cultivate for their own use or for small-scale marketing. The 1998 Law on Private Farms created a category of independent *dekhan* small-scale farms, exempt from state orders and enjoying inheritable use of land, but the land could not be sold or sublet. Even on leased "private" land,

10. Low farmgate cotton prices meant low wages for cotton picking or reversion to the Soviet pattern of forcing students and others to harvest the crop. Higher wages in Kazakhstan's more market-driven farm sector encouraged skilled cotton pickers to cross the border to South Kazakhstan at harvest time, despite the risk and the harassment of migrant laborers.

11. President Karimov's popularity and reputation for maintaining stability may have been declining since the late 1990s, but with restricted freedom of expression that is difficult to gauge. After a series of assassinations of public officials in 1997, the government arrested hundreds of people in a 1998 crackdown. In February 1999, five bombs in downtown Tashkent, the biggest one apparently targeted at the president, killed several people and injured over a hundred; the subsequent crackdown targeted "religious extremists" (Whitlock, 2002, 242–64). In August 1999, some 650 Islamist gunmen were caught entering Uzbekistan; attempts to bomb the insurgents' bases hit the wrong targets, killing several Kyrgyz civilians and Tajik cows and undermining Uzbekistan's reputation for military effectiveness.

farmers had to grow what they were told to grow and sell to prescribed buyers at fixed prices, with payment into bank accounts from which they had difficulty withdrawing cash. In sum, most of the irrigated arable land remained in farms whose official descriptions changed, but over which the former state farm managers or local administrators retained considerable authority. [12]

Sluggish economic performance after the mid-1990s impeded the government's ability to match its claimed commitment to social sectors with delivery of social services. In education, there were increasing complaints of inefficiency, corruption and falling standards. In 1997, the government announced replacement of the eleven-year Soviet school system by a nine-year system followed by two-year colleges preparing students for university or providing technical training (Nazarova et al., 2015). In 1999 funds were allocated to building new colleges with the goal of completing the reform by 2009, but there were shortages of textbooks and other materials; adoption of the Latin script in 1996 added to the need to replace worn-out or obsolete textbooks. More important, the college system was rife with corruption, as grades were traded for bribes in well-organized markets, especially in the new colleges, but also in many universities and secondary schools, where underpaid teachers felt the need to supplement their state salaries. The government feared that relaxing its grip on the education system by allowing private schools or colleges might undermine political stability.

Health sector reform was initiated in 1996 with a presidential decree that signaled a shift away from hospitalization towards primary healthcare and a reduction in the number of tiers of health facilities. This was a positive shift from the Soviet system's overemphasis on capital-intensive hospitals and specialist services and towards greater reliance on general practitioners and access to out-patient facilities. As with education, concerns about the effectiveness of reform and the quality of services grew, as public-sector resources available for the health sector declined and accountability mechanisms were weak. Private financing of health increased, both officially through the introduction of a prepaid rather than a free system and unofficially as people paid to gain preferential treatment, raising concern about access to healthcare for the poorer and most vulnerable groups in society. Health problems such as drug addiction and the spread of HIV/AIDS became more serious after independence, although data are unreliable.

The system of official residence permits, *propiskas*, remained from the Soviet era. Enforcement varied, and Tashkent's population swelled from just

---

12. Muradov and Ilkhamov (2014) argue that this and later land reforms were not intended to give farmers independent land rights. The goal was to remove farm workers from the state payroll without changing how land was used, so that the state could determine the amount of land sown with cotton and increase its share of revenues.

over 2 million at independence to around 3.5 million a decade later. In July 2004, the mayor of Tashkent announced a cleanup of illegal migrants, which was accelerated after July 30 bomb attacks on the US and Israeli embassies and on the office of the Prosecutor General. People expelled from the city for lack of *propiskas* included skilled workers who had been living there for years, and all were deprived of fundamental labor rights, e.g., by law people losing their jobs are entitled to two months' pay but this was denied to the illegals.

5.3. Economic Reform and Social Unrest

By the turn of the century many in the government recognized the costs of the exchange controls and need for economic reforms. After September 11, 2001, a window of opportunity for reform opened, as the USA provided aid and backed renewed IMF and World Bank engagement in Uzbekistan. Starting in early 2002, the government used tight monetary policy to gradually reduce the black-market premium on foreign currency. Inflation halved to 12% in 2003. Restrictions on foreign exchange availability for current account transactions were abolished at the end of 2003. However, a requirement to preregister all import contracts with the Agency for Foreign Economic Relations and other restrictions meant that bureaucratic hurdles on access to foreign currency remained.[13]

In the run-up to the removal of foreign exchange controls, the government introduced trade barriers to protect domestic producers of import substitutes who might be hurt by increased competition. The restrictions were particularly strict on the shuttle-traders who went on shopping trips to China, Turkey, and neighboring countries, and who stocked many of the stalls in the bazaars. The government even sought to close the bazaars in November 2002. The immediate effects of the restrictions were higher prices for many consumer goods and increased purchases in border areas of Kazakhstan or the Kyrgyz Republic of goods, which were brought legally or illegally into Uzbekistan.[14]

In 2003, the government introduced measures to free up the economy or improve efficiency. State procurement on wheat and cotton was increased to

13. Gemayel and Grigorian (2005) describe problems of currency convertibility faced by enterprises and households after 2003. The problems included delays in processing requests for foreign exchange, a de facto limit of $5,000 on availability of foreign currency, and required completion of long forms of which people were distrustful, fearing the information might be passed on to the government and used to their disadvantage. The EBRD Transition Indicator for the trade and forex regime increased from 1.00 in 2000 to 1.67 in 2001–4 and 2.00 after 2005, but remained at this low level (table 2.2).

14. The main effect was displacement of a legal tax-paying shuttle trade by an illegal bribe-paying shuttle trade; the ICG (2004a, 17) reported that $350 in bribes could ensure that a car full of goods from the Kyrgyz Republic could reach Tashkent without problem.

50% of the crop, but applied to the actual harvest, which often reduced the burden and improved transparency. The government began serious moves towards reforming delivery of energy and water. Power sector tariffs were increased by 60% in 2002 and by 40% in 2003, although they were still well below cost-recovery levels, and a metering program and other steps to improve collection rates was under way. In 2003, the government announced its aim of moving towards more targeted social assistance. However, pressure on the state budget (in part from funding the quasi-fiscal deficits of the energy sector) led to reduced funding in the early 2000s for the *mahallahs*, which became increasingly seen as an instrument of political control rather than of decentralized social assistance (Sievers, 2002).

The reforms suggested a renewed commitment to measures aimed at more efficient delivery of public services, but also a reality of very slow and gradual change. There were internal contradictions, e.g., the growing perception of the *mahallahs* as a mechanism for social control undermined the attempt to decentralize water management after 2000. At the same time, ever-tightening security measures stifled economic activity. The human rights record came under international scrutiny when Uzbekistan hosted the 2003 EBRD annual meetings in Tashkent. President Karimov refused to countenance requests that he renounce the use of torture. EBRD involvement in Uzbekistan was substantially reduced in 2004, and other multilateral institutions reconsidered their programs in Uzbekistan.

Even in their attenuated post-2002 form the bazaars were harassed by the authorities who saw them as hotbeds of illicit activities. The crackdown on bazaars in Uzbekistan contributed to the Dordoi (in Bishkek) and Kara-Suu (near Osh) markets in the Kyrgyz Republic becoming by 2004 the largest in Central Asia, and they were catering overwhelmingly to customers from Uzbekistan. The merchants at the Kara-Suu market were largely ethnic Uzbeks with Kyrgyz citizenship who acted as wholesalers between merchants from western China and shuttle-traders from Uzbekistan. Despite the official restrictions from Uzbekistan, this business was so profitable that similar markets developed in other towns in the southern Kyrgyz Republic such as Jalalabad and Uzgen and in Khujand in northern Tajikistan, all located close to the Uzbekistan border.[15] Ironically, Uzbekistan was now outsourcing the small-scale

15. Borders, especially in the Fergana Valley, were subject to irregular and unannounced closures, which became more general after March 2004 and imposed high costs on the small-scale cross-border trade in the Fergana Valley. After masonry bridges were blown up to prevent Uzbekistan residents from going to the Kara-Suu market, the locals established rope bridges and pulley systems, which allowed cross-border trade to continue to some extent, but also claimed several lives. Where the border near Osh is a narrow stream, Uzbek border officials helpfully placed a plank across the stream and charged each person using the plank 100 sum (Megoran et al., 2005).

entrepreneurial activities that had characterized the first phase of transition from central planning, and in which Uzbekistan had been the leader in Central Asia in 1992.

Closure of bazaars in March and November 2004 was associated with the worst rioting since independence.[16] The most serious of these incidents occurred in Andijan on May 13, 2005, when government troops opened fire on demonstrators, killing 187 by government estimates and hundreds or even thousands by other estimates. The demonstrations were in support of members of *Akromiya* who had been imprisoned. Verme (2006) describes *Akromiya* as an SMEs' association and demonstrators saw local entrepreneurs being victimized, but the government called *Akromiya* an Islamist organization and arrested hundreds of "Islamist militants" in a crackdown after the massacre. Human Rights Watch (2005) paints a grim picture of a peaceful demonstration ending in a massacre, and some reports add to the death toll hundreds killed trying to flee the country, especially across the Kyrgyz border. The Andijan death count is the largest from a peaceful demonstration in the post-Soviet space. President Karimov refused to accept any external investigation and most aspects remain controversial, but the clear signal was that dissent would be punished.

The May 2005 Andijan events stimulated a revision of Uzbekistan's external relations. In the face of strident criticism from the West, Uzbekistan gave notice for the USA to vacate its military base, realigned with Russia and China in the Shanghai Cooperation Organization, and quit its connection with the GUAM (Georgia, Ukraine, Azerbaijan, Moldova) group in favor of the Russian-led Eurasian Economic Community. Uzbekistan soon had second thoughts about realigning with Russia, and in 2008 Uzbekistan left the Eurasian Economic Community and quietly cooperated with the USA over the northern supply network to Afghanistan. The external situation subsequently stabilized (see part 3).

Apart from the relaxation of foreign exchange controls, and virtual disappearance of the black-market premium on foreign currency between 2003 and 2008, the economic strategy changed little. The government continued to control cotton marketing and developed other primary exports largely through domestic companies. Uzbekistan enjoyed steady economic growth led by energy self-sufficiency and by exports as the value of cotton, minerals, energy, food, and car exports all increased (Popov, 2013; Cornia, 2014).[17]

16. The details of both sets of events are unclear. The March 2004 violence, ascribed by the government to Islamic extremists, featured four days of gun battles in Tashkent and Bukhara, in which fifty or more people died, and two suicide bombs in Tashkent's Chorsu bazaar. The November 2004 riots in Tashkent and in Fergana Valley towns were more spontaneous and directly related to new regulations on small-time traders.

17. In the World Bank's World Development Indicators, Uzbekistan's GDP increased from

TABLE 5.1. Sectoral Composition of Value-Added, Uzbekistan, 1987–2010

	Agriculture	Mining, Utilities, & Construction	Manufacturing	Public & Private Services
1987	27.6	10.3	28.0	34.1
1994	37.4	12.2	14.2	36.2
2000	34.4	13.7	9.4	42.5
2004	30.8	15.7	10.2	43.3
2010	19.5	26.4	9.0	45.1

Source: Cornia (2014, 5), based on World Bank World Development Indicators.

TABLE 5.2. Major Exports, Uzbekistan, 2000 and 2010, Share of Total Exports

	Cotton	Energy products[a]	Fruit and vegetables	Precious metals[b]	Copper	Cars	Textile products
2000	31.9	11.9	2.5	25.1	4.5	2.2	5.4
2010	13.5	25.4	9.3	23.7	4.6	4.1	5.0

Source: Ganiev and Yusupov (2012), based on national statistics.
Notes: (a) mostly natural gas; (b) mostly gold.

Table 5.1 highlights the increase in the share of gas and minerals in value-added after 2000.

Despite an inward-looking development strategy based on import substitution, the export/GDP ratio increased, led by exports of natural gas as world energy prices soared. Gas exports initially went to Russia and other CIS destinations, but after completion of the Turkmenistan-China pipeline in 2009, Uzbekistan could also sell gas to China. The changing export shares in table 5.2 were associated with shifts in the direction of trade as the gas, cars, and fruit and vegetables were primarily sold in Russia, whose share of Uzbekistan's exports increased from 17% in 2000 to 33% in 2010 (displacing the EU as Uzbekistan's major export market), and in Kazakhstan, whose share increased from 3.2% in 2000 to 7.2% in 2010. The export shares of China, Turkey, and Bangladesh also increased, mostly associated with cotton (and uranium to China). The origin of Uzbekistan's imports changed by less, although the share of Russia increased from 16% to 22%, China from 3% to 14%, and South Korea from 10% to 16% (mainly auto parts to the Daewoo/GM factory).

Cotton continues to be a major export, although its relative importance has been in decline. Cotton production, which by 2003 had halved from the late 1980s peaks of around eight million bales, recovered in 2004–7 to around

---

$14.3 billion in 2005 to $56.8 billion in 2013, although there is some doubt about the reliability of these data (Bologov, 2016).

five million bales, before falling to around four million bales in 2009–15. The lower output partly reflected an ongoing policy of pursuing food self-sufficiency by controlling how much land is devoted to cotton and to wheat production. At independence, about 1.7 million hectares were sown with cotton and about 0.5 million hectares with wheat. In 2009 wheat acreage overtook cotton acreage, after which the area sown with wheat was about 1.4 million hectares and cotton 1.3 million. In addition, incentives for cotton growers were blunted by state pricing policies. Cotton yield per acre declined slightly between 1991 and 2015, while yields were increasing in all major competitors outside Central Asia (Golub and Kestelman, 2015, 24).

Cotton production remains highly regulated. During January and February, quotas are allocated to districts whose governors appoint local officials who assign quotas to individual farmers. Production is closely monitored, and governors whose districts fail to meet the quota risk being fired. Farmers failing to meet their quota suffer economic and administrative punishment, even facing criminal prosecution (Muradov and Ilkhamov, 2014). After harvesting, farmers must immediately transport the raw cotton to one of the 127 gins, and after logistical costs have been deducted the farmer will eventually receive the state procurement price. [18]

Farmers are responsible for securing their inputs, many of which are supplied by state monopolies and financed by banks in paper transactions. The system offers many opportunities for corruption as officials determine access to inputs and as farmers misreport their land's fertility in a bid to secure more subsidized inputs. Input quality varies, e.g., irrigation channels are maintained by the state, but are often in a poor condition. Between 2007 and 2015, the government undertook a modernization program of the cotton gins, upgrading forty-five and closing twenty-five. However, the ginning outturn ratio at the end of the program was 32%, while the global norm was 39%; Golub and Kestelman (2015, 25) estimate that the productivity gap cost about $370 million at world prices. Overall, it is difficult to value the benefits to farmers from state-supplied inputs due to nontransparent pricing, but on balance they are surely insufficient to offset the cost to cotton farmers of low procurement prices for their output.[19]

Although farmers benefitted from higher state procurement prices after 2003, especially if these are valued before 2003 at the parallel exchange rate (table 5.3), the farmgate prices were still well below the world price or prices

18. MacDonald et al. (2015) provide a good overview of the cotton sector. Ganiev and Yusupov (2012, 9) estimate that the cotton marketing monopoly "was tantamount to imposing a tax of approximately 25% on cotton fiber exports in 2011."

19. For more details on supply and cost of cotton farmers' inputs see Muradov and Ilkhamov (2014) and Golub and Kestelman (2015, 20). The conclusion of this paragraph is consistent with the anecdotal evidence from Shtaltovna and Hornidge (2014) presented in table 3.4.

TABLE 5.3. World Cotton Prices, and US and Uzbekistan Farm Prices, 1999–2012

Marketing Year	Farm Price			World Price
	SPP_O	SPP_P	USA	
1999/00	29.4	7.2	45.0	52.8
2000/01	22.3	8.2	49.8	57.2
2001/02	17.8	8.4	29.8	41.8
2002/03	19.5	15.5	44.5	55.7
2003/04	27.9	27.7	61.8	69.2
2004/05	29.8	29.9	41.6	53.5
2005/06	30.5	30.8	47.7	56.1
2006/07	34.9	34.2	46.5	59.1
2007/08	38.6	37.1	59.3	72.9
2008/09	43.4	37.9	47.8	61.0
2009/10	42.0	30.7	62.9	77.5
2010/11	50.2	35.3	81.5	165.0
2011/12	38.0	25.8	90.5	103.5

Source: MacDonald (2012, 10).

Notes: Prices in US cents per pound of cotton fiber. Uzbekistan state procurement prices (SPP) for seed cotton are converted into fiber-equivalents assuming a 32% ginning output. SPP_O and SPP_P convert the Uzbekistan farm price into US dollars at the official and parallel exchange rate respectively.

received by US cotton farmers. After 2007, as a currency black market re-emerged, the gap increased once more, especially when cotton prices spiked upwards in 2011. Golub and Kestelman (2015, 18–19) estimated that, at the official exchange rate, the gap between Uzbek and US farm prices for cotton almost disappeared in 2013/14 and 2014/15, but at the black-market exchange rate Uzbek farmers received only 62% of the US farmgate price.

The willingness of the government to cede control was brought into question by the way in which the "second wave" of land reform was implemented. Khan (2007) estimated that in the 2002–7 land reform large commercial farms received 85% of sown area while smaller *dekhan* farms only received 12%.[20] The commercial farms were on average several hundred times larger than the private *dekhan* farms, which mostly relied on family labor.[21] The expectation

20. Farmers received land-use rights that cannot be sold, mortgaged, or exchanged, while the state retains the right of expropriation if deemed necessary (Lerman, 2008). The government also retains control over water allocations, which in many cases are critical for land use. When water distribution was devolved to local Water Management Units, the units were inadequately financed and had insufficient authority to prevent continuing deterioration of irrigation and drainage (Abdullaev et al., 2009; Golub and Kestelman, 2015, 6).

21. This description is not fully consistent with that found in fieldwork in Khorezm by Djanibekov et al. (2012) who report excessive fragmentation of land by 2007. This led to the state requiring holders of less than thirty hectares to return their land for redistribution to large farms.

was that the best farmers would run the large commercial farms that might also reap economies of scale, although this seemed to be based on Soviet-era prejudices rather than current evidence.[22] The distribution of land meant that over 90% of rural households had no land beyond their household plot, which, as elsewhere in Central Asia, remained crucial for home food consumption and for the supply of milk, and this pushed many rural workers to migration.

As gas production increased, Uzbekistan became an energy exporter and benefited from high energy prices and new transit routes. The Turkmenistan-China gas pipeline, completed in 2009, passed through Uzbekistan, which could tap into the pipeline as a relatively low-cost export option for gas. In 2012 gas and other energy exports exceeded $5 billion, while cotton export revenues were $1.25 billion; for comparison, remittances from Russia, as reported by the Russian Central Bank (Cornia, 2014, 8), totaled $5.7 billion.

Uzbekistan's most notable minerals are gold, copper, and uranium, while other significant mineral resources include bentonite, coal, fluorspar, gypsum, iodine, kaolin, lithium, oil and natural gas, silver, sulfur, tungsten, and zinc (Safirova, 2012). Mineral production is concentrated in a handful of state enterprises whose data are generally not published. Navoi GMK is the largest gold producer with a rumored output of sixty tons per year, and it also had a monopoly on uranium mining until 2010 when a joint venture with a Chinese partner opened a new mine. Almalyk GMK is the dominant copper producer and produces 90% of the country's silver and 20% of gold. Copper and gold enjoyed high world prices during the first decade of the twenty-first century. Copper exports increased from $126 million in 2000 to $600 million in 2007, before collapsing and then recovering to $536 million in 2010 (Ganiev and Yusupov, 2012, 32). While data problems make it difficult to decompose the dramatic increase in the value of mining output with any precision, it is clear that gas, gold, and copper were major contributors.

The UzDaewoo automobile joint venture, the largest manufacturing foreign investment in Central Asia in the 1990s, suffered from Daewoo's financial

---

This stage was rapidly implemented in 2008 leading to a similar outcome to that reported by Khan but a year or two later.

22. Increased yields in China, Brazil, and India highlight benefits from liberalization and decentralization of decision making. Chinese farmers have experimented successfully in double-cropping cotton and wheat, which in Uzbekistan is inhibited by top-down decisions about what to grow. Chinese cotton farmers have adopted simple techniques, such as plastic mulching (covering rows with polyethylene film to reduce evaporation and hence better control salt levels), which spread quickly once shown to work, but is discouraged in Uzbekistan by state control over the input supply process. In sum, substantial scope to increase productivity in cotton farming exists, especially by farmer education and extension services; Inna Rudenko and colleagues (Rudenko and Lamers, 2006; Martius et al., 2011) illustrate this with fieldwork in Khorezm.

difficulties and bankruptcy. Daewoo's car division was sold to General Motors in 2001, and the Uzbekistan operation became a joint venture with General Motors; the restructured joint venture has been known as GM Uzbekistan since 2008. The decision by GM to keep the factory in production was helped by extensive state support in the domestic market, not only through tariff protection, but also by excise taxes and a 6% road fund tax levied only on imported cars (and that would be illegal if Uzbekistan were a WTO member).[23] By 2013, the factory was producing about two hundred thousand vehicles per year, had 94% of Uzbekistan's new car market, and exported to Russia and Kazakhstan.[24] In 2014, however, car exports to Russia fell by 35%, which Uzbek sources ascribed to discrimination against nonmembers of the Eurasian Economic Union, including abuse of technical barriers to trade such as introduction of safety regulations that targeted Uzbek cars. In 2011, a GM Powertrain joint venture between GM and UzAvtosanout opened in Tashkent, with projected capacity of 225,000 1.2 and 1.5 liter engines a year, suggesting that GM may have plans to incorporate the previously isolated Uzbekistan operations into its global supply network.[25]

The car industry has fared better than the aircraft industry, represented by the Chkalov factory that moved to Tashkent in 1941.[26] After 1991 the factory's future was seen in large cargo planes (Ilyushin, 76) and smaller passenger planes (Ilyushin, 114), but both aircraft relied on research conducted at the Ilyushin center in Moscow and on a network of suppliers in Russia. President Karimov thought that Uzbekistan was in control because final assembly was in Tashkent and the factory was modernized in the 1990s, but when six Il76 orders were placed from India in 2001 disagreement arose over revenue-sharing. In 2006, all Russian aircraft producers merged into the United Aircraft Corporation (OAK), and from December 2006 OAK envisaged that all Il76 assembly would shift to Ulyanovsk in Russia. In 2010 Chkalov declared

23. The excise tax is levied at $2.5–7.2 per cubic centimeter of engine displacement, with the rate depending on the size of the car and the date of production. It has been exempted on cars imported from Russia in a reciprocal deal that helps to explain the export sales to Russia.

24. UNECA (2016, 96–101) cited Uzbekistan's car industry as an import-substitution success story, but this was not a valid conclusion from the papers that the report referred to (notably, Ganiev and Yusupov, 2012). The industry exists only due to the high levels of public support that impose high costs on domestic car-buyers, while exports are artificially supported by bilateral trade agreements and are not competitive on open international markets.

25. GM Uzbekistan continues to rely on supply chains developed by Daewoo, mostly involving Korean suppliers and a twice-weekly container train from Lianyungang, China, to Uzbekistan. Rastogi and Arvis (2014, 24) report that GM was planning to use its own supply network to source inputs from North America and Southeast Asia through Korea, and Brazilian and EU inputs by rail through Russia. They also suggest that local content is small because potential suppliers are discouraged from investing in Uzbekistan.

26. This paragraph draws heavily on Fazendeiro (2015).

bankruptcy. The last Il114s were delivered to Uzbekistan Air in 2013. The Chkalov company was released from bankruptcy and in January 2014 became the Tashkent Mechanical Plant, part of the car industry.

Despite the good economic performance after 2003, there were some threats. World commodity markets are volatile, and it is uncertain how much of the minerals and energy boom was due to higher prices rather than increased real output. In 2006, the government set up a Fund of Reconstruction and Development to collect boom-period revenues from extractive industries, which could be used in future to cofinance strategic projects such as those identified in the 2011–15 industrial and infrastructure modernization program. However, the focus on capital-intensive industrial and mining sectors and the nature of the 2002–7 land reform did little for equity and contributed to increased unemployment.[27] Inadequate employment creation was reflected in the growth of migrant labor going primarily to Russia, estimated at almost two million workers in 2011.[28]

The large numbers of migrant workers also reflect the fast-growing population, which is putting strains on the education system and creates risk of serious youth unemployment problems in the coming years as well as potential environmental pressure as the rural population expands. The government recognized the need to maintain education and health standards in the 2007 Welfare Improvement Strategy (Olimov and Fayzullaev, 2011), but implementation was problematic. There is a sense that widespread use of patronage to fill public offices has been associated with declining quality of public officials, and public services are being maintained (or not maintained) by continuous increases in the number of officials.[29] According to Said (2014, 7), "a dramatic increase of the government bureaucracy in the past two decades has coincided with a steep decline in its capacity to effectively implement policies."

By 2007–8 the black market had practically disappeared, but it reappeared in 2009 as the government responded to a dip in remittances by tightening de facto exchange controls (Horton et al., 2016). All legal entities had to obtain the central bank's permission to access forex, and all forex transactions were

27. Using the national poverty line, poverty fell from 45% in 1994–95, to 27% in 2001, and 15% in 2012. Inequality is hard to assess because Gini coefficients vary widely depending on the data source, and some of the reported changes are implausible (Cornia, 2014, 10).

28. Estimates of migration are approximate because much is unofficial and remittances are underreported because they are often carried or sent as cash. The cost of sending remittances fell dramatically as more companies offered the service, with fees dropping from around 10% in 2002 to 2–3% by 2009, increasing the financial attractiveness of temporary migration to Russia. During the cotton harvest season, there is considerable short-term migration in response to higher wages in South Kazakhstan than in the adjoining Tashkent oblast.

29. Perceptions of corruption are increasing; Uzbekistan ranked 153 out of 167 in Transparency International's 2015 Corruption Perceptions Index, which is worse than 79 out of 90 in 2000 if we assume that the additional coverage tends to bring in poorer and more corrupt countries.

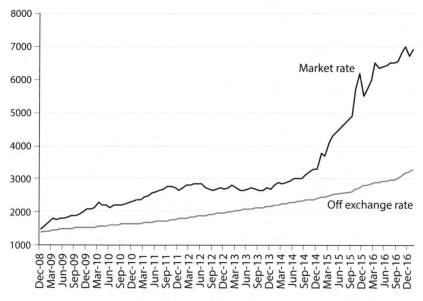

5.1. Exchange rate, sum/USD, December 2008–December 2016. Source: Ben Slay, private correspondence, based on Central Bank of Uzbekistan data and UNDP calculations.

subject to extensive red tape. Commercial banks had an actual rate for selling sum, and authorized importers could obtain forex through commodity exchanges where the rate might vary. Individuals had the legal right to exchange up to $2,000 per quarter, but faced long queues at the bank and were often told the bank had no money; in practice, the forex was usually loaded on to debit cards rather than given as cash, with a two- or three-month delay before the transaction was completed. A variety of exchange rates coexisted: in July 2014, the central bank's official rate was 2,320 sum/USD, the commercial banks' actual rate was 2,362, and at the commodity exchange the rate was around 3,700.

From 2009 until mid-2014, the black-market premium was stable, with a roughly one-third premium on trading sum on the black market rather than at the official rate (figure 5.1).[30] A sharp increase in the number of sum per dollar (depreciation of the sum) began in the second half of 2014, after which the premium became more volatile and larger in 2015 and 2016. The timing is similar to the exchange rate history for the other major labor exporters in the CIS (Armenia, the Kyrgyz Republic, and Tajikistan). The increasing black-market premium and multiple exchange rates of 2014–16 indicated that

30. Black-market efficiency was complicated by illegality that was intermittently enforced, e.g., a high-profile crackdown in February 2013 saw traders at several popular locations arrested but within a few days the black market was back in business. Black-market rates varied substantially, with wide spreads between buying and selling rates.

the government was resorting to stricter implicit forex controls in a de facto return to the pre-2003 situation, despite Uzbekistan's formal acceptance of convertibility.[31]

5.4. Responding to Crisis and Facing New Challenges in 2014–16

As elsewhere in Central Asia, Uzbekistan felt the impact of falling world prices after mid-2014 for key resources, directly for gold and copper and indirectly for oil through the threat to remittances from migrant workers in Russia. Uzbekistan's vulnerability was increased by the fact that in the first decade of the twenty-first century Russia displaced the EU as the country's top trading partner. The Russian economy went through a deep recession between mid-2014 and late 2016, which had consequences for import demand and for the derived demand for migrant workers. The impact on Uzbekistan was exacerbated by the deepening of the Eurasian customs union into the Eurasian Economic Union (EAEU) in January 2015, and explicit, favored treatment in the Russian markets of Kazakhstan and the Kyrgyz Republic relative to Uzbekistan. Treatment of migrant labor was an especially contentious issue, as the benefits for labor from EAEU member countries were strengthened, and conditions for labor from nonmembers deteriorated. Uzbekistan remained committed to staying outside Russia's sphere of influence, but paid an economic price for this independent stance.

Meanwhile, the government gave some signs of easing its emphasis on control of the domestic economy. In December 2012, the Uzbek State Committee for Geology and Mineral Resources reached an agreement for Rio Tinto to engage in geological survey studies at the Gava site. In 2014, the government shifted towards encouraging PSAs for oil and gas, but with limited response due to perceived problems of forex access and pipeline options. Meanwhile, the economic situation was fueling discontent (Fumagalli, 2016). The government may be correct that militants organized some of the demonstrations, but the economic and policy situation provided a fertile breeding ground for discontent.

In an autocratic regime, the ability to respond to difficult challenges depends critically on the president. In August 2016, Uzbekistan's first and only president died. After the announcement of President Karimov's death on Sep-

31. In nonrecognition of inflation (or to curb cash transactions), the government was unwilling to print high denomination notes. In the 1990s and early 2000s, the one-hundred-sum note was king. In the early and mid-2010s, the one-thousand-sum or five-thousand-sum notes were the highest value banknotes, despite being worth less than a US dollar on the black market by 2015. The inconvenience of having to carry bags full of sum for large or multiple transactions further encouraged use of dollars or euros, even though such use was generally illegal.

tember 2, 2016, Shavkat Mirziyoyev, who had been prime minister since 2003, became interim president. He won the December presidential election with 88% of the vote.

5.5. The Karimov Era in Retrospect

In the uncharted waters of transition, a wait-and-see approach was not a bad option, especially for a new country. Any government of a newly independent country, whose economists were Soviet-trained with no experience of a market economy, was bound to make mistakes.

The import substitution strategy led to many consequences familiar from the pursuit of such policies across the Third World of the 1950s and 1960s. Initially, the protected industries grow quickly, although because they tend to be capital-intensive output grows faster than employment. Relative incentives matter; favoring manufacturing for the domestic market disfavors agriculture and export activities. Apart from the artificially supported car exports, Uzbekistan has not succeeded in diversifying its exports away from a handful of primary products. Despite many advisors pointing to a tradition of small and medium-sized manufacturing enterprises, such activities are not flourishing in twenty-first-century Uzbekistan. Foreign investment has increased since 2000, but much of this is tariff-jumping, as foreign firms find it difficult to export to Uzbekistan and establish production facilities that can serve the protected market. The most striking symptom of failure is the several million migrant workers who have gone to Russia to find work. This may be better than the emergence of slums or bread riots that characterized countries pursuing import-substituting industrialization in the 1950s and 1960s, but selective emigration (i.e. mostly males) adversely affects the rural social structure and their concentration in Russia leaves Uzbekistan vulnerable to changes in Russia's policies towards foreign workers.

Uzbekistan's economic policymakers have now been exposed to market economies and to non-Soviet economics by international travel and a variety of training programs. Nevertheless, even when policymakers understand reform to be necessary, it is difficult to push through. The system put in place during the decade after independence created opportunities for self-enrichment by a small elite who are now wary in case any change might undermine their hold on power or their sources of income. Vested interests resisting reform include the former state farm managers and state enterprise managers, but because of the lack of large-scale privatization there is no group comparable to the Russian oligarchs. Ostentatious consumption by some members of the elite became more visible in the 2000s. An especially high-profile figure of hate was the president's daughter Gulnara Karimova, who led an ostentatious lifestyle (with a $600 million fortune in Swiss bank accounts, according to Said, 2014, 5) until she was placed under house arrest in 2013.[32]

The revenue stream from cotton, minerals, and energy exports reduced the pressure to reform, and sharp decline in these revenues, as in 1996 or 2009, was a catalyst for strengthening controls rather than implementing reforms. Nevertheless, as President Karimov's articulation in 2012 of an *Uzbekistan Vision 2030* implied, reform was essential if the goal of becoming a middle-income country was to be achieved. Import substitution is not a viable strategy for promoting long-run growth.

The exchange controls imposed in 1996 were a major policy error, although the severity of the consequences was substantially reduced by the 1999–2007 resource boom. The multiple exchange rates that reemerged after 2009 weakened incentives to invest in innovation and efficiency as a launchpad for exports, hampering diversification and encouraging participation in the informal economy, and complicated foreign investors' operations. People are discouraged from holding domestic currency, which boosts dollarization and reduces monetary policy effectiveness. The banking sector is distanced from financial intermediation by its focus on implementing government programs and collecting state revenue, and households are discouraged from holding bank deposits that may be difficult to access.

Despite the negative consequences of strict forex controls that were recognized by the government in the early 2000s and again in the 2010s, the instinct of President Karimov's regime was to turn to controls when faced with an economic crisis. The distrust of market mechanisms and unwillingness to decentralize decision making to producers or to households ensured that the variety of market-based economy established in the 1990s underperformed for the rest of Karimov's rule. Even in the favorable conditions of booming world markets for gold and copper and with gas and oil reserves sufficient to cover domestic demand and increasing exports, Uzbekistan living standards improved but did not boom, especially outside the main urban centers.

5.6. Prospects for the Mirziyoyev Era

Uzbekistan's cautious approach to reform means that there is still time to loosen overstrict regulation and to reverse the bias against exports, much as South Korea did in 1964 after a decade of mild import substitution. The change in presidency in 2016 offered an opportunity for transformation by a relatively

---

32. Gulnara Karimova gained widespread business interests, especially in the new sectors of finance, media, and mobile phone services (section 10.7). Cooley (2017) provides more information about the wealth of the elite.

youthful leader.[33] In the first year of his presidency, Shavkat Mirziyoyev signaled new directions in both foreign economic relations and domestic economic policy. The areas were well chosen: the adoption of foreign exchange controls and the high costs of conducting international trade were the two outstanding flaws in the Karimov economic model.

Between Karimov's death and the end of 2016, Mirziyoyev hosted working visits from Vladimir Putin and Nursultan Nazarbayev in September, Alexander Lukashenko in October, Recep Tayyip Erdogan in November, and Almazbek Atambayev in December, as well as separate state visits from Presidents Nazarbayev, Atambayev, and Ghani. In 2017, President Mirziyoyev made frequent international trips, starting with state visits in March and April to Turkmenistan, Kazakhstan, and Russia, and in May to Beijing where he attended the "One Belt, One Road" international forum. Later in May he went to Riyadh for the Arab Islamic Summit. In June, he attended the Council of the Heads of State of the Shanghai Cooperation Organization (meeting, inter alia, the prime ministers of Pakistan and India) and he opened EXPO-2017 in Astana. In September, Mirziyoyev attended the United Nations General Assembly in New York, and in October the CIS Summit in Sochi. In October and November, he made state visits to Turkey, South Korea, and Tajikistan. The list goes on.

The schedule looks hectic, but it was far from random. First working meetings with the presidents of Russia and Kazakhstan indicated Uzbekistan's priorities; Russia is too important for a Central Asian leader to ignore, even if Uzbekistan maintains its distance from the Eurasian Economic Union and even if Uzbekistan and Kazakhstan can cooperate as the main centers of Central Asia. Three visits to Turkmenistan stressed the need to improve relations with a neighbor that is critical for connectivity to Iran and the Middle East. The Beijing visit highlighted China's economic importance for Uzbekistan, as well as Uzbekistan's interest in the Belt and Road Initiative. South Korea has been an important investor in Uzbekistan and is a potential partner in mining and energy joint ventures. Finally, attendance at the United Nations in New York, an Islamic summit, and the SCO meeting signaled Uzbekistan's intention to assume a more active role on the world stage.

The meetings with Turkmenistan and Kazakhstan highlighted connectivity, and hence Uzbekistan's reintegration into a regional (and wider) economic

33. Mirziyoyev was born in 1957, Karimov in 1938. Nazarbayev (born 1940), Rahmon (born 1952), Berdimuhamedov (born 1957), and Atambayev (born 1956) are slightly older than Mirziyoyev, but there are signs of a generational shift among Central Asian presidents. Nevertheless, the last four are all men who were into their thirties before the collapse of central planning (as is Jeenbekov, born 1958), and it may be the next generation, born after 1970, that will produce the first leaders to feel comfortable with market mechanisms rather than instinctively turning to economic controls.

circle. In their March 2017 meeting at the Turkmen-Uzbek border, Presidents Berdymuhamedov and Mirziyoyev opened rail and road bridges across the Amu Darya River. In Astana in March, Presidents Nazarbayev and Mirziyoyev announced the first scheduled high-speed passenger rail service between Tashkent and Almaty, and in July the direct Tashkent-Samarkand road passing through Kazakhstan was reopened. In April 2017, Uzbekistan Airways resumed Tashkent-Dushanbe flights after a quarter-century gap, and in November 2017 direct flight connections between Tashkent and Kabul were initiated.[34] The words and symbolism spoke of reintegration of Central Asia.

Mirziyoyev and Nazarbayev issued warnings to upstream nations that any water projects must follow international norms in recognizing downstream nations' rights. Nevertheless, Mirziyoyev extended an early welcome to Kyrgyz president Atambayev in Tashkent and made a state visit to Bishkek in September 2017; both countries value cooperation with China and seek China's support for a rail link from Kashgar through Osh and the Ferghana Valley to Tashkent. In November 2017 President Mirziyoyev made a state visit to Tajikistan, the main target of the warning on water rights.

Changes in domestic economic policy were less immediately clear after President Karimov's death, and commentators speculated about whether the new presidency would lead to reform or continuity. In the campaign leading to the December 2016 presidential election, Mirziyoyev called for a transition from "a strong state to a robust civil society," by strengthening the role of the parliament and local elective councils, and for thoroughgoing decentralization, expansion of the mass media, and a strong and truly independent judiciary. On the economy, he enumerated specific industries and agricultural products that he would boost to international levels of quality and competitiveness, to be achieved by reducing the role of the state in the economy and by promoting private property. This sounded like a major change, but some commentators saw continuity; e.g., ICG (2016) reported that Mirziyoyev's presidential election campaign in many respects resembled Karimov's 2015 program, stressing no foreign alliances, less state involvement in the economy, and more support for businesses and farmers.

In February 2017, Uzbekistan adopted a *2017–2021 National Development Strategy,* which was a more thoroughly articulated reform manifesto. The *Strategy* identified five priority areas: reform of public administration; reform of the judiciary and strengthening the rule of law; parliamentary reform; combating corruption; and strengthening human rights. These all address areas in

---

34. The first direct flight from Kabul to Tashkent, on November 29, 2017, took 1.5 hours; previously passengers from Kabul had to travel to Tashkent via Istanbul or Dubai, taking 17–32 hours. The twice-weekly schedule is designed to connect with flights to Germany, the UK, and other countries, as well as with flights to Samarkand, Bukhara, and Urgench.

which Uzbekistan had slipped down the global rankings. The establishment of the office of ombudsman to protect the interests of domestic and foreign businesses, and the creation of partnerships with the multilateral development banks, may foreshadow significant improvements in governance that should positively affect economic development. At the same time, early moves against corruption and poor administration focused on the demotion or removal of figures who were widely unpopular and perceived as being corrupt, notably Gulnara Karimova, or potential rivals for power such as minister of finance and deputy prime minister for macroeconomic development and foreign investment Rustam Azimov.[35]

President Mirziyoyev extended the existing ban on child labor in cotton picking to include education and health workers, and in September 2017, even as the cotton harvest was underway, he ordered all forced labor to be sent home (Lillis, 2017). The plan is to increase wages to the point that voluntary labor will suffice for cotton picking, and gradually to increase the role of cotton-picking machines.[36] While it is unclear whether machine-harvesting will prove to be economically practical, the timing is favorable for reform, as cotton has already lost the dominant role in the economy that it had enjoyed in the 1990s (table 5.2).

The reduced importance of cotton gives President Mirziyoyev more room for maneuver on water issues. Despite Uzbekistan's joint statement with Kazakhstan on upstream hydroelectric projects, Tajikistan's massive Rogun Dam is progressing and the Kyrgyz Republic has plans for more hydroelectric projects. In June 2017, President Mirziyoyev issued a decree that called for eighteen new hydropower projects and the modernization of fourteen existing hydroelectric plants at a cost of $2.65 billion over the period 2017–25, indicating that Uzbekistan itself intends to use the waters of Central Asian rivers for hydroelectricity as well as for irrigation. In a July interview, Foreign Minister Abdulaziz Komilov signaled the end of Uzbekistan's adamant opposition to Tajikistan's Rogun Dam project, stating that "the position of principle remains that during the construction of such dams, the interests of both upstream and downstream countries should be considered. We do not say that our Tajik

35. Azimov was seen by outsiders as the major reformer in President Karimov's governments and a potential presidential successor. After announcement of his resignation/dismissal in early June, there were no reports of what Azimov was doing. Uncertainty about Gulnara Karimova's situation also reflected ongoing limited transparency in Uzbekistan. Gulnara's sister Lola posted on her website in August 2017 that she would shortly be giving up her position as ambassador to UNESCO in Paris, but there was no official statement and she continued to be listed on the UNESCO website as Uzbekistan's representative.

36. Planning for increased mechanization had begun under President Karimov. A World Bank team, working with the Ministry of Labor, visited Tashkent in June 2015 and April 2016 and the final report was released in May 2016 (Swinkels et al., 2016).

friends should stop the construction of the Rogun Dam. Go ahead and build it, but we hold to certain guarantees in accordance with these conventions that have been signed by you."[37]

By far the most significant measure of economic reform came on September 5, 2017, when the Central Bank of Uzbekistan reunified Uzbekistan's exchange rates, and President Mirziyoyev promised freely floating market-determined rates for the future. The sum immediately dropped from the official USD rate of 4,210 to 8,100, and the black market disappeared. If rigorously implemented over the long term, a unified market-determined exchange rate will remove the single largest obstacle to the efficient operation of a market-based economy in Uzbekistan.

Simultaneously, restrictions on currency convertibility were lifted for legal entities and individuals. Legal entities can purchase foreign currency in banks without restrictions for payment on current international transactions, i.e. the import of goods, workers and services, repatriation of profits, repayment of loans, travel expenses, and other nontrade transfers. Individual entrepreneurs and farmers are allowed to withdraw foreign currency from their bank accounts. Individuals can buy foreign currency on plastic payment cards, which can be used abroad without restrictions. In December, banks launched a service to transfer money abroad, e.g., for relatives who are studying or being treated abroad; citizens have to go to banks with the national currency, which will be automatically converted into foreign currency and sent abroad.

The currency reform was followed by increased activity in foreign financial markets. During the visit of an Uzbekistan governmental delegation led by Prime Minister Abdullah Aripov to Germany on November 14–17, 2017, Uzbekistan's National Bank for Foreign Economic Activity reached loan agreements worth €950 million with German banks.[38] Earlier, the National Bank

37. The foreign minister was referring to two UN conventions that set out mechanisms for resolving contentious issues and provide guidelines for compensation in the event of harm being caused. "It is in this way that disputes between the US and Canada and between the US and Mexico were resolved. Even in the Middle East disputes are resolved this way," he said. While he mainly spoke in Uzbek throughout the televised event, Komilov made a point of addressing the Rogun issue in Russian, so that he might be more easily understood by foreign listeners, particularly those in Tajikistan. See "Uzbekistan Breaks Silence on Tajik Giant Dam Project," *Eurasianet,* July 8, 2017 (http://www.eurasianet.org/node/84281).

38. The €500 million agreement with Deutsche Bank aimed at supporting large-scale investment projects in Uzbekistan and other agreements were with Commerzbank (€350 million) and with AKA Bank (€100 million). Announcements of new German foreign investment projects in Uzbekistan such as VW-MAN investing in 2018–19 in facilities to produce Amarok pick-up trucks and intercity MAN-Lion coaches may reflect a more optimistic view of Uzbekistan's economic prospects. However, this project builds on an existing joint venture that produces MAN trucks in Samarkand and may have happened without the change in president. Peugeot is also constructing facilities to begin production of cars and minibuses after December 2018.

of Uzbekistan signed agreements with the EBRD for a $100 million line of credit line for small business projects,[39] with Russia's Gazprombank to finance investment projects worth $153 million, and with Turkey's Türk Eximbank for export credit worth $44 million.

One effect of the currency reform was to squeeze importers like the monopoly importer of oil and gasoline, Uzbeknefteprodukt, which before the reform bought foreign currency at a preferential foreign exchange rate and after the reform had to import fuel at the market rate. Motorists began to anticipate price increases by keeping their fuel tanks full, and when fuel was unavailable at service stations they bought it from hawkers selling gasoline in plastic bottles. The state-run television station, Uzbekistan-24, suggested that allowing gas stations to charge more might cause speculative middlemen to disappear[40] On November 15, motorists arrived at filling stations to find AI-80 gasoline was selling for 3,800 sum ($0.40) per liter, more than one-third higher than the previous rate of 2,800 sum, and higher-grade AI-91 for 4,300 sum per liter, an increase from 3,000 sum.

The government was not a passive bystander. On November 16, President Mirziyoyev ordered the Finance Ministry to extend an interest-free $250 million loan to two oil refineries to fund an increase in the import of crude oil. He also decreed that the import duties on crude hydrocarbons would be waived until January 1, 2020, and that excise taxes on the sale of gas would be cut by half. Earlier in November the government had been active in securing contracts for oil deliveries from Kazakhstan and Russia, to be transported initially by rail to the Shagyr oil loading point and in the longer term via a Shymkent-Jizzak oil pipeline to be built by 2021.[41]

39. In October 2017, the EBRD approved a $10 million loan to private fruit juice company Agromir, and the next day in a letter to President Mirziyoyev, EBRD president Suma Chakrabati described this as "an important milestone in the 'new beginning' in relations between Uzbekistan and the EBRD"; reported in *The Tashkent Times*, October 24, 2017. In November 2017, two EBRD vice presidents opened an EBRD office during their visit to Tashkent. A November IMF mission said that the liberalization of the foreign exchange market in early September was a significant first step that was welcomed by all stakeholders (IMF, "Statement at the Conclusion of an IMF Staff Mission to Uzbekistan," Press Release No.17/444, November 16, 2017). Such positive engagement with the IMF and EBRD was in stark contrast to President Karimov's frosty relations with international financial institutions.

40. According to Uzbekistan-24, the cheapest grade AI-80 was selling on the street for 4,000–5,500 sum, compared to 2,800 sum at the service station. See "Currency Reform in Uzbekistan: Pain Precedes Gain," *Eurasianet,* November 16, 2017 (http://www.eurasianet.org/node/86061).

41. Negotiations in November 2017 also included a contract with Saint Petersburg based Silovye Mashiny (aka Power Machines, one of the world's biggest power engineering companies) to upgrade over the period 2018–20 six power units at the Syrdarya Thermal Power Plant, the largest in Central Asia. As in other areas, there is difficulty in distinguishing between policy innovation and continuity. Silovye Mashiny modernized two of the Syrdarya TPP's power units in

The gasoline crisis and other energy-related policies suggested that the government was taking a cautious approach to reform in a key sector.[42] The government is actively involved in market regulation in the short term and in investment promotion for the long term, but appears set on a medium-term objective of moving towards market-determined prices for gasoline consumers. Reforming a regulated and underpriced gasoline market is politically challenging; drivers everywhere are aware of and respond to increases in the price at the pump. The initial steps have not created free pricing and competition in fuel, because the centralized management and pricing system remains in place. This example highlights the multifaceted needs (e.g., enterprise reform and institutional change as well as price liberalization) if market mechanisms are to function well. In general, economic reform rarely yields immediate benefits, and requires some degree of patience.

On December 22, 2017, President Mirziyoyev addressed the national parliament on the main outcomes of the past year and the priority areas for socioeconomic development in 2018. The setting was symbolic; it was the first time an Uzbekistan president had given such an address before parliament. The first half of the address focused on improving the functioning of the state and establishment of the rule of law to strengthen the rights and freedoms of citizens. The president then stressed that the governance and legal reforms, as well as promised social improvements, required a sustainable economy. The willingness to recognize weaknesses in the economy suggested that the president is aiming for economic change rather than continuity. He reminded the listeners of the major reform achievements in 2017 with respect to the foreign exchange regime and improving regional economic relations, and highlighted the need to reduce regulation and to facilitate trade, e.g., by introducing green channels at the border in 2018 and emphasizing risk assessment rather than control.

There were echoes of past practice in his address. Recognizing the need for innovation, he announced the creation of the Ministry for Innovative Development in 2018, which would be declared "The Year of Support of Active Business, Innovative Ideas, and Technologies." Recurring themes from 2017 of supporting small business and entrepreneurship and promoting the rural

---

2013–15 and completed modernization of the Charvak Hydro Power Plant in the Tashkent region in 2016.

42. Energy-related project news included a $2.2 billion oil refinery announced in May 2017, and a $4 billion Uzbek-Korean joint venture to build the Ustyurt Gas Chemical Complex, with capacity to produce 3.5 bcm of natural gas and five hundred thousand tons of polyethylene and polypropylene a year. Companies like Hyundai and Denmark's Haldor Topsoe were working with state-owned enterprises on projects to develop fossil fuel derivatives like gas-to-liquid methanol-to-olefins and methanol-to-gasoline. In March 2017, General Electric announced investments of $388 million over two years in industrial equipment and home appliances.

sector were prominent, but with little analysis of how the goals would be achieved, beyond establishment of high-tech poultry farms, specialized livestock complexes, and greenhouses. With respect to the manufacturing and mining sectors, the president listed output and investment achievement and plans. The slogans and quantitative results and targets for specific products were redolent of the planning past rather than a market-oriented future.

Nevertheless, the balance sheet for economic modernization in 2017 was clearly positive. President Mirzyoyev had the right priorities and made impressive steps in addressing the two biggest weaknesses of the economy that he inherited. His year-end address promised further measures to improve regional connectivity and enhance Uzbekistan's integration into the global economy through improved hard and soft infrastructure. He committed to restart in 2018 negotiations for WTO membership. The social measures—increased housebuilding, improved health, and education services—promised for 2018 are desirable and important for long-term economic health. Entrepreneurship, rural development, and the rule of law are all central to creating a well-functioning sustainable market-based economy, and it is appropriate that President Mirziyoyev focuses on these areas, although these are areas in which change is inevitably drawn out with few opportunities for instant results.[43]

Long-term prospects will depend on the extent to which President Mirziyoyev delivers on his election call for a transition from "a strong state to a robust civil society," and implements the priority areas identified in the *2017–2021 National Development Strategy* and restated in his year-end address. Legal and judicial reforms inevitably take time.[44] Despite the government's attempts to promote more active citizen involvement, there continues to be little evidence of an independent civil society. Signs of increased flexibility in the political arena in 2017 have to be tempered by the limited response, with no indication that parliament might serve as a check on executive power. Although the state media showed willingness to report on more controversial issues in 2017, there was no sign of an independent media sector within Uzbekistan.

Following the smooth succession after President Karimov's death, there was uncertainty about Uzbekistan's future course. Many outside observers,

---

43. Establishment of a Ministry of Pre-School Education and commitment to build "thousands of new kindergartens over the next 3–4 years" are especially laudable. School started at seven in the Soviet era, preceded by preschool provided by the parents' enterprise, but after the collapse of central planning enterprises quickly cut back on this activity. However, positive economic impact of improved preschool access will not be seen until the 2030s.

44. However, the president's condemnation of torture and other forms of intimidation of citizens may, like the ending of forced labor for cotton harvesting, have a positive impact on the country's external image with economic implications for foreign investment or for boycotts of goods made with Uzbek cotton.

burned by enthusiasm for a new start in Turkmenistan after President Ni-yazov's death a decade earlier, were cautious in predicting major reforms. Others saw a basis for optimism in Mirziyoyev's tenure as prime minister, even though in that position his freedom of action had been limited. The Karimov era was not without evolution: there were reforms especially under Mirzi-yoyev's prime ministership after 2003, in both economic and political areas. In Karimov's final years, positive moves included measures on rural development and housing, and some loosening of restrictions on bazaars and small enterprises. However, the government always held back from making the currency convertible and from opening up trade and transit, and in the Karimov era efforts at political or social reform were overshadowed by political repression (highlighted by the 2005 Andijan incident), unwillingness to abjure the use of torture (as at the 2003 EBRD meetings), and foot-dragging on abandoning child labor. The negative international image discouraged foreign investment and other collaboration with high-income countries, but the government gave the impression of not being too concerned by missed opportunities.

In 2017, President Mirziyoyev introduced major economic change by energetically reversing two fundamental traits of Uzbekistan's economy since independence. First, he undertook a full travel and meeting schedule to restore the country's international links and, in particular, to repair Uzbekistan's fractured relations with Central Asian neighbors. Figurative bridge-building was accompanied by concrete steps to rebuild connectivity by bridges to Turkmenistan, flights to Tajikistan, high-speed trains to Kazakhstan, and a rail link to China via the Kyrgyz Republic. Second, he removed the millstone around Uzbekistan's economy by unifying the exchange rate and liberalizing access to foreign exchange. These steps appear to have been harbingers of a shift from economic control to greater confidence in market mechanisms, although it is too early to be certain.[45]

In his end-of-year address, President Mirziyoyev signaled that the direction taken in 2017 was the correct one and promised further reforms along the path set out in the *2017–2021 National Development Strategy*. In the economic sphere, these include specific commitments on WTO accession and on trade facilitation that will reinforce the two main changes in 2017. The payoff from the enacted and promised reforms could be large, especially if Uzbekistan reestablishes its central position on routes between East Asia and the Middle East and Europe, and can diversify the economy by trading along those routes.

---

45. The opposite signal was sent by President Mirziyoyev at a November 20, 2017, meeting about ensuring food supplies over the winter, where he announced a state order system for the purchase of fresh fruit and vegetables, potatoes, melons, and grapes for 2018, and ordered officials to ensure that sufficient storage facilities would be available. (Reported on the official website at https://ouzbekistan.fr/en/information-digest-of-press-of-uzbekistan-november-22-2017-2/.)

6

Turkmenistan

Turkmenistan is the least populous and most closed of the Central Asian countries. Among all the former centrally planned economies, Turkmenistan has regularly ranked last by transition indicators measuring speed of reform or degree of economic liberalization. Although it is often linked with Uzbekistan as the least reformed and most repressive of the former Soviet republics, there are important differences of degree and intent. Whereas Uzbekistan could reasonably be described as a gradual reformer, with strong state control over the economy, Turkmenistan sought to conserve the economy as it was, but with the rents from cotton and gas going to the president rather than to the Soviet state. By this criterion, the transition (from Communism to Nationalism) was smooth and rapid.

Nationhood was embodied in the leader Saparmurat Niyazov, who, after the metamorphosis from first secretary of the Turkmen Soviet Republic to president of Turkmenistan, assumed the name "Turkmenbashi"—leader of the Turkmen. President Niyazov relied on revenue from exports of cotton and natural gas to sustain an inefficient economic system, and to maintain popular support by initially generous social services and by an extensive security service. In the middle of the otherwise drab, dry, and dusty capital city, he built a sumptuous marble-clad palace surrounded by gardens and fountains, as well as erecting numerous statues and other monuments and having, inter alia, a city, the main airport, yogurts, vodka, and a French perfume named after himself. International coverage of the reclusive country focused on the grotesque personality cult, and information about the economic, political, and social system was limited.

In the years after independence, Turkmenistan could sell its cotton on world markets, and like Uzbekistan benefited from buoyant world cotton prices until 1996. Exacerbated by falling output, cotton export revenues declined sharply; like Uzbekistan but with a delay, Turkmenistan imposed draconian forex controls in 1998. Extracting rents from gas exports was harder because the pipelines all led north to Russia, and the ultimate customers in Ukraine and Azerbaijan were delinquent in paying. In 1997 Turkmenistan cut off gas supplies and the payment issue was only resolved, and the gas started to flow again, in 1999. Resumption of gas exports coincided with the start of the commodity boom. Over the next decade, Turkmenistan benefited from increasing revenues, although with limited gas pipeline options the price received by Turkmenistan failed to keep up with world oil prices or with the price at which Russia was supplying gas to the EU.

Apart from the cotton and gas exports, Turkmenistan remained the most closed and least reformed of the Central Asian countries during the 1990s and early 2000s. President Niyazov rarely traveled until 2006, when he went to Beijing. The trip was important because it led to the signing of a contract for China to build a gas pipeline from Turkmenistan to China. The pipeline, completed in 2009, broke Russia's monopsony position, and China quickly became Turkmenistan's primary export market. The year 2006 was also important because President Niyazov died in December, leading to the first peaceful presidential succession in Central Asia. The smooth transfer of power to the health minister, Gurbanguly Berdimuhamedov, was followed by expectations of reform, but initial changes were cosmetic rather than substantive.

A decade later, economic fundamentals had changed little. Although President Berdimuhamedov set aside the most egregious personality cult and other damaging polices of Turkmenbashi, "With little incentive for systemic change, in virtually all areas targeted for reform by Berdimuhamedow—from governing institutions and education to healthcare and culture—the government prioritizes appearance over substance" (Bohr, 2016, 90). In foreign affairs, President Berdimuhamedov retained his predecessor's emphasis on neutrality, but emphasized positive neutrality and greater engagement with neighbors. The size of the country's natural gas reserves, especially after confirmation by an international audit in 2008, continued to attract attention, but the country's antipathy towards investment by the energy majors stymied their involvement and effectively left Turkmenistan dependent on a single customer, although after 2009 the customer switched from Russia to China.

After the 2014–16 collapse in energy prices, Turkmenistan was left in a vulnerable position, facing lower global energy prices, to which the government responded by reducing subsidies on basic goods and strengthening exchange controls. Long-term prospects were overshadowed by the rise of liquefied natural gas as a more flexible option to pipeline delivery of gas, heralding an era in which landlocked gas producers are unlikely to be able to compete with the offshore gas fields being exploited by Brazil, Australia, and others (Denison, 2012). The pressure to diversify the economy, and a concomitant greater opening, were reflected in cautious reinvolvement in international organizations and in projects such as the Kazakhstan-Turkmenistan-Iran railway that was completed in December 2014.

6.1. The Turkmenistan Economic Model

At independence, Turkmenistan's economy was dominated by two products: cotton and natural gas. The Karakum Canal, begun in 1954, allowed an increase in the total sown area from 368,000 hectares in 1950 to over 1.3 million hectares in 1990, when over half of the arable land was devoted to cotton. The natural gas sector was developed in the late Soviet era, and in 1985 the Turkmen republic produced 75 bcm, an amount exceeded only by the USA, Canada, and the Russian republic. The pre-independence industrial sector was very small, apart from two oil refineries and the cotton gins. Given the dependence on cotton and gas, both of which were underpriced by Soviet planners in 1990, Tarr (1994) estimated that Turkmenistan would be a big gainer from the move to world prices (table 2.1). However, all the cotton and gas was delivered within the Soviet Union, and the extent to which Turkmenistan could realize a shift to world prices varied.

Turkmenistan moved cautiously through the early stages of nation-building and replacing the planned economy. Russia's January 1992 price liberalization was followed by necessity, while retaining many price controls. In November 1993, the national currency, the manat, was introduced apparently as a planned step towards economic independence rather than as a first step in establishing monetary control; annual inflation remained around 1,000% in 1995–96, when it was falling in other transition economies. Small-scale privatization (mostly in consumer services and retail trade) was completed in 1994–96, but larger-scale privatization was put on hold. Housing was not privatized. The 1997 decree on land privatization divided state and collective farms into individual plots, leased out to farmers who could obtain ownership rights subject to satisfactory output performance (Lerman and Brooks, 2001). In practice, farmers remained subject to severe restrictions; to obtain a lease they had to contract to fulfill specified state orders, and government control over essential inputs, notably water and fertilizer, locked farmers into such arrangements. For a brief period in 1996–99 the Central Bank was permitted some independence, and it succeeded in bringing inflation down to 17%; however, the inflation rate mattered little, because outside the petty trading of the bazaar relative prices did not determine resource allocation. After 1999, the president reestablished control over the Central Bank, which henceforth passively monetized budget deficits. Public finances were nontransparent, with a large proportion not recorded in the state budget but passing into funds directly controlled by the president.[1]

In essentials, the post-independence economic system changed little from the Soviet-era dependence on cotton and gas, even though the mechanisms of central planning disappeared. The government controlled the resource rents, which were used for populist measures to garner public support, for import substitution measures aimed at promoting national self-sufficiency, and for prestige and security to maintain the position of the president. Some of the revenues were used to maintain the universal benefits from the Soviet era such as pensions at age fifty-seven for women and sixty-two for men, and to supplement them with free provision of gas, electricity, heating, water, and salt for residential use and with extensive housing and other subsidies. During the early 1990s this may have gained some popular support for, or at least acquiescence to, the regime.

Turkmenistan embarked on an economic program of import-substituting industrialization. The familiar symptoms of misallocated resources, artificial exchange rate, and financial repression were evident, although lack of publicly available data impedes precise analysis. In a drive towards self-sufficiency in food, the area under wheat increased from two hundred thousand hectares in 1990 to eight hundred thousand hectares in the early 2000s, some of which was newly cultivated land but mostly wheat was grown at the expense of fodder, vegetables, or cotton (Peyrouse, 2009, 5). In consequence, and also due to poor irrigation maintenance, increased salinization, and promotion of cotton textiles factories, cotton exports fell.[2] The reversal of the relative size of cotton and wheat output is clear from official production figures (table 6.1).

In the early 1990s Turkmenistan, like Uzbekistan, benefitted from buoyant world cotton prices, and through state control of cotton marketing the government extracted a large share of the rents. The two main crops, cotton and wheat, remained subject to state orders at prices well below world prices. Export earnings were subject to surrender requirements and foreign exchange controls were universal and restrictive after December 1998, when the official exchange rate started to become increasingly artificial. Key inputs such as

---

1. According to Global Witness (2006) and Cooley and Sharman (2015), President Niyazov had amassed over $3 billion in a Deutsche Bank account before it was frozen on his death. This was the largest fortune of any Central Asian presidential family member or other elite figure.

2. The profligate use of irrigation water inherited from the Soviet era continued and contributed to increased salinization, leading to substantial declines in agricultural yields and rural incomes (O'Hara and Hannan, 1999). With declining monitoring and shortening time horizons, the situation was exacerbated by opportunistic behavior such as piercing to withdraw water illegally from irrigation channels.

TABLE 6.1. Cotton, Wheat, and Rice Production, Turkmenistan, 1992 to 2014 (Thousand Tons)

	Cotton	Wheat	Rice
1992	390	377	64
1993	402	509	88
1994	385	675	92
1995	379	695	79
1996	131	453	41
1997	190	707	27
1998	158	1,245	14
1999	234	1,506	33
2000	233	1,60	27
2001	360	1,760	39
2002	230	2,326	80
2003	235	2,487	110
2004	330	2,600	110
2005	330	2,834	120
2006	230	3,260	135
2007	313	2,700	111
2008	330	2,200	110
2009	220	1,700	110
2010	225	1,200	113
2011	195	1,300	127
2012	198	1,200	129
2013	198	1,600	132
2014	195	1,200	130

Source: FAO at http://faostat.fao.org/faostat/ (accessed November 1, 2017).
Note: The cotton data have been subject to large revisions, and are inconsistent with other sources; the wheat figures between 2000 and 2006 are also inflated (see text).

water and fertilizer were subsidized, but because access to them was tied to fulfillment of state orders, farmers were constrained in their choice of output to the mandated wheat or cotton mix.

During the second half of the 1990s, Turkmenistan pursued a statist development strategy in which growth was led by construction of infrastructure and monuments and by import-substituting industrialization. Starting in 1995 the government financed development of a modern textile industry processing domestic cotton and silk, which became the centerpiece of import-substituting industrialization. The process was directed and implemented by the government, with the private sector playing a passive role, largely restricted to contract work by foreign firms. The financial sector remained heavily repressed, doing little more than allocating government-directed credits.

A high investment to GDP ratio was maintained: 45% in 1996, and 49–51% over the remainder of the decade. The investment was directed to three types of projects: unproductive, infrastructure, and industrial.

The most striking construction works were in the national capital, with its grand statues and new public buildings. These were financed off-budget through funds whose details are not publicly available. Some projects were intended to be productive, such as the row of theme hotels south of the capital constructed in the mid-1990s for a flood of business people and tourists who never came. Others, such as the huge statues of the president and of his mother, had no value beyond feeding the personality cult.

The government tried to diversify external transport links and improve the domestic network. A rail link to Iran in May 1996 and a small gas pipeline to Iran in 1997 were completed—the first railway or pipeline south from former Soviet Central Asia. In the late 1990s the government embarked on an ambitious road-building program, connecting all the nation's major towns by divided highways and, in the case of the north-south highway from Dashoguz to Ashgabat, accompanied by a parallel rail link. Another rail project connected Kerkishi directly to Turkmenistan's rail network rather than via Uzbekistan. The Caspian Sea port of Krasnavodsk was renamed Turkmenbashi and upgraded, and a new national airport opened in Ashgabat. These projects yielded potential social benefits, but the railway and gas pipeline to Iran, the Ashgabat airport, and the new roads all operated far below capacity.

The industrial investments focused on a $1.5 billion upgrade of the Turkmenbashi oil refinery and associated development of petrochemicals, and the creation of a cotton textile industry. Petrochemicals and capital-intensive textiles did not fit well with the comparative advantage of a country in which average rural incomes in 1998 were around $200 per year or less. Between 1995 and 2000 the share of cotton processed domestically rose from 3% to 35%. The mills were typically joint ventures with Turkish partners, with the state purchasing most of the equipment and providing cotton at below world prices; yet, despite generous treatment of depreciation, the mills were not making high profits. The government's response to these problems was to use export credits from Japan and an EBRD loan to fund what was claimed to be the world's largest textile complex, the Turkmenbashi Jeans Factory, which was equipped with state-of-the-art equipment. Although their accounts are not in the public domain, it is likely that many of the textile factories had negative value-added.[3]

3. Pomfret (2001a) estimated that the Turkmenbashi Jeans Factory probably had negative value-added, i.e. the value of the output (measured by the cost of importing equivalent amounts of jeans) was less than the value of the cotton used as inputs (measured by its value if exported). As well as displacing imports, the textile industry was supposed to generate exports, but in 1999 these amounted to only $21 million, mostly to Turkey, Russia, and Iran.

Regardless of the social desirability of individual projects, the degree of centralization and lack of tendering suggest that resources were extravagantly used. Much construction was based on simple cash contracts negotiated with a single firm, and some projects were financed by directly assigning part of the cotton crop to a foreign contractor. Some large contractors undertook social projects without payment, in return for being granted a large construction deal or other privilege.[4] In a nontransparent society much of the evidence is hearsay, but the projects were real and the payments were large. Beyond these three areas, the capital-intensive oil and gas sector dominated, while the share of investment going to the agricultural sector, where half the population works, declined from 15% in 1994 to 2% in 1999 (Pomfret, 2006, 97).

The effectiveness of policies to promote wheat production in Turkmenistan is apparent in official statistics: output of wheat and to a lesser extent rice increased while cotton output was volatile around a declining trend (table 6.1). In Turkmenistan, however, for wheat as for cotton, there is doubt about true output levels. With domestic demand for wheat around two million tons (1.7 million for flour and 0.3 million for seed), according to the official output levels the country should have been exporting wheat by the middle of the first decade of the twenty-first century. By October 2006, it became clear that official figures of a three-million-ton harvest were false by a large margin, and the president fired two of the country's five regional governors. In a TV broadcast President Niyazov stated that "in 2007 there won't be enough bread for everyone" and that "wheat-sowing amounted to less than 50%" of the target in each of the five provinces, before claiming that he had had difficulty sleeping since he heard the news; in November, the new governors were given two days to achieve the winter sowing targets, despite subzero temperatures in those days. Whatever the true harvests, output seems certain to have been below two million tons despite the president's threats and exhortations. Moreover, relying on command with no input from agronomists contributed to poor land use, e.g., crop rotation would have replenished soils, and to declining seed stock quality.[5] The drive for self-sufficiency in food grains led not only to less fodder but also to poorer quality of wheat available for human food.[6]

---

4. Werner (2001, 128) describes the $40 million heart clinic and $27 million kidney clinic built by Siemens primarily for the president's own use. Siemens had earlier arranged the president's heart bypass operation in Munich in 1997. The French firm Bouygues aired a complimentary TV program on their TV network TF1, in return for construction projects (Garcia, 2006).

5. President Niyazov's frequent purges included farm managers as well as local and provincial officials, and the lost expertise was not replaced by newly trained experts. As with the destruction of the tertiary education system and nonrecognition of foreign qualifications, the president placed loyalty above competence throughout his country.

6. Consumers prefer the hard wheat grown in Kazakhstan. The government was unwilling to authorize use of foreign exchange for imports of wheat or flour, and, as the quality of domestically

After cotton prices dropped in late 1996 and Turkmenistan began to restrict gas supplies to delinquent customers, the sustainability of the economic model was in doubt. Revenue constraints led to cutbacks in social benefits, e.g., through limited supply of electricity. Perhaps more importantly as a catalyst for discontent, the president's megalomaniacal construction projects in the center of Ashgabat involved the bulldozing, with little notice or compensation, of people's houses. The security services arrested thousands of suspected dissidents, so that an increasing number of people had been, or had known somebody who had been, badly treated by the authorities. The threat of arrest, torture, imprisonment, or forced labor in the uranium mines ensured that open dissent was extremely rare within the country. The boom in world energy prices after 2000 dissipated concerns about the sustainability of the system.

The political system established by Turkmenbashi was characterized by a strong presidency, with centralized decision making and supported by a pervasive personality cult and security services. The president, who was also prime minister and chaired the only political party, controlled selection to the "Khalk Maslakhty" (People's Council), which had sole power to alter the constitution and which in December 1999 unanimously extended the president's term of office without limit. The legislature ("Majlis") and judiciary, as well as specialized bodies, including the Central Bank, were subordinate to the president's authority, and major decisions at all levels of government had to be cleared by the president's office. Like the economic system, the political system changed little from the Soviet model, apart from changes in institutions' names:

> In order to consolidate his control over the government, as well as all aspects of society and the economy, Niyazov manipulated the structural remains of the disintegrating Soviet system to create a political machine based on coercion, fear and patronage (Gleason, 2011, 81).

The political system became even more repressive after an apparent assassination attempt on the president in November 2002. Strict censorship made it difficult to gauge popular sentiment.

6.2. External Relations

President Niyzazov had a positive attitude towards the United Nations, as an institution that imposes no constraints on domestic policy-making and which he viewed as the guarantor of the country's neutrality. The UN General As-

---

produced flour deteriorated, the price of imported flour in Turkmenistan's bazaars—if available—skyrocketed.

sembly formally recognized Turkmenistan's neutrality in Resolution 50/80 of December 12, 1995 (Anceschi, 2008). In 1999, the Arch of Neutrality was erected in Ashgabat as a national symbol; a thirteen-meter-high gold statue of Turkmenbashi, which rotated so that the ruler always faced the sun, topped the Arch.

The president's attitude towards other international institutions was more cautious. Turkmenistan joined the IMF and World Bank in 1992, but beyond provision of some technical assistance the actual operations of these institutions were minimal. The IMF provided technical advice, but Turkmenistan was the only post-Soviet state not to have borrowed from the IMF during the 1990s (Boughton, 2012, 387); lack of cooperation led the IMF to withdraw its resident representative in 1999. World Bank loans approved between 1994 and 1997 were frozen between 1997 and 1999 due to misprocurement. Turkmenistan joined the Islamic Development Bank and the EBRD in 1994 and the ADB in 2000, but the operations of the development banks in Turkmenistan were limited.

Turkmenbashi was suspicious of any foreign commitments that might interfere with his power. From the start, Turkmenistan viewed the CIS as a consultative grouping and nothing more; Turkmenistan refused to supply statistical data to CIS agencies, and in 1999 the country withdrew from the CIS visa-free zone. President Niyazov carefully avoided siding with the Eurasian Union or the GUUAM group, which each contained five of the twelve non-Baltic Soviet successor states. Turkmenistan remained outside all projected regional trade arrangements within the former USSR, and the only regional trade grouping that it joined was the Economic Cooperation Organization, which has been economically ineffectual, although relations with Iran, Turkey, and Pakistan provided a counterweight to Russia's still-powerful influence (see chapter 9). Turkmenistan is the only Soviet successor state, and one of the few countries in the world, not to have initiated negotiations to join the WTO.

6.3. Economic Performance, 1991–2006

Tracking Turkmenistan's output performance is complicated by poor data, but the general pattern is clear. Real GDP fell substantially during the first half of the 1990s and in 1996 stood at less than 60% of its 1991 level, before experiencing another big drop in 1997.[7] The big decline in 1997 reflected falling cot-

---

7. Mercer-Blackman and Unigovskaya (2000, 4) report IMF staff estimates. Several international agencies stopped publishing GDP estimates in the mid-1990s. The EBRD in *Transition Report 1999* (277) reported a 26% decline in Turkmenistan's real GDP in 1997, but six months later in the May 2000 *Transition Update* (83) the decline was revised to 11.3% (as in table 2.3).

ton prices, a poor cotton harvest, and the cessation of gas exports in March 1997: cotton export earnings were down to $84 million from $791 million in 1995 and $332 million in 1996, and gas export earnings were $70 million, compared to around $1 billion in the two previous years. This was the backdrop to the tightening of forex controls in 1998.

Problems with gas exports arose from the inherited pipeline network, which only led to Soviet markets. After independence, the Russian pipeline monopolist Gazprom refused to export Turkmenistan's gas to Western European markets, and Turkmenistan remained dependent on CIS markets. Several countries fell behind in payments, but Turkmenistan's export data recorded the contract value of gas exports, whether paid for or not, while arrears entered into the national accounts as increased foreign assets. In March 1997 Turkmenistan cut off gas supplies to its main debtor, Ukraine. After negotiations with Russia and gas importers over debt rescheduling and future payment arrangements, large-scale gas exports were resumed in January 1999 (Sagers, 1999).

The first decade after the dissolution of the USSR saw Turkmenistan sustain its political and economic independence, and the president consolidate his personal position. Economic independence was incomplete; the country still depended on the Russian-controlled pipeline system for much of its gas exports, and cotton exports were subject to volatile world prices. Self-sufficiency in grain and textiles involved substantial resource costs. Increases in the acreage under grain, combined with loss of land to salinization as a result of poor irrigation practices, reduced the area under cotton in the early 2000s to less than half what it had been in 1990. The agricultural sector absorbed most of the increase in the rapidly growing labor force, and by the late 1990s employed about half of the economically active population. Low state prices for the major crops provided little incentive for farmers, who were discouraged from shifting their output mix beyond cotton or wheat or from experimenting with new methods to increase yields. The limited information on rural living standards, and casual observation, suggest that by the turn of the century rural households were significantly poorer than urban households and that public services, such as water supply, had been declining more in rural areas.

As in other Soviet successor states, real per capita GDP was lower at the end of the 1990s than at the beginning. In the comparative estimates of poverty rates by Milanovic (1998), Turkmenistan experienced a substantial increase in poverty after the dissolution of the USSR, but was not an extreme. The World Bank's poverty assessment, based on the 1998 Living Standards Measurement Study (LSMS) survey, was more cautious, concluding that poverty was not as serious in Turkmenistan as elsewhere in Central Asia, but a large segment of the population was living not much above the poverty line.[8] The free provision of gas, water, electricity, and salt to households, plus public housing at low cost and other subsidized basic goods and services undoubtedly protected poorer members of society. Such untargeted social assistance is, however, costly and may be regressive; richer households have more electric appliances and are most likely to have indoor toilets, benefiting more than poor households from free electricity and water. Disruption of electricity supply appears to have been frequent, especially in rural areas. The lack of basic individual and social rights was universal.

Officially Turkmenistan allocated 10% of GDP to health and education. Official statistics are positive but unreliable. External sources report anecdotal evidence, which can diverge widely, but is generally negative, e.g., visiting epidemiologists report hepatitis A to be endemic and hepatitis B widespread, largely due to poor upkeep of water and sanitation services. In the face of unpleasant statistics (e.g., evidence of high morbidity or HIV infection), the official response was often to deny a problem or take extreme measures. Reported HIV cases in Turkmenistan before 2000 were zero.

Reports on education pointed to deteriorating facilities, lack of textbooks, and curricula heavily focused on the presidential personality cult. The government increasingly encouraged schools to focus on teaching "native traditions" and "natural spiritual values," while abandoning "subjects of minor importance" such as algebra or physics. Knowledge of Turkmenbashi's thoughts, collected in the book *Ruhnama*, was required for an increasing number of jobs, and in 2004 was introduced as part of the driving test, while standards in previously mainstream subject areas fell drastically after independence. In 2001, twelve thousand teachers were dismissed and the Academy of Sciences closed, reportedly for failure to teach or follow the president's thoughts. The number of years required to complete school was reduced from ten to nine years, and some university degrees required two years' study instead of four, with admissions, grades, and degrees reported to be for sale. Gleason (2011, 82) concluded that "Niyazov virtually eliminated public education."

As those who could afford it studied outside the country, most commonly in Moscow, the number of students in higher education fell from forty thousand in 1991 to less than ten thousand by 2004.[9] However, in the 2000s

8. The LSMS data are not in the public domain so independent assessment of the result is not possible. Comments on the survey's findings are based on reports in World Bank and IMF publications, which refer to 7% of the population living below $2.15 at purchasing power parity. The United Nations *Common Country Assessment* (UN Office in Turkmenistan, February 2004, 11) concluded that "the country does not have overall precise or updated figures on poverty."

9. These are the official enrollment statistics. Other sources reported estimated enrollment in 2004 as low as 3,500 students, e.g., "Turkmenistan wrestles with Child Labor Issue as Cotton

declining high school standards led a growing number of universities in other CIS countries to turn down students from Turkmenistan. From September to November most students above fifth grade were forced to harvest cotton. Textbooks were strictly censored, and closure of the State Library in 2000 and almost total censorship of foreign media limited access to information and ideas. The government clearly placed social control above human capital formation, fearing educational institutions as potential centers of dissent.

Environmental constraints on sustainability also increased in the 1990s. Over-irrigation of land where the natural salt level is high led to severe salinization problems, especially in the Dashoguz and Lebap regions, which are major agricultural producers. The desiccation of the Aral Sea also had dramatic consequences for Dashoguz, where according to the government's own National Environmental Action Plan of 2002, between 70 and 85% of the population did not have access to safe water.[10]

The economic crisis in spring 1997 led to acknowledgment of the need for policy reform and announcement of the *Thousand Days* economic program in April 1997. However, the lack of will to reform was reflected in the president's official view that the economic achievements of the 1990s would be a springboard for greater progress by 2010. Little happened during the thousand days, and the seriousness of the problem in 2000 was reflected in failure for the first time to meet payment deadlines on construction projects and other expenditures. In 2001, the rating agency Fitch-IBCA downgraded Turkmenistan's long-term debt from B– to CCC– and its short-term debt from B to C.

Another danger signal was the end of a surplus in the state budget in 1999 and 2000, and a deficit in 2002 equal to 2.7% of GDP, although this measure is opaque because many state transactions are through off-budget funds whose contents are secret. The World Bank stopped reporting the unreliable data on Turkmenistan's public finances (table 2.4), but according to EBRD data, the debt/GDP ratio exceeded 100% in 1999. In most years, the consolidated state budget required some financing by money creation, although due to extensive price controls inflation is repressed and inflationary pressures are inadequately reflected in the official consumer price index figures (in table 2.10). A better guide to long-term inflation is the value of the currency in foreign exchange markets, where it started at two manat to the dollar in November 1993 and by 2003 had reached 21,000 manat to the dollar on the black market.

Harvest approaches" (posted at www.eurasianet.org, September 1, 2004). The government's response to the exodus of students was to declare that after June 2004 degrees obtained abroad since July 1993 would not be recognized. This led to many newly "unqualified" teachers and academics losing their jobs in the educational system, adding to the impact of the dismissals in 2001.

10. Reported in the United Nations System in Turkmenistan, *Common Country Assessment*, February 2004, 21.

The lack of financial reform was another symptom of economic malaise. Although two-tier banking was quickly introduced after independence, the financial system remained in many respects the Soviet monobank system, with the central bank's functions not clearly separated from those of the state banks that control most of the deposits. All these entities acted as agents of the government's directed credit policies.

The currency black market and the unreformed financial system both reflected that Turkmenistan was far from a market-driven economy, with the two key prices in such an economy (exchange and interest rates) having no economic function in Turkmenistan. More fundamentally, the economy remained tightly controlled through a single person, which often led to nondecision and made real coordination difficult. Such a system was likely to have the stultifying negative consequences of the centrally planned economy without achieving the degree of organization that allowed the planned economies to survive so long. However, pressure for change was reduced by a revival of economic growth (table 2.3), in 1999 and 2000 as a rebound from the artificially low levels of 1997–98 and then driven by buoyant energy and cotton prices in 2001–4.

The recidivist influences were reflected in official suspicion of the private sector, which was only really permitted in petty retailing. Signs of entrepreneurship were evident in Ashgabat's huge outdoor Sunday market and in the shuttle trade,[11] but otherwise private activity was quickly discouraged by excessive red tape and by a widely held belief that any successful business would be heavily taxed or nationalized. Freedom of movement of individuals and travel outside the country was limited, which preempted temporary migration to work in Russia. All media outlets were censored, and access to the internet was heavily controlled. The EBRD (in *Transition Report 2003*) described the president's December 1999 program for the socioeconomic development of Turkmenistan up to 2010 as a "Soviet-style ten-year plan." With its relatively simple production structure, Turkmenistan could postpone reforms as long as energy revenues were sufficient to satisfy the president's needs and ability to maintain power, but it was unlikely that the unreformed economic system could supply the range of goods and services appropriate to the more diversified economy envisioned in the presidential program for socioeconomic development.

From 2002, reports of Turkmenbashi's bizarre behavior became more frequent. In March 2002, he began a purge of the security service, which

11. The shuttle trade, believed to be equal in value to 10–20% of official trade in 1999 and 2000, involved small traders flying, especially to Istanbul. Carpet sellers and clothing buyers traded their baggage rights on outward and return flights, and appeared to have quasi-formal arrangements with customs officials.

increased his reliance on the extra-legal and unpredictable Presidential Guard. In August 2002 he renamed the months, with January becoming Turkmenbashi. A reported assassination attempt in November 2002, which may have been a set-up, was the signal for increased repression; political rivals, journalists, and religious leaders were tortured, imprisoned, and killed. External relations atrophied; disputes with Azerbaijan and Iran over demarcation of the Caspian Sea often turned violent, and relations with Uzbekistan reached a low when Turkmenbashi accused President Karimov of complicity in the assassination attempt. Turkmenbashi eliminated dual citizenship in April 2003, forcing the ninety-five thousand ethnic Russians in Turkmenistan to renounce their Russian citizenship or leave the country. In February 2004, he announced that Turkmen men should not grow beards. The education system was destroyed by a series of measures, reflected in the June 2004 invalidation of all qualifications from outside the country; by that time teaching at all levels was in Turkmen, which excluded many qualified teachers and professors, and the main textbook was *Ruhnama* (the thoughts of Turkmenbashi). In 2004 Turkmenbashi replaced fifteen thousand healthcare workers by military conscripts and banned diagnosis of infectious diseases such as tuberculosis, cholera, or dysentery, which were usually diagnosed as simple viruses.[12] In March 2005, he announced the closure of hospitals and libraries outside the capital.

Nevertheless, Turkmenbashi's power remained absolute as he continued to rotate or fire ministers and senior security officers. Any popular discontent was dealt with by a ruthless security apparatus. There were questions of why he needed semipermanent attendance by a group of German doctors, and in mid-2005, after his attendance at sixtieth anniversary of VE Day celebrations in Moscow, reports of his frailty and poor health circulated widely, although the official media touched up photos to make him look healthier. His hair had turned from gray to black several years earlier.

In the early 2000s, Turkmenbashi became increasingly reclusive. He rarely traveled or met other leaders.[13] In April 2006, he made a rare official foreign visit, to Beijing to negotiate a pipeline to China that would reduce Turkmenistan's dependence on Russian pipelines. In December 2006 the president died, apparently of natural causes.

12. When typhoid broke out in Dashkoguz, the response of the senior local official (*hakim*) was to build a wall around the hospital containing the infected people (*Eurasia Insight*, "Reported Plague Outbreak Renews Concerns about Turkmenistan's Healthcare System," posted at www.eurasia.org on July 21, 2004).

13. Following proactive US military policy against tyrannical regimes in nearby Afghanistan and Iraq, Turkmenbashi's summits with President Putin of Russia in Ashgabat in April 2003, where major long-term agreements for gas supply and for Russian investment in Turkmenistan were announced, and with President Karimov of Uzbekistan in Bukhara in November 2004 were attempts to build bridges with leaders less concerned about human rights.

6.4. Natural Gas: Part One

Turkmenistan has gas reserves second only to Russia in the CIS, and often described as the fourth or fifth largest in the world.[14] At independence, the country inherited recently constructed Soviet facilities, and in the 1990s and early 2000s the government appeared content to maintain existing capacity and live off the rents. Dependence on gas revenues was exacerbated by the decline of cotton earnings when world cotton prices fell after 1996 and cotton output was in long-term decline. Nevertheless, with the start of the global energy boom in the late 1990s and the related settlement of nonpayment, gas rents seemed to be sufficient for the president's needs, at least until 2006.

There are substitutes for gas, and in periods of low energy prices the bargaining power is with the buyers. In the 1990s Turkmen sales to captive markets through the ex-Soviet pipeline network ran into payment arrears and were renegotiated to the supplier's disadvantage, often by incorporating barter components that reduced the true price of the gas; when large-scale gas deliveries to Azerbaijan and Ukraine resumed in 1999, the price of just under $36 per 1,000 m³ was payable 40% in cash and 60% by barter. With rising energy prices, bargaining power shifted to gas suppliers after 1999. The terms of Turkmenistan's gas deals were generally opaque, but the sharp turnaround in the country's economic growth in 1998–99 can only be explained by increased gas receipts, probably reflected in better payment records.

Construction of new pipelines was an obvious solution to Turkmenistan's problems with nonpaying customers, but organizing pipeline construction to new markets was not easy. Neither Russia nor Iran had a strong interest in providing pipeline facilities for Turkmenistan's natural gas to become a competitor to their own natural gas supplies to Turkish or European markets.[15] Thus, Russia was happy to continue shipping Turkmenistan's gas to CIS markets, including Russia itself, where it was bartered or collecting payment was difficult, while Russia's own natural gas supplies were exported to hard currency destinations. A route across the Caucasus to join Turkey's pipeline network was stymied by jurisdictional disputes over delimitation of the Caspian Sea, which prevented underwater pipeline construction.[16] Negotiations in

---

14. Oil production was small, less than ten million tons (0.3% of world output).

15. The 200 km Korpedeke-Kurt-Kui gas pipeline built by an Iranian company became operational in December 1997 with a projected annual capacity of 8 bcm, although it only carried five billion in 1999. The main attraction for Iran was that a pipeline from Turkmenistan reduces the cost of supplying the domestic demand in northern Iran while freeing for export Iran's own natural gas supplies in the south. However, it never operated at full capacity, and more substantial projects through Iran were stymied by the nonparticipation of US companies or of other companies concerned about the reach of sanctions.

16. This was a bigger obstacle for gas than for oil because gas could only be shipped across the

1995–97 with Unocal of California to construct a pipeline through Afghanistan to the energy markets of South Asia collapsed in 1998, as the US government drew back from relations with the Taliban government.

In the 1990s and early 2000s Turkmenistan remained dependent on the inherited pipeline network run by Gazprom.[17] Contracts with Turkmenistan's captive customers in the CIS included barter terms, and anecdotes of low quality or unusable goods being supplied to satisfy the barter terms abound. In one 1990s deal, Ukraine supplied twelve million galoshes in payment for gas; this was to a nation of four million people living in the desert! The 2003–5 gas contract with Russia was worth $44 per 1,000 m³ with half to be paid by barter. As a rule of thumb, the true value of barter may be half its contract value, which would bring the true price for the gas in 2003–5 down to $33 per 1,000 m³.

Once in place barter deals proved hard to terminate, and until as late as 2005 some 50–60% of Turkmenistan's gas exports were paid for by barter (Global Witness, 2006). Barter deals were valued by insiders because of their lack of transparency and potential for large-scale corruption. The use of intermediaries in the Turkmen-Ukraine gas trade was an additional component of a lack of transparency that enriched some insiders, who would obtain unsalable goods from Ukrainian factories, supply these goods to Turkmenistan as the barter component of the gas deal, and sell the gas to Ukraine's national gas supply company, Naftohaz Ukrainy, with a large gap between the price paid for the export goods and the price received for the imported gas.[18]

A peculiar aspect of the Turkmen-Ukraine gas deal was that, despite owning the crucial pipeline, Gazprom allowed an intermediary, Itera, to handle

---

Caspian with expensive investment in liquefication capacities and specialized boats (and such technology was still primitive before the 2000s). A proposal for a TransCaspian pipeline had been floated within the Economic Cooperation Organization in the early 1990s, when it was considered economically infeasible (probably due to low energy prices). In 1999–2000 the US government funded a $750,000 feasibility study by Enron for a pipeline supplying gas from Azerbaijan and Turkmenistan to Turkey, but the project fell afoul of poor relations between Turkmenbashi and President Heydar Aliev of Azerbaijan (Cutler 2003), and the project was eventually limited to the Baku-Tbilisi-Erzurum gas pipeline from Azerbaijan to Turkey, which opened in late 2006.

17. Here and at several later points Russia and Gazprom are used interchangeably. Gazprom became a joint stock company in 1993 with the government as the main shareholder; the government share was gradually increased until it reached 51% in 2005. While Gazprom at times operates as an arm of Russian foreign policy, there are also occasions when Gazprom is serving its own interests or those of its top officials (who may be serving the interests of senior Russian politicians). No attempt is made to disentangle these skeins of decision making within the Russian gas sector.

18. Especially in the 1990s the energy trade in Ukraine was a giant system of monopolies that disposed of their output and obtained their energy supplies through a system of transfer pricing "designed to suck all the profits from the Ukrainian economy into foreign bank accounts" (*Financial Times*, December 9, 1998).

the sales, even buying back some of the gas from Itera at a higher price than that which Gazprom could have paid Turkmenistan for it.[19] After Vladimir Putin came to power in Russia and the Gazprom senior management was revamped in 2001–2, Itera lost the contract, which was taken over by an even more shadowy company, TransUral Gas.[20] TransUral Gas was in turn displaced in 2004 in favor of RosUkrEnergo, a fifty-fifty joint venture between Gazprom and a consortium of unnamed Ukrainian and Russian businessmen represented by Austria's Raiffeisen Bank. On the Turkmenistan side, most of the revenue went into nontransparent off-budget funds, including Turkmenbashi's Deutsche Bank account in Frankfurt. The impression is that despite an effort at cleaning up the Russian side after 2002 and the Ukrainian side after the 2004–5 Orange Revolution, large profits continued going to unnamed Ukrainians and perhaps to Russians connected to Gazprom, and Turkmenistan's leadership also profited from the arrangements. Intermediaries were finally eliminated from the Russia-Ukraine gas trade and from Turkmenistan's gas sales to Ukraine in March 2008 when Naftogaz Ukrainy and Gazprom signed a new agreement.

The barter system did not terminate until 2005. In December 2004 Turkmenistan stopped gas supplies to Russia and demanded a price of $58 per 1,000 m³, expecting that Gazprom's inability to meet its export and domestic commitments without Turkmen gas would force it to offer better terms, but Gazprom survived the rest of the winter without Turkmen supplies. In April 2005 Russia and Turkmenistan agreed that Gazprom would make all payments in cash instead of the earlier barter arrangements, but the price remained $44

19. In 2000 Itera bought Turkmenistan gas for $35.37 per 1,000 m³, and sold about a third of it to Gazprom for $45 per 1,000 m³ (Global Witness, 2006). Itera originated as a US-registered company (International Trading Energy and Resources Association) whose founder and main shareholder, Igor Makarov, was a Turkmenistan citizen with good connections in Ukraine and Turkmenistan. Gazprom claimed that Itera's special relationships enabled it to ensure payment by Ukraine. By 2001 the main holding company of Itera was registered in the Dutch Antilles and over 60% of the shares were held in trust for unnamed individuals, one of whom turned out to be a former deputy prime minister of Turkmenistan and others were believed to include high-ranking Gazprom managers (Global Witness 2006).

20. According to Blank (2003), under Moscow's 2003 gas deal with Turkmenistan: "A large quantity of Turkmen gas will be shipped through Russia to Ukraine by a little-known gas company, TransUral, whose major stockholder, Semyon Mogilevich, is one of Russia's most notorious criminal kingpins. The Trans-Ural firm will earn from $320 million to $1 billion from this deal alone. And all the firms involved, including Gazprom, already are contributing to Putin's reelection." Mogilevich was also reputed to have a major interest in RosUkrEnergo. He was put on the FBI's most wanted list in 2003 for fraud, but lived with apparent impunity in Moscow until he was arrested in January 2008 on tax evasion charges. The arrest was welcomed by Ukrainian leaders and appeared to be a prelude to the March 2008 agreement that eliminated intermediaries from the Russia-Ukraine gas trade. It may also have been connected to Russia's March 2008 presidential election won by Dmitry Medvedev, who had been chairman of Gazprom since 2000.

per 1,000 m^3. Following the November-December 2004 Orange Revolution, the new head of Naftohaz Ukrainy announced that the contract with Turkmenistan active from July 1, 2005 would involve no barter terms. The January 2006 Russia-Ukraine energy dispute ended with what appeared to be a definitive movement towards cash payments on gas transactions involving Russia, Ukraine, and Turkmenistan, although the role of the intermediary RosUkrEnergo remained unclear.

The dynamics of the gas trade among CIS countries were driven by the price Russia received for its gas exports to the EU. The delivery price of Russian gas to Western Europe varies according to a formula, which includes oil prices; as oil prices increased, the price of Russian gas exports to the EU tripled between 2002 and 2006. After 2005, the shift in favor of sellers became more transparent as payment for Turkmenistan's gas in hard currency rather than barter became normal. The greater transparency was accompanied by increasing conflict over price increases, as gas suppliers tried to benefit from continuing increases in oil prices and concerns about energy security. For the EU, this was dramatized in the January 2006 dispute involving Russia increasing its gas price to Ukraine, when cuts in Russian gas supply to Ukraine had short-run spillover effects on European supplies. The conflicts often had a geopolitical component as well as pure commercial interests, with Russia more willing to put pressure on Georgia or Ukraine after the Rose and Orange Revolutions of November 2003 and November 2004, which in Russia's view were Western-inspired and contrary to Russia's interests.

The paradox is that long-term agreements on quantity and price are considered necessary to ensure the profitability of expensive gas pipeline projects, but large swings in energy prices undermine attempts to set gas prices into the future and renegotiation is always either a confrontational zero-sum game or subject to indirect consequences as price hikes are passed on. The January 2006 Russia-Ukraine gas dispute initiated an era when prices became negotiable. Before 2006, intra-CIS trade had been largely insulated from the rapidly increasing prices paid for Russian gas at the EU border. The price that Turkmenistan received from Gazprom was increased to $65 in January 2006.

Turkmenbashi seemed content with these arrangements at least up until 2005. However, with the accelerating global energy boom, he started to look for higher output and for alternative customers that would put pressure on Russia to increase the price paid for Turkmenistan's gas. In January 2005, the Turkmenistan government claimed that the country had recoverable gas reserves of 20.42 trillion cubic meters (tcm). However, the BP *Statistical Review of World Energy* continued to give almost identical numbers (c. 2.7 tcm) for every year after their reserves estimates begin in 1997, reflecting Turkmenbashi's lack of international credibility. A second sign of increasing dissatisfaction with the current arrangements was Turkmenbashi's April 2006 visit to

Beijing, where agreement on a new gas pipeline to China was reached. In May 2006 construction began on the 7,000 km pipeline from Turkmenistan through Uzbekistan and Kazakhstan to join China's domestic pipeline network.

6.5. From Turkmenbashi to Berdymuhamedov

The timing of President Niyazov's death in December 2006 was unanticipated and, at least to outside observers, there was no heir apparent. Nevertheless, the succession went smoothly. The designated caretaker ruler, the president of the senate, was arrested and the health minister, Gurbanguly Berdymuham-edov, became acting president. In the February 2007 presidential election Berdymuhamedov won almost 90% of the vote, and in the remainder of 2007 he consolidated his power. The personality cult was reduced and some of the extremes of Turkmenbashi's final years were reversed, but the initial changes appeared to be cosmetic rather than substantive. With a super-presidential regime similar to that of his predecessor, Berdymuhamedov's Turkmenistan remained close to the bottom of any ranking list of countries by political or economic freedom.[21]

A sense of change was created by reversal in 2007 of three of Turkmen-bashi's worst recent policy decisions on education, pensions, and foreign exchange markets. These changes cut back some of the most egregious threats to economic growth, social harmony, and economic efficiency.

Education reforms such as reducing the number of years of compulsory schooling or the years needed for a university degree, the nonrecognition of foreign qualifications, and the emphasis on *Ruhnama* were all discarded in a return to the 1990s (Horák, 2013). The symbolism was clear, but the impact on education was less so; the teachers and old-fashioned teaching methods

---

21. The succession is described by Peyrouse (2012, 108–31). In the Freedom House world ranking by political rights and civil liberties Turkmenistan has always received the lowest score in both categories; in 2008, this was shared only by Burma, Cuba, Libya, North Korea, Somalia, Sudan, and Uzbekistan, and in 2015 by the Central African Republic, Equatorial Guinea, Eritrea, North Korea, Saudi Arabia, Somalia, Sudan, Syria, and Uzbekistan—the ten "worst of the worst." In Transparency International's 2007 Corruption Perception Index Turkmenistan ranked 162nd out of 179 countries and in 2015 it ranked 154th out of 168 countries. In the Reporters sans Frontières index of press freedom for 2015, Turkmenistan's media ranked 178th out of 180 countries, only beaten by North Korea and Eritrea. UNESCO (2015, 382–84) provides a more positive assessment that reads like a paean to the current president, who "is far more committed to science than his predecessor" and who has "restored the legislative powers of the *Majlis*" and is "giving greater freedom to the media." Bohr (2016, 20–21) argues that the power of the Majlis was reduced in the 2008 revision of the constitution, and power shifted to the State Security Council, a small group dominated by defense and security officials; the 2008 constitution revision also abolished the "Khalk Maslakhty" (People's Council).

remained the same, and *Ruhnama* continued to be an important textbook. Some of the educational changes have since been extended, e.g., recognition of foreign degrees, introduction of a twelve-year education system in 2013/4, study of *Ruhnama* formally made noncompulsory in 2013, and extension of periods of higher education (although university students were subject to dress codes, curfews, and driving bans). The use of students for cotton harvesting is reported to have increased (Bohr, 2016, 43).

In January 2006, Turkmenbashi signed a new pension law that strengthened the relationship to contributions. Some groups, such as farm workers or petty traders with no contribution record, suffered from reduced pension rights. Berdymuhamedov reinstated the rights of the disentitled pensioners, although the average monthly payment of 500,000 manat ($20–25) was still low.

Reform of the exchange rate system was initiated by announcing that from January 1, 2008, banks would be able to open foreign exchange points and use exchange rates close to the previous black-market rate for most transactions. The exchange rate was fixed at 19,800 for buying and 20,000 for selling US dollars, nearly killing the black market, and the official exchange rate was raised from 5,200 to 6,250 manat to the dollar. A step toward unification of exchange rates came on April 19, 2008 when the open market rate was lowered to 17,400 for buying and 17,600 for selling dollars. On January 1, 2009, the currency was redominated with one new manat (TMT) replacing 5,000 old manat (TMM).

Because Turkmenistan functions as an integrated economic and social system, which keeps the population docile through a mix of basic needs satisfaction, benefits for the presidents' clients, and a pervasive security apparatus, piecemeal reforms can be counterproductive. Turkmenbashi's 2006 pension reform, although a step towards a more rational system, was chaotic because many people, who were not recorded as having made contributions, lost their pension rights; these people had previously been dependent on many nontransparent benefits, which accompanied the status of pensioner and whose loss left people in penury. The untargeted subsidization of necessities is inefficient and inequitable (e.g., free electricity or water provide the largest benefits to those with the biggest houses), but announcement in January 2008 that free petrol would be limited to 120 liters a month led to such strong concerns among ministers that the proposal was withdrawn; farmers who had relied on selling their vegetables in urban markets, for example, faced a huge cost hike, while urban motorists who supplemented their income by providing taxi services lost that source of income.

Other changes in 2007 or 2008 were cosmetic or worse. Among the cosmetic changes, in spring 2008 the country officially reverted to the conventional names for the months of the year and the largest gold statue of Turkmenbashi was moved from the city center to the outskirts of Ashgabat. The opening of internet cafes was publicized internationally as ending quarantine on information. About a dozen internet cafés were opened in various towns in 2007, all operating under Turkmentelkom, but the official affiliation discouraged many people from accessing them for fear of surveillance;[22] internet usage in 2014 was the lowest in Central Asia (table 2.9), despite Turkmenistan having the second highest per capita income. Less dramatically, President Berdymuhamedov began a program to reduce the number of satellite dishes, which cluttered up apartment blocks across the country. Although the dishes are unsightly, they were the population's true information lifelines, and the negative impact of reducing access to Russian or Kazakh TV stations more than offset the positive effect of the internet cafés on information access.

Heavy-handed regulation continues to characterize almost all economic life. In agriculture, farmers still grow what they are directed to grow, with unrealistic targets set for cotton and wheat output. Changes in controlled prices have been trumpeted as liberalization, e.g., in 2012 the government canceled flour rationing and increased the maximum price of bread, but these are far from creating market-determined prices. Water, electricity, gas heating, and other essentials continued to be either free or heavily subsidized, although bread subsidies were removed in 2012. The government reports that hospitals are providing better social services, but the hospitals often lack staff and supplies, and the good ones are only available to the elite, for a fee; rural hospitals remain unrenovated, often without running water (Bohr, 2016, 45).[23]

There is little incentive to start a business, because even when a would-be entrepreneur has passed all the regulatory hurdles there is a widespread belief that a successful business would be confiscated. The banking system remains state-dominated, with only one small private bank among the eleven domestic banks; the two foreign banks (Turkish and Pakistani) concentrate on remittance outflows. The only other roles for foreign investors are as partners in oil and gas exploration and exploitation, as partners in textile joint ventures, and

22. In June 2008 Turkmenistan opened up citizens' access to the internet, with the state-run fixed-line provider beginning some home installations and Russia's MTS starting wireless coverage, but with government control of controversial websites, slow connections, and costs beyond the reach of most Turkmen, the circle of users is unlikely to widen much beyond the government officials and foreigners who used the internet in the past. In December 2010, the license of MTS Turkmenistan was suspended, although this was reversed in 2012 when MTS agreed to work jointly with the Altyn Asr subsidiary of Turkmen Telecom. MTS and Altyn Asr have a duopoly in mobile phone services (section 10.7).

23. When Médecins sans Frontières produced a critical report in 2010, the president reacted by seeking out and punishing healthcare workers who had cooperated with the foreign NGO. A fundamental problem appears to be lack of public funding for health, reflected in hospitals being expected to be self-sufficient or even contribute to the state budget and in restrictions on pharmaceutical imports (Peyrouse, 2012, 136–41).

on construction projects. Unlike elsewhere in Central Asia, immigration and emigration are generally prohibited, and remittance inflows are negligible. This removed the safety valve of unemployed youths working temporarily in Russia.

The construction projects remained lucrative for foreign companies as President Berdymuhamedov maintained the building boom in Ashgabat as well as encouraging tourism projects on the Caspian Sea. Completed construction projects include a $60 million 185-meter high carpet-themed Monument to the Constitution, a $140 million Palace of Happiness for wedding ceremonies, and a $184 million TV tower in the shape of an eight-pointed star, which is in the *Guinness Book of Records* as the world's largest star-shaped structure. Estimated costs for the 2017 Asian Indoor and Martial Arts Games complex, a new Ashgabat airport, and a new house of parliament are each in the billions of dollars. The contracts continue to be awarded to French (e.g., Bouygues and Vinci) and Turkish (e.g., Çelik and Polimeks) companies without tendering, and in a bizarre twist the only permitted color is white.[24]

Financial reforms and relaxation of forex controls in 2011–12 also seem more form than substance. The small banking sector is dominated by state-owned banks, the six largest of which account for over 90% of the market, and over half of "commercial" bank lending is directed to state-owned enterprises at below-market rates. Privately owned nonbank financial intermediaries such as insurance companies remain virtually nonexistent. A stabilization fund was established in 2008, but its investment rules and governing principles have not been published, and a significant part of gas revenues continue to go to the Foreign Exchange Reserve Fund that is off-budget, nontransparent, and under the president's personal control.

Like his predecessor, Berdymuhamedov pays little attention to environmental issues. Turkmenbashi's Lake of the Golden Age, intended to create a lake 103 km long and 18.6 km wide that will solve the country's irrigation problems, is being constructed at a cost of $4.5 billion. The project is more likely to lead through massive evaporation to further environmental problems as sand and chemicals are dispersed (Kalyuzhnova and Kaser, 2006; Peyrouse, 2010, 62).

Control over media makes it difficult to assess social and political conditions. A September 2008 shooting incident in the northern suburbs of Ashgabat was initially reported outside the country as involving Islamic fundamentalists and resulting in the deaths of at least twenty policemen. Within a few hours, the story had been rewritten as a drugs-related shoot-out.[25] Neither

---

24. In 2014, the government banned import of black cars and advised importers to only buy white cars. Further details are in online reports such as *Hurriyet Daily News*, February 24, 2013, and *BBC*, January 27, 2015.

25. The first version originated in an Associated Press report that was picked up by newspapers and online news services. The second report came from an official source in Turkmenistan.

version reflected well on the country's economic and political stability. Turkmenistan's long-standing role as a transit country for Afghan opium has been replaced by the growth of clandestine laboratories producing heroin, and an associated fall in the street price of heroin and estimates of about a fifth of Turkmen youth consuming heroin (Peyrouse, 2012, 140–41). Rising drug use is occurring against a backdrop of deteriorating social conditions and a health system shrouded in secrecy.

In foreign relations, the new president made a cleaner break with his predecessor. After Turkmenbashi's initial activity in joining the United Nations, IMF, World Bank, EBRD, and ECO in 1992, he became skeptical of multilateral institutions and regional organizations as a threat to his prized neutrality. Especially in his later years, Turkmenbashi seldom traveled. In contrast President Berdymuhamedov was everywhere in his first year, visiting New York, Brussels, Moscow, and Tehran, welcoming Recep Tayyip Erdogan, Vladimir Putin, and Hu Jintao to Ashgabat, and sending observers to SCO and CAREC meetings.

The thrust of being more engaged in the wider world was clear, but the main change in substance was the tilt towards China that had been foreshadowed by Turkmenbashi's April 2006 trip to Beijing. China offered billions of dollars for investment projects in which it supplied practically state-of-the-art turnkey factories at a fraction of the price charged by European or Turkish suppliers, and Chinese loans at 3% undercut other potential lenders.[26] Natural gas exports were increasingly directed to China after completion of the pipeline in 2009, until China was practically the sole buyer in 2015.

Relations with international organizations warmed after Turkmenbashi, but beyond the United Nations they remain minimal. The UN continues to be the country's principal foreign policy partner, and Turkmenistan hosts the UN Regional Centre for Preventive Diplomacy in Central Asia in Ashgabat. The World Bank limited its support to technical assistance and had no financing operations. The EBRD welcomed the May 2008 exchange rate unification as improving conditions for the private sector, and in 2010 signaled a rapprochement by adopting a "calibrated strategic approach," which set political and economic benchmarks against which reform could be measured and responses tailored, but by the 2014 review none of the three political criteria (progress

---

The BBC posted the first report, but within a few hours it disappeared from the BBC website (www.bbc.co.uk) to be replaced by the second version, although it is doubtful whether there was any reliable way to check the veracity of the two versions.

26. In 2009 China Development Bank provided a loan of $4 billion followed by a $4.1 billion loan in 2011 for development of the South Yolotan gas field. The Chinese Import-Export Bank provided smaller loans for transportation and communications projects. Chinese firms have invested in the silk industry, pharmaceuticals, fertilizers, construction, and telecommunications (Bohr, 2016, 78). China has a "debt for delivery" policy whereby Turkmenistan repays loans through gas deliveries.

towards political pluralism, greater media freedom, and improvement in human rights) had been met. Relations with the ADB have been slightly warmer, but Turkmenistan did not join CAREC until 2010, more than a decade after the four other Central Asian countries

6.6. Natural Gas: Part Two

Turkmenistan played an important role in Russia's gas strategy in the early 2000s, because Turkmenistan's sales to Russia freed up Russian gas for export to Europe at a higher price.[27] Thus, although Turkmenistan remained dependent on Russian pipelines, it did have some bargaining power. The price paid by Gazprom to Turkmenistan was increased to $65 per 1,000 m^3 at the start of 2006, and in September 2006 Turkmenistan negotiated an increase in the price to $100 per 1,000 m^3 for 2007–9.

Following Turkmenbashi's trip to Beijing and China's agreement to build a pipeline, Russia made a counteroffer to build a pipeline along the Caspian coast from Turkmenistan to Russia. As additional incentives for Turkmenistan to sign the pipeline contract, Russia-connected companies provided capital, e.g., Itera was a lead investor in the $4 billion development project to turn the area around the Caspian port of Turkmenbashi into a tourist center. In May 2007 Russia, Turkmenistan, and Kazakhstan signed an agreement to build a 10-bcm-a-year pipeline along the eastern coast of the Caspian, the Prikaspiisky route, feeding into the Russian pipeline network, and in addition to the 50+ bcm a year already flowing to Russia. This was widely seen as a preemptive move to forestall Caspian gas going to China, but it did not stop the Turkmenistan-China agreement; in July 2007, China signed a contract to buy 30 bcm a year of Turkmenistan's future gas output, and the China National Petroleum Corporation was granted drilling rights in Turkmenistan.[28] In December 2007, the proposed Prikaspiisky pipeline capacity was doubled, to carry 10 bcm from each of Kazakhstan and Turkmenistan, and in July 2008 it was increased further to accommodate larger deliveries from Turkmenistan. However, on the ground nothing happened.

In November 2007, as a sweetener for the Prikaspiisky pipeline deal, Russia's price was raised to $130 for the first half of 2008 and $150 for the second half of 2008, which was still less than the price Russia received from Europe.

---

27. A similar displacement effect, with profit to the middleman, was at play in Iran. Turkmenistan supplied 27 million m^3 per day at a price of $75, which enabled Iran to release 30 million m^3 of its own gas for sale to Turkey at a higher price than it paid Turkmenistan.

28. China's heightened interest in Caspian energy (Kazakhstan's oil as well as Turkmenistan's natural gas) was, in turn, born out of frustration with Russia's failure to guarantee supplies of its Far East energy to China. Proposals around this time for an energy club within the SCO aimed at moderating Russia-China energy conflicts made no headway.

In January 2008 China agreed to pay $195 for the gas that it would obtain from Turkmenistan; this included a $50 premium to finance the Turkmenistan-China pipeline, but was still higher than the $130 paid by Russia.[29] As the oil boom approached its peak, in a March 2008 agreement between Naftogaz Ukrainy and Gazprom, Ukraine agreed to pay $179.50 per 1,000 m³ for gas supplied between March and December. On March 11, 2008 Gazprom announced that it would pay European prices for Central Asian gas in 2009, i.e. in the range of $200–300 per 1,000 m³. The following day Russia signed an agreement to transfer to the Turkmenistan government Soviet-era geological data covering Turkmen energy deposits that had been kept in Moscow.

Russia was keen to discourage Turkmenistan from supporting non-Russian pipeline prospects, which would reduce Russia's monopoly power and influence. The Prikaspiisky pipeline deal, the gas price hikes, and the data transfer appeared to be a package deal to keep Turkmenistan within the Russian energy network. It was, however, too little too late. The pipeline to China was completed in 2009, while Gazprom was unprepared to take any steps towards constructing the Prikaspiisky pipeline

Meanwhile, the attractiveness for Russia of buying Turkmenistan's gas was being eroded as Russia reduced the historic underpricing of domestic gas prices between 2008 and 2011 in anticipation of WTO accession, which was finalized in 2012.[30] Even more dramatically, after oil prices plummeted in the second half of 2008, the price paid by the EU for Russian gas collapsed in 2009. A pending gas glut in the CIS further reduced Russia's eagerness to buy Turkmen gas.[31] Russia appeared to have second thoughts about the March 2008 deal, and an unexplained explosion in the existing Turkmenistan-Russia pipeline in April 2009 was widely interpreted as a Russian strategy to avoid taking delivery of what had become overpriced gas.

29. At the same time, Turkmenistan was receiving $75 per 1,000 m³ from Iran; when Turkmenistan tried to raise the price, Iran offered a super-premium price (reportedly $300) to Azerbaijan in February 2008 to teach Turkmenistan that Iran was not a captive market.

30. Between 2008 and 2011 Russia gradually introduced netback pricing for gas, i.e. linking Russia's domestic price to the export price minus transport costs. Gazprom intended to bring prices for all CIS customers up to levels that provided equal profitability to sales to EU customers by 2011; prices were increased for the Baltic countries in 2005, for Ukraine, Moldova, Armenia, Azerbaijan, and Georgia in 2006, and for Belarus in 2007.

31. Gazprom's 2006 production (548 bcm) was boosted by unrepeatable acquisition of the assets of independent producers (Itera, Novatek, TNK-BP) in 2004–7. Russia's gas production was about to shift from the fields in Western Siberia, which were past their peak, to the large Yamal Peninsula and Shtockman gas fields in the Russian Arctic, but difficult conditions delayed their development. Uzbekistan's gas production (55 bcm in 2006) was not much lower than that of Turkmenistan, but with its much larger population most of Uzbekistan's gas was used for domestic consumption; under a 2002 agreement Uzbekistan supplied about 12 bcm a year to Russia until 2012. Kazakhstan's gas production was much lower, but large new gas fields (e.g., Kashagan) are located close to the Russian border.

In January 2008, President Berdymuhamedov announced an independent audit of Turkmenistan's gas reserves, probably as a signal that Turkmenistan was willing to play by international rules in order to attract foreign investment. In March, the British firm Gaffney, Cline, and Associates was selected to conduct the survey, and they essentially confirmed the high-end Turkmen estimate of reserves. The 2015 BP *Statistical Review of World Energy* gives proven reserves as 17.5 tcm, ranked fourth in the world behind Russia, Iran, and Qatar, and ahead of fifth-placed USA. However, exploitation of Turkmenistan's gas is hampered by geography and by technology. Unlike the Soviet-era gas fields, which are in the east of the country, the unexploited gas reserves tend to be in the west, mostly under the Caspian Sea. Disputes over delimitation of the Caspian Sea have delayed exploitation of some fields such as the Serder field, which is also claimed by Azerbaijan where it is called Kapaz. The technically more difficult exploration and exploitation of offshore fields highlight the need for cooperation with foreigners possessing the necessary expertise, an area in which Turkmenistan has had little experience.[32]

The prospect of higher gas output and higher energy prices increased interest in other gas pipelines in Berdymuhamedov's early years. After Turkmenbashi's death, relations between Turkmenistan and Azerbaijan warmed; in 2007, Turkmenistan reopened its embassy in Baku, which had been closed since 2001, and in June proposals were announced for joint exploration of the Serdar/Kapaz field under the South Caspian Sea. In August 2007, the USA granted $1.7 million to Azerbaijan for a feasibility study on TransCaspian oil and gas pipelines that would link up to the Baku-Tbilisi-Erzurum gas pipeline and the proposed $5–6 billion Nabucco pipeline from Turkey to Hungary via Bulgaria and Romania; the feasibility of the TransCaspian and Nabucco projects was linked because Turkmen supplies were needed to justify Nabucco's planned capacity of 30 bcm a year. In March 2008, a delegation from Turkmenistan visited Baku and reached an agreement on debt disputes between Azerbaijan and Turkmenistan,[33] but the Caspian demarcation question remained unanswered.[34] In 2014, the TransCaspian pipeline, Nabucco, and the proposed South Stream pipeline from southern Russia to Italy via Serbia were shelved.

32. ExxonMobil and Monument signed PSAs in the early 1990s but cut their activities in the late 1990s due to high costs and dissatisfaction with the regime. In 2000 Monument sold its interest to Burren and in 2002 ExxonMobil pulled out. After that Turkmenistan dealt with small energy companies (Burren, Dragon, and Petronas). Schlumberger provided oil and gas services under contract. In 2007, Eni purchased Burren for reasons unrelated to Turkmenistan.

33. Although both countries acknowledged the debts arising from gas shipped from Turkmenistan to Azerbaijan as far back as 1991, in 1991–93 they both still used the ruble, whose hard-currency value was disputed. Turkmenistan sought $56 million while Azerbaijan offered $18 million; under the March 2008 agreement Azerbaijan agreed to pay $44.8 million.

34. The TransCaspian pipeline was strongly opposed by Russia. Both Azerbaijan and Turkmenistan were drawn into a Caspian arms race (Kucera, 2012). In 2015 Turkmenistan's navy had

Major energy companies (Unocal, Chevron, ExxonMobil, Total) have shown interest at various times in a Turkmenistan-Afghanistan-Pakistan-India (TAPI) pipeline, but nothing has happened. A TAPI pipeline route is still on Turkmenistan's agenda, but until Afghanistan's (and Pakistan's) government can provide reasonable security guarantees and become an acceptable counterpart for the major energy companies and their governments a trans-Afghanistan pipeline remains a distant prospect. Anceschi (2017) calls TAPI a "virtual pipeline," that is a continuous topic for diplomatic discourse without any real existence.[35]

Despite all the talk, Turkmenistan's actual gas pipeline options were restricted to Russia, Iran, and China. Between 2006 and 2008 there was a substantial upward shift in the prices agreed on gas trade involving Turkmenistan and its major customers, Russia and Ukraine, but Turkmenistan was still receiving substantially less than the price in the EU, which exceeded $300; how much Turkmenistan was underpaid is difficult to assess because it is hard to know the true transport costs from the Turkmen border to the EU border. Turkmenistan's attempts to increase the price it received from Iran met with an angry reaction, which would eventually lose that market for Turkmenistan's gas.[36] Price disputes eased after completion of the China pipeline as world oil prices recovered in 2009–10 and stayed above $100 per barrel in 2011–14. Turkmenistan's customers adopted a wait-and-see approach. However, once the collapse in oil prices was under way in 2014, both Russia and Iran announced their intention to cease buying Turkmen gas, leaving the country dependent on China's continuing purchases.[37] In sum, between 2009 and 2015 Turkmenistan replaced its dependence on Russia by dependence on China.

6.7. Conclusions

During the first decade after independence, Turkmenistan's government gave low priority to economic reform, while emphasizing the country's neutrality and minimizing internal political change. The country's abundant resource endowment, based on cotton and natural gas, provided favorable

---

nineteen patrol and combat boats and around five hundred servicemen (Kuchins et al., 2015, 9, citing the International Institute for Strategic Studies).

35. Similar lack of progress has dogged proposals for a Turkmenistan-Uzbekistan-Tajikistan-Afghanistan-Pakistan Interconnection electricity project (Kuchins et al., 2015, 26).

36. Despite the opening of a second pipeline in 2010, trade with Iran has been hampered by sanctions that limited Iran's access to hard currency. The sanctions have eased since 2016, but Turkmenistan's (disputed) claim that Iran owes $1.8 billion in arrears jeopardizes future deals.

37. In 2014 Turkmenistan completed its domestic East-West Connector gas pipeline that allows gas to be switched between alternative export pipelines, but without increased output and foreign demand gas exports will continue to go to China.

initial conditions for pursuing this agenda. In 1997, the unreformed economy suffered a deep decline and the economic strategy appeared to be unsustainable. After 1999, however, the economy was rescued by high world energy prices. Nevertheless, Turkmenistan has been poorly run since independence. The inherited natural resource wealth has been dissipated by mismanagement of the cotton sector and by misuse of the huge rents from cotton and especially natural gas.

Turkmenbashi's prized neutrality in effect left the country dependent on Russia, which controlled the country's important transport and pipeline outlets. Turkmenbashi appears to have been content with this situation, which generated large rents from opaque gas transactions once energy prices started to increase in 1998–99 and customers paid up. The situation changed in 2005–6, perhaps associated with new discoveries or more likely with a desire to take greater advantage of soaring world energy prices. Turkmenbashi traveled to Beijing to bring in China as a major gas customer, who could also help in developing new gas fields. In addition to gas exploration, Chinese companies have invested in light industries (e.g., silk, pharmaceuticals, and fertilizers), the Chinese Export-Import Bank has provided loans for transport and communications projects, and Chinese companies tender for construction projects at lower rates than the previously dominant French and Turkish companies (Bohr, 2016, 76). The change in trade partners coincided with the change in presidents, but the overall impression is of continuity since Turkmenbashi's 2006 trip to Beijing, especially as President Berdymuhamedov continued to deal with some of his predecessors' preferred intermediaries such as Itera.[38]

Despite some hopes for reform in his first years, Berdymuhamedov has followed in his predecessor's footsteps, with a slightly less outrageous personality cult, but still with absolute presidential power.[39] State control of the economy remains pervasive. In February 2012, Berdymuhamedov was re-elected president for another five-year term, with an increased majority: 97% of the vote on a 96% turnout. In February 2017 the victory was repeated, and

38. In 2007–8 Itera extended its role in Turkmenistan to construction of hotels and resorts, and won the exclusive right to the Avaz Tourist Development Project on the Caspian Sea, where the first hotels opened in 2009 and "in 2014 some 30 hotels and holiday homes were under construction" with a target capacity to cater for seven thousand tourists by the scheduled completion date of 2020 (UNESCO, 2015, 382). In 2008, the company gave President Berdymuhamedov a €60-million luxury yacht that is parked next to the presidential residence at Turkmenbashi.

39. The personality cult is only slightly less extreme. Niyazov styled himself *Beyik Türkmenbasy* (Great Father of the Turkmen People) while Berdymuhamedov is *Hormatly Prezident, Arkadag* (Most Honorable President, Protector of the Nation), or "Arkadag" for short. While his thoughts are not glorified to the extent of the *Rukhnama*, President Berdymuhamedov's collected writings have been translated into English and Czech (Meurs, 2015, 129).

the term in office extended to seven years. Constitutional restrictions on the president's age were abolished, paving the way for a lifetime presidency.

In 2014, Turkmenistan like other energy exporters saw the start of a drastic decline in oil prices that would surely spill over into gas prices. The president announced that gas meters would be installed in homes to rationalize the use of gas, and a charge was levied on households for gas consumed beyond 50 m³ per person. Owners of trucks, buses, and tractors lost the right to free gasoline, which was restricted to drivers of cars and motorbikes. Apart from the world price of oil and gas, technological changes—such as fracking that has increased global gas supply or improved technology for producing and shipping liquefied natural gas (LNG) that favors offshore deposits over land-locked producers such as Turkmenistan (see chapter 3.2)—may be even more harmful to the gas-dependent economy.

In January 2015, the manat was devalued from 2.85 to the US dollar to 3.5, where it remained for the rest of the year.[40] In September 2015, the Council of Elders proposed that free supply of electricity, gas, and water should be terminated as part of the process of establishing a market economy, effectively ending a key component of the compact introduced by President Niyazov in 1993.

There were signs, starting in 2014, that Turkmenistan was reintegrating into the regional and global communities. President Berdymuhamedov attended the 2014 SCO summit as an observer. Turkmen delegates spoke at 2015 and 2016 events such as the OECD's Eurasia Week and ESCAP's annual meetings, although participation was limited to prepared statements. The Kazakhstan-Iran railroad along the Caspian coast was opened by the three countries' presidents in December 2014, and construction of a railroad line through Afghanistan to Tajikistan began in June 2013. Such links are, however, only helpful if accompanied by reforms to facilitate domestic activity and international trade, e.g., the 1997 rail link to Iran has remained underutilized due to the absence of economic reform.

In sum, Turkmenistan's future could lie in continued gas exports, perhaps directed beyond China, if its huge reserves can be exploited. However, the assumptions underlying that scenario are by no means assured in an era unlikely to repeat the energy boom of the 2000s; even if natural gas demand does expand, it will be satisfied primarily by LNG exports from countries with large gas fields accessible to ocean-going ships. In that scenario, Turkmenistan will be left with stranded assets, and no customers for suboptimally located gas.

40. In January 2016, the government halted the sale of foreign currencies, and the black-market premium widened to 20%, with a rate of 4.2 manat to the dollar; "Turkmenistan Halts Sale of Foreign Currency in Panic Measure," at http://www.eurasianet.org/node/76781 (posted January 12, 2016).

Turkmenistan would be transformed from a resource-abundant to a resource-scarce economy that will have to find other areas of specialization if it is to foster prosperity. However, it is difficult to see prospects of Turkmenistan developing international competitiveness in any product other than gas without major domestic reforms to provide the setting for soundly based economic diversification, and neither president has shown any appetite for economic change. Even with presidential will, reform will be difficult because destruction of the education system and frequent purges of public servants have left the country bereft of administrators who could implement policy changes effectively (Stronski, 2017). More than any other Central Asian country, Turkmenistan risks following the model of the insulated and backward pre-Russian khanates, whose leaders lived well but whose people were mired in poverty, rather than the outward-looking "Silk Road" future beckoning the region in chapter 11.

7

The Kyrgyz Republic

The Kyrgyz Republic was the most explicit of the Central Asian countries, and to some extent of all former Soviet republics, in attempting a rapid transition from central planning. It became identified with the "Washington consensus" advocated by the IMF and the World Bank, and was the first of the Soviet successor states to join the WTO. Although it followed the common political path to a superpresidential regime, when opposition became strong in 2005 the president stepped aside with minimal bloodshed. Since a second uprising in 2010, the Kyrgyz Republic has been the only Central Asian country to attempt to create a balance between parliament and president. In 2017, for the first time in Central Asia, power was peacefully transferred from one elected president to another.

Economic performance was, however, disappointing due to limited resources and poor institutions. The country became highly dependent on revenues from a single goldmine, Kumtor, while other mineral and hydro resources remain poorly developed. The open economy allowed the country to become an entrepôt in the 2000s, and this stimulated other activities. However, as a development model it was vulnerable to changes in external circumstances, and the entrepôt function became less viable in the 2010s. A quarter century after independence, economic performance appears to have been poorer than that of Uzbekistan and little better than that of Tajikistan.[1] The biggest symptom of economic distress was the rise in number of Kyrgyz

1. This is the picture drawn by tables 2.1 and 2.8, although casual empiricism suggests that living standards are higher in the Kyrgyz Republic than in Tajikistan, and little different from Uzbekistan (especially if measured by private consumption at purchasing power parity exchange rates). Harder to measure is the greater freedom of expression and access to competing news sources; the Kyrgyz Republic ranked 89th in the Reporters sans Frontières World Press Freedom

migrating to Russia for work; by the end of the oil boom the numbers were commonly thought to be around a million people and in 2014 the Kyrgyz Republic's remittances to GDP ratio was the third highest in the world. This left the country susceptible to Russian pressure to join the Eurasian Economic Union, which it did in 2015, and vulnerable to downturns in the Russian economy.

This chapter starts by describing the policies and performance of the economy in the transition to a market-based economy during the 1990s. The Kumtor gold mine, which has been by far the largest enterprise in terms of contribution to GDP and government revenue since 1997, and the Manas transit center, leased to the USA from 2001 to 2014, have been the most high-profile and controversial items in political debate, largely due to perceived misuse of revenue or corruption. The main long-term economic developments of the twenty-first century have been the growth of trade and associated linkage effects and labor migration and remittances. The final sections assess economic developments since the 2010 revolution and draw conclusions. Prospects of the Eurasian Economic Union are analyzed in chapter 10.2.

7.1. Creating a Market Economy[2]

The Kyrgyz republic was one of the poorest of the Soviet republics. The mountainous terrain and artificial Soviet borders meant that after independence the new country did not have an integrated national economy. The capital Bishkek, the Chu Valley, and northern towns such as Talas were connected to Kazakhstan rather than to other parts of Kyrgyzstan, while the southern cities of Osh and Jalalabad in the Fergana Valley were better connected to Khujand (Tajikistan) or Tashkent than to Bishkek; road or rail travel from Bishkek to Osh typically involved transiting Kazakhstan, Uzbekistan, and Tajikistan. At independence, ethnic Kyrgyz accounted for just over half of the population; the biggest minorities were Russians, concentrated in Bishkek and the north, and Uzbeks, concentrated in the south (table 7.1). After ethnic violence between Kyrgyz and Uzbeks led to several hundred deaths in 1990, Mikhail Gorbachev fired the first secretary of the Communist Party in the Kyrgyz republic, and turned to an outsider, Askar Akayev, a physics professor, to clean up the republic's administration.

The population was primarily rural, based on cotton in the south, grain-farming in the north, and livestock. Industry consisted of some military-

---

Index for 2017, well ahead of the other four Central Asian countries, which ranked between 149th and 178th out of 180 countries covered.

2. Pomfret (2006, 73–88) provides more detailed analysis of the economy in the 1990s, as well as discussion of health, education, and other social sectors that are ignored in this chapter.

TABLE 7.1. Ethnic Composition of the Kyrgyz Republic, 1989 and 2015

	1989 Census	2015
Population	4.36 million	5.89 million
Kyrgyz	52.4%	72.8%
Russian	21.5%	6.2%
Uzbek	12.9%	14.5%

Source: 2015 data from the National Statistical Office, reported in ICG (2015, 2n).

related enterprises, for which the location far from the Soviet Union's more vulnerable frontiers was an advantage, and a sugar refinery, the republic's largest single enterprise, which owed its existence to Soviet foreign assistance and regional policy; once transportation costs were taken into account and Cuba was abandoned, it made no sense to be refining sugarcane in the southeast part of Central Asia. Dissolution of the USSR left the sugar refinery and most of the military-related factories high and dry. Many Russians and almost all Germans left the country shortly after independence. The economy during the 1990s was characterized by substantial urban-rural migration (figure 4.1) as town-dwellers returned to their family villages, and by the reemergence of subsistence and informal activities.

The options available to the newly independent Kyrgyzstan were limited. Harnessing the water flowing down from some of the world's highest mountains for hydroelectricity generation required large investments with long payback periods and grids to take the electricity to reliable markets. Moreover, any hydro project would be opposed by downstream neighbors, who needed the water for irrigation and were unaccustomed to paying anything like an economic price for water. The country was known to have mineral deposits, but they had been little exploited in the Soviet era.

Whether due to limited options or to the chance event that the incumbent leader had come from the Academy of Sciences rather than through the Communist administrative hierarchy as in the other Central Asian countries, the Kyrgyz Republic had by 1993 become the most liberal country in the region. Practically all price controls were rapidly removed, apart from public transport, electricity, and municipal services. In May 1993, the Kyrgyz Republic became the first Central Asian country to leave the ruble zone and issue its own national currency, and thereafter it was the first to bring hyperinflation under control. International trade was liberalized as export controls were removed, and trade barriers were low; in 1998, the Kyrgyz Republic became the first of all Soviet successor states, including the Baltic countries, to accede to the World Trade Organization.

Privatization was comprehensive and rapid. Housing and small enterprises were mainly transferred to current occupiers and operators, and large- and medium-sized enterprises were transferred into private ownership through a voucher scheme. By the end of the 1990s the private sector was producing three-fifths of GDP.[3] The relative ease of privatization in the Kyrgyz Republic was assisted by the lack of valuable assets to be contested. Even among the small enterprises privatized in the early transition years, most failed to survive for more than two years (Anderson and Pomfret, 2001). By far the largest and most successful enterprise in the country since 1997 has been the Kumtor goldmine, developed as a joint venture between the government and Cameco of Canada. Among the few other dynamic enterprises in the 1990s, the most successful retailing and media businesses were associated with the president's family, who were believed to have received special privileges.

Agrarian reform was more difficult because of population pressure on the land and suspicion of the creation of a rich peasant (*kulak*) class. In the late Soviet era population pressure was a general problem in irrigated areas of Central Asia, but an added problem in the Kyrgyz Republic was the regional variation. Irrigated land per person was much less in the southern districts of Jalalabad and Osh than in the mountain areas or the northern districts, and this fueled ethnic tensions over land; the worst outbreak of violence in Central Asia during the Gorbachev era followed a reallocation in 1990 of land tilled by ethnic Uzbeks to ethnic Kyrgyz, when several hundred people were killed in the ensuing interethnic riots. Nevertheless, reform did proceed as the state farms were dismantled, and the approximately five hundred collective and state farms averaging over 2,500 hectares per farm at the time of independence were replaced by over sixty thousand farms averaging about 20 hectares per farm (World Bank, 2004, vol. II, 130). The successor organizations operated at first with long-term leases. Following a 1998 referendum, private land ownership was legalized, and by 2003 land was private property in a meaningful sense, with a functioning land market.

Despite ongoing disputes over land rights and establishment of formal ownership,[4] Mogilevskii et al. (2015) conclude their review of land reform with a positive assessment of the impact on the agricultural sector:

> a certain freedom granted to farmers stands out as one of the main achievements and an important reason for the sector's efficiency. Peasant farms are effectively protected from attempts to regulate crop structure or introduce any other types of market distortions should the government or other major player in the sector make any effort of this kind (p. 40)

3. These are the rounded figures quoted in EBRD *Transition Reports*. The extensive unofficial sector in the Kyrgyz Republic makes it likely that the private share was even larger.

4. Land disputes are important background issues in the 2010 film *Svet-Ake* (*The Light Thief*) or for interviewees in *The Interim Country*, a Canadian documentary of the 2010 events.

and

> It would not be an exaggeration to say that self-reliance of farmers is a major source of extreme poverty reduction and basic food security (p. 31).

They also find that post-2003 agrarian reforms, i.e. water users' associations to manage on-farm irrigation and transferring pasture management to communities, have had limited impact, because the water users' associations and pasture user unions have had difficulty collecting fees from members, and require further support if they are to succeed.

The results from rapid reform were not as good as anticipated. Even though the economy began to register positive growth in 1997 (table 2.3), inequality increased and poverty was widespread. The major source of the economic problems was the failure to create an environment in which market forces could produce socially desirable outcomes. Despite formal progress in establishing the rule of law and other market-supporting institutions, in practice market-unfriendly institutions such as the importance of personal contacts and the ubiquity of corruption dominated.[5] In the public sector, the initially tolerant president resorted to ruling by decree when he encountered obstacles in the mid-1990s. Subsequent elections, while not as outrageously manipulated as elsewhere in Central Asia, were not fair.

The general problem in the 1990s was lack of preparedness for transition to a market economy. This was to some extent true in all former centrally planned economies, but Frunze, as the republic's capital was then known, was a particularly sleepy and backward Soviet capital. Attempting a Big Bang transition was far more fraught in this setting than in Warsaw or Prague or than in Tallinn or Moscow.[6] Licensing and certification requirements remained widespread, increasing the costs of doing business. The banking system was weak; the August 1998 Russian crisis triggered the failure of three of the four largest

5. In the 1999 BEEPS survey, on the headline measure of perception of corruption as an obstacle to doing business, Kyrgyzstan was rated the worst of the twenty transition economies covered. In the 2002 survey, which covered twenty-six transition countries, Kyrgyzstan moved up to sixteenth place on the same measure, but it still ranked below the three other Central Asian countries in the survey—Uzbekistan, Kazakhstan, and Tajikistan (Gray et al., 2004, 12). The problem worsened in the twenty-first century; in the 2013 BEEPS survey 49% of firms reported that unofficial payments were needed when dealing with public officials, up from 37% in 2008, while the percentage of firms considering the court system uncorrupted fell from 34% in 2008 to an abysmal 9% in 2013. Spechler, Ahrens, and Hoen (2017, 31–51) paint a grim picture of state capture by corrupt or criminal men using government positions for enrichment and parliamentary privilege for protection against prosecution.

6. Mogilevsky and Hasanov (2004, 228–29) provide evidence on one symptom, the legal instability. They show that the lack of experience of policymakers, administrators, lawyers, and others led to laws quickly needing redrafting, and the subsequent legal uncertainty was especially high for legislation directly affecting enterprises and business.

banks, but the fundamental problem was the banks' poor balance sheets. Banking sector assets fell from $160 million before the crisis to $90 million by the end of 2000 (Pomfret, 2004, 89), and when the banking system was restructured in the early 2000s it was dominated by foreign banks from Kazakhstan. The episode engendered widespread distrust of banks; two decades later, less than one-fifth of the population over age fifteen held an account with a formal financial institution.

The government was trapped between its desire to moderate the negative social impact of transition by limiting the decline in public spending and the need to establish macroeconomic equilibrium. In 1990–91 the Kyrgyz republic suffered from a substantial decline in transfers from within the USSR, and it had few domestic sources of funding for public spending. The extent of the real decline in public spending is difficult to measure given the hyperinflation and monetary disorder of the early 1990s, but the World Bank (2004, vol. 1, 13) estimated that, in US dollar terms, the value of public spending fell by 90% between 1991 and 2000 despite the large budget deficits.[7] The government tried to cushion the impact of reduced direct support via social policies or through indirect subsidies for state-owned enterprises and consumer goods by relaxing pricing of public services (e.g., offering discounts or by lax collection) such as district heating,[8] gas, public transport, water, irrigation, and electricity. These quasi-fiscal operations were often funded by running down assets and accounting sleight-of-hand;[9] their imputed cost, according to World Bank (2004) estimates, peaked at 17% of GDP in 1999. Understandable as such subterfuges might have been in the situation of rising poverty and general economic hardship, adding new price distortions to the economy and running down infrastructure assets were neither desirable nor sustainable.

International aid to the Kyrgyz Republic between 1992 and 2000 amounted to $1.7 billion, about one-fifth in grants and four-fifths in loans. Assistance started to increase when the Kyrgyz Republic established itself in 1993–94 as a leading economic reformer and relatively liberal country, with an urbane

7. The general budget deficit was reduced from a peak of 17% of GDP in 1995 to 9% in 1996, although it edged back up to 10–11% of GDP in 1999–2000 (Mogilevsky and Hasanov, 2004, 227). The source of table 2.4 gives different numbers, but they follow the same pattern.

8. District heating is the supply of heating to urban buildings from a central boiler. The system inherited from the Soviet era was extremely inefficient, often running through uninsulated pipes. The best solution is to allow the system to atrophy, but there is an equity issue, as the decrepit district-heating network is increasingly left serving poor urban dwellers who cannot afford to purchase alternative sources of heating for their homes.

9. The largest quasi-fiscal operations concerned electricity provision by the state-monopoly supplier Kyrgyzenergo, which faced estimated nonpayment of around 40%. During the late 1990s, income from releasing water to the downstream countries, Kazakhstan and Uzbekistan, was treated as revenue to Kyrgyzenergo, rather than as state revenue from exporting a public resource.

TABLE 7.2. Debt Indicators, Kyrgyz Republic, 1993–2000 (Million Dollars and Percentages)

	1993	1994	1995	1996	1997	1998	1999	2000
Public external debt stock	317	435	618	750	926	1,115	1,326	1,403
Share of GDP	30%	39%	41%	41%	52%	68%	106%	102%
Public debt service	4.5	18.6	95.8	75.9	43.4	5.8	53.4	77.6
Percent of budget revenue	3%	9%	39%	28%	16%	20%	26%	31%

Source: World Bank, 2004, vol. 1, 12.

and educated president.[10] In the Soviet era, the Kyrgyz republic had become accustomed to external assistance in the form of net flows from the rest of the USSR, but a big difference post-1991 was that the assistance led to accumulated debt; even if World Bank, ADB, IMF, and EBRD loans were provided on better than commercial terms, they still had to be serviced and eventually repaid. Yet, until the late 1990s, the government acted as though the foreign aid could be used to smooth out the consumption shock from transition and the dissolution of the USSR, without worrying about investing the funds to generate the foreign exchange earnings necessary to repay them. Access to soft loans from multilateral institutions reduced the pressure to bring current revenues in line with expenditures, and only around the turn of the century did the government become seriously concerned about the accumulation of external debt, which by 1999 exceeded 100% of GDP, the highest in Central Asia (table 7.2).

The aftermath of the 1998–99 banking crisis saw an apparent slowdown in major reforms, but more importantly the government addressed the underlying macroeconomic imbalances. Between 1999 and 2001 the general government deficit was reduced from 11% of GDP to 5% of GDP, and the quasi-fiscal deficit was reduced from an estimated 16% to 7% of GDP (World Bank, 2004, vol. I, 10). The latter was associated with some structural reform, especially in energy supply.[11] The crisis was followed by currency depreciation, import

10. During the second half of the decade annual aid flows averaged about $50–60 per head of population, which is high by international standards. Over half of the aid came from the major multilateral agencies: the World Bank provided 23%, the Asian Development Bank 15%, IMF 15%, and EBRD 5%. The major bilateral donors were Japan (15% of the total) and Germany, Switzerland, and the EU (each 4%).

11. Electricity tariffs were increased by over a fifth in each year from 2000 to 2002, and at the same time the number of users eligible for special tariff reductions was reduced and the tariff structure was modified to mitigate the impact on the poor. Nevertheless, the average billed tariff in 2002 was still no more than half of the cost-recovery level (Pomfret, 2004, 96). In 2001, the government divided Kyrgyzenergo into a generating company, a transmission company, and four distribution companies in order to increase transparency, and the subsequent increase in aggregate reported losses highlighted the complexity of the preexisting in-kind collection and offsets

contraction, and fiscal adjustment in 2000–2001, scaling back of external borrowing, and a March 2002 debt restructuring by the Paris Club that reduced debt service flows for 2002–4 from 20–24% of government revenues to 9–10%, a reduction of about $111 million in current value terms. After the turn of the century, with a more sustainable macroeconomic policy, reforms were resumed, especially in areas of deregulation and reduction in bureaucratic red tape.

Economic growth was not smooth, but it was higher in 2000–2004 than it had been in 1998–99. Economic recovery was helped by robust growth in Russia and Kazakhstan. After 2000, labor migration to those two countries and workers' remittances became significant. Nevertheless, popular frustration remained strong. Although President Akayev himself was not seen to be profiting as blatantly as President Nazarbayev in Kazakhstan, members of the president's family were perceived to be benefiting financially from their political connections. The frustration also had a regional dimension in a country divided by high mountains; in the poorer southern part of the country, people complained that the political system favored northern groups closer to the president.

Although political dissent was gathering force in the early 2000s, when political change came it happened remarkably rapidly. The parliamentary elections of February and March 2005 were widely perceived as unfair because leading opposition candidates were barred. Even so, the first round on February 27 went less smoothly than expected for the president's candidates, and the second-round run-offs were more clearly marked by dubious practices. The election of Akayev's son and daughter fueled fears that the president was planning a dynastic succession, amid widespread concerns about the corrupt practices of the family. Protests began in Jalalabad on March 10, and within a week both Jalalabad and Osh, the main cities of the south, were in opposition hands. The north was initially quiet, until on March 24 crowds converged on the White House, the seat of government, and the president fled. Despite the descent into autocratic rule during Akayev's last decade in power, he remained the least despotic Central Asian ruler. By ordering that force was not to be used against the protesters (in stark contrast to the events in Andijan two months later), he ensured a peaceful end to his reign. Akayev formally resigned on April 4, 2005, paving the way for the first peaceful transition of political power in Central Asia.[12]

---

by which the distribution segments had been deprived of capital in order to focus limited funds on maintaining upstream facilities.

12. Shishkin (2013, 1–44 and 92–233) provides a journalist's vivid eye-witness account of events in the Kyrgyz Republic as they unfolded in 2005–10. Lewis (2008, 119–59), who worked in the ICG Bishkek office in 2005, emphasizes the role of criminal elements in the 2005 election and its aftermath. Both accounts highlight the growing influence in the early 2000s of the presi-

7.2. Economic Development

The transition from central planning was characterized by economic decline and deindustrialization. In 1992–95, Kyrgyzstan exported machinery and equipment, while the output of the machine-building sector declined seven-fold (Mogilevsky and Hasanov, 2004, 233), indicating destruction of the nation's physical capital stock. During the 1990s, lack of private investment, apart from a spike in 1995–97 associated with the Kumtor goldmine, reflected low domestic savings rates and failure to attract foreign direct investment beyond the single project. Starting in 1999 public investment began to increase as the World Bank, Asian Development Bank, and other donors funded the Public Investment Program, which financed spending on roads (especially the Bishkek-Osh road connecting the north and south of the country), irrigation systems, and electricity transmission lines.

The workforce declined over the 1990s. The population growth rate fell from 2.0% per year in 1979–89 to 1.2% in 1989–2001, due to a decline in the birth rate from 3.0 in 1989 to 2.0 in 2001 and to emigration. Between 1989 and 1999, 393,500 people, 8.6% of the population, emigrated. Although part of the emigration reflected a desire of ethnic minorities to move to countries where their ethnic group was the majority, much of the emigration and the decline in the birth rate was driven by economic motives. The nature of the population change meant that the share of working-age people increased, as a disproportionate number of elderly people emigrated and fewer children were born. At the same time participation rates fell, from 85% in 1989 to 79% in 1999, reflecting return to the household (some of this was involuntary because provision of kindergarten services declined) and workers commuting to jobs in Kazakhstan or Russia.[13] The official data show that despite a larger working age population in 1999 than in 1989, the numbers employed were slightly lower in 1999 than a decade earlier (Pomfret, 2006, 79).

The rise of the unofficial economy made unemployment difficult to measure. The official unemployment figures understate the number of people losing their jobs, because low benefits and strict eligibility conditions weakened the incentive to register as unemployed (Babetski and Maurel, 2002). Especially during the mid-1990s and during the 1998 crisis, people resorted to informal employment in services or street-trading, and many turned to subsistence farming as a coping mechanism. The phenomenon of urban-rural emigration may be interpreted as a correction to the overindustrialization of

---

dent's wife Mayram Akayeva, son Aidar, daughter Bermet, and her husband Adil Toigonbaev, which infuriated other members of the elite and made the family members the faces of high-level corruption; Aidar and Bermet both stood for parliament in the 2005 election.

13. Unless otherwise stated, figures in this paragraph are from Mogilevsky and Hasanov (2004).

the Soviet era or as a symptom of the relatively good performance of the agricultural sector in the post-Soviet era. Between 1996 and 2000 the only two sectors in which employment increased were agriculture and trade and catering, while employment fell by a fifth or more in industry, construction, and transport (Babetskii, Kolev, and Maurel, 2003, 502). The trade sector continued to flourish in the early 2000s, as shuttle-traders brought consumer goods from China and elsewhere not just for the domestic market but also to be shipped on to Uzbekistan where the shuttle trade was more tightly controlled (section 7.5).

Hydroelectricity accounted for 10–15% of exports, but other energy sources had to be imported. The inherited arrangement, enforced by Moscow before 1992, was that the Kyrgyz Republic released water when required for irrigation in the downstream countries, in return for which Kazakhstan and Uzbekistan guaranteed energy supplies in the winter months. These arrangements became sources of dispute after the dissolution of the USSR. As the upstream country, the Kyrgyz Republic ostensibly controls the flow of water, but its economic might is less than that of either of its downstream neighbors, and Uzbekistan has occasionally flexed its economic muscle (e.g., in cutting off energy supplies to Kyrgyzstan in the winter of 1997–98) and threatened to wield its military power.

Geographical location and landlockedness hampered economic development. Air transport was not an effective option, apart from for gold exports. For much of the 1990s the country's airports were not operational for commercial flights, and the gateway airport to the northern part of the country was Almaty in Kazakhstan. Modernization of Bishkek airport was eventually completed in 2000 with the help of a $57 million Japanese loan. The national airline was corporatized in 1998 and separated from airport management in 2001, but its fleet consisted of aging Soviet aircraft.[14]

Political differences led to frequent closures of the Uzbek border. Even the day-to-day hassle of the border crossings became more onerous, to the extent that the Kyrgyz government built a new road between Osh and Jalalabad to avoid transiting Uzbekistan, even though the new road was 100 km long and through difficult terrain while the Soviet road was only 55 km across the Fergana Valley. Relations with Kazakhstan were friendlier, but the culture of bribes at the border and along the roads meant that transiting Kazakhstan was expensive during the first decade after independence.[15] Physical connections

14. When the EU published in 2006 a list of airlines failing to meet regulatory oversight standards of the EU and hence banned from entering the airspace of any member state, the list included all Kyrgyz airlines. The December 2016 update removed some previously banned airlines, but left all Kyrgyz airlines on the list.

15. The situation improved in the 2000s, partly because Kazakh banks with assets in the Kyrgyz Republic began to lobby in Astana for reducing the costs of exports from the Kyrgyz

with China were poor, with the few roads often impassible in winter. Trade with poverty-stricken Tajikistan was largely restricted to the illicit drug trade, for which the southern Kyrgyz city of Osh was a key transshipment point for Afghan opium en route to Europe.

Internal transport was poor. The Soviet system ignored republic boundaries. Although rail connections between Bishkek and Kazakhstan and between southern Kyrgyzstan and the Fergana Valley were of local importance, most domestic transport was by road (62% of freight and 86% of passenger traffic); however, the stock of lorries was aged, and many roads were in poor condition. The major project in 1999 and the early 2000s was the Bishkek-Osh road, linking the country's two major cities, so that by 2003 the journey could be completed in eleven to twelve hours, but the priority given to building this expensive road[16] plus the paucity of total public funds for transport projects meant that little money was left for maintenance of the country's roads. In the south, the tightening of border controls hampered traffic not only between Jalalabad and Osh, but also between Osh and Batken; in both cases the most direct route crosses Uzbekistan, but border delays, especially for trucks, encouraged use of circuitous alternative routes. For Batken, the mountainous road around the Uzbekistan enclave of Sokh is so slow that the province was economically almost cut off from both the rest of the Kyrgyz Republic and from the wider world.[17]

The economy in the early twenty-first century was dominated by three major developments: the Kumtor gold mine, the country's role as an entrepôt, and increasing dependence on remittances. After production came on stream in 1997, the Kumtor mine came to play a dominant part in the monetized economy.[18] The underdeveloped structure and vulnerability of the Kyrgyz economy was illustrated by the extent to which the aggregate rate of economic

---

Republic, but more fundamental was the domestic pressure for change as Kazakhstan's economy boomed. The ADB may have provided a catalyst by making its loan for upgrading the Almaty–Bishkek road conditional on Kazakhstan curbing unofficial levies on users of the road.

16. The ADB and Japan provided $220.8 million funding for the road, but required 20% counterpart funding from the Kyrgyz government.

17. The bazaars in Batken, unlike in other towns in the Kyrgyz Republic, did not have many Chinese consumer goods for sale. A response to the tightening of Uzbekistan's borders was to improve air services from Batken in 2003–4; the flights' economic viability was helped by the deterioration of transport facilities from northern Tajikistan, whose residents increasingly crossed into the Kyrgyz Republic in order to make international journeys as the once-efficient routes via Uzbekistan became unavailable.

18. Exports of precious metals are dominated by gold; in 2013, gold exports were worth $737 million, silver $3 million, and other precious metals $18 million (Mogilevskii et al., 2015, 7). The mining industry also produces some nonferrous metals (antimony, mercury, rare earth), and there are undeveloped deposits of gold, tin, tungsten, and other metals. Coal deposits and possible oil fields remain unexplored.

growth remained sensitive to a single enterprise; when a landslide shut down the Kumtor goldmine in 2002, GDP growth dropped to zero, recovering in 2003 after the mine reopened. More threatening to the country's long-term future was the widening north-south gap as Kazakhstan's wealth spilled over to Bishkek and to the Issyk-kul resort area in the north, while the south was stuck in the slow-growing and increasingly segmented Fergana Valley. The dynamic trade-related growth was concentrated in the north (section 7.5), and the controversial US airbase close to Bishkek (section 7.4) was perceived to benefit northern interests.

7.3. Kumtor

Kumtor is one of the world's largest goldmines, with estimated deposits of around seven hundred tons. Soviet geologists determined that the low recovery rates made exploitation infeasible. The newly independent Kyrgyzstan government sought foreign developers, and in December 1992 the Canadian uranium company Cameco submitted a feasibility study based on cyanide heap leaching technology, which can profitably process ores containing as little as .01 troy ounces per ton; the estimated production costs at Kumtor were around $200 per ounce.[19] The production sharing agreement signed with Cameco in 1994 led to substantial foreign investment in 1995–97 and production began in 1997, with an anticipated life of the mine to 2021. Cameco's initial investment was $452 million, but only $45 million came from its own resources; the remainder consisted of loans guaranteed by Cameco.[20] The Kumtor ownership structure was one-third Cameco and two-thirds Kyrgyzstan. Additionally, Cameco had a $100 million development contract for the decade 1997–2007.

Although Kumtor was the most obvious sign of productive activity in the Kyrgyz Republic, there were concerns about how much it was benefiting the country. The returns to Cameco were front-loaded, as is typical of a PSA for this kind of capital-intensive operation, and domestic critics asserted that the country gained little benefit. The mine's environmental impact also came under criticism, with accusations of cover-ups following hazardous materials

19. Cameco had been founded in 1988, as a joint venture between the Saskatchewan government (62%) and the Canadian federal government (38%). The federal government floated its shares in 1991, and by 2002 Cameco had been fully privatized. According to Baxter and McMillan (2012), by 1992 the company wanted to reduce its dependence on uranium in light of the end of the Cold War and concerns about the safety of nuclear power plants.

20. Lenders included private-sector investors led by Chase Manhattan, and public-sector investors such as the International Finance Corporation, the EBRD, and the Canadian Export Development Corporation.

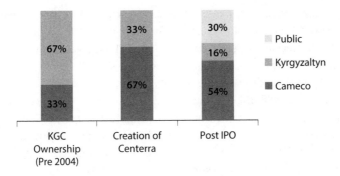

7.1. Evolution of Kumtor ownership structure in 2004. Source: Cameco Financial Statements.

spills; in 1998, a truck crashed on the road leading to the mine spilling nearly 1,800 kilograms of cyanide into the Barskoon River, two months later there was a spill of seventy liters of nitric acid, and in 2000 of 1,500 km of ammonium nitrate.

A financial restructuring of the joint venture in June 2004 created a new company listed on the Toronto Stock Exchange, Centerra; Kumtor's ownership was changed so that Cameco owned two-thirds and a Kyrgyz parastatal, Kyrgyzaltin, one-third. Cameco's interest in creating a new publicly traded company was to put a market value on their stake in Kumtor. Shortly after the Centerra IPO the Kyrgyz government sold 7.5 million shares, reducing its holding to 16% and raising C$116.25 million as current revenue. By the end of 2004, Cameco owned 54% of Centerra, Kyrgyzaltin 16%, the EBRD 4%, and other shareholders 26% (figure 7.1).

The restructuring was politically controversial in the Kyrgyz Republic, with accusations that high officials were personally benefiting. It contributed to the overthrow of President Akayev in the 2005 Tulip Revolution. After the 2005 change of power, President Bakiyev initially sought a simple revision of the 2004 arrangement to return Kumtor to a Kyrgyz-Cameco joint venture, with the Kyrgyz stake increased to 61%; this was, unsurprisingly, unacceptable to Cameco. The validity of the agreement was challenged in the Kyrgyz parliament in 2007, and in 2009 the government and Centerra reached a new agreement, which expanded the company's concession area to include the entire area under its license and simplified the tax structure governing the project. The government's ownership stake was increased from 16% to 29% by a transfer of Centerra shares from Cameco to Kyrgyzaltyn and creation of new shares, i.e. a dilution causing a one-time loss for other investors. The striking feature of the 2009 agreement was that for the first time a Kumtor deal was only reached after parliamentary approval. Nevertheless, the deal was widely seen as too favorable to the company, e.g., because its tax obligations were limited to 14% of gross revenues plus a small environmental fee ($310,000 per year).[21] Many Kyrgyz ascribed the favorable treatment to high-level corruption involving President Bakiyev's family and associates.

After resolution of the dispute in 2009, Cameco divested its ownership in a public offering of 88,618,472 shares, for which it obtained a price of C$10.25 per share, for a net return of around $872 million. The gains to Cameco over the fifteen years of its involvement included returns of $86 million in 1997–99, $641 million in 1999–2009, and an estimated net $756 million from the 2002–4 restructuring and the 2009 divestment. Cameco's total investment was reportedly $584 million, although it is unclear what share of this was loans and how much the company benefitted from the $100 million management contract.

The Kyrgyz government's net income from the project between 1997 and 2009 was $543 million, or about 20% of government revenue and 7–10% of GDP over this period (Baxter and McMillan, 2012, 21). Intangible benefits are difficult to assess. Cameco transferred skills and provided access to capital markets. There were concerns that close ties between Cameco and senior officials led to other projects being ignored, and it may also be true that the blatant corruption and physical danger surrounding gold-mining projects in the Kyrgyz Republic discouraged new investment. Projected returns to the Kyrgyz Republic between 2009 and 2021 were $850 million, although this projection is clearly sensitive to the price of gold. With subsequent discoveries, the expected life of the mine has been extended to 2026 and in 2012 the mine was estimated to contain 9.6 million ounces in proven and probable remaining reserves.[22]

The financial returns suggest that Kumtor was a project that benefited both the host country and the foreign investor. The Kyrgyz government may have been able to obtain a larger share of the pie with better negotiating of the PSA in the 1990s, but the risk was that a tougher line might have discouraged any foreign participation, as happened in Mongolia (Pomfret, 2011). Cameco took the risk of investing when major gold producers shied away.

More serious reservations are that the financial analysis excludes environmental costs or other negative externalities. The Kumtor mine has been associated with environmental disasters such as hazardous material spills and pol-

---

21. "Gold in the Hills," *Economist* (London), March 16, 2013. Mogilevskii et al., (2015, 13–14) provide more details and estimate Kumtor's effective tax rate, when all payments to the public budget are accounted for, to be 24%, which is higher than for other active foreign-owned mine companies.

22. "Kumtor Mine Reserves Increase 58% to 9.7 Million Ounces of Gold 5 Year Extension of the Life-of-Mine to 2026," November 7, 2012, at http://www.marketwired.com/press-release /centerra-gold-kumtor-mine-reserves-increase-58-to-97-million-ounces-of-gold-tsx-cg-1723106 .htm.

lution of rivers, whose full costs have never been publicized, and destruction of glaciers that affect water flows in the Aral Sea Basin (French, 2014). Additionally, the rents associated with a major gold mine are believed to have nourished corruption and undermined political institutions as well as social harmony. These are potentially major costs that underlie most case studies of resource abundance turning into a curse.

After President Bakiyev was ousted in 2010, Kumtor again became a source of controversy. In early 2011, in a series of sporadic demonstrations in the Issyk-Kul region, protestors claimed grievances over environmental damages dating back to the start of the mine's operations and criticized the company for not doing enough to develop the local economy.

The regional economic impact of Kumtor is complex. Centerra contributes to local development through employment and training opportunities, in 2013 employing 2,741 people, 95% of whom were local residents, and paying wages that are approximately ten times the national average.[23] Under the provisions of the 2009 agreement, the firm also pays 1% of its gross revenues into the Issyk Kul Regional Development Fund, an off-budget trust with few mechanisms for accountability or transparency; mismanagement of the fund has exacerbated tensions within the community and generated mistrust of Centerra.[24] On the other hand, after a careful inventory of Centerra's corporate social responsibility activities, Mogilevskii et al. (2015, 16–17) conclude that the company's voluntary contributions far exceed those of other mining companies.

Parliament responded by establishing a commission to assess Centerra's compliance with the 2009 agreement. The commission's chair, Sadyr Japarov, presented his findings a year later, and introduced a motion in the parliament to nationalize Kumtor. The motion was defeated, with most parliamentarians in support of changing the 2009 agreement, but not willing to go to the extreme of expropriation for fear of dissuading future foreign investors.[25]

---

23. "Kumtor Gold Company. Contribution to the Economy," May 13, 2013, at http://www.kumtor.kg/en/media-relations/contribution-to-the-kyrgyz-economy/ and Dmitry Solovyov, "Young Nation Kyrgyzstan Fights over Gold at Top of the World," April 3, 2013, at http://www.reuters.com/article/2013/04/03/us-kyrgyzstan-gold-insight-idUSBRE93207920130403,. The number of employees increased to over three thousand in 2014.

24. The former manager of the fund went on trial for charges of corruption. Aigul Akmatjanova, head of the Kyrgyz chapter of Transparency International, argues that the company has been too hands-off in ensuring that the funding goes to worthwhile projects despite having the right to veto selected projects (Trilling, 2013).

25. Prime Minister Satybaldiyev reassured Centerra and investors that the government had no intention of nationalizing the project and President Atambayev declared that the Kyrgyz Republic would become a "rogue state" if Kumtor were nationalized ("Almazbek Atambayev: "Kyrgyzstan Will Become a Rogue State by Nationalizing Kumtor," December 24, 2012, at http://kabar.kg/eng/economics/full/5909). Following the defeat of his motion to nationalize the mine,

A state commission led by Temir Sariev, the minister of economy and antimonopoly policy, reported in late 2012 and made allegations relating to "inefficient or improper management of the Kumtor mine regarding customs practices, tax and social fund payments, operational decisions, procurement practices and mill efficiencies." As a result, $467 million in fines were issued for alleged environmental damages, as well as for waste disposal and water treatment violations dating back to 1996. Centerra dismissed the allegations as "exaggerated or without merit" and stated that it would seek international arbitration if talks with the government broke down. In February 2013, the parliament adopted a decree giving legislators the option to invalidate the 2009 contract if the two sides failed to reach an agreement.

A memorandum of understanding between the government and Centerra was rejected by parliament in September 2013, but agreement appeared to have been reached in December. The deal let Kyrgyzstan trade its current 32.7% equity interest in Centerra for a 50% stake in a joint venture that would own and operate the mine. In February 2014, with sixty votes in favor and thirty-five against, the parliament approved creation of a joint venture splitting control of Kumtor fifty-fifty with the Canadian company.[26] The protracted negotiations reflected grandstanding in the newly strengthened parliament by parties and politicians appealing to Kyrgyz nationalism but often unclear about the goals of an agreement falling short of nationalization. The February 2014 vote, for example, targeted Kumtor control, but gave up the country's equity interest in Centerra without consideration of whether a 32.7% share in Centerra's profitable operations outside Kumtor would yield more or less revenues for the Kyrgyz Republic than creation of the joint venture. As late as April 2015, the parliament passed a nonbinding resolution calling the government's handling of Kumtor negotiations "unsatisfactory," even though parliament had acquiesced and offered no alternative nonnationalization strategy to adopt.

Public concerns about foreign mining companies exploiting the nation's mineral resources have led to violent conflict over the privatization of the country's resources and discouraged other investors. In October 2013, for ex-

---

Japarov was jailed for inciting violent protests in favor of expropriating Kumtor (Radio Free Europe, "Kyrgyz Opposition Protesters Demand Gold Mine's Nationalization," April 24, 2013, at http://www.rferl.org/content/kyrgyzstan-kumtor/24966987.html). Rejection of nationalization remained the policy despite changes of prime minster and apparent strengthening of resource nationalism in 2015 (Fumagalli, 2015, 2).

26. Cecilia Jamasmie, "Centerra and Kyrgyzstan Reach Agreement on Kumtor," December 24, 2013, at http://www.mining.com/centerra-and-kyrgyzstan-reach-agreement-on-kumtor -mine-11719/ and "Big Win for Centerra," February 6, 2014, at http://www.mining.com/big-win -for-centerra-kyrgyzstans-parliament-approves-kumtor-joint-venture-80619/. For more details and assessment see Gullette and Kalybekova (2014) and Fumagalli (2015).

ample, a crowd of about two hundred people attacked the local office of Z-Explorer, an Australian company developing a gold field in Batken province.[27] The crowd looted computers and other equipment from the company office and burned documents. The rioters protested about damage to water supplies and orchards, but the company expressed its concerns over the participation of local political leaders, presumably hoping to force renegotiation of the contractual terms. Doolot and Heathershaw (2015) argue that decentralization of political decision making after the fall of the Bakiyev regime in 2010 intensified these problems as local elites sought rents from mines but could not guarantee the security necessary for projects to go ahead successfully.

7.4. Transit Center Manas

After September 11, 2001, the USA supported its operations in Afghanistan from airbases in Uzbekistan (Karshi-Khanabad) and the Kyrgyz Republic (Manas). In 2005, following US criticism of the government after the Andijan massacre, Uzbekistan gave the USA six-months' notice to quit Karshi-Khanabad. The Manas transit center then became the main transit point for US troops serving in Afghanistan—especially after routes through Pakistan became more difficult in 2009—and a high-profile and controversial symbol of increasing US-Russia tensions in Central Asia. Rent from the airbase was a source of revenue for the Kyrgyz government, but its main domestic significance arose from public discontent over extraterritoriality and especially over corruption at the highest level of government, playing an important role in both the overthrow of Akayev in 2005 and the overthrow of his successor, Bakiyev, in 2010.

The December 2006 fatal shooting of a Kyrgyz civilian and failure to bring any person from the base to trial fueled nationalist discontent. Amid deteriorating US-Kyrgyz relations, closure of the base was announced in December 2009. However, the dispute was resolved, much to Russia's dissatisfaction, by negotiation, with redesignation from "base" to "transit center" and an increase in the rent paid by the USA from $20 million to $60 million. US-Kyrgyz relations continued to be rocky. Russia, whose own air base at Kant was not many kilometers from Manas, offered financial inducements such as debt write-offs and new project investment in return for termination of the Manas lease. As the scale of US involvement in Afghanistan wound down, the issue became less significant and the base closed in 2014.

27. Cole Latimer, "Aussie Mining Office Attacked in Kyrgyzstan," Australian Mining, October 21, 2013, at http://www.miningaustralia.com.au/news/aussie-mining-office-attacked-in-kyrgyzstan. A subsidiary of Australian-listed Manas Resources, Z-Explorer discovered the Shambesai deposit in 2010 and in 2013 received a license to develop the field, which holds estimated gold reserves of 8.8 tons.

The transit center was a voracious demander of fuel, during its life consuming over a billion gallons of aviation fuel that was mostly sourced from the Omsk refinery in Russia. The first fuel supply contract in November 2001 involved subcontracting to two companies, one controlled by the president's son Aidar Akayev and the other controlled by Adil Toigonbayev, the president's son-in-law. For 2002–7 the fuel contract was awarded to Red Star, but the subcontractors remained unchanged. After the overthrow of Akayev in 2005, President Bakiyev's son Maksim took control of the subcontracts (Toktomushev, 2015). McGlinchey (2011b, 95) reports that although Akayev's relatives made $40 million per year from the fuel supply contracts, Maksim Bakiyev was clearing $100 million per year. By 2010 Maksim Bakiyev was the most-hated man in the country.

7.5. Retail Trade and Value Chains

During the 1990s, an important element of Central Asia's international economic relations was the "shuttle trade" in which small-scale traders traveled to Turkey, China, the Gulf states, and elsewhere to buy consumer goods for resale in the bazaar upon returning home. Such trading, which was primarily carried out by women, helped many households to weather the transitional recession. Much of this trade was unmonitored and unregulated, and indeed it was lack of regulation that allowed the traders to be competitive given their small scale of operations. As governments tightened their borders or monitored bazaars more closely, transactions costs increased and the shuttle trade became less attractive by the end of the 1990s.

One consequence of the Kyrgyz Republic having adopted the most open economic system in Central Asia was that, when more organized bazaars replaced the shuttle-traders, the most important locations were in the Kyrgyz Republic. The bazaar merchants' stock came primarily from China; in 2001–13 the Kyrgyz Republic and China were the only countries in the neighborhood that were WTO members, and Kyrgyz trade barriers were low.[28] Many of the customers were from neighboring countries, and they took responsibility for traversing the more tightly regulated borders. The entrepôt trade brought substantial direct benefits as well as acting as a catalyst to other developments such as the garment and beans exports.

---

28. After the Kyrgyz Republic's WTO accession in 1998 was followed by a half decade of disappointing economic performance, many people in the region held it up as evidence of the costs of such a move. In fact, the shocks of the 1998 Russian crisis, the Kyrgyz Republic's own 2000–2002 debt crisis, and the 2002 temporary closure of Kumtor were all exogenous to WTO membership (Pomfret, 2007). The expansion of the country's entrepôt trade, on the other hand, was helped by WTO membership, especially after China also became a member in 2001.

During the 2000s the country's bazaars became major trading hubs. In 2008, the Dordoi bazaar in Bishkek employed fifty-five thousand people, with 40,300 sales outlets and annual sales of $2,842 million, of which $2,131 million are estimated to have been foreign sales (to ultimate customers in Uzbekistan, Kazakhstan, and Russia). The facilities at Dordoi included overnight accommodation and well-organized local and long-distance transport services. The smaller Karasuu bazaar in Osh (annual sales in 2008 of $684 million, of which $400–500 million went to Uzbekistan) involved mainly ethnic Uzbek traders with family connections on both sides of the border.[29]

The logistics developed around the bazaars facilitated production for export, notably the rapid growth in the early 2000s of an export-oriented clothing industry located primarily in Bishkek and to a lesser extent in Osh. At independence, textiles accounted for over 80% of light industry production in the Kyrgyz republic and clothing for 15%. Following disintegration of the unified Soviet economic space and the breakdown of supply chains, output of textiles and clothing collapsed in the 1990s. Reemergence in the 2000s was based on clothing exports to Russia and Kazakhstan of better quality items than were coming from western China and beating eastern China producers on price.[30] The clothing producers were mostly small and informal; official estimates are of exports of $170 million in 2008 falling to $155 million during the global recession in 2009, and of employment just over one hundred thousand, but the actual numbers for exports and employment are believed to have been three to four times higher. Material inputs were mostly imported, with a significant portion purchased at the Dordoi bazaar (Birkman et al., 2012).

The open Kyrgyz economy also had success in agricultural global value chains, importing know-how and inputs and benefitting from foreign intermediaries with knowledge of export markets. The Talas beans are the best-documented case.[31] Beans had been produced for home consumption by the small Kurdish ethnic community that had been moved to Talas oblast in the 1930s. Starting in 1995, Turkish firms identified beans as an export crop (Tilekeyev, et al., 2018). With the introduction of new bean varietals, primarily from Turkey, the land devoted to bean production in Talas oblast increased

---

29. Data in this paragraph are from surveys in summer 2008 (World Bank, 2009). On the operation of the bazaars, see also Kaminski and Raballand (2009) and Kaminski and Mitra (2010; 2012).

30. In contrast to the labor-intensive clothing industry, textile production never really recovered. Textiles accounted for less than a tenth of light industry production in 2010, and the largest textile firm went bankrupt in 2012.

31. Reports frequently refer to the prospects for fruit and vegetable exports from the Fergana Valley and some projects have received external aid, e.g., Swiss support for walnut forests (Ives, 2011) whose heritage was publicized by Deakin (2007). However, evidence of value chains involving such exports is scarce.

from five thousand hectares in 1999 to forty-five thousand hectares in 2012, as small-scale farmers became competitive producers supplying export markets in Turkey, Bulgaria, and Russia (Tilekeyev, 2013). A combination of forces may have been necessary to stimulate the technology transfer and investment from Turkey, but some degree of policy certainty related to WTO membership and liberal trade policies surely helped.[32] Tilekeyev uses household survey data from May–June 2011 to show that households specializing in beans were significantly better off than non-bean-producers.

The significance of the value chain lies in the emergence of many small and medium-sized enterprises offering intermediary services. Several local companies imported cleaning equipment, and they grade and pack the beans in standard 25 kg and 50 kg polypropylene bags and offer storage services. There is an active web-based market in transport services to Europe, Russia, and China.[33] By 2011 bean production generated employment for 162,000 people, and although still a minor player in the global market the Kyrgyz Republic was one of the world's top twenty bean exporters (Hegay, 2013, 25).[34]

7.6. Migration and Remittances

Despite the revenue from Kumtor and the success as an entrepôt and of nascent value chains, the economy was not providing sufficient jobs for the growing population. Growth was volatile and, compared to neighboring Kazakhstan and even Uzbekistan, relatively sluggish in the first decade of the twenty-first century. Increasing numbers of workers migrated to Russia or Kazakhstan in search of jobs. The number of people migrating for temporary work in Russia

32. Geography mattered as bean production was concentrated in two of Talas oblast's four rayons, Kara-Buura (72% of cropland devoted to beans) and Bakai-Ata (87% of cropland devoted to beans), both located between 1,000 and 1,400 meters above sea level, and with plentiful water and a hot-weather growing season (May–August); the other two rayons are lower and higher.

33. Before independence transport links from Talas went primarily to Dzhambul (now Taraz) in Kazakhstan, but by the early 2000s the upgraded Bishkek-Osh road facilitated access to inputs via the Dordoi market. Transport for exports was often arranged by internet with truckers who had space on their return journey to Europe, Russia, Turkey, or China; such logistics were facilitated by the improved road network, so that delivery to Bishkek could be complemented by pick-up in Talas for a return to Europe via Taraz.

34. On the negative side, an export-oriented monoculture exposes Talas to market volatility, especially as domestic consumption is low, and to risks of land degradation and disease (Tilekeyev, 2013, 6). Hegay (2013) reports that due to poor markets farmers do not always have access to clean seeds, and this is responsible for the spread of pathogens and declining yields. Reports in 2016–17 suggested that local authorities and others were trying to syphon off some of the bean revenues by forcing farmers to use a central marketing system, potentially creating a tragedy of the anticommons.

or Kazakhstan in the early 2000s is believed to have been around two hundred thousand to three hundred thousand, although no reliable estimates exist. In the official balance of payments, the forex inflow of remittances was $70 million in 2003, although unofficial estimates placed the figure at over $100 million; in any case offsetting the trade deficit of $76 million.

The number of migrant workers grew rapidly as the oil boom fueled demand in Russia and, to a lesser extent, Kazakhstan for unskilled or semiskilled workers on construction projects and elsewhere. The World Bank (2016b, 161) estimated the stock of emigrant workers from the Kyrgyz Republic in 2013 to be 738,300, of which 572,678 were in Russia. Other estimates are higher, e.g., up to a million by the Eurasian Development Bank research team. All should be taken with caution due to the difficulty of defining "migrant worker," duplicate counting of migrants who visit home during the year, and the fact that many migrants in Russia work illegally. Nevertheless, even the lower estimates are large for a country whose population was 5.8 million with a domestic workforce of 2.7 million in 2013 according to the World Bank *World Development Indicators*.

Remittance inflows increased to $1,223 million in 2008 before falling to $982 million in 2009, after which growth resumed to a peak of $2,278 million in 2013 (table 2.15), equivalent to over 30% of GDP, the second highest GDP/remittances ratio in the world after Tajikistan. As oil prices slid in 2014–15, remittances dropped to $1,688 million, equivalent to 26% of GDP. The recovery in 2016–17 may reflect Russia's favorable treatment of Kyrgyz workers, relative to migrants from Tajikistan or Uzbekistan, after Eurasian Economic Union accession.

Remittances appear to have been used primarily by poor households to lift their consumption above the poverty line. The National Statistical Commission has estimated that in 2012 the poverty rate using the national poverty line was 38%, but would have been 45% without remittances. More generally, and from across Central Asia, there is evidence that remittances are used to support consumption, rather than, say, investment in small businesses.

7.7. Economic and Political Developments in 2010 and After

Economic growth during the first decade of the twenty-first century was disappointing. According to World Bank data, real per capita GDP increased by a third, which was the smallest increase in Central Asia. The entrepôt-related activities and revenues from the Kumtor goldmine were an insufficient foundation for the entire economy. Tourism was growing, but slowly, and still represented less than 5% of GDP. Emigration provided a safety valve, but, when Russia was hit by falling oil prices in 2009, remittances fell sharply and men returned home, providing background to the violent overthrow of the country's second president, Kurmanbek Bakiyev, in April 2010.[35]

Unlike Akayev in 2005, Bakiyev tried to suppress the revolt by force. The security forces' response was ineffective, although sixty-eight protesters died, and the president fled first to his stronghold in the south and then to Belarus. The interim government with Roza Otunbayeva as president dissolved the parliament, and announced that elections for parliament and president would take place under a new constitution giving greater power to parliament. Otunbayeva announced that she would not be a candidate in the 2011 presidential election.

In June 2010 the most violent episode of ethnic conflict in post-Soviet Central Asia erupted in southern Kyrgyzstan.[36] There were long-standing divisions between Uzbeks and Kyrgyz in Osh and Jalalabad, e.g., violence had erupted in 1990 over access to land, but the outbreak of conflict in 2010 was sudden and violent, with over four hundred deaths and over a hundred thousand Uzbeks fleeing across the border into Uzbekistan as well as many temporarily internally displaced people (ICG, 2012, 2).[37] About three-quarters of those who died were Uzbek and the majority of buildings destroyed were Uzbek-owned in traditional Uzbek districts, although in subsequent trials most of the defendants were Uzbeks accused of initiating violence. Justice perceived as biased in favor of Kyrgyz views plus official opposition to any

35. Another catalyst was reduced electricity subsidies, which made good economic sense, but increases in electricity prices contributed to popular unrest.

36. McGlinchey (2011a; 2011b) blames the provisional government for dismissing parliament, which was the only institution in which regional powerbrokers could interact peacefully. After Almazbek Atambayev, a northerner, won the 2011 presidential election, his authority was defied by Kyrgyz nationalists in the south, such as the mayor of Osh, Melis Myrzakmatov. ICG (2012, 2) took a more agnostic stance: "The causes of the June 2010 events are complex and not yet fully understood, and there is little sign that the current Kyrgyz government is making any effort to do so." The ICG account relates the violence to Bakiyev's overthrow via conflict between Bakiyev loyalists and oppositionists in the president's hometown of Jalalabad; many Kyrgyz, who may have opposed Bakiyev, were even more opposed to Uzbeks destroying property of the deposed president's family. Pro-Bakiyev groups remained powerful in the south, many forming the Ata-Jurt party, which won the largest number of seats (28 out of 120) in the October 2010 parliamentary election, and became more virulently Kyrgyz nationalist.

37. Perceptions of whether Uzbeks are richer or less rich than Kyrgyz in southern Kyrgyzstan are difficult to verify. Using household survey data, Esenaliev and Steiner (201xamineor long-term economic devld the growth of labor migration and remittances.f the twenty-first century, the growth of trade a2) conclude that the answer depends on the welfare criteria used. They find that Uzbek households have lower per capita expenditure than Kyrgyz households, but Uzbeks in urban areas have more valuable and larger houses, and this visible evidence may drive Kyrgyz perceptions of Uzbeks being disproportionately wealthy. Lack of participation in local government decision making and lack of local budget transparency may fuel misperception.

international inquiry suggest that the sources of ethnic-based discontent have not been addressed. The October 2011 presidential election was won by a northerner, Almazbek Atambayev, who generated suspicion among southern Kyrgyz and won lukewarm support from Uzbeks in the south.

President Atambayev brought some stability by changing the egregious corruption of the Bakiyev family and associates into "a system that gives more equitable opportunities for monetary gain at least to a larger group of elite politicians and business families" (ICG, 2015, 5). The parliamentary system is dominated by "party clans" designed to benefit from the system, rather than by parties distinguished by their platform.[38] Voters select party lists rather than choosing representatives whom they expect to best represent their interests. Parties cannot be identified by religion or ethnicity, which appears to deter extremism and racism but in practice makes it difficult for Uzbeks and other groups to organize within the political system, and the composition of parliament after the 2011 elections was overwhelmingly Kyrgyz. In 2013 parliament set Kyrgyz language competency as the cornerstone of national identity, and in 2014 the option of taking the school graduation exam in Uzbek was discontinued, making it more difficult for Uzbeks to gain university admission.[39]

An external challenge to the country's economic model came from the formation of the Eurasian customs union by Belarus, Kazakhstan, and Russia (to be analyzed in section 10.2). The immediate effect was to increase trade barriers at the Eurasian Union's boundaries, including the Kazakhstan-Kyrgyz border. Some of Kazakhstan's tariffs increased as the union's common external tariff was most closely aligned to the previous tariff of Russia, but more importantly nontariff barriers became stricter and border delays lengthier. All of this had a negative impact on shipments of goods from Dordoi north to Kazakhstan and Russia, and on imports from China that had previously transited Kazakhstan.

The intention of the Eurasian Economic Union is to have free movements of labor and capital as well as of goods. At the same time, restrictions on migrant workers are being tightened.[40] The message for the Kyrgyz Republic, as

38. After the 2011 election the threshold for a party to enter parliament was increased from 5% to 7% of the vote and the deposit to enter an election was increased from five hundred thousand to five million som (roughly from $7,200 to $72,000), making it harder for a new party to challenge the incumbent parties.

39. Perceived US support for Uzbek rights, e.g., giving the 2015 Human Rights Defender Award to an Uzbek imprisoned since 2010, fueled continuing deterioration of US-Kyrgyz relations (ICG, 2015, 8).

40. From January 1, 2015 Russia required migrants from outside the Eurasian Economic Union to take tests in Russian language and history, while the fee for work permits in Moscow was tripled ("Contagion," *Economist* (London), January 17, 2015). The article quotes Talant Sultanov, director of the Kyrgyz National Institute for Strategic Studies, as saying, "The old model

well as for Tajikistan and Armenia, was that remittances would plummet if they remained outside the Union. Within the Kyrgyz Republic, and in outside reports on the issue, the Union is generally expected to have negative economic consequences compared to the recent past,[41] but Russia is saying that the recent past is no longer an option. The Kyrgyz Republic formally acceded to the Eurasian Economic Union in August 2015.

Russia also offered positive inducements for closer ties. Under 2012 agreements, Russia's UES was to build the Kambarata Dam at a cost of $2 billion, and RusHydro was to build the smaller Upper Naryn Cascade. In April 2014, Gazprom purchased the Kyrgyz state gas company and gas network for a symbolic $1, guaranteeing stable supplies and spending $609 million over five years to upgrade of the country's energy infrastructure, as well as assuming Kyrgyzgaz's debt. Such moves exacerbated tensions between the Kyrgyz Republic and Uzbekistan, which opposed dam projects and fears increased Russian presence in Central Asia.

Among Kyrgyz, there is concern about the ability of Russian companies to deliver on commitments, and about the potential for Russia to use promised investments for political ends, e.g., a $1.7 billion credit for Kambarata-1 promised in 2009 was withdrawn when President Bakiyev failed to terminate US use of the Manas transit center. In January 2016, Kyrgyzstan's parliament voted overwhelmingly to cancel the construction deals with the Russian companies, citing lack of progress in work, although unilateral cancellation of the dam deals left the country with a $37 million bill. In April 2016 Kyrgyz deputy prime minister Oleg Pankratov met with representatives of China's State Power Investment Corporation to discuss plans to build a cascade of four hydropower stations on the Naryn River, expected to generate around 4.6 billion KwH annually—more than either of the canceled Russian projects. The Kyrgyz government continues to court Chinese involvement in the country, e.g., in "link D" to the Turkmenistan-China gas pipeline and a proposed rail link between Osh and Kashgar.

7.8. Conclusions

The Kyrgyz Republic is the most liberal Central Asian state, and the openness of the society is in stark contrast to that of Uzbekistan or Turkmenistan. This has also meant that better and more reliable information is available for the Kyrgyz Republic, which makes it the most analyzed of Central Asian transition

---

does not work any more," and Prime Minister Djoomart Otorbaev as stating there is "no alternative" to joining the Union.

41. The World Bank (2014) forecasted that joining the EAEU in 2015 would hurt the Kyrgyz tailors by increasing the price of their imported inputs.

economies. Some phenomena, such as resurgence of infectious diseases, are not necessarily absent from other countries, but their extent elsewhere may be either deliberately suppressed or simply undocumented.

The Kyrgyz Republic also has a relatively free market economy, matched only by that of much richer Kazakhstan. Despite the reform slowdown around the turn of the century and the institutional shortcomings emphasized in this chapter, the Kyrgyz Republic developed vibrant markets. The two largest bazaars, Dordoi in Bishkek and Kara-Suu near Osh, cater not only to domestic customers but are also entrepôts where Uzbekistan's citizens come to buy imported consumer goods unavailable in their own country. Tajikistan's citizens cross the border into Batken, despite it being the poorest province in the Kyrgyz Republic with the worst stocked markets, to do their shopping or to catch flights to the outside world.

The Kyrgyz Republic and Tajikistan started independent life with the most difficult initial conditions of all Soviet successor states. They were resource-poor and landlocked, and a significant percentage of the better-educated were from ethnic groups who were likely to emigrate. Despite internal peace and generally good policies, the economic performance of the Kyrgyz Republic during the 1990s was awful, as living standards were eroded, both in terms of consumption levels and the availability of social support, education, and health services. In Central Asia only the truly desperate situation in Tajikistan was worse.

Emigration of Slavs and Germans after the dissolution of the USSR left the formerly heavily Europeanized north more Kyrgyz in ethnic composition, but economic developments have tied the north more closely to Kazakhstan. Among the foreign investment inflows after the recovery from the 1998 crisis were not only the Kazakhstan banks, which now dominate the banking sector, but also investors in the Issyk-Kul resort area, which increasingly caters to Kazakh tourists. The links between the northern part of the Kyrgyz Republic and the Almaty and Jambyl regions of Kazakhstan were threatened by the Eurasian customs union, but are likely to strengthen following Kyrgyz accession to the Eurasian Economic Union. The south is less changed since independence, remaining much poorer than the north and with a deep post-2010 cleavage between the Kyrgyz and Uzbek population, but the south is increasingly disaffected due to perceived neglect by the northern elite, which dominates the country's politics. Poverty and a deep regional schism create a political tinderbox, even though the country's economic policies have been the best in the region.

The 2010 constitutional reform limited the power of the president by increasing accountability to parliament. The parliament elected in 2011 immediately went on a spending spree as members authorized use of public policy for one another's pet projects. When there were debates, the parliament split along geographical lines or by personal ties rather than by parties with national programs. Some parliamentarians took populist positions, e.g., on Kumtor and resource nationalism or on strengthening the status of the Kyrgyz language, rather than engaging in substantive debate. Nevertheless, the rough balancing of power within the parliamentary regime brought stability such that by the mid-2010s investment was picking up, most visibly in a construction boom in Bishkek.

The country's physical infrastructure has also gradually improved, with help from international financial institutions and bilateral donors, most recently in Chinese road construction. The road from Bishkek to Naryn and on to Torugart at China's border, for example, is now a mostly four-lane all-year highway. One consequence is the increased traffic of Chinese trucks from Kashgar to Bishkek, avoiding the need to transit Kazakhstan. Another response has been the flourishing of the At-Bashy bazaar, halfway between Naryn and Torugart and near the Silk Road fortress of Tash-Rabat, as a new entrepôt where Chinese goods are traded alongside a traditional livestock market.[42]

Overall, the record is a mixture of greater economic and political freedom than elsewhere in Central Asia, but continuing high corruption and pervasive clientelism as well as increasing Kyrgyz chauvinism. Economic performance in the twenty-first century has been disappointing, compared to high hopes from the rapid reform of the 1990s. Reforms as drastic as creating a new system from the ashes of central planning may take time to have an impact. The fundamental reforms of agriculture between 1992 and 2003, relatively good macroeconomic policies, and ease of doing business may only reap returns when a generation without memory of the centrally planned economy and with horizons beyond local rent-seeking options becomes the entrepreneurs. The confidence-driven boom since the mid-2010s may be a harbinger of such a change. The Kyrgyz Republic remains bound by the actions of its far larger neighbors; joining the Eurasian Economic Union may not have been a happy decision, but China's road-building, construction of a spur from the Turkmenistan-Xinjiang gas pipeline to the Kyrgyz Republic (Line D), and promise of a railroad through southern Kyrgyz Republic to Osh and the Fergana Valley could all be helpful in opening up new activities and passed-by regions.[43]

42. The government has established a logistical center at At-Bashy, which helps local firms to become formal and to export. Although still far smaller than Dordoi, At-Bashy represents an alternative that will become more attractive if importers from China continue to experience problems transiting Kazakhstan.

43. The railroad is controversial because funding is unclear. If the Kyrgyz Republic takes a loan to finance the railroad and revenues do not cover the cost of servicing the loan, then the country could experience a second debt crisis (see section 11.1 for further discussion).

8

Tajikistan

Tajikistan is the only Central Asian country whose political transition from Soviet republic to independent nation was not peaceful. Open civil war in 1992–93 simmered on for several years before peace negotiations led to the June 1997 Agreement on Peace and National Reconciliation. During this period about fifty thousand to one hundred thousand people lost their lives and over half a million people were displaced as a result of warfare, mostly in the hot-war period of 1992–93 when atrocities were committed by all sides. Even after the peace agreement the central government did not have full control over the territory, and until 2001 bandits were operating within 50 km of the capital city. Between 2001 and 2007 President Rakhmonov stabilized his power, creating a powerful presidency with limited opposition much as in the other Central Asian countries, but it had taken a decade longer in Tajikistan.

Tajikistan was the poorest republic in the Soviet Union, with the highest proportion of underprovisioned households (table 2.1). During the 1990s, economic progress was massively disrupted by the civil war, which completed the destruction of central planning but prevented introduction of institutions such as the rule of law and contract enforcement that are essential for a well-functioning market economy. The first serious reform program, with support from the international financial institutions, was introduced in 1996, and was partially reversed later in the year as the security situation deteriorated. Even after the 1997 peace agreement, the economy suffered from the 1998 Russian crisis and from a cruel mix of floods and droughts in 1998–2000. By the end of the 1990s, Tajikistan was among the poorest countries of the world. The rapid growth that could be expected in the recovery from civil war did not begin until 2000 (table 2.9), and Tajikistan remains the poorest country in Central Asia.

The Tajik republic was poorly integrated—both into the Soviet space and internally. The mountainous eastern half of the country, Gharm and the autonomous region of Gorno-Badakhshan, is sparsely populated, poor, and culturally distinct. The western half of the country is divided by east-west mountain ranges that separate the northern province of Sugd (formerly Leninabad) from the rest of the country by high mountains that are impassable in winter. The capital Dushanbe was predominantly a Russian city until the 1980s when rural-urban migration brought Tajiks into the city and 1992–93 when most of the Russians emigrated. The southern province of Khatlon was created in 1993 by amalgamating Kulyab and Qurgan Teppe; the latter had been developed as a cotton-producing area by major irrigation projects in the 1960s, and many workers from the poor mountain region of Gharm had been brought into the region to work on the farms that produced over half of the republic's cotton.

The only exploitable natural resource was water, which was used to irrigate cotton and to generate hydroelectricity. The main economic development in the late Soviet era was the South Tajik Territorial Project whose centerpiece is the aluminum smelter built in the final years of the Soviet Union. Since independence, production has been erratic and maintenance poor, but the smelter survives as the country's prime earner of foreign currency. The only other significant export is cotton, although output has fallen drastically since independence (section 3.5).

The dire state of the national economy in the early twenty-first century was illustrated by the increase in migrant labor, primarily to Russia where the oil boom created demand for manual workers in construction and other sectors. Much of this movement is undocumented, but at least a million Tajiks are working abroad, out of a population of seven million. Remittances became a major source of income for those remaining in the country, and the ratio of remittances to GDP became the highest in the world.

Tajikistan has enjoyed high rates of economic growth in the twenty-first century. During the recovery years 2001–4, annual growth in real GDP was over 10% and growth rates were 6–8% after 2004, apart from the slowdowns in 2009 and 2015 related to the impact of falling oil prices on the Central Asian regional economy (table 2.9). Between 2000 and early 2015, poverty fell from over 83% to about 31%, although the country has done less well in reducing nonmonetary poverty; microdata suggest that the main contributors to nonmonetary poverty are limited or no access to education (secondary and tertiary), heating, and sanitation, and that these three are the most unequally distributed services, with access to education varying by income level and heating and sanitation by location.[1]

---

1. World Bank assessment in October 2016, posted at http://pubdocs.worldbank.org/en /707131475782010877/Tajikistan-Snapshot-October2016FINAL.pdf. Some 70% of the population suffers from severe electricity shortages during the extremely cold winters (Swinkels, 2014), forc-

An ambitious National Development Strategy to 2030, announced in 2016, envisages even higher growth, 8–9% on average, to increase real GDP by 250%. The government emphasizes promotion of food security, improved communications connectivity, and achievement of the UN Sustainable Development Goals and climate commitments. To achieve these goals, gross domestic savings are to rise from 8.5% to 30.0% of GDP and the private investment share of GDP from 3.0% to 25.0%, exports of goods and services are to increase, and economic diversification is to take place. Industry's share of GDP is to increase from 12.3% to 22.0% (mainly hydroelectricity and coal) and, although the GDP share of services is to remain unchanged, services are to become more sophisticated. Export concentration in the three largest items is to fall from 83% to 58%. Attaining these goals would help expand the middle class from less than a quarter of the population to half. The cost of financing the programs needed to attain these objectives is estimated at $118.1 billion.

8.1. Civil War and Its Aftermath

The civil war that broke out as Soviet rule dissolved was a struggle for power with regional and ideological dimensions.[2] The incumbent leader, Rahmon Nabiyev, was slow to adapt to the new situation after independence, e.g., by adopting a more nationalist posture and recognizing the country's Islamic heritage as Karimov astutely did in Uzbekistan. Nabiyev was deposed in September 1992 and in November, Emomali Rakhmonov was chosen as the new leader of the Popular Front, the alliance centered on the old Communist elite. With the help of Russian and Uzbek troops, tanks, and military aircraft, forces loyal to Rakhmonov recaptured Dushanbe in December, and by the end of January 1993 the Popular Front was militarily victorious all over the country. In September 1994, a UN-monitored ceasefire was arranged, and in November 1994 Rakhmonov was elected president. The losers regrouped in northern Afghanistan as the United Tajik Opposition (UTO). Negotiations between the UTO and the government moved slowly, and were deadlocked in 1995–96. In 1995, many displaced people returned to their homes, and in early 1996 the government began to implement economic reforms, but later in 1996 renewed fighting broke out across the country. In December peace negotiations were resumed between the government and the UTO, and an agreement was finally signed in June 1997. Although the agreement formally ended the civil war, the security situation remained tenuous until 2001 when government forces killed

---

ing use of internal fires for heat and creating domestic internal pollution that is among the worst in the world.

2. See Epkenhans (2016) on the civil war, and the summary in Pomfret (1995, 98–102; 2006, 62–65). The old elite was based in Khujand in the north. Rakhmonov came from Kulyab in the south. Allied against these two regions were leaders from Garm and the Gorno-Badakhshan autonomous oblast in the east and from Qurgan-Tepe in the south.

prominent rebel leaders, and law and order was more or less restored by the end of 2001.

Between 2001 and 2004 President Rakhmonov worked systematically to reduce the power of local warlords, including those in the Popular Front who had helped to put him in power in 1992. Despite the 1997 power-sharing agreement, the power of the main religious opposition group was also undermined. By the mid-2000s the result of these political maneuvers was a powerful presidency much as in the other Central Asian countries. Rakhmonov came to power as a regional warlord, but by 2004 appeared to have reinvented himself as a national leader. In 2007, after a decree banned Slavic name endings and other Soviet-era practices, the president changed his name to Emomali Rahmon.

Liberalization of domestic prices and foreign exchange was rapid and extensive in 1992, but rather than a conscious policy of Big Bang transition this reflected loss of government control in the most severe part of the civil war. Tajikistan continued to use the Soviet ruble even after all other countries abandoned the currency in 1993, and the elsewhere-worthless Soviet banknotes ended up in Tajikistan. Macroeconomic stabilization was exceptionally slow, and inflation was still over 400% in 1994 by which time most Soviet successor states were tackling hyperinflation. A national currency was finally introduced in May 1995, but the Tajik ruble depreciated rapidly. Only after replacement of the Tajik ruble by the somoni in October 2000 was macroeconomic stability addressed seriously and inflation brought down to 12% in 2002.

Privatization was much slower than elsewhere, with small-scale privatization completed in 1999 (Umarov and Repkine, 2004, 208), and privatization of medium and large enterprises only really begun in 1998. However, much spontaneous, forced, or illegal privatization took place. In agriculture, privatization probably occurred faster than elsewhere in Central Asia because the war situation disrupted supplies to state farms. Presidential decrees authorizing privatization of land reflected both recognition of the actual situation and a way of encouraging farm production. The process of land reform in 1995–99 created *dehkan* farms as a mid-sized alternative to the Soviet system of large collective or state farms and tiny household plots, but Lerman and Sedik (2008) caution that perhaps a third of *dehkan* farms simply perpetuated the Soviet farm structure with a new name and that most of the agricultural productivity increases over the next decade were on household plots. Although acreage devoted to grains and horticultural crops increased after the land reform, the cotton sector was little affected because local governors were able to enforce cotton cultivation.

In retail trade, the main development was the emergence of new enterprises, especially the shuttle-traders whose activities were legalized in 1996 and who accounted for three-quarters of employment in the retail trade sector by 1999 (Umarov and Repkine, 2004, 210). In both agriculture and trade, however, the new production units struggled in the face of declining domestic demand and their lack of access to credit, as well as government regulations imposed on small and medium-sized enterprises.

Trade policy has been liberal. In 1996 remaining export taxes, export surrender requirements, and export and import licenses were abolished. Between 1999 and 2002 import tariffs fell by three-fifths, and in 2002 they were unified at 5% with few exceptions. In 2001 Tajikistan applied to join the WTO, although accession negotiations would last for twelve years. There was a minor reversal in 2003, when the government sought to align its tariffs with those of other members of the Eurasian Economic Community and this led to an increase in the average tariff from 5% to 7.7%.[3] In 2004, the government removed the final restrictions on currency convertibility for current account transactions.

Foreign debt was a major problem in the first decade after independence, and by 1999 it exceeded 100% of GDP. Over half of the debt was bilateral, two-thirds of which was incurred from Russia during the civil war. In December 2002 debt owed to Russia was restructured, and arrangements were also made with other bilateral creditors. Combined with faster growth, this reduced the debt/GDP ratio to 73% by the end of 2003. A larger debt-reduction step occurred during the October 2004 visit by Russian president Vladimir Putin, who wrote off a large part of the bilateral debt in return for military base rights in Tajikistan. Multilateral debt was mostly borrowed after the end of the civil war.

Output fell drastically during the civil war period, 1992–97 (table 2.3), especially for products requiring any kind of marketing chain, such as cotton, coal, cement, or commercially milled flour; the decline was less pronounced for home-consumed crops such as wheat (Pomfret, 2006, table 4.1). Especially during the war years of 1992–97, the industrial sector was plagued by outright theft (Umarov and Repkine, 2004, 202). As the country was divided under competing armies, military authority was used to sell off enterprises and equipment, and much of what was of any productive value left the country. The absence of new investment meant that any physical assets remaining by the end of the 1990s were likely to be obsolete or so poorly maintained as to be worthless.

The only significant industrial enterprise to survive the 1990s was the aluminum smelter that had been built in the final years of the Soviet era as the centerpiece of the South Tajik Territorial Project. Although production was

3. Tariffs and other taxes are commonly evaded. The extent of evasion is by its nature unknown, but under-invoicing of imports is believed to cost the government substantial loss of tariff revenue.

erratic and maintenance poor, the smelter survived as a prime earner of foreign currency and thus as the economic prize for the central government. Its significance was reflected in the share of nonferrous metals in total industrial output, which increased from 8% in 1991 to 31% in 1996 and 56% in 2000.[4] Hydroelectric power, generated from the Nurek power station just south of the capital, also remained under central government control.

In contrast, the central government lost control over the cotton sector in the 1990s. The cotton ginneries were privatized in 2001. Farmers were free to sell their cotton directly to foreign buyers, but in the two main cotton-growing regions, Khatlon (60% of output) and Sugd (30%), local officials used their control over inputs to enforce output quotas, which were sold through them at artificially low prices (Luong, 2004b, 221), raising revenue at the local level in much the same way as the central government was doing in Uzbekistan. However, in contrast to Uzbekistan, the state provided minimal support through input supply or irrigation maintenance.

Trade in drugs and weapons was rampant. The narcotics trade was related to the increased production of opium in Afghanistan, which overtook the Southeast Asian Golden Triangle to become the major producer in Asia by the late 1990s. Tajikistan became a major transit route to Russia and perhaps Europe. Initially the trade was small-scale involving poor couriers, although military leaders also used the drug trade to finance their armies. One aspect of these quasi-legal or outright illegal activities was the participation of many officials, which undermined the rule of law and contributed to the country's poor governance.

Social indicators in the Tajik republic were the worst in the Soviet Union, and they declined substantially after independence. Lower standards of education[5] and healthcare[6] provision especially hurt the poor, as the better off could afford to pay to obtain better services. Social protection measures had become

---

4. Official data from the Tajik Statistical Committee, reported in Umarov and Repkine (2004, 203). Aluminum output in the 1990s is understated because hundreds of tons were smuggled out of the country under the protection of bribed officials. The only other functioning nonferrous metal activity in 2000 was a small goldmine.

5. Many school buildings were in poor condition. A World Bank survey of 1,845 schools found that a quarter of them lacked heating and a quarter were without water supply and over a third without toilets. Preschool enrollment rates dropped from 16% in 1989 to 5.5% in 2000 and the proportion of fifteen- to eighteen-year-olds enrolled in education fell from 40% in 1989 to 23% in 2000 (Falkingham, 2004, 163). The Soviet-era curriculum was largely unchanged during the 1990s, and curriculum reform was hampered by lack of funds to purchase textbooks. The four institutions for teacher retraining were closed in 2003 for lack of funds, despite an estimated shortage of ten thousand teachers at all levels (from the government's 2003 progress report on Tajikistan's Poverty Reduction Strategy, available as *IMF Country Report 04/280*, August 2004, 30).

6. After the civil war, Tajikistan appeared to have an oversupply of hospitals, beds, and even

ineffective by the end of the 1990s, and pensions had fallen to about a third of the value of salaries. Lack of infrastructure investment or maintenance left the country exposed to natural disasters; pumping stations were clogged with silt and pipes corroded, to the extent that the poor quality of drinking water contributed to typhoid outbreaks in Dushanbe in 1997, 2002, and 2003.[7] The 1999 Tajikistan Living Standards Survey, based on the LSMS methodology, revealed the greatest inequality and the highest levels of poverty in Central Asia.

8.2. The Economy in the Twenty-First Century

Increased foreign remittances and higher prices for the traditional exports of cotton and aluminum helped to promote growth in the twenty-first century, but merchandise exports encountered obstacles due to the poor transport infrastructure and border restrictions. The physical infrastructure, massively destroyed during the civil war, was in terrible state, exacerbated by worsening interstate relations with Uzbekistan through which all international rail and much road transport must pass. There are frequently long delays at road borders, or they are closed. In winter, the road from Dushanbe to Khujand is impassible (and even in summer it is in poor shape), so that much of the overland transport between the country's two largest cities must pass via Uzbekistan. The road from Dushanbe to Khorog, the main town in the east, takes twelve to fifteen hours when the road is open. Flights between Tajikistan and Uzbekistan were suspended until 2017, and people in Khujand wishing to travel abroad often made the four- or five-hour road trip to Batken's airport in the Kyrgyz Republic. New road links to northwest China and northern Afghanistan may provide some minor relief of this constraint (section 10.3).

Nevertheless, good trade policies and improved transport infrastructure will only have a positive impact on trade flows and economic growth if the government reduces the red tape that boosts the costs of international trade. The multiple border checks on trucks entering Tajikistan include requirements of sixteen to twenty inspections and documents, some of which are little more than excuses for the inspectors to collect bribes. Failure to harmonize standards means that medicines from India or China, which have met Russian or Kazakhstan's standards, are still required to satisfy Tajikistan's standards.

The major economic prize in the civil war, Talco, is an ongoing source of rents. Control and financial performance are opaque. After a 2004 restructur-

---

trained personnel inherited the Soviet health system, but an absence of medical equipment, supplies, and pharmaceuticals (World Bank, 2000, 9).

7. Typhoid outbreaks also occurred outside the capital (e.g., in the village of Kolkhozabad 120 km south of Dushanbe more than fifty people contracted typhoid in late 2004), but these cases are less likely to make the news headlines.

ing of the company, the director and another senior official absconded, and were sued in London by Talco over claimed missing profits of $500 million. The case was settled out of court in November 2008, most likely because too many operational details were being exposed. At the time of the trial, the Norwegian company Hydro Aluminum supplied alumina to Talco, or more precisely to CDH (registered in the British Virgin Islands), which contracted Talco to process the raw materials and return the metal, which was sold back to Hydro Aluminum; the judge concluded that Hydro made a reasonable profit, and of the remaining annual net profit about $1.8 million went to Talco, $3 million in tax to Tajikistan, and $94 million to CDH.[8] Profits were boosted by very low electricity charges and guaranteed delivery by the state electricity company, Barqi Tojik. This structure seems to have been stable, with slight changes of personnel (e.g., the involvement of RusAl in 2004 was terminated in 2007 and CDH was replaced in 2008 by another BVI-registered shell company). Although the beneficial ownership of CDH and its successor is unknown, the financial arrangements were controlled by Orien Bank, which is controlled by President Rahmon's brother-in-law, and the World Bank has reported that the president was directly supervising the aluminum business.[9] Apart from the conflict with RusAl, Talco is a source of tension with Uzbekistan because of cross-border pollution from the smelter, and because the smelter is being used to justify further investment in hydroelectricity projects that are anathema to Uzbekistan.

The government hopes to promote hydroelectricity projects. Most of Tajikistan's electricity comes from the Nurek Dam, built between 1961–80 with a current generating capacity of 3,015 MW. The remainder comes from the Sangtuda-1 Dam, which became operational in 2009 with Russian investment of c. $500 million (and 75% Russian ownership) and has 670 MW capacity, Sangtuda-2, constructed in 2010–11 with $180 million in Iranian investment and 220 MW capacity, and several smaller dams.[10] The priority customer is Talco, which receives about 40% of the country's electricity.

8. Heathershaw (2013, 190) estimates that in 2005–8, a period when world aluminum prices tripled, "Talco, and thus the Tajik state, lost US$1.145 billion in revenues due to this trading scheme . . . a massive amount for a country with a GDP of just US$3.7 billion in 2007."

9. This paragraph draws on an article "IMF Blows Whistle on Tajik Corruption," in *Asia Times Online*, March 26, 2008, at http://www.atimes.com/atimes/Central_Asia/JC26Ag01.html. The *Economist* (London) has stated in "Folie de grandeur: A President with an Edifice Complex Is Screwing the Motherland," July 27, 2013, that "Mr Rakhmon personally oversees TALCO." Heathershaw (2013, 187–91) makes a similar statement about beneficial ownership and provides further details of the case.

10. Operation of Sangtuda 1 has not been smooth, with frequent allegations by the Russian owners that Barqi Tojik is not paying for its electricity and by the Tajikistan government that the company is not paying its taxes, creating a vicious circle whose driver is Tajikistan's electricity

A major public policy goal has been financing the Rogun Dam, which upon completion would be the world's highest at 335 meters, and with 3,600 MW capacity would almost double Tajikistan's electricity supply of around 4,000 MW.[11] Construction of Rogun began in 1982, but stopped in 1991 when the dam was only 61 meters high. After a flash flood in 1993 washed away the upper section, and amid the general neglect of the 1992–97 civil war, nothing remained of the $800 million construction work by the end of the century. Construction resumed in 2005 following a deal with RusAl, which included renovation and upgrading of the Talco aluminum smelter. It gained greater urgency when frequent blackouts occurred during unusually cold winters in 2007/8 and 2008/9. However, RusAl pulled out over disputes about the operation of Talco. A joint stock company was launched in January 2010 in which citizens were enjoined, or forced, to purchase shares by sacrificing part of their salary or, for students, as a prerequisite to taking exams. By 2011, two million shares had been sold, raising $170 million, but this was less than 10% of the amount required to complete the dam (Menga, 2015, 486). Work was discontinued in 2012.

The project was strongly opposed by Uzbekistan, which has closed borders, delayed border crossing, and even started dismantling rail lines into Tajikistan. The World Bank was brought into the debate when its 2012 report on *Tajikistan's Winter Energy Crisis: Electricity Demand and Supply Alternatives* concluded that Rogun offered a lower-cost option for meeting Tajikistan's electricity demand than any alternative.[12] Tajikistan hosted UN conferences on energy, and signed on to proposals such as the 2011 US New Silk Road proposal whose centerpiece was electricity exports through Afghanistan to South Asia (see chapter 10), and in which Rogun could play a pivotal role. None of this helped Tajikistan to finance the estimated $6 billion construction costs. In sum, despite the prospect of alleviating winter power shortages, pro-

---

tariff, which is among the lowest in the world (and Talco paid an even lower preferential rate until July 2014).

11. Nurek was the world's highest dam at 300 meters, until completion in 2013 of the Jinping-1 Dam on China's Yalong River. In 2005, President Rahmon contracted a German engineering firm, Lahnmeyer, to prepare a feasibility study for Rogun, but canceled the contract when the firm recommended 285 meters as the optimal height for the dam (Menga, 2015, 484). Being number one is important. In 2011 at a cost of $3.5 million, Tajikistan erected the world's tallest freestanding flagpole, at 165 meters overtaking competitors in Azerbaijan, North Korea, and Turkmenistan, but in 2014 Saudi Arabia erected the 170-meter Jeddah Flagpole to take the world record. Dams are harder to supersede.

12. By contrast, the World Bank report by Fields et al. (2013) recommended that Tajikistan's electricity problems could be resolved by a set of low-cost measures combined with a 50% increase in electricity prices. The measures include Talco doing repairs and maintenance in winter when electricity is in high-demand elsewhere and other energy-saving measures at Talco, but under current pricing arrangements Talco has little incentive to economize on electricity at any time.

TABLE 8.1. Area under Cotton, Output and Yield, Tajikistan, 1990–2010

	Area: thousand hectares	Output: thousand tons	Yield: tons per hectare
1990	304	840	2.8
1997	220	353	1.6
2007	255	419	1.6
2010		301	

Source: van Atta (2009, table 1).

viding electricity for Talco, and generating sufficient electricity for export to Afghanistan and South Asia and the increasingly favorable climate for renewable energy, Rogun appeared to be thwarted by the huge financing costs for an impoverished country. Nevertheless, in July 2016 Tajikistan's state commission in charge of the project picked the Italian company Salini Impregilo to carry out the construction for $3.9 billion, and in October 2016 President Rahmon officially relaunched construction.[13]

The cotton sector has declined dramatically from its 1989 output of almost a million tons, the twelfth highest in world. Output fell during civil war, and recovery since then has been mixed; area under cotton increased after 1997 but yield per hectare remained low (table 8.1). After privatization of cotton gins, "futurists" gave loans to farmers with the crop as collateral. When farmers failed to produce the contracted amounts, they accumulated debts and became tied to the gins (Van Atta, 2009; Hofmann and Visser, 2014, 21). Gin ownership became increasingly concentrated, with local monopolies; one of President Rahmon's brothers-in-law was reputed to control 80% of cotton deliveries, until he was shot by the president's son in 2008. State directives persist, e.g., in Sughd province 60–70% of irrigated land has to be planted with cotton (Mukhamedova and Wegerich, 2014, 14).

The first land reform laws were in 1992 and 1995, but the first land certificates were only issued to members of collective farms in 1998. In practice, management and use of land remained with the old collective farm managers. The 2002 Law on Dehqon Farms led to the emergence of private farms, but the numbers were few and implementation varied across regions; genuine individual farms became more common in the highland regions, while the

13. The project was announced and lauded on the company website at https://www.salini-impregilo.com/en/projects/new-contracts/rogun-dam.html. Meanwhile, Uzbekistan has tempered its opposition, but remains concerned about a project that could take at least six years to fill the lake behind the dam, with serious consequences for downstream countries during that period. Despite positive signs on international relations in general, President Mirziyoyev has insisted, with support from President Nazarbayev, that any dam-building must recognize downstream countries' interests.

TABLE 8.2. Remittance Inflow, Tajikistan, 2002–17 (Million US Dollars)

2002	2003	2004	2005	2006	2007	2008	2009	2010
79	146	252	467	1,019	1,691	2,544	1,748	2,306

2011	2012	2013	2014	2015	2016	2017[e]	remittances/ GDP	
3,060	3,626	4,219	3,854	2,259	1,867	2,031	41.7% (2014)—28.8% (2015)	

Sources: World Bank (2016b, 244), and World Bank Migration and Remittances database (accessed November 3, 2017).
Notes: No entries in the source before 2002; 2017 = estimate.

larger farms in lowland regions made cosmetic changes but without real restructuring.[14] The increase in individual farms was supported, at least in principle, by the creation of decentralized water management institutions, the Water Users Associations (WUAs), but in practice the WUAs did not serve all farms and were biased towards the old collective farm managers and community settlements' representatives. A striking feature of the agricultural sector, related to the international migration of working age males, was the feminization of the rural workforce (Mirzoeva, 2009; Hegland, 2010; Mukhamedova and Wegerich, 2014).

The principal symptom of economic failure is the massive emigration, especially of males seeking temporary work abroad, mainly in Russia. This started in the 1990s, partly as people sought an escape from the civil war, but it became more prominent after the turn of the century. Since many of the workers have a precarious legal status and fear repatriation, their numbers are difficult to assess, but already in 2002 estimates of the number of Tajiks working in Russia in 2002 were around eight hundred thousand, sending remittances of $400 million to their families back home—an amount exceeding the government's budget. The more cautious estimates of the World Bank (table 8.2) show the value of remittances rising rapidly as the Russian and Kazakhstan economies boomed between 2002 and 2008.

Tajik workers in Russia have been subjected to frequent crackdowns, in part due to local resentment of foreigners but sometimes as part of national policy. In November 2002, high-profile summary deportation of two hundred Tajiks by military aircraft, in flagrant disregard of the 2000 bilateral agreement on visa-free travel, appeared to be connected with Tajikistan's improved relations with the USA after September 11, 2001. The Tajik government is in a

14. Hofmann and Visser (2014) emphasize the role of geography in explaining regional variation in actual land reform, but there also seems to have been a large within-region variance depending on local governance and on personalities, and reflecting the weak central control of the country, especially before c. 2007. In 2007 the government began a process of debt forgiveness, aimed at the unpopular futurists, and the World Bank actively assisted in registering land usage.

difficult position; because so many of its citizens depend upon remittances to make ends meet, the government does whatever it can to ease the way for migrant workers, making official protests to Russia against the deportations or lack of rights for temporary workers and trying to facilitate the movement of workers, e.g., in January 2003 passenger rail fares to Russia were cut by about a sixth. The continuing importance of good relations with Russia was underlined in March 2003, when Tajikistan's government was the only one in Central Asia to criticize US military action against Iraq.

Russian influence was strengthened in 2004 by writing off $250 million in official debt in return for military bases. At the same time, RusAl invested $600 million in the aluminum smelter and $560 million in the Rogun Dam, and UES invested $250 million in the Sangtuda hydroelectric facility; these payments for a foothold in the economy's commanding heights should be seen in the context of an economy whose 2004 GDP at market prices was only a little over $2 billion. However, the foothold has at times been precarious as Sangtuda electricity is sold to the state electricity-distributing monopoly, Barqi Tojik, which has not always been able to pay, largely because Tajikistan's electricity tariffs are amongst the world's lowest; the vicious circle is completed by the Tajik tax authorities freezing Sangtuda's bank accounts for nonpayment of taxes, which Sangtuda blames on Barqi Tojik, to which the tax authority turns a deaf ear. In 2007, RusAl pulled out of Tajikistan and successfully sued Talco in Switzerland and New York, but Talco rejected foreign court rulings.

Remittance earnings can be volatile, and they fell by about a third in 2009 as the oil boom ended and the world economy stuttered. However, they quickly recovered and by 2013 exceeded $4.2 billion, equivalent to over two-fifths of Tajikistan's GDP, the highest remittance-dependence ratio in the world. How do the recipients use remittances? Using household survey data from the three LSMS waves of 1999, 2003, and 2007, Buckley and Hofmann (2012) conclude that in 1999 in the wake of the civil war remittances were a survival mechanism for poor families. In 2003 and 2007, as living standards recovered, households receiving remittances continued to use them to maintain consumption levels rather than to invest in education for their children or in setting up a small business. These findings were confirmed in later LSMS waves (Danzer et al., 2013; Gang, et al., 2017). In sum, remittances help poor households in the short run, but are not offering a pathway to long-run development.

Remittance dependence brought major social problems. The great majority of migrants are male, leaving their villages populated by women, children, and old people.[15] Boys have few role models, and may be brought up to see

---

15. For more information on the composition of migrants and their employment, see ILO (2010). In the 2007 LSMS, 93.5% of migrants were men, 76.4% of migrants were from rural areas, and over 98% went to Russia (half of them in Moscow). The median spell outside the country was

working in Russia or Kazakhstan as a rite of passage. The outcome may be satisfactory to those in power as it removes the social group most likely to protest actively against low living standards, corruption, or other sources of dissatisfaction.

Tajikistan's rapid growth after 1999, ongoing reforms, and improved internal security were all positive signs. On the other hand, Tajikistan remained the poorest country in Central Asia, with many acute problems. The economy relies heavily on earnings from aluminum and cotton exports and labor remittances. The physical infrastructure, heavily damaged by civil war, has remained in poor shape. Social collapse was highlighted by the drug problem and migration, which divide the once-strong family structure. Institutional change has been slow, and governance remains poor.[16]

8.3. Narcotics and Governance

Poverty and social disintegration contributed to a major drugs problem. With 1,400 kilometers of porous borders with Afghanistan, Tajikistan has become since the early 1990s a major transport route for opium and heroin. Before 1992 the border between the USSR and Afghanistan was fairly well sealed, but as Afghanistan's opium production increased during the 1990s, the route through Tajikistan became a major outlet for Russia-bound heroin. From 1993 to 2005 the border was patrolled by Russian troops, but there were reports that they facilitated and participated in the drug trade. For fighters on all sides in the 1992–97 Tajikistan Civil War, the drug trade provided a source of funds. Petty couriers also flourished in the wartime chaos. Even after 1997, the state's limited ability to collect taxes reduced its ability to build up costly institutions such as the army, police, and border controls (Engvall, 2014, 56).

The civil war provided a fertile ground for the drugs trade as the competing factions financed their military activities from drug money, and this continued after the 1997 peace agreement. In 2000, following a crackdown by the Taliban regime, opium production plummeted in Afghanistan, but the harvest rebounded rapidly after the fall of the Taliban regime, from 16 tons in 2001 to 3,600 tons in 2003 (equivalent to about 300 tons of heroin). This was about three-quarters of the world's opium production, and with tightened security on the borders of Iran and Pakistan a large share passed through Central Asia, mostly via Tajikistan and then the Kyrgyz Republic. Huge potential profits plus

---

seven months, and only one-fifth stayed away for more than a year. In 2011, 99% of returned migrants brought money, and 78% of those still living abroad sent remittances (Gang et al., 2017, 4).

16. The question of whether Tajikistan is a narco-state or a failed state—or both or neither—is debated in, for example, Paoli et al. (2007), Driscoll (2008), ICG (2009), Nakaya (2009), Heathershaw (2013), and Engvall (2014).

poverty brought many Tajiks into the drug trade, and as much as a third of the population is thought to have become dependent on the drug trade.[17]

The 1997 peace treaty could be interpreted as a division of spoils among the warring factions. The president himself appears to have stayed largely outside the drugs trade, focusing on aluminum and cotton for his revenue. Participation in the drugs trade provided income for regional barons and other powerful men, but also left them exposed to charges of corruption, which President Rakhmonov frequently used after 2000 to pick off rivals or powerful opponents. The removal of political and military heavyweights took until 2007, at which point Rahmon had created a single patron-client pyramid of power similar to that elsewhere in Central Asia (Engvall, 2014; Driscoll, 2008).

After 1997, the drug trade evolved from small-scale couriers to more organized larger-scale operations (Paoli et al., 2007, 966). Engvall (2014, 65) cites estimates that the annual income from drug-trafficking in Tajikistan was worth between $500 million and $1 billion, which as a share of GDP may have been the highest narcotics dependence in the world, even though Tajikistan is not a producer (in Colombia, for example, the cocaine industry never accounted for more than 5% of GDP).[18] The government's official position is strict, with heavy penalties, including the death penalty, for participating in the drug trade, but high officials are among the participants.[19] Tajikistan's authorities are considered to have a relatively good record in the number of drug seizures, but they are all small scale. Despite an estimated annual total of around a hundred tons of heroin being smuggled across the Afghanistan-Tajikistan border by around 2010, no major drug cartel has been brought to trial.[20]

17. Most of the local traffickers were paid in kind, creating about twenty thousand addicts in Dushanbe alone. Street prices, with low-grade heroin available in Dushanbe for $2 a dose, were low enough to displace vodka, but high enough to lead addicts into crime. Women and girls were especially used as couriers, because they were thought to appear less suspicious; negative consequences included increasing abuse of females at borders, criminalization of females, and transition to people-trafficking for the sex trade. Another negative consequence of the burgeoning drugs trade was the spread of HIV, whose primary mode of infection in Central Asia is intravenous drug injection. The ambivalent attitude of the authorities, who on the one hand support NGOs' distribution of clean syringes but on the other hand often treat drug-takers as criminals subject to police harassment, led to a lack of a consistent policy and uncontrolled, and unmonitored, spread of HIV.

18. De Danieli (2013, 146) gives a smaller estimate of "profit" from drugs-related operations of $200–250 million but says that "higher estimates are not unrealistic." From 2007 fieldwork, he reports prices in Afghanistan of $1,000–1,200 per kilogram of 70% pure heroin and $2,500–3,000 for 100% pure, and in Osh the prices were $3,000–3,500 and $5,500 respectively.

19. Tajikistan's ambassador to Kazakhstan was twice caught carrying substantial quantities of heroin into Kazakhstan before being expelled. During the second arrest Kazakh police found 62 kg of heroin and one million US dollars cash in the ambassador's car (Engvall, 2014, 62–63).

20. De Danieli (2011/2013) and Paoli et al. (2007). Engvall (2014) quotes an estimate by the

The flourishing of the drug trade and the multipolar power structure between 1997 and 2007 had important consequences for state functioning. The existence of networks within various ministries and within law enforcement agencies such as police, customs, military, and so forth undermined the state's ability to carry out normal tasks of government and the state's legitimacy. Positions within the civil service were openly bought, and it was widely recognized that those with any connection to the drug trade would be the most expensive, although they could be risky if the government chose to press charges. According to official sources, between 2000 and 2005 eight hundred civil servants were arrested on drug-trafficking charges, as well as more senior officials (De Danieli, 2011, 133). On the other hand, well-connected individuals were immune; in a case that received publicity when a US embassy cable of October 4, 2007 was released by *Wikileaks*, a senior antinarcotics officer was fired because he arrested the occupants of a state security vehicle carrying 60 kilograms of heroin and those arrested included a distant relative of the president.

Since 2007, President Rakhmon has wielded uncontested authority. Instead of distributing government positions among powerful figures, they are being more narrowly allocated to his family and close associates. The president seems anxious to satisfy his extended family, but also to avoid unseemly family feuds such as the 2008 killing of his brother-in-law by his son in an apparent conflict over control of cotton rents. The dismissal of his son-in-law, Amonullo Hukmatullo, the head of Tajik Railways, for embezzling $46 million reflected concerns over Hukmatullo's failure to keep his family's behavior on a lower profile; an older son was imprisoned in Russia for drug-trafficking, and a sixteen-year-old son liked showing off his guns and luxury cars—when he killed three people with his BMW, the president was reportedly furious.

President Rahmon likes to keep a low profile, but the spreading influence of his extended family is clear.[21] The following examples, as of 2014, are from Esfandiar (2014). The president's elder son, at age twenty-six, was head of the customs service and of the Tajik Football Federation (a valuable position in the corrupt FIFA). The president's eldest daughter's husband, Makmadzoir Sohibov, was head of the state procurement agency until 2011, when he moved into private business. His brother Zainullo Sohibov was head of the Tajik Cement factory, a state-owned enterprise that is the lead contractor on Rogun

UN Office on Drugs and Crime of ninety tons, or about a quarter of Afghanistan's production, passing through Tajikistan in 2009.

21. The president has two sons and seven daughters. The elder son, Rustum Emomali, is thought to be being groomed as a successor. Positions in the power hierarchy can change. In 2016, the Sohibov clan, the in-laws of the eldest daughter, Furiza, appeared to be in the ascendancy, while the Hukmatullo (previously Hukumov) clan related by marriage to another daughter was in decline. The president's wife's family, the Sadulloevs, are increasingly influential.

Dam, and another brother, Narzullo Sohibov, was deputy director of the state agency responsible for managing state property and enterprises. The president's daughter Ozoda was first deputy minister in the Foreign Ministry and her husband first deputy minister of finance. Another son-in-law, Ashraf Gulov, was consul general in Russia. The president's wife's brothers also hold key positions; Amonullo manages electricity sales in the state energy company Barqi Tojik, Hasan controls Orienbank and is involved in aluminum, cotton, and oil exploration, and Amirullo is mayor of Qurghonteppa (formerly Qurgan-tepe).

Favoring relatives is not uncommon in Central Asia and powerful or rich presidential children have become unpopular in the Kyrgyz Republic, Uzbekistan, and Kazakhstan, but the extent of the presidential extended family's grip on key positions in the government and the economy is greatest in Tajikistan. Moreover, the qualifications of many appointees are unclear, e.g., Ashraf Gulov's position as consul general in Russia, still the most important foreign posting, raised doubts about how well he would be able to represent Tajikistan's interests. If government is left in the hands of President Rakhmon's abundant relatives, not just as figureheads but in key executive positions (e.g., at Barqi Tojik), then governance suffers and the prospect of Tajikistan being a failed state increases. The considerable wealth in a country suffering widespread poverty might trigger protests, but the part of the government over which President Rahmon seems to exert effective control is security services.[22]

8.4. Conclusions

Ben Slay (2011) has argued that Tajikistan's economy is a simple one based on export of two resources: labor and water. More than half of the water used in Central Asia comes from rivers whose headwaters rise in Tajikistan, but Tajikistan is limited in producing hydroelectricity from these waters by conflict with downstream nations, notably Uzbekistan, and by difficulties of exporting electricity. Three-quarters of exports come from aluminum and cotton, both of which "can be seen as algorithms for reprocessing water" and exporting it embodied in aluminum ingots and cotton fiber. However, the value of these exports is dwarfed by the remittances sent home by migrant workers; in 2010 goods exports amounted to $1.2 billion, but remittances were roughly twice that size. With a healthy surplus on the BOP current account, Tajikistan, for all its economic problems, enjoyed growth during the oil boom and weathered global slowdowns in 2008–10.

---

22. This extends beyond Tajikistan's borders as the government has been effective in obtaining extradition of regime-opponents from other CIS countries, and one prominent critic, Umarali Quwatov, was assassinated in Istanbul.

With such a narrow economic base, the foundations for future growth do not seem solid. Although poverty has fallen, much of the population relies on close to subsistence farming, supplemented by remittances from relatives working in Russia. With deteriorating economic conditions in Russia, the remittance flow fell precipitously in 2015 (table 8.2). Although few households fell into poverty when remittances dropped in 2009 (Gang et al., 2017), the 2015 fall in remittances exposed Tajikistan's institutional frailty. Reduced forex revenues caused balance of payments pressures and depreciation of the somoni, which was met by heavy-handed regulatory changes, such as stricter enforcement of a law that payments within Tajikistan must be made in the national currency (highlighted by the publicity surrounding the arrest of ten people involved in an unlawful car sale in March 2015) and sudden closure in April 2015 of over eight hundred private exchange offices across the country. The ineffectiveness of such measures in the face of declining forex inflows and Tajikistan's limited reserves was addressed by President Rahmon firing all the central bank's senior staff on May 5, 2015 (Ishankulov, 2015). The clumsy response to a standard monetary challenge reflected the low technocratic capacity of the government after the post-independence churning of positions and clientelism.

By late 2016 the somoni had depreciated by almost 50% since the start of 2015, causing problems for the banking system. With over 70% of loans denominated in foreign currency, firms and banks faced currency mismatch risks. The ratio of nonperforming loans, which had been under 30% at the start of 2015, reached 55% by September 2016, when four banks faced insolvency. The banks managed cash-flow by limiting access to deposits and by delaying payment settlements and tax bills. In December, the government recapitalized the banks, at a cost of nearly $500 million. The episode illustrated not only the weakness of the financial sector, but also weak corporate governance and poor risk management with a high concentration of loans in construction and agriculture, and minimal identification of sound new productive ventures.

More positive views of Tajikistan's economic drivers are offered by Tilekeyev (2014), who highlights the performance of a sample of micro-, small-, and medium-sized enterprises, and by Azevedo et al. (2014), who focus on the reduction of poverty. Beyond doubt, the economy achieved overall progress in the two decades after the 1997 peace agreement. The ambitious 2030 Strategy presumes continuation of this pattern to create a middle-income economy with a substantial middle class. The challenge is whether this is possible given the constraints of the water-based economy, relations with neighbors that limit the options for exporting electricity, and most of all the state of governance in both the private and the public sector in Tajikistan.

PART III

The External Context

9

Regional Problems
and Opportunities

In 1990, the Soviet Union was one of the world's two superpowers, with an integrated economy, planned as a single unit. The trauma of the 1990s involved not only falling living standards and increased inequality and poverty, but also the disintegration of the Soviet economic space. To some extent regional disintegration in Central Asia was a corollary of nation-building, in which previously open borders were monitored and transport networks nationalized. Nevertheless, the extent of regional disintegration was viewed by national leaders as something to be reversed, at least in principle; Kyrgyz president Akayev complained in the early 2000s that he had signed over two hundred regional agreements, not one of which had any practical effect in restoring the common economic space in Central Asia.

The five Central Asian countries all remain open economies, in that trade/GDP ratios are high. In the early 1990s, the Central Asian countries' trade was heavily oriented towards CIS markets, due to inherited input and output links and infrastructure (especially pipelines and railways). However, the main exports were redirected to global markets, most easily for cotton, and more slowly for minerals and oil, and least rapidly for natural gas. By 1996, over half of the Central Asian countries' foreign trade was outside the old Soviet area. In addition to goods trade, the region is characterized by large international labor migration flows, although these continue to be primarily within the CIS.

This chapter analyzes the choices between regionalism and multilateralism. In the 1990s and 2000s, despite the actual multilateralism, only the Kyrgyz Republic joined the World Trade Organization (section 9.1). At the same time, a number of regional agreements were signed, both among the Central

Asian countries and between Central Asian countries and their neighbors, although none had much influence, until the Eurasian Economic Union was constructed after 2009 (section 9.2). High costs of international trade in Central Asia are a symptom and a cause of regional disintegration (section 9.3). Section 9.4 briefly examines three, largely noneconomic, areas of conflict that require regional cooperation. The final section draws conclusions and assesses the situation in the 2010s. Bilateral relations with Central Asia's two large neighbors, Russia and China, and other external powers are analyzed in the next chapter.

9.1. The Central Asian Countries' Trade Patterns and Policies

Before independence, the Central Asian countries had open economies, but their trade was overwhelmingly oriented to former Soviet markets and any trade outside the Soviet Union was handled through Moscow.[1] Trade/GDP ratios remain high despite adoption, especially in Turkmenistan and Uzbekistan, of import-substitution policies (table 2.12),[2] but by 1996 over half of the Central Asian countries' international trade was with non-CIS countries (Kaser, 1997, 179; Islamov, 2001,173). The lead was taken by Uzbekistan, primarily reflecting its ability to sell cotton on world markets. Kazakhstan was slower to diversify markets, unsurprisingly given its reliance on oil pipelines and mineral-processing links and its proximity to Russia, but the CIS share of Kazakhstan's trade had fallen to half in 1997 and dropped substantially further in 1999 during the export boom following devaluation of the currency. Intra-Central-Asian trade flows are very small. To some extent this is a consequence of the lack of regional cooperation and high trade costs described in this chapter, although it also reflects the similarity of the five economies, and greater opportunities for trade with complementary economies outside the region.[3]

1. In 1988, the trade/GDP ratios of the Central Asian republics were similar to those of Canadian provinces, but the provinces' trade was roughly equally divided between trade within and trade outside Canada, whereas 85–90% of the Central Asian republics' trade was within the USSR, and most of the rest was restricted to Eastern Europe and other Soviet allies (IMF, 1992, 37).

2. The decline in Tajikistan's export/GDP ratio reflects the decline of the country's traded goods sector, but the economy remains highly open and the ratio of remittances to GDP is among the highest in the world.

3. Breaking non-CIS trade down by destination country is not very interesting. Most cotton exports went to cotton exchanges in the UK or Switzerland, and the ultimate destination was unknown (and of little concern to Uzbekistan). Kazakhstan's oil also became anonymous once it left the country; in 2002, according to the IMF *Direction of Trade Statistics*, over a fifth of Kazakhstan's exports went to Bermuda.

TABLE 9.1. Average Import Tariff, 2002 and 2010 (Percent)

	2002	2010	
	Simple average	Simple average	Trade-weighted average
Kazakhstan	7.8	6.2	2.4
Kyrgyz Republic	5.1	4.7	1.3
Tajikistan	8.0	7.9	3.6
Turkmenistan	na	5.1	2.9
Uzbekistan	15.3	15.4	6.9

Sources: IMF data reported in Elborgh-Woytek (2003, 18); Mogilevskii (2012a, 9).
Note: na = not available in the source.

Trade policies, as with other elements of the transition strategy, have changed little since being established in the mid-1990s. The Central Asian countries have, in general, levied low tariffs with an average of 5–15%, and for all five countries trade-weighted applied tariffs are much lower than the simple average (table 9.1). The Kyrgyz Republic bound most tariffs at 10% as part of commitments made during WTO accession negotiations, but other countries have had higher peaks, e.g., Uzbekistan's July 1995 tariff schedule had an average tariff of 18% but included a 100% tariff on automobiles to protect the Uz-Daewoo joint venture. There have been recurring complaints of ad hoc impositions of taxes on imports that make trade policy less predictable, and countries have charged different rates for excise and other taxes on domestic and imported goods, which is in effect a tariff.

Border crossings have been temporarily closed; in the twenty-first century, the main source of tension has concerned Uzbekistan-Tajikistan border crossing points.[4] Such actions are often unpredictable and may be discovered only upon arrival at the border. Reintroduction of foreign exchange controls by Uzbekistan in 1996 and Turkmenistan in 1998 made other import restrictions largely irrelevant. When world wheat prices spiked in 2008, Kazakhstan introduced temporary restrictions on grain exports, and food security became a policy concern in several Central Asian countries. Customs officials operate with considerable discretionary power, and bureaucratic requirements impose substantial costs.[5]

4. Even after common EAEU membership was supposed to reduce border controls, the Kazakhstan–Kyrgyz border could have long delays, e.g., in the weeks surrounding the 2017 Kyrgyz election, when bilateral relations deteriorated after the Kyrgyz president accused Kazakhstan of interfering.

5. Formal health, safety, and technical requirements can be onerous. There are, of course, good reasons for enforcing some of these standards, but their complexity is in many cases an excuse for customs officials to extract bribes in return for smoothing the process. In Turkmenistan

TABLE 9.2. Status of WTO Accession Negotiations

	Applied	Member
Kazakhstan	January 1996	November 2015
Kyrgyz Republic	February 1996	December 1998
Tajikistan	May 2001	March 2013
Turkmenistan	Not applied	
Uzbekistan	December 1994	
China	1986	December 2001
Russian Federation	June 1993	August 2012

Source: www.wto.org.

Despite their participation in the global economy and multilateral trade, Central Asian governments have been cautious in accepting world trade law by joining the World Trade Organization. The main obstacle to WTO membership has been Central Asian governments' unwillingness to formally abjure the nontariff barriers to trade described above. The Kyrgyz Republic in 1998 became the first former Soviet republic to join the WTO (table 9.2). Uzbekistan and Kazakhstan also lodged applications in the 1990s, but they allowed the accession process to drag on inconclusively. Turkmenistan has not yet made a formal application for WTO membership, and is one of only fourteen UN members, mostly microstates, that have not done so.[6] The benefits of WTO membership were accentuated by China's accession in 2001 and by Russia's 2012 accession, after which WTO trade law provided a common framework for formal trade policies and dispute resolution with respect to both of the region's most economically important neighbors. Tajikistan applied for WTO membership in May 2001 and became a member in 2013. Kazakhstan finally completed its accession in 2015. Most of the practices described in the previous paragraph are illegal for WTO members, and should have ceased after countries acceded to the WTO, although it is difficult to monitor what actually happens at border crossing points.

The Kyrgyz Republic's WTO experience became a disputed element in trade policy debates elsewhere in Central Asia and in Azerbaijan. Opponents of WTO membership cited the Kyrgyz Republic's poor economic perfor-

---

restrictions can appear capricious, e.g., the 2014 ban on imports of black cars because the president found the color depressing.

6. The fourteen United Nations member countries that did not have WTO membership or observer status in 2017 were Democratic People's Republic of Korea, Eritrea, Federated States of Micronesia, Kiribati, Marshall Islands, Monaco, Nauru, Palau, San Marino, Somalia, South Sudan, Timor-Leste, Turkmenistan, and Tuvalu.

mance after 1998 as evidence of a harmful effect of WTO membership (e.g., Trend, 2003, 55–60), but there are many other explanations for the country's disappointing economic performance around the turn of the century; the 1998 Russian crisis, Kazakhstan's large currency devaluation, and the Kyrgyz Republic's banking and external debt crises were major negative shocks to the Kyrgyz economy, which coincided with WTO accession. The weakened economy failed to reap much in the way of immediate benefits from WTO membership, but it is hard to demonstrate that the Kyrgyz Republic suffered harm from accession.[7]

The benefits from WTO membership are long-term rather than immediate. WTO accession signals a commitment to abide by accepted world trade law. In this context, it is worth emphasizing that the basic WTO principles (nondiscrimination, transparency, and so forth) are good rules for any country, and the WTO's dispute settlement mechanism offers small countries some protection against abuse of these principles by large countries. The commitment together with China's WTO accession provided an institutional foundation for the Kyrgyz Republic's emergence as the entrepôt for Central Asia, described in chapter 7.

The most important benefit from current nonmembers' WTO accession would be to place all Central Asian trade on a common basis of international trade law, and potentially to separate trade from politics. WTO accession could bring further benefits by encouraging liberal policies and punishing backsliding on commitments. Such an environment would help to attract foreign direct investment, as well as making domestic investment more attractive. Without good policies and good governance, the impact of WTO membership will be largely nullified. With a positive domestic environment, WTO membership helps to ensure that a country can reap benefits from specialization and trade with diminished fear of protectionist responses in foreign markets. WTO membership would also grant some leverage to reduce existing illiberal polices in export markets, e.g., Uzbekistan would want to join Brazil and West African countries lobbying for reduced subsidies to cotton producers in the USA and EU.

Less controversial was accession to the World Customs Organization (WCO). In the 1990s, WCO membership was uncontroversial, as the WCO was a technical talking shop that imposed little requirements on members. All five Central Asian countries became members (table 9.3). In the twenty-first century, the WCO has assumed greater saliency as trade facilitation has largely

---

7. In a study of twenty-five transition economies during the period 1990–98, Campos (2004) found no robust relationship between WTO membership and the rate of economic growth, although he did find a positive effect of WTO membership on domestic reform; see also, Bachetta and Drabek (2002).

TABLE 9.3. Dates of WCO Accession

	Member
Kazakhstan	June 1992
Kyrgyz Republic ·	February 2000
Tajikistan	July 1997
Turkmenistan	May 1993
Uzbekistan	July 1992

Source: WCO website at http://www.wcoomd.org/~/media
/wco/public/global/pdf/about-us/wco-members/list-of
-members-with-membership-date.pdf.

displaced tariff reduction as the main subject of international trade policy negotiations.

9.2. Regionalism

Central Asian leaders signed many agreements during the 1990s and early 2000s to promote regional economic cooperation or restore the common economic space, but without any appetite to follow up on commitments. Despite reservations about joining the WTO, the countries' international economic relations were multilateral, selling resources on the world market to the highest bidder and importing from the most competitive supplier. Turkmenistan was the only exception, constrained by pipeline availability to export its natural gas through Russia. Notwithstanding the many declarations of intent, regional integration atrophied. The decade and a half after independence was a period of regional disintegration. The nadir came around 2005, when two reports sponsored by multilateral institutions (UNDP, 2005; ADB, 2006) highlighted the costs of regional disintegration and potential benefits from regional cooperation.

This section reviews regional organizations involving one or more of the five Central Asian countries.[8] The assessment of regional organizations focuses on arrangements within the former Soviet space, new organizations with an exclusively Central Asian membership, relations with southern neighbors in the Economic Cooperation Organization, and relations with Russia and China within the Shanghai Cooperation Organization. Other groupings involving Central Asian countries and their neighbors are based on cultural or geographical affinity (e.g., the Turkic Group, the Organization of the Islamic Conference, and the Black Sea and Caspian Sea organizations) and contain no trade mandate.

---

8. Pomfret (2009) and Laruelle and Peyrouse (2012) provide more details.

9.2.1. ARRANGEMENTS WITHIN THE FORMER SOVIET SPACE

The Commonwealth of Independent States (CIS), which replaced the Soviet Union on December 25, 1991, was conceived as a framework in which to maintain economic ties among the Soviet successor states.[9] However, in both the political and the economic spheres, the replacement of the Soviet Union by sovereign nations created tensions and conflicts that the CIS framework was unable to contain. From the mid-1990s Russia appeared to view the CIS as a vehicle for exerting political leadership in the former USSR and saw the Collective Security Treaty Organization (CSTO) as the main instrument.[10] Meanwhile, Russia showed little interest during the 1990s in pursuing closer economic ties, even with Belarus, which sought economic union, and still less with the Central Asian countries. Russia's economic weakness was confirmed by the country's 1998 economic crisis and default on foreign loans.

In the early years of the CIS many agreements to form economic arrangements were signed, but had zero impact. In 1993, Armenia, Azerbaijan, Belarus, Kazakhstan, Kyrgyzstan, Moldova, Russia, Tajikistan, and Uzbekistan signed a treaty to set up an economic union (Georgia signed some of the provisions, and Ukraine became an associate member), but neither the economic union nor subsequent proposals involving the CIS as a group made any practical progress (Sakwa and Webber, 1999, 386–90). The reality of intra-CIS economic relations was more complex. During the early 1990s, goods and people continued to pass practically unimpeded across poorly monitored national borders.

The situation gradually changed over the second half of the 1990s with the erection of formal customs posts, and by the early 2000s several CIS member states had introduced visa requirements for citizens of other CIS countries. The most important was Russia, which generally tolerated freedom of movement prior to the outbreak of the second Chechen war in 1999, but then began to view illegal immigrants as a security risk. Russian officials estimated that

9. President Nazarbayev of Kazakhstan was a key mover in ensuring that the successor to the Soviet Union would include all the non-Baltic republics rather than just the three Slavic republics. Aitken (2009) provides an account based on Nazarbayev's own recollections.

10. Between 1992 and 1994, Russia opted for a primarily unilateral solution to regional conflicts in the Caucasus and in Tajikistan. After 1994 Russia sought more multilateral approaches, but the decline in Russian power exposed by the first Chechnya conflict and the freezing of the main intra-CIS conflicts encouraged the emergence of alternative political initiatives, such as the GUAM grouping of Georgia, Ukraine, Azerbaijan, and Moldova, which came to reflect a long-lasting split. In 2014, secession struggles in eastern Ukraine meant that in all four GUAM countries pro-Russian governments controlled part of their internationally recognized territory. Georgia formally left the CIS in 2009, and in 2014 Ukraine and Moldova initiated, but did not formally ratify, legislation to terminate their CIS membership.

perhaps four million illegal immigrants were working in Russia in 2002 (compared to three hundred thousand guest workers with proper documentation). Legislation, which took effect on November 1, 2002, expanded law enforcement officers' powers to deal with illegal immigrant labor, and the position of migrant workers became more precarious.[11]

President Nazarbayev of Kazakhstan tried to deflect Russian dominance into a more cooperative structure by promoting the CIS as a formal regional trading arrangement (Kalyuzhnova, 1998, 49–50). In December 1994, Kazakhstan announced a treaty for the formation of a customs union with Russia and Belarus, which came into effect on July 15, 1995. The Kyrgyz Republic acceded in 1996 and Tajikistan in 1999 making it a Union of Five. Despite the formal agreements between 1994 and 2000, there was little implementation; the Kyrgyz Republic's president Akayev was quoted in 1999 as saying that the customs union agreements existed "on paper only" (Zhalimbetova and Gleason, 2001, 4). Indeed, members were operating in contradictory directions in terms of their actual policies; the tariff bindings that the Kyrgyz Republic agreed to in its 1998 WTO accession would for Russia or Belarus have been unacceptably low as part of a custom union's common external tariff.

Uzbekistan and Turkmenistan were more overtly resistant to Russian regional designs, and to falling too much under the influence of any multilateral organization. In 1995–96 Uzbekistan became the most prominent regional ally of the USA, and in July 1996, President Karimov was warmly received by President Clinton in Washington, DC. Uzbekistan withdrew from the CSTO in 1998 and aligned itself with the GUAM grouping. Turkmenistan, with substantial export earnings from cotton and natural gas, adopted an autarchic political position; President Niyazov prized the 1995 UN declaration of Turkmenistan's neutrality, and skipped CIS summits in 2000 and 2001.[12] President Karimov, by contrast, sought to portray himself as Central Asia's regional leader; concerns about potential Uzbek hegemony tended to push Kazakhstan and the Kyrgyz Republic, which also feared Uzbek irredentist claims to its territory, closer to Russia.[13] After President Rakhmonov emerged as the victor in Tajikistan's civil war, with military support from Russia, Russian troops remained at bases in the country and patrolled the southern border, but Ra-

11. After 2010, improvement of migrant workers' position was an important incentive offered by Russia to induce Tajikistan and the Kyrgyz Republic to join the EAEU.

12. Turkmenistan's relations with Russia were briefly revived by Russian assistance in bringing Boris Shikhmuradov, a leading dissident who had been in exile in Moscow, to trial in Ashgabat in connection with the November 2002 assassination attempt on Turkmenistan's president. However, as energy prices rose, the price paid by Russia for Turkmenistan's gas became an increasing source of disagreement.

13. There was also an older political split insofar as Yeltsin, Akayev, and Nazarbayev opposed the August 1991 coup, while Karimov and Niyazov initially supported it.

khmonov worked to reduce Russian control and in 2005 Tajik troops replaced Russian soldiers on the border.

A February 2000 agreement by the Union of Five countries envisaged a common external tariff (CET) consisting of tariff lines that were common to Belarus, Kazakhstan, and Russia with the remaining tariff lines to be set at a subsequent stage in a five-year implementation period, but by 2005 the CET covered only 6,156 of the 11,086 tariff lines identified in the union's classification system (Tumbarello, 2005, 9). In October 2000, the Union of Five was renamed the Eurasian Community and a new treaty was signed in Astana. In practice, Eurasian Community integration plans stalled in 2003, and in June 2004 Belarus president Lukashenka told the Community's general secretary that "member states have got practically nothing from the Eurasian Community." In 2005 Uzbekistan joined the Eurasian Community, and then exited in 2008.

Arrangements within the former USSR remained opaque; people still crossed some borders unimpeded, but the pattern was towards more and more onerous barriers.[14] The major exception is the evolution of the Eurasian Community since 2009, when Russia adopted a less inclusive view of CIS relations and took a more assertive stance in leading regionalism in the former Soviet space. Starting in 2010, a customs union was established between Russia, Belarus, and Kazakhstan, and in 2015 this was superseded by the Eurasian Economic Union, which formally displaced the Eurasian Community. The Eurasian Economic Union will be analyzed in the next chapter.

9.2.2. ORGANIZATIONS WITH AN EXCLUSIVELY CENTRAL ASIAN MEMBERSHIP

Between 1993 and 2004 Kazakhstan, the Kyrgyz Republic, Tajikistan, and Uzbekistan made several declarations aimed at creating an integrated economic space. The Tashkent Declaration of January 1994 and the Cholpon-Ata Treaty of April 1994 led to the Central Asian Economic Union, which evolved into the Central Asian Economic Community (CAEC) in 1998. The CAEC was viewed as a forum for resolving disputes within Central Asia, and as a vehicle for promoting collaborative projects; one initiative of the CAEC was the creation of an Interstate Central Asian Bank of Cooperation and Development, which was founded in June 1994, but it was underfunded and only granted some small credits. The CAEC had minimal impact on intraregional

14. Many of the Soviet successor states have bilateral trade agreements, but these vary in implementation and even when bilateral trade is tariff-free there is little guarantee that the agreement will continue to be observed, as for example with Uzbekistan's car exports to Russia described in chapter 5.

trade. In February 2002, the four leaders proclaimed the Central Asian Co-operation Organization (CACO) as the successor to the CAEC, but despite lofty aspirations little changed. After Russia's accession to the CACO in May 2004 and Uzbekistan's accession to the Eurasian Community in the following year, the CACO became redundant as its members were all in the Eurasian Community.

The Special Programme for the Economies of Central Asia (SPECA) was launched in 1998 with the support of the two United Nations regional organi-zations, the Economic and Social Commission for Asia and the Pacific (ESCAP) and the Economic Commission for Europe (ECE), as an alternative forum for regional cooperation. The presidents of Kazakhstan, the Kyrgyz Republic, Tajikistan, and Uzbekistan signed the Tashkent Declaration on March 26, 1998, creating SPECA, and Turkmenistan, Afghanistan, and Azer-baijan subsequently joined SPECA. The existence of SPECA is symptomatic of the proliferation of institutions for regional cooperation in Central Asia; if the CAEC/CACO had been an effective regional organization, there would have been little need for SPECA. SPECA's achievements have been limited, in part because it has no self-funding mechanism, but also due to incomplete participation. SPECA continues to exist as a forum for interstate meetings under UN aegis, but has little practical impact.

In 1997, Central Asia Regional Economic Cooperation (CAREC) was founded by Kazakhstan, the Kyrgyz Republic, Uzbekistan, and Xinjiang Au-tonomous Region of China, who were joined in 1998 by Tajikistan. Six multi-lateral institutions support CAREC countries in mainstreaming regional co-operation in the areas of transport, trade, and energy—the Asian Development Bank, which hosts the secretariat in Manila, the European Bank for Recon-struction and Development, the International Monetary Fund, the Islamic Development Bank, the United Nations Development Programme, and the World Bank. Despite slow progress after its launch in 1997, CAREC estab-lished a Trade Policy Coordinating Committee, which had its first meeting in September 2004. CAREC members now include Azerbaijan and Mongolia (since 2002), Afghanistan (since 2005), Turkmenistan and Pakistan (since 2010), and Georgia (since 2016). It is difficult to assess the value of CAREC. It has certainly been more effective than SPECA in bringing together the Central Asian countries' governments at regular meetings, probably because it oper-ates at ministerial and senior officials' level rather than at the heads of state level, but also because it has proven flexible in focusing on areas in which progress may be feasible. While much of the multilateral partners' investment under CAREC would likely have happened in its absence and CAREC has had only limited success with respect to specific goals such as promoting WTO accession, it has been successful in monitoring trade facilitation (see section 9.3) and running workshops.

Although the formal agreements have had little impact, the CAREC and SPECA organizational structures survive because the need for regional cooperation is self-evident. Transport and transit matters require some degree of regional cooperation, although the individual countries' needs vary and neighboring countries should also be involved. The Central Asian regional organizations have, however, made no attempt to coordinate trade policy, and since 2004 there has been no effective regional organization composed solely of the five Central Asian countries.

9.2.3. RELATIONS WITH SOUTHERN NEIGHBORS

The Economic Cooperation Organization (ECO) offered to the newly independent countries a regional trading arrangement that could promote a southward reorientation of their trade from the patterns imposed within the Soviet economy. ECO's founding document is the 1977 Treaty of Izmir, signed by Iran, Pakistan, and Turkey, although the organization was dormant between the 1979 Iranian Revolution and 1985. The three founding members then attempted to revive the organization by offering preferential tariff treatment to one another, but the list of eligible products was extremely restricted. In 1992, the five Central Asian countries, together with Afghanistan and Azerbaijan, became ECO members. The expanded organization contained over three hundred million people from the non-Arab Islamic countries west of India.

The ECO heads of state met frequently after 1992, and the summits typically included grand declarations. In 1993 ECO gained observer status at the United Nations General Assembly, and it was later accorded observer status at the WTO. In 1996, the Council of Ministers approved a restructuring that included establishment of a permanent ECO secretariat in Tehran. They established eight regional institutions (a trade and development bank, an insurance institute, a shipping company, an airline, a reinsurance company, a chamber of commerce, a science foundation, and a cultural/educational institute), but amidst bickering over location and funding, implementation proceeded slowly.[15] The poor implementation record is highlighted by the ECO members' failure to agree on and implement transit agreements.

Although ECO has survived, its practical impact has been limited. As with the CAEC/CACO, a fundamental obstacle to regional integration is the similarity of the member countries' economies, which all tend to be specialized on a small group of primary products (oil, gas, minerals, and cotton). Trade

---

15. The shipping company operated two leased multipurpose cargo vessels in the Persian Gulf and some ships plying the Caspian Sea, but despite being the sole profitable ECO project the shipping line ran into financial difficulties due to some ECO members' failure to make their contributions to the capitalization fund (Afrasiabi, 2000, pt. 2).

between the five Central Asian countries and their southern neighbors has expanded since 1992, but from a low base and more slowly than many observers expected. Moreover, it has done so on a nondiscriminatory basis rather than within a regional trading arrangement such as the ECO founding members appear to have envisaged in the early 1990s.

9.2.4. THE SHANGHAI COOPERATION ORGANIZATION

The Shanghai Cooperation Organization (SCO) is the only international group formed by China, and it receives extensive press coverage in China. The SCO emerged from a meeting in 1996 of China, Russia, Kazakhstan, the Kyrgyz Republic, and Tajikistan (dubbed the Shanghai Five)—intended to demilitarize borders—and the extension of the Shanghai Five's mandate at a July 2000 summit in Dushanbe. At the latter, China, Kazakhstan, the Kyrgyz Republic, Russia, and Tajikistan (with Uzbekistan as an observer) took up themes related to trade facilitation and discussed issues such as countering Islamic terrorist groups. With the extension from security issues into economic areas, the group changed their name to the Shanghai Forum and invited other countries to join them.

From 1998 to 2001 the organization evolved into a Sino-Russian vehicle for opposing US hegemony and for mutual tolerance of antiseparatist measures in Chechnya and Xinjiang.[16] In 1998–99 Central Asia divided into two opposing camps as Uzbekistan aligned with GUAM and Kazakhstan, the Kyrgyz Republic and Tajikistan joined Russia in the Union of Five and its successors. China played a catalytic role in bringing the Central Asian countries together in 2000 and 2001, in part in response to the incursion of Islamic fighters into the Fergana Valley, presenting a common security problem to Uzbekistan, Tajikistan, and the Kyrgyz Republic. At a June 2001 summit, Uzbekistan became the sixth member and the group was renamed the Shanghai Cooperation Organization. Although Russia saw the SCO as a vehicle for its leadership in Central Asia, for the Central Asian leaders, especially Uzbekistan, the SCO was palatable because of China's counterweight.

16. In 1997–98 China had been an economic anchor in East Asia and had sought closer relations with the USA, but it gradually came to resent a perceived asymmetry in this rapprochement, which brought little gain to China. After the US bombing of the Chinese embassy in Belgrade in spring 1999, China pursued a more anti-US course, embracing Japanese proposals for Asian monetary cooperation (which were opposed by the USA) and promoting the SCO (Pomfret, 2005b). Joint operations planning in 2001 represented the first cooperation between the Russian and Chinese military since the early 1960s. Russia and China were united in their support for the 1972 Anti-Ballistic Missile Treaty and opposed to US plans to revise the ABM Treaty; the final statement at the June 2001 summit called the ABM Treaty "a cornerstone of stability, peace and nuclear deterrence," and cooperation against terrorism was a major theme.

The euphoria of the June 2001 summit did not last. The SCO failed to respond to the September 9 assassination of Ahmad Shah Massoud or the September 11 terrorist acts in the USA. The decision to establish an antiterrorist center in Bishkek was postponed; SCO experts did not meet until December 2002 to discuss the rules, activities, funding, and staffing of the antiterrorist center, and in September 2003 it was announced that the Bishkek center had been canceled and a Regional Anti-Terrorist Structure (RATS) would be opened in Tashkent in 2004. Chiefs of SCO national border guard services met in Almaty on April 24, 2002, to coordinate responses to terrorism, the drug trade, and illegal migration, but there were doubts about the sincerity of such meetings when the Russian military and influential Central Asians were believed to be participating in the drug trade. Earlier in the year Chinese Foreign Ministry official Zhou Li called for a coordinated response against "the three forces" (i.e. radical Chechen, Uighur, and Uzbek organizations), but it is unlikely that China would welcome foreign troops in Xinjiang. More fundamentally the Central Asian governments did not share the Sino-Russian agenda of opposing US hegemony; after September 2001, the Central Asian governments preferred to cooperate with the USA, providing bases and supply networks, rather than coordinating antiterrorist action under the aegis of the SCO.

Despite the roadblocks, the SCO survived and has evolved. Although Russia pursues its own Central Asia strategy, primarily through widening and deepening of the Eurasian Economic Union, and China primarily operates through bilateral relations with Central Asian governments (discussed in chapters 10 and 11), the SCO has proven flexible enough to be useful to its members. The SCO is sometimes viewed as a counterweight to NATO, and joint military exercises (the "Peace Mission" war games) have been a regular feature. However, proposals to unite the SCO and CSTO or to combine the SCO's Regional Anti-Terrorist Structure with the CSTO's rapid reaction antiterrorist force have not gained traction, suggesting limits to the extent to which Russia or China is willing to commit to joint military action in Central Asia.

Mongolia was admitted as an observer at the 2004 SCO summit, and India, Iran, and Pakistan at the 2005 summit. At the fifth SCO summit in Astana in 2005, with representatives of India, Iran, Mongolia, and Pakistan attending an SCO summit for the first time, the host country president, Nursultan Nazarbayev, greeted the guests with the words: "The leaders of the states sitting at this negotiation table are representatives of half of humanity." In 2009 Belarus and Sri Lanka were granted SCO dialogue partner status, meaning they share the goals and principles of the organization, and Turkey became the third dialogue partner in 2012. Also in 2012, Afghanistan became an observer. Armenia and Cambodia in 2015 and Azerbaijan and Nepal in 2016 were granted dialogue partner status. Applications by India and Pakistan for full membership were accepted at the June 2015 summit, paving the way for observers to become members; India and Pakistan became SCO members in 2017.[17]

SCO enlargement will increase its weight, certainly if measured by population. However, expansion is reducing the Central Asian countries' role, perhaps shifting the organization to one where large neighbors discuss Central Asia or discuss issues beyond Central Asia. The SCO has sometimes positioned itself as a counterweight to Western-led multilateral institutions, especially in the wake of the financial and economic crises of 2008–10, but this involved sniping at the IMF and other institutions rather than proposing constructive alternatives.[18]

The future of the SCO is uncertain. The large member countries see a value in the organization, at least as part of their diplomatic toolbox. It could prove a useful meeting place, in much the way that Asia-Pacific Economic Cooperation (APEC) has since 1989, with possibilities for coordinated action in specific areas. However, the SCO appears to be more directed towards security or diplomacy than economic matters. Although China sometimes announces Central Asian projects in an SCO context, the projects are essentially bilateral, and the organization has no economic institutional arrangements to coordinate projects. For Russia, the Eurasian Economic Union is by far the dominant instrument for economic relations with Central Asia.

9.2.5. OVERVIEW

Table 9.4 summarizes the membership of the regional arrangements described in this section. A striking feature is the absence since 2005 of a purely Central Asian organization. The principal organizations contain powerful external countries and have their secretariats outside Central Asia: Moscow for the CIS, EurAsEc, and the EAEU, Tehran for the ECO, and Beijing for the SCO. The arrangements sponsored by multilateral agencies also have their principal secretariats outside the region, e.g., SPECA in Bangkok and Geneva or CAREC in Manila, although the agencies also have offices within or close to Central Asia (such as the UN Special Office for North and Central Asia in Almaty, or the CAREC Institute in Urumqi).

The regional arrangements have often been in implicit competition, reflecting differing and mutually exclusive political pacts. The evolving patterns

17. Iran's membership application was blocked by an SCO requirement that no new member can be admitted while subject to UN sanctions, but was revived in 2016.

18. There is an issue of overlapping fora, as Russia, India, and China are three of the BRICS (together with Brazil and South Africa), a group that also sees itself as a counterweight to the established economic powers' role in international economic governance.

have incorporated Central Asian leaders' concerns for closer or more arms-length relations with Russia and, to a lesser extent, China as well as internal competition for and suspicion of hegemonic leadership within Central Asia. Such ebbing and flowing of interest in alternative regional permutations has inhibited the institutional development of any regional organization involving the Central Asian countries.[19] Although most have had an economic content, at least in their stated goals, their economic impact was minimal before 2010 when the Eurasian Customs Union was formed.

A turning point was the gas pipeline built by China between 2006 and 2009 from Turkmenistan through Uzbekistan and Kazakhstan to western China. The project required cooperation among the three Central Asian countries and was clearly win-win for the three countries, who could export gas or earn transit fees. This reflected the growing influence of China, but was also the first major example of plurilateral cooperation among Central Asian countries. Russian attempts to thwart the pipeline or to offer an alternative were ineffective, but with its economy benefitting from the oil boom Russia was becoming increasingly assertive and exasperated with the CIS; this was reflected in Russia's 2008 war with Georgia and implementation of the customs union with Belarus and Kazakhstan that in 2015 became the Eurasian Economic Union. China's influence continued to grow, but in 2015 it was unclear to what extent China was working in partnership with Russia in the region or bilaterally with Central Asian countries or pursuing its own agenda. By 2015 the Eurasian Economic Union and SCO appeared stronger than a decade earlier. Bilateral relations with Russia, including the Eurasian Economic Union, and with China will be analyzed in the next chapter.

9.3. Why Are the Costs of International Trade So High in Central Asia?

The trade situation in Central Asia in the 1990s represented a tragedy of the anticommons, where excessive ability of official and unofficial regulators to tap the gains from trade forestalled potential win-win situations.[20] A practical example (and just one of thousands) concerned Kyrgyz onion exports to

19. Allison (2008) argues that the true aim of "virtual regionalism" in Central Asia has been to assert political solidarity, e.g., with Russia and China in the Eurasian Community or the SCO as protection against Western pressure on human rights or democracy.

20. The tragedy of the commons arises from too many people having access to a common resource, such as fisheries; each fisher has an incentive to catch as much as possible, because any individual conservation strategy will be ineffective as fish left in the water will be caught by other fishers. The tragedy of the anticommons arises when too many people have the potential to hold up an activity by levying taxes or imposing other costs. As in the tragedy of the commons, each hold-up agent will ignore potential externalities of their actions and try to maximize their own

TABLE 9.4. Membership of Regional Agreements Involving Central Asian Countries (x = Member; O = Observer; d = Dialog Partner)

	CIS	CSTO	Eurasian Community	EAEU	CACO	CAREC	SPECA	ECO	SCO
Kazakhstan	x	x	x	x	x	x	x	x	x
Kyrgyz Republic	x	x	x	x	x	x	x	x	x
Tajikistan	x	x	x		x	x	x	x	x
Turkmenistan	(x)				x	x	x	x	
Uzbekistan	x	(x)	(x)		x	x	x	x	x
Russia	x	x	x	x	x				x
China						x			x
Iran								x	O (x)
India									x*
Pakistan						x		x	x*
Turkey					O			x	d
Afghanistan						x	x	x	O
Azerbaijan	x					x	x	x	d
Armenia	x	x	O	x					d
Belarus	x	x	x	x					O
Georgia	(x)				O				
Moldova	(x)		O						
Ukraine	(x)		O						
Mongolia						x			O
Sri Lanka									d
Nepal									d
Cambodia									d

Notes: CIS: Turkmenistan and Ukraine are associate members; Georgia withdrew in 2009; Ukraine and Moldova initiated withdrawal legislation in 2014, but the legislation was not approved by parliament—in September 2015 the Ukrainian Ministry of Foreign Affairs confirmed Ukraine will continue taking part in the CIS "on a selective basis," and since then Ukraine has had no representatives in the CIS Executive Committee building.

CSTO: The Collective Security Treaty was signed by Russia, Armenia, Kazakhstan, Kyrgyzstan, Tajikistan, and Uzbekistan in 1992 and by Azerbaijan, Belarus, and Georgia in 1993. In 1999 Russia, Armenia, Kazakhstan, Kyrgyzstan, Tajikistan, and Belarus renewed the treaty, and in 2002 they renamed the military alliance the Collective Security Treaty Organization. Uzbekistan was a CSTO member from 2006 to 2012.

Eurasian Community: The treaty establishing the Eurasian Community was signed in 2000 by the presidents of Belarus, Kazakhstan, the Kyrgyz Republic, Russia, and Tajikistan. Uzbekistan joined the Eurasian Community in 2005, but suspended its membership in 2008. The Customs Union of Belarus, Kazakhstan, and Russia was formed in January 2010, and later renamed the Eurasian Customs Union. The Eurasian Economic Community was terminated on January 1, 2015 with the launch of the Eurasian Economic Union (EAEU). Armenia and the Kyrgyz Republic acceded to the EAEU in 2015.

CACO: Central Asia Cooperation Organization—successor to the Central Asian Economic Union (1994–98) and Central Asian Economic Community (CAEC, 1998–2002). With Russia's accession to CACO in 2004 and Uzbekistan's accession to the Eurasian Community in 2005, CACO became redundant.

SPECA: UN Special Programme for the Economies of Central Asia—launched in 1998 by the UN regional bodies (ESCAP and ECE), includes the five Central Asian countries, Azerbaijan, and Afghanistan.

CAREC: Central Asia Regional Economic Cooperation—founded in 1997 by Kazakhstan, the Kyrgyz Republic, Uzbekistan, and Xinjiang Autonomous Region of China, and supported by six multilateral institutions (ADB, EBRD, IMF, IsDB, UNDP, and World Bank). Tajikistan joined in 1998, Azerbaijan and Mongolia in 2002, Afghanistan in 2005, Turkmenistan and Pakistan in 2010, and Georgia in 2016. Secretariat in Manila.

ECO: Economic Cooperation Organization—founded in 1977 by Iran, Pakistan, and Turkey, dormant from 1979–85. The five Central Asian countries, Afghanistan, and Azerbaijan joined in 1992. Secretariat in Tehran.

SCO: Shanghai Cooperation Organization—successor to the Shanghai Five (1996–2000, China, Russia, Kazakhstan, the Kyrgyz Republic, and Tajikistan) and the Shanghai Forum (2000–2001), renamed SCO after Uzbekistan's accession in 2001. Mongolia was admitted as an observer in 2004, and India, Iran, and Pakistan in 2005. Belarus and Sri Lanka were admitted in 2009, Turkey in 2012, Armenia and Cambodia in 2015, and Azerbaijan and Nepal in 2016 became "dialog partners," i.e. they shared the SCO's goals and principles. Membership of India and Pakistan was approved in 2015 and confirmed in 2017. Iran's membership application in 2008 was blocked due to the country being under UN sanctions; following the lifting of sanctions in 2016, China announced support for Iran's membership. As of 2017, Afghanistan, Belarus, Iran, and Mongolia have observer status, and Armenia, Azerbaijan, Cambodia, Nepal, Sri Lanka, and Turkey are dialog partners. (Armenia, Azerbaijan, Bangladesh, Egypt, Nepal, Sri Lanka, and Syria have been reported to have applied for observer status, and Egypt, Israel, Maldives, and Ukraine to have applied for dialog partner status.) Secretariat in Beijing.

Russia. The numerous individuals with the power to levy a fee along the road from the farm in the Kyrgyz Republic to the onion market in Russia thought only of maximizing their own returns. Given that the trader has started out on the enterprise, he or she will be willing to pay the extra cost as long as the shipment retains value, but at some stage the trader will look at the total costs and decide it is not worth making a new shipment; by the late 1990s the high shipment costs across Kazakhstan made the onion trade unprofitable. When Kyrgyz onions were not exported, Russian consumers missed their onions, Kyrgyz producers swamped the domestic market driving down prices, and Kazakhstan received no transit charges; both Kazakhstan and Russia were absolute losers.

Why do these lose-lose situations arise? There is a coordination problem, because each levier of fees will not consider the effect of their combined actions. The solution in more established areas of flourishing intraregional trade is for the government to exert its influence to prevent a tragedy of the anticommons. In the 2000s the situation along Kazakhstan's roads improved, as trucks were no longer pulled over by police or at weigh-stations or quarantine check points with the sole purpose of extracting a bribe. However, once trade has been cut off for some time, it is no simple matter to restart it, because connections will have been lost and new channels to Russian wholesalers will have to be established.

A related problem arises when fees are levied or regulations imposed in differing countries, especially when information on each national set of regulations is difficult to access. This is most apparent for Uzbekistan, which is double-landlocked and hence any exports must cross at least two other countries in order to reach an ocean port, but in practice it also applies to much of the trade of the other Central Asian countries due to the nature of the inherited transport system. The problem is complicated because there are genuine reasons to charge fees for road and rail use or to regulate axle size of lorries and so forth, but, if the sum of the fees or the heterogeneity of the rules chokes off trade, then nobody benefits.

How large are the social costs of impediments to trade within the region? Measurement of something that does not happen is always difficult, and even rough estimates are hard to make when we have little idea of potential areas of comparative advantage or of the relevant demand and supply curves. The burdens of trade impediments are likely to be heaviest in markets where supply is elastic. If demand is also elastic, then even small impediments will cut trade volumes far below potential. This best describes household or labor-intensive activities, like the Kyrgyz onion farmers, underlining the regressive

---

current benefits, in this case leading to too little rather than too much of the activity taking place (Buchanan and Yoon, 2000).

TABLE 9.5. Ease of Doing Business, June 2014, June 2015, and June 2016

Country	Overall Ease of Doing Business[a,b]			Ease of International Trade[b]		
	June 2014	June 2015	June 2016	June 2014	June 2015	June 2016
Kazakhstan	77	41	35	185	122	119
Kyrgyz Republic	102	67	75	183	83	79
Tajikistan	166	132	128	188	132	144
Uzbekistan	141	87	87	189	159	165

Source: World Bank at www.doingbusiness.org.
Notes: (a) overall rank based on unweighted average of scores in ten areas; (b) 189 countries in 2014 and 2015, and 190 countries in 2016. Turkmenistan not included.

impact of trade impediments that are likely to hit the poor hardest. Apart from the basic needs of the poorest citizens, the demand for nonluxury consumption goods is likely to be more price elastic than demand for luxury goods, so that the nonrich members of the community will be hit as consumers.

The costs of conducting international trade in Central Asia are acknowledged to be high. The most frequently cited supporting evidence is from the World Bank's *Doing Business* database. In *Doing Business 2015*, the four Central Asian countries covered ranked between 77 and 166 out of 189 countries for overall ease of doing business, but they were among the seven worst places for ease of conducting international trade (table 9.5). Turkmenistan was not covered, but would probably have been lower than the other four Central Asian countries. In *Doing Business 2016*, which assessed performance in June 2015, the four Central Asian countries had moved to substantially higher ranks for both overall ease of doing business and ease of international trade.

The pictures offered for both 2014 and 2015 are misleading. The situation was not so bad as the June 2014 rankings imply. The *Doing Business* methodology is based on asking informed people in national capitals about the cost of shipping a container in dollars and in time from the country's commercial center, which may be appropriate for a country like Singapore but is less appropriate for the Central Asian countries where a small share of trade is by container and where there is a large variance between what an observer in the capital city may hear and what happens on the ground. The huge improvement in costs of international trade between 2014 and 2015 is unbelievable, although the relative position of the five countries in June 2015 and in June 2016 is plausible and corresponds to casual observation. However, the *Doing Business* numbers tell us little about the magnitudes of costs of international trade in Central Asia.[21]

21. The *Doing Business* (*DB*) indicators have come under increasing scrutiny and the trading across border component has been especially criticized for appearing to give concrete numbers

The Corridor Performance Measurement and Monitoring (CPMM) program conducted by freight forwarders under the aegis of the CAREC secretariat (ADB, 2014) produces the most convincing measures of high trade costs in Central Asia and some neighboring countries. The program has been in operation since 2010, with between two and three thousand observations each year, e.g., the 2015 sample consisted of 2,784 trips, of which 75% were by road and 25% by rail.[22] For each trip, a reporter in a truck or on a train traveling along major corridors tracks the cost and time taken. The CPMM indicators of cost and speed provide detailed information about the difficulties of conducting overland trade in the CAREC region, and the large number of observations helps to address the uncertainty and variability of costs and time.

The overall picture is that, even when the physical infrastructure is good, journeys are slow and costly with especially long delays at border crossing points (BCPs). Table 9.6 provides data for twelve road BCPs and four rail BCPs. CPMM 2015 identified the key problems for transport and transit to be lack of harmonized transit or BCP procedures with no best-practice benchmark in the region, little effective interagency cooperation and absence of "single window" BCPs, low adoption of risk-management techniques, and persistent unofficial payments. These problems reflect the poor soft infrastructure for international trade in Central Asia.

Improvements in the hard infrastructure (roads, railways, etc.) without improved soft infrastructure can only lead to limited improvement in the time and money costs of international trade. By 2012, for example, the Tashkent-Beyneu corridor (part of the E40 route to Berlin and Brussels) had been upgraded so that speeds of 100 kph were possible in parts and 60 kph on most of it (a big improvement over the Kungrad-Beyneu section, which was a rough dirt road a few years earlier), but crossing the border took on average thirty hours at the Kazakhstan BCP and fourteen hours at the Uzbekistan BCP (CPMM, 2012, 24).

In the early 2010s, delays became longer at many BCPs, apart from those between Russia and Kazakhstan, which shortened after the establishment of the customs union. The average border-crossing time for trucks leaving Kazakhstan for Russia fell from 7.7 hours in 2011 to 2.9 hours in 2012, but the aver-

---

for time and cost. Behar (2010) documented large discrepancies between *DB* estimates and numbers from the World Banks's *Enterprise Surveys,* e.g., exports from Kazakhstan took a bottom-ranking thirty-four days according to *DB,* but the response to the same question for the same year in *ES* was only eight days. Researchers continue to use *DB* rather than *ES* because the country coverage is greater and the *DB* indicators are more standardized, but *ES* are based on surveys of actual traders whereas *DB* estimates are from people who are mostly not traders such as consultancy or law firms (Sourdin and Pomfret, 2012, 26–28) and they refer to laws and regulations on the books, rather than their implementation on the ground or at the port.

22. References to CPMM data in the text are to annual reports.

TABLE 9.6. Average Border-Crossing Time in Hours, Inbound Traffic, Selected BCPs

	from–to	2010	2011	2012	2013	2014	2015
ROAD							
Khorgos	PRC/KAZ	16.0	12.7	17.3	11.2	6.8	5.8
Tazhen	UZB/KAZ	9.7	10.3	12.5	8.6	7.8	7.8
Konysbayeva	UZB/KAZ	8.2	8.7	7.8	6.8	7.5	7.5
Chaldovar	KAZ/KRG	36.9	5.1	4.9	6.6	6.5	6.5
Irkeshtam	PRC/KRG	4.5	12.0	9.9	7.2	6.1	5.2
Dusti	AFG/TAJ	8.7	5.4	4.6	5.3	5.8	5.8
Karamyk	KRG/TAJ	na	3.9	3.6	1.9	2.3	4.7
Fotehobod	UZB/TAJ	8.0	4.8	4.4	5.1	6.6	7.1
Sarah	IRN/TKM	6.4	6.5	10.5	8.8	6.1	6.1
Farap	UZB/TKM	8.6	7.8	8.5	6.6	7.3	7.1
Alat	TKM/UZB	3.7	5.3	5.8	4.6	5.3	5.4
Dautota	KAZ/UZB	3.9	4.8	12.8	6.1	5.8	5.9
RAIL							
Altynkol	PRC/KAZ				4.5	37.4	na
Dostyk	PRC/KAZ	34.5	43.6	28.3	64.8	59.7	42.3
Farap	UZB/TKM				14.5	14.9	4.7
Keles .	KAZ/UZB				4.9	0.8	5.7

Source: CPMM, 2015, 42–43.

age border-crossing time for trucks entering Kazakhstan from outside the customs union increased from 8.6 to 21.5 hours, with "waiting in queue" the biggest part (CPMM, 2012, 38–39). The longest delays were on the corridor with the highest volume of freight, the railway between China and Kazakhstan; at the border between China and Kazakhstan the average time at the Chinese BCP (Alashankou) was 353 hours and at the Kazakhstani BCP (Dostyk) 54 hours in 2012.[23] The exception to the long delays in 2012 was the Chongqing-Duisburg train (see chapter 11), which is subject to speedy gauge change and simplified border formalities. This last observation and the changes at the Kazakhstan-Russia border suggest that governments could facilitate trade, but the political will to do so for intra-Central-Asian trade has been lacking.[24]

23. Some of this is associated with the change of gauge, but delays are mostly associated with customs, quarantine, and other issues. It is difficult to allocate the time to one BCP rather than the other because delays at one BCP lead to back-up of trains at the other, e.g., delays entering Kazakhstan lead to backup at the Chinese BCP. There is a suspicion that these 2012 data are influenced by the customs union's hardline towards goods entering from China (CPMM, 2012, 21).

24. Although there is anecdotal evidence that the level and frequency of corruption has declined, the CPMM annual reports consistently find a 30–35% chance that "unofficial payments" would be demanded at BCPs. Coulibaly and Thomsen (2016) provide specific examples of unofficial payments along the main Tajikistan-Kyrgyzstan-Kazakhstan route that were paid to avoid

For road transport, major sources of delay are trans-loading, customs inspection, and waiting in queues. Restrictions on trucks crossing borders are common, whether due to bonded carrier requirements (China-Kazakhstan), to "bilateral" BCPs that third-country vehicles cannot cross (Karamyk BCP in the Kyrgyz Republic), or to requirements to offload trains from Afghanistan and ship goods by ferry to Uzbekistan where they are loaded onto trucks. Requirements for trucks in transit can also be costly and lead to delays waiting for a convoy to be formed.[25] Customs inspection is rarely based on risk assessment, and a requirement to offload the entire shipment invites bribery. Absence of single windows exacerbates the delays from exhaustive customs checks.

The principal corridor from Central Asia to South Asia is through Afghanistan. Apart from security risks, the two main bottlenecks are the BCPs between Pakistan and Afghanistan, and trucks may face lengthy delays due to convoy requirements on segments of the route in either country (CPMM, 2014, 34).[26] Road upgrading could shorten travel times, the BCPs could be better designed to separate passenger traffic from goods, and improvement in the security situation would also reduce some concerns. However, the principal source of delays is customs procedures.[27]

In the 2010s, for a conjuncture of reasons, physical connectivity of Central Asia to surrounding regions improved markedly, as some projects were implemented and even grander ones proposed (see chapter 11). The key question raised by this section is whether potential benefits from improved hard infrastructure will be nullified by the region's high trade costs. Hard and soft infrastructure are interconnected in that, as potential traders face more alternatives, there could be a race to the bottom in reducing obstacles to trade. The Kyrgyz onions case remains a stark warning of the dangers of a tragedy

---

higher official fees, e.g., for excessive axle load or breaking ecological rules, or to forestall a lengthy check, e.g., paying quarantine officials not to open refrigerator doors on a truck.

25. The TIR system is used for about a third of international road journeys, but for many hauliers it is too expensive. CAREC has proposed alternative systems, with a comprehensive guarantee mechanism open to authorized economic operators.

26. The route from Karachi to Kabul, via Sukkur-D.I.Khan-Peshawar-Torkham, has better roads than the southern route to Kandahar via Chaman and Spin Boldak. However, the segment from D.I.Khan to the border is prone to delays, and truckers report a high level of demands for unofficial payments. In 2014, trucks took an average 34 hours to pass though the Peshawar BCP, and 39.5 hours at the Afghan BCP, Torkham; at both BCPs, most of the delay was associated with customs procedures, and the queuing led to large variance in time. In 2015, following easing of the convoy requirement, at both Peshawar and Torkham average border-crossing time fell to thirty-two hours. Crossing times were longer at the Chaman-Spin Boldak BCPs, thirty-six and sixty hours respectively in both 2014 and 2015, i.e. four days and nights to cross the frontier, and security on this route is poorer than on the Kabul route.

27. The two authorities have difficulty sharing information about freight because Afghanistan uses ASYCUDA World, while Pakistan uses the proprietary Web-Based One Customs System.

of the anticommons, and Central Asian policymakers are generally more aware of these dangers and of potential gains from trade in the 2010s than in the 1990s.

9.4. Water Disputes, Border Clashes, and Security

The most glaring regional water issues concern upstream/downstream disputes over the Syrdarya and Amudarya Rivers and desiccation of the Aral Sea.[28] Since independence, increased cooperation at the local level within a context of differing institutional set-ups at the national level has been accompanied by conflict and intransigence with respect to international agreements. National water systems remain state-controlled to ensure that some water reaches all users and implicitly to forestall outright water wars, with new institutions such as water users' associations limited to local management. The conflict between upstream and downstream countries about timing and magnitudes of water release from reservoirs, in winter for hydroelectricity or in spring for agriculture, perpetuates the region's major environmental disaster, desiccation of the Aral Sea.

The Aral Sea, the world's fourth-largest lake in 1960, had shrunk by 90% in the early twenty-first century. Fishing and associated activities disappeared in the 1980s, salts and toxins from the newly-exposed sea bed were carried as far as 500 km in dust storms 150–300 km wide causing animal mutations and chronic human health problems, and the reduced water area contributes to regional climate change (adding to global warming in the region).[29]

The origins of the problem lay in the expansion of irrigation projects during the 1950s and 1960s to support increased cotton output. The flow varies from year to year, but after 1960 the trend was of less and less water from the Amudarya and Syrdarya Rivers reaching the Aral Sea. The shrinking of the sea was already acknowledged as a major ecological problem before independence, and Soviet planners had grandiose schemes to divert rivers flowing into the Arctic Ocean into the Aral Sea, although nothing happened. Data from the early 1990s clearly identifies irrigated farming as the cause of the problem (table 9.7). The per capita use data highlight the profligate use of water in Turkmenistan, whose cotton sector was reliant on the long and inefficient Karakum Canal, and to a lesser extent in the other cotton-producing areas.

28. Kazakhstan has a water conflict with China over the Ili and Irtysh Rivers, from which China plans to extract water in order to stimulate the Xinjiang economy. The Ili River feeds Lake Balkhash, which is in danger of shrinking like the Aral Sea. The Irtysh provides water for large industrial towns in northeastern Kazakhstan, Oskemen, Semey (formerly Semipalatinsk), and Pavlodar as well as the national capital, Astana, before entering Russia and joining the Ob River.

29. With desiccation of the Aral Sea, Vozrozhdeniya Island, a major bioweapons research and storage facility abandoned with little care in the 1990s, is no longer an island. Anthrax spores and other weaponized pathogens are no longer contained (Gorvett, 2017).

TABLE 9.7. Use of Water from the Aral Sea Basin, Early 1990s

A. BY SECTOR, KM³ PER YEAR

	Water intake	Water diversion	Net use
Municipalities	3.1	1.6	1.5
Industry & power generation	8.3	6.4	1.9
Rural sector	0.9	No data	No data
Irrigated farming	114.0	26–39	75–88
Total	c. 127	35–49	79–94

B. BY COUNTRY, KM³ PER PERSON PER YEAR

	Annual use
Turkmenistan	4,044
Uzbekistan	2,596
Kazakhstan	1,943
Tajikistan	1,843
Kyrgyzstan	1,371

Source: Kasperson et al. (1995), chapter 3.

The situation was exacerbated after the dissolution of the Soviet Union, when central control of water use lapsed. In principle, the same division of water between the Central Asian states was observed, but post-independence with poor monitoring there were more opportunities for free-riding (e.g., by farmers piercing irrigation channels to obtain additional water). The obvious approach of pricing water was opposed by downstream countries that continued to view water as a free resource, an attitude that perpetuated overuse of water contributing to a tragedy of the commons.

The disaster was self-evident, and soon after independence the five presidents, with the support of many international donors, launched the International Fund for Saving the Aral Sea in 1993. The World Bank opened a well-funded office dedicated to managing the Aral Sea Basin Program in 1994, but it closed in 1997 due to mismanagement of funds. With lack of local initiatives and widespread corruption, donors' interest and participation lagged, and the Aral Sea continued to shrink. The major cotton-producing countries were unwilling to seriously countenance reduction of land devoted to cotton, and almost all cotton lands were irrigated. Incentives for farmers to adopt more appropriate techniques, such as drip irrigation were low in the absence of water-pricing, and countries were reluctant to unilaterally curb water use.

Failure to cooperate led Kazakhstan to take the drastic action of building a barrage across the sea in 2005, so that it could work on a national policy towards rejuvenation of the northern part of the Aral Sea. The Dike Kokaral was feasible because the Syrdarya River still fed the northern Aral Sea, whereas the Amudarya River, which passed through a greater cotton-growing area, no longer reached the Aral Sea in most years. The fish catch increased to 5,596 tons in 2014, some reintroduced and some naturally migrating, but this was still well below the 1961 catch of 34,160 tons (Bland, 2015). In sum, Kazakhstan appears to have abandoned hope of a multilateral solution to the Aral Sea, and has built a dike across the sea so that it can focus on regeneration of the northern portion, while leaving treatment of the southern portion to Uzbekistan.

Apart from the overuse of the water in the Aral Sea basin, there is an upstream-downstream issue about seasonality. The upstream countries, Tajikistan and the Kyrgyz Republic, want to develop their hydroelectricity capacity by building new dams, but this would mean releasing water year-round and especially in winter to meet peak heating demand, while the downstream water users want the water to be released in spring when demand for irrigation is highest. For two decades after the dissolution of the Soviet Union, the issue was in limbo because no country was willing to consider serious negotiation. In 2012, Presidents Karimov and Nazarbayev agreed that any dam construction in Tajikistan and the Kyrgyz Republic must be approved by the downstream states in accordance with expert consensus and international conventions. Uzbek-Tajik relations had long been poor; if Tajikistan ignored the warning, many observers feared that would be a potential cause for war, especially as Uzbekistan had the biggest army in Central Asia. The situation may be easing since President Karimov's death. Tajikistan relaunched construction of the Rogun Dam in October 2016, and President Mirziyoyev gave tacit acquiescence. He went further in supporting Kyrgyz dam plans, offering to collaborate in managing river flows.

After the creation of the new independent states in 1991, border tensions were inherent in the imprecise delimitation of republican borders within the Soviet Union. The introduction of visas added to border tensions. Especially in the southern part of Central Asia, a vicious circle of heightened security concerns, more onerous visa restrictions and border-crossing procedures, and violent clashes emerged. Policy statements emphasize coordinated action against terrorism, but border closures and international incidents remain frequent. Nevertheless, in Central Asia, unlike in most other parts of the CIS, there have been no official claims of other countries' recognized territory nor serious secession movements.

The situation is most complicated in the densely populated Fergana Valley where the arbitrary borders were meaningless until 1991, but are now national boundaries and include several enclaves (Starr, ed., 2011). The largest enclave, Sokh (population fifty thousand), a piece of Uzbekistan's territory surrounded by the Kyrgyz Republic's Batken province, has been viewed by Tashkent as a potential base for Islamic Movement of Uzbekistan (IMU) militants, and even as a potentially seceding Islamic republic. To counter the perceived threat, Uzbekistan has sought a corridor along the Sokh River that would link the enclave to the rest of Uzbekistan, but an agreement in 2001 with the Kyrgyz government in Bishkek to provide such a corridor in return for a similar corridor to a smaller Kyrgyz enclave surrounded by Uzbekistan was denounced by Batken provincial officials and residents because of the impact on water rights and the splitting of the province. Similar conflicts over access to enclaves arise between Tajikistan and the Kyrgyz Republic, e.g., residents of the two Tajikistan enclaves, Vorukh and western Kalacha, that are both surrounded by Batken province of the Kyrgyz Republic have long complained about their isolation from the rest of Tajikistan and Tajikistan has informally sought land corridors, but the Kyrgyz Republic opposes such proposals as interfering with the movement of Kyrgyz citizens. Apart from the enclave issue the hardening of borders has split families and negatively influenced local cross-border markets and patterns of migrant livestock farmers whose summer and winter pastures are now in different countries (Murzakulova and Mestre, 2016).

Governments have been concerned about the threat of insurgents since the 1990s, and especially since 2001 when US support could be sought in countering Islamic threats. Invasions have been sporadic and small scale. Several hundred guerrillas invaded southern Kyrgyzstan in summer 1999 under the aegis of the IMU allegedly seeking to create an Islamic state in southern Kyrgyzstan as a springboard for jihad in Uzbekistan. These, and similar invasions in 2000 and in 2006, were defeated by Kyrgyz military forces, sometimes with Uzbek and Kazakh air support. In late 2010 and early 2011 members of Jamaat Kyrgyzstan Jaish al-Mahdi (the Kyrgyz Army of the Righteous Ruler) bombed a synagogue and a sports facility, attempted to bomb a police station, and killed three policemen, before security forces killed or apprehended a dozen or more members of the group including its leader. Kazakhstan established a national antiterrorism center in 2003 and at various times claimed that jihadist plots had been thwarted; in 2011–12 suicide bombs and other fatal incidents occurred in Atyrau, Aktobe, Almaty, and Taraz,[30] and the government blamed terrorists for fomenting the December 2011 violence in Zhanaozen. In Tajikistan over two dozen people, mostly opposition fighters from the civil war who had been arrested in 2009, escaped from jail in August 2010 and launched attacks across the country. Over two dozen people were killed by a car bomb

30. In response to criticism from the president that over a hundred terrorism-related crimes had been committed and dozens of people had died, the Kazakh National Security Committee reported in February 2013 that security forces had neutralized forty-two extremist groups and prevented thirty-five violent actions in 2011 and 2012, but failed to prevent eighteen extremist actions (Nichol, 2014, 23).

in Khujand, for which the Tajik branch of the IMU claimed responsibility. In July 2012, a security force's general was killed near Khorog in the Gorno-Badakhshan autonomous oblast, and the government's response involved a force of over three thousand.[31]

In Uzbekistan, explosions in Tashkent in 1999 killed between sixteen and twenty-eight people, and were followed by arrests of opposition leaders. In March-April 2004 a series of suicide bombings led to forty-seven deaths, for which a breakaway part of the IMU claimed responsibility. The IMU claimed responsibility for explosions at the US and Israeli embassies in July 2004. The biggest incident was the 2005 Andijan massacre, after which some defendants at the trial claimed they were members of a branch of Hizb ut-Tahtir. In a 2009 shoot-out in Tashkent the government claimed that three of the dead were IMU terrorists. The USA designated the IMU as a Foreign Terrorist Organization and added related groups to the list in 2005, and in 2008 strengthened financial and travel sanctions against individual leaders.[32] In August 2009 the IMU leader, Akram Yuldashev (founder of the Akramiya group allegedly behind the Andijan events), and in September 2009 the head of the Islamic Jihad Group, Najmiddin Jalalov, were killed in Pakistan by US predator drone missiles, and IMU military commander Abbas Mansur was killed by a US drone in 2011.

The CSTO's Central Asian rapid reaction force headquartered in Bishkek was a small force of three to five thousand troops between 2001 and 2009, but in 2009 the force was expanded to twenty thousand mostly Russian troops based in Tajikistan. CSTO consensus behind Russia is not assured. In September 2008 CSTO members condemned Georgia's aggression against the breakaway region of South Ossetia, but they refused Russia's request to extend diplomatic recognition to South Ossetia and Abkhazia. Uzbekistan declined to participate in the rapid reaction force in 2009, citing concerns that it could be used in disputes between member states. In 2012 Uzbekistan suspended its CSTO membership and sought closer links with China and the USA. President Rahmon's May 2013 visit to China, where he and President Xi Jinping signed a strategic partnership agreement that included cooperation on security issues, suggested that Tajikistan too wished to have China as a counterweight

---

31. The events are disputed, especially the number of civilian casualties. Among those killed by security forces was a former UTO leader, Imomnazar Imomnazarov, whose memorial service attracted a large crowd. Some commentators alleged that the fighting was for control over narcotics trade, or to destroy opposition in the GBAO region prior to the 2013 presidential elections (Nichol, 2014, 28).

32. The dichotomy between the US Departments of State and Defense was reflected in the cuts in development assistance and increases in military assistance after the Andijan events. Uzbekistan was a destination for prisoners from Afghanistan to be sent for questioning ("extraordinary rendition"); the Bush administration claimed that it had received assurances from the Uzbek authorities that torture would not be used.

to Russia. However, after Presidents Rahmon and Putin met in August 2013 Tajikistan's parliament confirmed the Russian base agreement in October 2013. In June 2010, an urgent request from Kyrgyz president Roza Otunbayeva for CSTO assistance in dealing with ethnic violence in southern Kyrgyzstan was not met due to lack of consensus. The institutional situation is complicated by the coexistence of CSTO's Central Asian rapid reaction force, the SCO's antiterrorism center in Tashkent, and the UN Regional Centre for Preventive Diplomacy established in Ashgabat in 2007 at the request of the Central Asian countries.

9.5. Conclusions

All five of the Central Asian countries that became independent in late 1991 are export-oriented economies, and thus trade relations have been an important policy element. Although all declared their intention to participate in the global trading system, they have, to varying degrees, pursued trade policies incompatible with WTO rules and were, except for the Kyrgyz Republic, cautious about accepting the obligations imposed by WTO membership. At the same time, the Central Asian countries signed on to myriad regional agreements in the 1990s and early 2000s. In practice, the Central Asian countries in their trade policies chose the path of policy autonomy combined with nondiscriminatory multilateralism; buying imports from the global least-cost supplier and selling exports in the best market makes considerable economic sense, and is supported by the failure of the many discriminatory trading arrangements in Latin America and Africa during the second half of the twentieth century (Pomfret, 2001b, 99–104). None of Central Asia's regional integration agreements had much economic impact before 2010.

From the dissolution of the Soviet Union until the mid-2000s, Central Asia was a region of economic disintegration. The combination of nation-building with increasingly strict border-crossing procedures and governments that were unwilling or unable to control petty corruption by customs and other officials increased the costs of doing international trade, while no Central Asian government showed much interest in facilitating trade. The CAREC data in table 9.6 show that the legacy of high trade costs continued in the 2010s.

The policy situation changed after 2010, when Russia, together with Belarus and Kazakhstan, implemented the customs union that would lead in 2015 to the deeper integration of the Eurasian Economic Union. Meanwhile, China saw the SCO as an umbrella organization, within which it would pursue bilateral economic relations with the Central Asian countries, illustrated most vividly in President Xi Jinping's Central Asian tour en route to the September 2013 SCO summit in Bishkek, during which he unveiled the One Belt One

Road concept of an overland route connecting China to Europe via Central Asia.

The next chapter will examine the evolution of relations between Russia and China and Central Asia. Despite its 2012 WTO accession, Russia places its political and security goals ahead of compliance with WTO obligations, as shown in its willingness to disregard WTO norms in restricting imports from Ukraine in 2013–14 and from Kazakhstan in 2015 on flimsy technical grounds.[33] China's vision of the SCO as a framework for bilateral economic relations under WTO norms contrasts with Russia's approach to the region, and the One Belt One Road program is presented as a win-win opportunity to reduce trade costs. A key question is whether the two organizational norms can be complementary or are irreconcilable.

In the twenty-first century, the situation is fluid. There is some fatigue with regional arrangements that have had little effect, but the need for regional cooperation on water or security is widely recognized. The national governments can also benefit by implementing policies to reduce nontariff impediments to trade such as cumbersome visa regulations, poorly developed financial systems, and capricious changes in border crossings, but that requires an appreciation that many of the foregone trade opportunities represent win-win situations. If the Central Asian governments feel that they have completed the nation-building task that was their top priority after 1991, then perhaps they can now move on to discuss regional cooperation with less fear of their sovereignty being undermined. This prospect will be discussed in chapter 11.

---

33. The Sanitary and Phytosanitary (SPS) and Technical Barriers to Trade (TBT) Codes of the WTO acknowledge members' rights to enforce safety, environmental, or other regulations that may impose nontariff barriers to trade. However, SPS regulations must be based on science, be applied only to the extent necessary to protect human, animal, or plant life or health, and should not arbitrarily or unjustifiably discriminate between countries where identical or similar conditions prevail. Similarly, the spirit of the TBT agreement is that regulations, standards, testing, and certification procedures should not create unnecessary obstacles to trade.

10

Central Asia in the Wider World

For the first decade after independence, the new countries operated in a foreign policy vacuum. External involvement was low key and small scale, despite speculation about the emergence of a New Great Game with external powers competing for power in Central Asia. Russia continued to be the dominant economic and political partner, but the government was focused on domestic issues, and organizations in which Russia played a leading role, the CIS and the Eurasian Community, were weak. The USA opened embassies in all the new independent states, but Central Asia was a low foreign policy priority; US economic influence was limited to the activities of a few companies such as Chevron, Mobil, Unocal, or Haliburton in oil or John Deere in farm equipment. The EU became a major trading partner, but relations were characterized by lack of clear strategic goals, and EU technical assistance had limited impact. China and Central Asia, amidst mutual suspicion, focused on border demarcation and demilitarization. The influence of Islamic countries, notably Turkey and Iran, increased but by less than most observers had anticipated. Japan, Korea, and others had a minor presence. External interest in Central Asia during the 1990s centered on pipeline politics, although issues such as how to get Tengiz oil to market at reasonable cost appear to have been mainly about economics and use or abuse of monopoly power rather than national policies.

The twenty-first century saw dramatic changes in external relations. After September 11, 2001, the USA sought logistical support for its military operations in Afghanistan. The Central Asian countries granted overflight rights and Uzbekistan and the Kyrgyz Republic provided air bases, until Uzbekistan's withdrawal of base facilities in 2005 and closure of the transit base in the Kyrgyz Republic in 2014. After 2009, Central Asia also assumed importance as a

TABLE 10.1. Ten Major Export and Import Markets, 2000 and 2010 (Billion US Dollars)

	Exports			Imports	
	2000	2010		2000	2010
EU	3.7 (23.8)	31.9 (37.7)	Russia	3.1 (27.2)	17.2 (27.3)
Russia	3.6 (23.3)	13.8 (16.4)	EU	2.2 (19.0)	11.1 (17.5)
China	0.7 (4.8)	12.4 (14.6)	China	0.3 (2.4)	6.8 (10.7)
Iran	0.5 (3.3)	4.0 (4.8)	USA	0.6 (5.1)	4.1 (6.6)
Turkey	0.4 (2.5)	2.7 (3.1)	Turkey	0.5 (4.6)	2.5 (4.0)
Switzerland	0.6 (4.1)	1.7 (2.0)	S. Korea	0.4 (3.8)	2.2 (3.5)
USA	0.2 (1.5)	1.1 (1.3)	Pakistan	0.2 (1.3)	1.9 (3.1)
Japan	0.1 (0.5)	0.6 (0.7)	Iran	0.2 (2.0)	1.8 (2.8)
S. Korea	0.1 (0.9)	0.4 (0.4)	Japan	0.3 (3.0)	0.9 (1.4)
India	0.1 (0.4)	0.3 (0.3)	India	0.1 (0.9)	0.8 (1.3)

Source: Mogilevskii (2012a, 30–1), based on data from COMTRADE and national statistical offices.
Notes: Totals include Afghanistan as well as the five Central Asian countries; numbers in parentheses are percentage shares.

link in the Northern Distribution Network (NDN) for nonlethal supplies to US forces in Afghanistan. The USA remains an important player due to its global political and military weight, but the long-term economic impact of its dozen years of physical involvement in Central Asian bases and the NDN is minimal.

A more lasting development has been the steady rise in importance of China as an economic partner. This relationship has a firm foundation in the comparative advantage of China and of Central Asia and was buttressed by China's adoption of a policy to strengthen economic development in its western provinces. In 2013, China's profile in Central Asia was raised by announcement of the One Belt One Road initiative and of the Asian Infrastructure Investment Bank, which promise major investment by China in Central Asia.

In the first decade of the twenty-first century, the EU was Central Asia's largest trade partner and China was the fastest growing (table 10.1).[1] The establishment of EU-China railroad links promises to connect these economic developments. However, external relations are also subject to Great Power politics. EU-Russian relations deteriorated in 2013, and both the EU and the USA imposed sanctions on Russia after the latter's annexation of the Crimean Peninsula. Russia imposed countersanctions, and moved closer to China,

1. The EU's position as Central Asia's largest export market was partly a statistical illusion because primary products like cotton or oil were often recorded as sold on European exchanges or to European companies, irrespective of their ultimate destination. Measures of bilateral economic relations often reflect individual companies' activities (e.g., Bouygues in Turkmenistan, Daewoo in Uzbekistan, Chevron in Kazakhstan, Cameco in the Kyrgyz Republic, or RusAl in Tajikistan) rather than national policies.

although the extent to which Russia's pivot is reciprocated by China is unclear. Meanwhile, Iran was reintegrating into the global community as UN sanctions were eased in 2016, and Turkey's relations with both the EU and Russia became volatile in 2016 and 2017. Amidst all of this, the Central Asian governments try to pursue multivector diplomacy.

This chapter focuses on economic relations. It addresses them one partner at a time—Russia, China, the EU, the USA, and the rest—although clearly interactions among the partners and the chronological evolution must be kept in mind.[2] The chapter starts by analyzing the pipeline politics that dominated international economic relations in Central Asia in the 1990s and 2000s. It ends with analysis of non-oil foreign investment.

10.1. Pipeline Politics

In the 1990s, competition among outside powers for Central Asian energy resources was the major driver of external relations. In oil, the USA appeared to be in a good position due to Chevron's role as lead firm in the Tengiz oil field, but Russia controlled the pipelines that were the dominant transport mode for oil. In the context of oil prices below $20 a barrel in the 1990s, producers wanted to use the Russian network in order to avoid the large costs of new pipeline construction, and the only new pipeline in the 1990s was a small gas pipeline from Turkmenistan to Iran. The Russian oil pipeline monopoly, Transneft, had a window of opportunity in which to cement its incumbent's advantage by securing long-term arrangements with Chevron and others, but instead Transneft chose to maximize short-term returns.

Chevron and BP, the lead operator of Azerbaijan's major oil field, sought alternative pipeline options. An upgrade of the Soviet-era Baku-Supsa pipeline by Kvaerner (Norway) was completed in 1998, and by the late 1990s Tengiz oil mainly went by rail and barge to the Georgian Black Sea port Supsa. The cost of the pipeline and Supsa Oil Terminal to Chevron and its partners in the Azerbaijan International Operating Company amounted to $556 million.

When oil prices increased after 1999, oil producers were more willing to spend on new pipelines, and they sought lower-cost and more reliable trans-

---

2. Cooley (2012) analyzes the interaction between the USA, Russia, and China between 2001 and 2011 with three main themes: (1) for the USA and China interest in Central Asia was primarily because it bordered a region of instability that mattered to them (Afghanistan for the USA and Xinjiang for China), while Russia was interested in Central Asia as a historical sphere of influence, (2) the three powers' interaction was a mix of competition (e.g., over military bases or pipelines) and cooperation (e.g., over the Northern Distribution Network or the China-EU rail link through Russia), and (3) the Central Asian governments have not been passive, adopting multivector diplomacy as well as balancing bilateral relations among the three external powers.

port options. First, the Caspian Pipeline Consortium (CPC) built a 1,500 km oil pipeline through southern Russia to the Black Sea coast that was completed in 2003 at a cost of $2.6 billion and was controlled by non-Russian oil companies. Initial capacity was 450,000 bpd, which the consortium intended to expand to 1.35 million bpd, but Russia was uncooperative. The 1,768 km Baku-Tbilisi-Ceyhan (BTC) pipeline was built in 2003–5 at a cost of $3.9 billion and with a capacity of one million bpd. The first oil was delivered to Ceyhan on the Mediterranean coast in May 2006, by which time the price of oil easily covered the transit fees (c$62 million per year to Georgia and $200 million to Turkey) and port fees in Ceyhan.

Oil pipelines are no longer an issue for Kazakhstan. The Transneft monopoly had been broken by CPC, and the Russian route monopoly was broken by BTC. The pipeline built across Kazakhstan to China between 2003 and 2009 provided further route diversification. Delivery of Kazakhstan's oil remains relatively high cost (a TransCaspian pipeline would help to lower costs), but routing is not a problem as long as world oil prices justify the delivery costs. Having options via Russia, Turkey, and China ensures that none of those countries wields power over Kazakhstan through its pipeline.

Gas is different. The only feasible method of transporting Central Asian gas is pipelines, and once built a pipeline creates a situation of mutual dependency between the buyer at one end and the supplier at the other end of the pipeline. Seeking diversity of outlets to avoid a Russian monopsony has been more difficult for gas. Gazprom's situation was more complex than that of Transneft; it supplied gas to the EU at a formula-based price that was related to the (lagged) price of oil and, for domestic policy reasons, had to supply the Russia domestic market at a much lower price. Import of Central Asian gas into Russia allowed Gazprom to fulfill its domestic market obligations and to supply more gas to the EU, which was especially attractive when Russia could use its monopsony power to pay Turkmenistan a low price, but also gave Turkmenistan some bargaining power. As energy prices increased, the arrangement became unstable (chapter 6). Construction of a gas pipeline from Turkmenistan through Uzbekistan and Kazakhstan to Beijing in 2006–9 broke Russia's monopsony, but by 2015 left China as the dominant purchaser of Central Asian gas.

In their assessment of Central Asian pipeline politics in the 1990s and 2000s, Chow and Hendrix (2010, 39) conclude that "international politics can sometimes help development, but do not determine the outcome and more often block sensible commerce." They emphasize the economics, such as the need for "bankable volumes" and price fundamentals, of profitable pipelines. Although Western energy companies such as Chevron and BP were critical in pushing along the CPC and BTC pipeline projects, Chow and Hendrix criticize the hubris of Western policymakers and commentators who thought that theirs was the home team in a new Great Game. The real home team consisted of the Central Asian governments who gained in confidence to cooperate on the 2006–9 gas pipeline to China, while China, which initially missed out on the big oil and gas fields in Kazakhstan (Tengiz, Karachaganak, Kashagan), used its trump card of a large and growing market contiguous to Central Asia (and Russia misplayed all its cards).[3]

In sum, for gas as for oil, pipeline politics had ceased to be of great importance by the 2010s (Calder, 2012). Some EU members were still dependent on Russian gas and concerned about energy security, but it was no longer a Central Asian issue. As with oil, a TransCaspian pipeline would provide an attractive alternative outlet for Central Asian gas, as would the long-mooted TAPI route, but they do not have the salience of pipeline politics in the 1990s. The development of LNG technology favoring offshore gas deposits relative to landlocked suppliers of natural gas reinforced the sense of "game over" (Denison, 2012) for pipeline politics.

10.2. Russia and the Eurasian Economic Union

Russia under Boris Yeltsin willingly precipitated the independence of the Central Asian republics. During the 1990s Russia collaborated in decommissioning Kazakhstan's nuclear weapons, and made treaty commitments to Kazakhstan's territorial integrity (similar to the commitments given to Ukraine). President Yeltsin seemed more concerned about holding the Russian Federation together, as the economy suffered severe transitional recession and as he increased democracy with elected regional governors who, in the North Caucasus and elsewhere, challenged Moscow's authority. The Chechnya conflicts pointed to Russia's military shortcomings, and Russia's August 1998 financial crisis and debt default highlighted the country's economic weakness.

The Central Asian leaders' reaction to dissolution of the USSR and Russian independence was not uniform. President Nazarbayev was a close ally of President Yeltsin, and he worked hard to maintain close economic and political relations within the CIS. President Rakhmonov was dependent on Russian military support for victory in the Tajik Civil War, and Russian troops continued to man Tajikistan's border with Afghanistan throughout the 1990s. In contrast, President Niyazov obtained the UN Declaration of Neutrality in 1995,

3. In its handling of delivery promises for gas from the Russian Far East, the Russian government seemed to be playing off China and Japan between 2003 and 2005, while harassing the most competent international company in the region, BP, which had bought half of TNK and gained what turned out to be temporary control over the huge Kovykta gas field in East Siberia. Against this background, China turned in 2004–6 to Kazakhstan and Turkmenistan as more congenial energy partners. Mihalka (2008, 130) wrote of the perception "that Russia has become a corrupt backward petrostate incapable of generating the capital necessary to develop its own energy infrastructure." Blank (2011; 2017) also emphasizes "Russia's Failure."

and President Karimov distanced Uzbekistan from Russian influence and became a close US ally. A visible sign of the split was the adoption of the Turkish/Latin alphabet by Turkmenistan and Uzbekistan and retention of the Cyrillic alphabet by the other three Central Asian countries.

In December 1999 Boris Yeltsin resigned as Russian president, and was succeeded by his prime minister, Vladimir Putin, who won the 2000 presidential election. When US interest in Central Asia mounted after September 11, 2001, Russia and China acquiesced to NATO's war in Afghanistan and the US need for bases to supply troops in Afghanistan. However, President Putin showed increasing nostalgia for the Soviet (or tsarist) empire and concern about US bases in Central Asia. When the USA criticized Uzbekistan's handling of the May 2005 Andijan events, Uzbekistan terminated its base agreement and joined EurAsEc. However, there is little evidence of increased Russian influence in Central Asia in 2005–8, e.g., the Central Asian countries did not follow Russia in recognizing Abkhazia or South Ossetia in 2008. Despite strong Russian pressure and some vacillation, the Kyrgyz Republic refused to close the US base at Bishkek airport, and Manas transit center remained operational until 2014 when the USA was winding down its military presence in Afghanistan. In 2008 Uzbekistan quit the Eurasian Community and gradually reestablished warmer relations with the USA (Blank, 2011).

Starting in 2009 Russia became more assertive towards Central Asia. The revival of Russian influence can be ascribed to Putin's nostalgia for Greater Russia, but it also reflected changing economic circumstances for Russia and their impact on Central Asia. The resource boom allowed Russia to pay off its debts in the first half of the 2000s and increasingly use money to modernize and upgrade its military. The most direct impact on Central Asia of the oil boom was the rapid increase in employment of migrant workers in Russia. Threats of changes to migrants' status gave Russia huge influence over Tajikistan and the Kyrgyz Republic, and the position of migrants was one of the principal carrots offered for Eurasian Economic Union accession.

Meanwhile, Russia reset its policy focus from the CIS to bilateral or plurilateral relations with preferred partners from the former Soviet Union. This policy moved fastest vis-à-vis Belarus and Kazakhstan who formed a customs union with Russia that began operating in mid-2011, and involved active bilateral dealings with Armenia, the Kyrgyz Republic, and Tajikistan as putative customs union members. The speed and level of implementation of the customs union were in stark contrast to the many paper proposals discussed in the previous chapter. After 2010 Russia also began taking a harder line on security matters, e.g., bolstering its Caspian Sea flotilla[4] and gaining agreement

4. In 2011 Russia announced an increase in the size of the Caspian fleet to twenty ships by 2020. In 2015 two frigates, nine corvettes, seven smaller military patrol boats, three minesweepers, and six landing craft operated out of two military ports, Astrakhan and Makhachkala. Kucera

of the other littoral states that Caspian Sea security would be the exclusive concern of the littoral states (i.e. ruling out US-led maritime security initiatives). In 2012 Russia crossed some "red lines" vis-à-vis Uzbekistan by increasing its military presence in the Kyrgyz Republic and in Tajikistan and in providing financial support for hydroelectric projects in those two countries. Russia was even more confrontational in other parts of the CIS: Russian absorption of Crimea and support for secessionist areas in eastern Ukraine in 2014–15 meant that all four GUAM countries now had frozen conflicts in which areas outside the central government's control were succored by Russia.

The customs union between Belarus, Kazakhstan, and Russia was important because implementation was rapid, and further deepening and widening were credibly promised.[5] The common external tariff was weighted towards the Russian tariff, which had little impact on Belarus, but led to significant increases in Kazakhstan's tariffs. Russia kept 82% of its customs tariffs unchanged, lowered 14%, and increased 4%; the corresponding shares for Kazakhstan were 45%, 10%, and 45% (Libman and Vinokurov, 2012, 49). Kazakhstan's average tariff increased from 6.5% to 12.1%, and the weighted average tariff increased from 4.3% to 12.7%, with the highest protection granted to the car, furniture, tobacco, textiles, clothing, leather, wood, and food producers (Jandosov and Sabyrova, 2011).

In July 2011 customs controls at the members' common borders were abolished, and common external commercial policies were implemented in areas such as antidumping duties, and sanitary and phytosanitary (SPS) and technical barriers to trade (TBT) rules. The border arrangements clearly privileged internal trade over trade with nonmembers. Average border-crossing time for trucks leaving Kazakhstan for Russia fell from 7.7 hours in 2011 to 2.9 hours in 2012, and the average border-crossing time for trucks entering Kazakhstan from outside the customs union increased from 8.6 to 21.5 hours, with "waiting in queue" the biggest part (CAREC, 2012, 38–39). Such delays primarily affected Kazakhstan's trade with the Kyrgyz Republic and with China.

Raising the external tariff while allowing duty-free imports from Russia was a recipe for trade destruction and trade diversion; both involved economic costs for Kazakhstan.[6] Moreover, the negative trade impact was exac-

---

(2012) saw this as the start of a Caspian arms race as other littoral nations responded by increasing their Caspian fleets (see chapter 6 on Turkmenistan).

5. The analysis of the customs union draws on Pomfret (2014). On the EAEU, see also Vinokurov (2017), Alimbekov et al. (2017), Khitakhunov et al. (2017), and EDB (2017).

6. The theoretical implications are clear (Pomfret, 2001b). A simple but plausible model by Tumbarello (2005) estimated substantial welfare loss for Kazakhstan from such tariff arrangements. Mogilevskii (2012c, 22) emphasized the number of contemporary exogenous shocks that obscured empirical identification of pure customs union effects. The negative impact may be

erbated by administrative changes and increased nontariff barriers, which further reduced trade with nonmembers, e.g., newly designed SPS rules made it harder for the Kyrgyz Republic to export its farm products to Kazakhstan (Djamankulov, 2011), and tighter controls on the customs union's external borders discouraged informal, or currently poorly monitored, imports into Kazakhstan from the Kyrgyz Republic and China (Mogilevskii, 2012b).[7] Laruelle and Peyrouse (2012, 44) highlight the drastic effect of the customs union on the Kyrgyz Republic's role as a platform for re-exporting Chinese goods and claim that the number of Kyrgyz wholesale traders fell by 70–80% in 2010–11.

Why did Kazakhstan take this step when economic studies suggested that the customs union would yield negative returns to Kazakhstan? Laruelle and Peyrouse (2012, 44–45) see the empirical literature as indicating potential short-run benefits for Kazakhstan, but a long-term negative impact as foreign investment, technology, and knowledge transfer flows decline. Mogilevskii (2012c, 33) highlights the immediate increase in Kazakhstan's tariff revenue, by at least $1.4 billion in 2011. The EBRD study (Isakova et al., 2013) foresaw small negative short-term effects on Kazakhstan, but uncertain long-term effects. None of these is fully convincing in explaining Kazakhstan's accession to the customs union, when many Kazakh economists were pointing to the negative implications, suggesting that forming the customs union was a political, rather than economic, decision.

In January 2012, the creation of a common economic space began. The aims included creation of a common market in goods, services, labor, and capital; coordination of monetary, financial, and tax policies; development of unified transport, energy, and information systems; and unification of systems of state support for innovation and priority sectoral development. In July 2012 the Eurasian Economic Commission, a supranational executive body comprising deputy prime ministers, was established. In May 2014, the three countries signed a treaty establishing the Eurasian Economic Union (EAEU) in January 2015. In October 2014, Armenia signed an accession treaty to join the EAEU in January 2015.

Russia targeted the Kyrgyz Republic and Tajikistan, both members of EurAsEc, as future EAEU members. In 2010–11 Russia provided stabilization grants and loans to the Kyrgyz Republic and Tajikistan to help them weather

---

reduced as Russia implements its obligations under its 2012 WTO accession (Shepotylo and Tarr, 2012).

7. Silitski (2010) argued that the main reason for Russia promoting the customs union was to control imports from the EU and China, which were evading tariffs, taxes, and other restrictions by routing via Belarus and Kazakhstan respectively. The first three antidumping duties were imposed in 2013 on (1) stainless steel pipes from China, (2) cast iron bath tubs from China, and (3) light commercial vehicles from Germany, Italy, and Turkey (Yalbulganov, 2014).

the global economy's downturn. In September 2012 Presidents Putin and Atambayev signed a fifteen-year extension to Russian military facilities in the Kyrgyz Republic, including the Kant airbase, while Atambayev confirmed that the US Transit Center at Manas would be closed in 2014 and converted to civilian use. Other accords at the meeting included cancellation of $190 million Kyrgyz debt to Russia, restructuring of a $300 million loan given by Russia to the Kyrgyz Republic in 2009, and promised assistance in building hydroelectric projects including the Kambarata-1 Dam and hydroelectric power station. A steering committee for integrating the Kyrgyz Republic into the customs union met and a road map was approved at the customs union members' October 2013 summit, although reconciling Kyrgyz WTO commitments with the external tariff of the customs union was an apparent obstacle.[8] The Kyrgyz Republic signed an association agreement with the EAEU in December 2014, agreed in May 2015 to join as a full member, and completed accession in August 2015.[9]

In 2011 and 2012 Russia and Tajikistan started on a similar path. The two countries' 2004 agreement on a Russian base was renewed for forty-nine years in 2012, and in 2014 the base became Russia's largest foreign facility after the Black Sea Fleet base in Crimea was nationalized. Tajikistan also sought greater financial assistance for the Rogun Dam, and Russian support in case of conflict with Uzbekistan, while postponing any decision on EAEU membership.

The beyond-trade aspects of the EAEU are especially valuable for the poorer Central Asian countries.[10] Both the Kyrgyz Republic and Tajikistan would benefit from regularization of the status of migrant workers and resolution of issues such as those workers' pension rights (EDB, 2013a; 2013b), as well as from improved north-south transport corridors. EAEU agreements on labor migration reduce the number of documents required by migrant work-

8. According to WTO (2013, 25), 30% of Kyrgyz duties align with those of the customs union, 21% can be realigned without violating WTO commitments, and 49% would require renegotiation of WTO terms (and potentially compensation to affected WTO members) before they could be aligned. Armenia faced similar issues to the Kyrgyz Republic. Both countries have delayed implementation by insisting on a transition period.

9. The foot-dragging was clear in an interview that President Atambayev gave to the Russian News Agency Tass in October 2014—available online at http://tass.ru/en/economy/756666. The report's headline was "No Option for Kyrgyzstan but to Join Customs Union—Kyrgyzstan President" In 2015–16 there was substantial dissatisfaction with the outcome, e.g., Sharsheev (2016) criticized Russian border officials' impounding Kyrgyz bell peppers and Kazakhstan banning Kyrgyz potatoes on SPS grounds despite Kyrgyz official denial of the charges. Sharsheev's broader criticism relies heavily on the decline in Kyrgyz trade after accession, but much of this decline was due to reduced import demand in Russia and Kazakhstan after the 2014 fall in commodity prices.

10. Using a computable general equilibrium model of the Kyrgyz economy, Mogilevskii, Thurlow, and Yeh (2018) estimate that the reduction in profits from re-exporting will be greater than the benefits from higher remittances and tariff revenue, although the impact is likely to favor poorer households.

ers, increase the timeframe for registration and permissible period of uninterrupted stay, grant social rights to the migrant's family (especially in education), and provide guarantees about information availability to migrants. In January 2015, Russia introduced new regulations for labor migrants, who now had to pass tests on Russian language, history, and legislation basics, as well as undergo a medical examination and buy health insurance, while local governments increased their fee for work permits, e.g., in Moscow from 1,200 rubles to 4,000 rubles per month. Citizens of EAEU member countries are not affected by the new regulations. Thus, Kyrgyz workers in Russia should have a big advantage over migrants from nonmembers such as Uzbekistan, while the new regulations gave Tajikistan an extra incentive to join the EAEU. If Uzbekistan and Turkmenistan remain outside a deepening EAEU, this will exacerbate the fault-line running across Central Asia and likely hamper economic integration within Central Asia.[11]

The future of Russian influence in Central Asia, and of the EAEU, is uncertain. Russia's absorption of Crimea and support for secessionists in eastern Ukraine cast a shadow over relations with Kazakhstan, which has a similarly large and geographically defined Russian-speaking population near its border with Russia. Western sanctions and Russian countersanctions raised questions about the functioning of the customs union given the possibility of routing Russian imports and exports through Kazakhstan (Khitakhunov, et al., 2017). Long-term oil prices below $50 would pose a serious economic threat to Russia, although it is unclear how President Putin would respond to the challenge.[12]

Russia's relations with Central Asia are intertwined with Sino-Russian relations. Détente was sealed in 2008 by final resolution of border disputes that dated back to the mid-nineteenth century. Russian and Chinese leaders share grievances about humiliation dating back to the dissolution of the USSR for Putin and to the 1840 Opium War for Xi, and both presidents perceive promotion of Western values as attempts to obstruct restoration of their countries' past greatness. However, in contrast to Russia's "big brother" role in helping China establish central planning in the 1950s, in the twenty-first century the bilateral relationship is lopsided in the other direction: China's GDP, $11.8

---

11. Uzbekistan's 2012 withdrawal from the CSTO was an indicator of deteriorating political relations with Russia, although economic relations appear to have remained strong. Non-EAEU members are likely to suffer from trade diversion, and there may be other dimensions, e.g., the loss of access to Russian markets for Uzbekistan's car exports.

12. Some observers question Russia's commitment to the EAEU relative to other avenues for reasserting the country's status as a great power, such as intervention in Syria. Dragneva and Wolczuk (2017) argue that while Russia was keen to launch the EAEU and set up the customs union, it has no commitment to deep economic integration and refuses to be constrained by EAEU rules. Vinokurov (2017) agrees that the EAEU has not been an impeccable success story and that progress has slowed since 2016, but the EAEU is a functioning customs union and slowing down of the integration progress during the shift to deeper integration is normal.

trillion in 2015, dwarfs that of Russia, $1.3 trillion in 2015.[13] Russia seeks to diversify its economy, but exports to China remain dominated by oil, gas, and arms.[14] The two countries are becoming competitors in supplying nuclear reactors, which had been one of Russia's few internationally competitive commercial items (Itoh, 2017, 37–39).[15]

Following the hosting of the 2012 APEC summit in Vladivostok and oil and gas deals with China in 2013 and 2014, Russian leaders talked of a "pivot to Asia." Deteriorating relations with the USA and EU following the start of the Ukraine crisis in late 2013 provided a catalyst for Russia to seek better relations with Asian powers.[16] In 2014–15 Russia-China relations visibly warmed. President Xi attended the Sochi Winter Olympics in February 2014, President Putin visited Beijing in May 2014, and a year later President Xi was in Moscow to celebrate seventy years since the end of World War II. China abstained in the UN vote on Russian intervention in Ukraine (in contrast to its more explicit unwillingness to recognize the breakaway regions from Georgia in 2008) and did not support sanctions against Russia. At their May 2015 meeting the two presidents underlined the complementarity of the EAEU and China's One Belt

13. For both countries, the other is not a major trading partner. At its peak in 2014 Sino-Russian trade was $94 billion, compared to Sino-US trade of $659 billion in 2014. Russia's exports to China in that year were less than a quarter of Russian exports to the EU. Although both countries promote bilateral cultural and educational exchanges and the number of Chinese students studying in Russia had increased to around twenty-five thousand by 2015, this number was overshadowed by the one hundred thousand Chinese students in Australia and three hundred thousand in the USA (Yahuda, 2017, 8).

14. Russia also supplies arms to India and Vietnam, sometimes of superior quality to the weaponry sold to China and against China's interests (Yahuda, 2017, 6), e.g., the main purpose of Kilo-class attack submarines sold to Vietnam is to check Chinese claims in the South China Sea. Swanström (2014, 491–93) reports that Russia supplied 84% of China's imported weapons between 1992 and 2006, but the trade declined dramatically after that as China found alternative suppliers. He also reports that China has become a serious competitor for Russian arms suppliers, including a contract to replace Tajikistan's aging Russian military aircraft.

15. Nuclear power plant had been a symbol of Sino-Russian cooperation in the late 1990s and two Russian-built reactors went into operation in Jiangsu Province in 2007. A decade later China had thirty-six nuclear reactors in operation and twenty-one under construction. In 2016, export of nuclear reactors was on the agenda during President Xi's visits to Iran, Saudi Arabia, and Egypt, all countries that had previously bought nuclear reactors from Russia.

16. Blank (2011) highlighted Russia's weakness, e.g., failure to compete with China on Central Asian pipelines in 2007–9 reflected financial constraints on Russia as oil prices fell, and he argues that cooperation with China may have been a defensive response to the challenge of selling Russia's oil and gas. The Eastern Siberia Pacific Ocean oil pipeline, completed in 2010, included a spur to Daqing in northeastern China, and a second spur to China was added in 2017. Russian oil exports to China increased from 0.16 mbd in 2005 to 0.77 mbd in 2015, but still accounted for less than 15% of China's oil imports. A 2013 oil deal with Rosneft was worth $270 billion over twenty-five years and a 2014 gas deal with Gazprom to deliver 38 bcm per year through a 4,000 km pipeline (Power of Siberia) from the Sakha republic to northeastern China was reportedly worth $400 billion, but it is unclear whether either has been ratified (Itoh, 2017).

One Road Initiative and their intention of working towards a cooperative outcome in Central Asia. In 2015, President Putin hosted the first Eastern Economic Forum, with China as a prominent guest.

The pivot to Asia may be more about Russia seeking to consolidate relations with the three major East Asian economies after the post-Crimea confrontation with Western powers than about single-minded cooperation with China. At the 2016 Eastern Economic Forum in Vladivostok, China had a lower profile than either Japan or South Korea, which were both represented by heads of government; the Japan Bank for International Cooperation proposed a $400 million investment in a project to ship LNG from Russian Arctic ports. However, in the face of Russian intransigence on the Kuril Islands / Northern Territories territorial dispute, Japan was scaling down other proposed investments in the Russian Far East from $9 billion offered in May 2016 to $2.6 billion in December 2016 (Yahuda, 2017, 9).

Russia's crude oil export to the three northeastern Asian countries increased from around 0.2 mbd in 2005 to 1.3 mbd in 2015, and since 2009 Russia has exported LNG to Japan. The oil and gas trade reflects a natural complementarity between Russia's Siberia and Far East and the energy-importing northeast Asian countries, but bargaining power now lies with energy importers. China is the largest importer with growing energy demand, unlike Japan whose demand may have peaked, and has well-developed plans for alternative energy sources.[17]

For Russia, China remains a more important trading partner than either Japan or South Korea, and relations with the latter are constrained by the fact that they both remain close allies of the USA. In light of the limited practical steps, however, some observers question the strength of the pivot and of Sino-Russian cooperation.[18] China remains Russia's major competitor for regional influence in Central Asia.

10.3. China and Central Asia

Following the Sino-Soviet split in the early 1960s, economic relations between China and Soviet Central Asia were practically nonexistent. Roads were

17. China has gas pipelines from Turkmenistan since 2009 and from Myanmar since 2015, and plans to produce 30 bcm of shale gas in 2020 and 80–100 bcm by 2030. Improvements in LNG technology have made pipelines less attractive than summer shipping from the Arctic; the 2014 Sakhalin pipeline is less important for China than for Russia, which is paying the construction costs. By 2015, China had built thirteen LNG terminals with many more under construction, and intends to purchase LNG from the USA, Australia, and other new offshore fields (Itoh, 2017).

18. Contributors to Saalman (2017) identify areas in which Russia and China remain competitors rather than cooperators. Blank (2017) argues that Russia turned to China because it had no alternative after the collapse of energy prices in 2014 and in the face of Western sanctions, but Russia is clearly the junior partner, a situation that Blank ascribes to Russia's failure to implement economic reforms.

closed, apart from two that reopened in 1983. The first connecting railroad only opened in 1990 as relations thawed under Mikhail Gorbachev and Deng Xiaoping. Other border posts opened during the 1990s, including river ports, but they could be closed unilaterally at short notice, and air services operated between Urumqi and Central Asia. After 1992, there was considerable mutual suspicion as the Central Asian countries feared an influx of millions of Chinese and China feared Central Asian support for Uighur separatists. Border delimitation and demilitarization negotiations in the 1990s provided a basis for confidence-building that was institutionalized in the Shanghai Five in 1996, and subsequently the SCO.

Trade between Central Asia and China grew in the 1990s, although it was from a low base and there are serious data issues. The main Central Asian exports to China were coal, iron, steel, and other primary products. Kazakhstan was by far China's largest trading partner in Central Asia at the turn of the century. Some commodity trade involved bulk state purchases that could fluctuate from year to year, e.g., Uzbekistan's cotton sales to China rose to $133 million in 1997 and fell to $29 million in 1998. In the 1990s and early 2000s, apart from minerals entering China by rail from Kazakhstan and cotton deals with Uzbekistan, much of Central Asia's trade with China was unmonitored and small scale, conducted by so-called shuttle-traders. Wiemer (2000) estimated China's unrecorded shuttle exports to have been worth $300–600 million in 1998, when Chinese customs statistics reported exports to Central Asia of $456 million. Even with the highest shuttle trade estimates, trade with Central Asia accounted for under 1% of China's total exports. Trade with China was perhaps 5% of Central Asian countries' total international trade, but no more.

The shuttle trade became less attractive by the end of the decade, as Central Asian governments tightened their borders or monitored bazaars more closely and transaction costs increased. In Uzbekistan, life for domestic traders became increasingly difficult after the tightening of forex controls in 1996. Following the negative impact of the 1998 Russian crisis, Kazakhstan closed border posts and devalued its currency substantially, cutting demand for imported Chinese goods. As both a consequence and a cause of the decline in the shuttle trade, around this time the Kyrgyz Republic emerged as an entrepôt, importing goods from China and elsewhere, to be sold in huge bazaars outside Bishkek and Osh to customers from across Central Asia (see chapter 7.5).[19]

19. Recorded trade between the Kyrgyz Republic and China stagnated after 1998, but the high values, relative to population or GDP, of Kyrgyz imports from China that appear in the Chinese trade data as early as 1997 (e.g., imports of $172 million in 1998 when total Central Asian imports from China were only $456 million) indicate a particular role for the Kyrgyz Republic.

China's economic influence in Central Asia increased rapidly in the 2000s, based on China's demand for energy and on Central Asian markets for Chinese manufactures. Around 2002, China ceased to be energy self-sufficient, and became worried about energy security and vulnerability to choke points on maritime routes from the Middle East and other oil-producing regions. Investment in oil fields in Kazakhstan was accompanied by construction in stages between 2003 and 2009 of oil pipelines linking western Kazakhstan to Xinjiang. In 2005, the Chinese National Petroleum Corporation became owner of PetroKazakhstan, Kazakhstan's largest independent oil producer. Even more dramatic was the pipeline agreement during Turkmenbashi's 2006 trip to Beijing, and completion of the gas pipeline through Uzbekistan and Kazakhstan by 2009. Thereafter China quickly became the dominant purchaser of Turkmenistan's natural gas.

The potential for increased trade between Central Asia and China was substantial given their differing factor endowments and natural resources, but realizing the potential depended upon a favorable trade environment and improved physical infrastructure. China's WTO accession in 2001 provided predictable conditions for trade, although at that time only the Kyrgyz Republic in Central Asia was a WTO member. Also in 2001, China launched the "Go West" policy to stimulate economic development in western China.[20] The Kyrgyz Republic did not closely monitor imports from China, e.g., in 2008 China reported exports to the Kyrgyz Republic of $9,213 million, while the Kyrgyz statistics indicated imports of $728 million from China (Mogilevskii, 2012b), or re-exports to neighboring countries, e.g., a World Bank (2009) analysis of 2008 mirror statistics found that the Kyrgyz Republic had "excessive" imports and Uzbekistan "under-imports." Nevertheless, Chinese-Kyrgyz trade was large, and the Chinese goods were not destined solely, or even primarily, for Kyrgyz customers.[21] In 2004 China created a special zone on the Kazakhstan border to promote cross-border trade, and this was also a setting for substantial small-time unrecorded trade. Table 10.1 shows the rapid growth of recorded Chinese trade with Central Asia between 2000 and 2010, and the unrecorded trade was much larger with respect to imports from China than for any other entry in that table.

China's "Go West" policy bore fruit slowly. Improved connectivity within China encouraged Hewlett-Packard and Foxconn (assembler of Apple prod-

20. Officially called the Western Development Program, it covered the municipality of Chongqing, the provinces of Gansu, Guizhou, Qinghai, Shaanxi, Sichuan, and Yunnan, and the autonomous regions of Guangxi, Inner Mongolia, Ningxia, Tibet, and Xinjiang.

21. Two articles by Gaël Raballand capture the rapid evolution of trade between China and Central Asia. Raballand and Andrésy (2007), based on data up to 2004, emphasize the importance of Kazakhstan's exports to China, of which over four-fifths consisted of oil and minerals. Kaminski and Raballand (2009), based on data up to 2006, emphasize small-scale traders exporting manufactured goods from China, with the Kyrgyz Republic as a re-export center.

ucts) to invest $3 billion to build printer and laptop manufacturing bases in Chongqing, opening the prospect of western China joining the boom in production along global value chains.[22] They and other exporters in Chongqing began searching for alternative export routes to the congested Yangtze River, and after some experimental starts in 2010 and 2011 with individual trains, regular rail service between Chongqing and Duisburg was established in 2013; routes from other Chinese cities to Europe were also being explored (table 11.1). To electronics firms in western China supplying EU markets (e.g., HP, Acer, and Foxconn) and to EU firms shipping parts to their operations in China (e.g., Volkswagen, Audi, and BMW), the Eurasian Landbridge rail link through Kazakhstan, Russia, Belarus, and Poland offers an attractive price/time option, faster than by sea and at lower cost than by air. This development is analyzed in the next chapter.

In 2012, the Central Asian countries still imported more from Russia than from any other single country, but China had become by far the region's most important export destination (table 10.2).[23] China has been active in Tajikistan and the Kyrgyz Republic as an investor and had been providing aid in the form of road-building and so forth (Kassenova, 2009). The Eurasian Economic Union hurt China's exports by increasing Kazakhstan's external trade barriers and by cutting off part of the Kyrgyz Republic entrepôt trade (and potentially all of it after the Kyrgyz Republic's accession to the EAEU in 2015). However, the underlying complementarities are so strong that it seems likely that China's trade with Central Asia will continue to increase in the longer term, and it would be even more substantial if transport connections were better and trade costs lower.

China's growing economic presence was highlighted by President Xi Jinping's September 2013 tour when he visited four Central Asian countries before attending the SCO summit in Bishkek. President Xi met all five Central Asian presidents, and he pledged over $50 billion in Chinese funding for energy and infrastructure projects. At the summit, he proposed a Silk Road Economic Belt as a way of integrating the region through new infrastructure, increased cultural exchanges, and more trade. The Asian Infrastructure Investment Bank, formalized in 2014–15, stood ready to provide funding.[24]

---

22. The decisions of Hewlett-Packard and Foxconn to locate in Chongqing were stimulated by establishment of a bonded train service from Shenzhen, which could bring components to Chongqing. Exporters from Chongqing intended to use the Yangtze River to Shanghai as the major export route, but this quickly became congested, especially at key locks.

23. China was the most important export market for Kazakhstan, Turkmenistan, and Uzbekistan largely because of the oil and gas pipelines completed in 2009. Turkey was Tajikistan's largest export market. For the Kyrgyz Republic it was Switzerland, primarily due to gold with unknown final destination.

24. The fifty countries signing the AIIB's Articles of Agreement in June 2015 included Ka-

TABLE 10.2. Central Asian (CA) Countries' Exports to and Imports from Russia and China, 2012 (Million US Dollars)

	Russian Federation (RF)			People's Republic of China (PRC)		
	Exports from CA	Imports from RF	Total trade	Exports from CA	Imports from PRC	Total trade
Kazakhstan	6,747	17,110	23,857	16,484	7,498	23,982
Kyrgyz Republic	219	1,785	2,004	61	1,210	1,271
Tajikistan	45	738	783	99	1,923	2,022
Turkmenistan	165	1,209	1,374	7,290	1,870	9,160
Uzbekistan	689	2,457	3,146	992	1,962	2,954

Source: From data in ADBI (2014, 46–56) based on IMF, *Direction of Trade Statistics*.

In contrast to Russian and EU interaction with Central Asia, most of China's activities have been low key—at least until President Xi's September 2013 visit. Pipelines and other investments are presented as business arrangements, and the focus on roads contrasts with Russian involvement in controversial hydroelectricity projects. Politically, China presents itself as a good neighbor, with similar concerns to Central Asian governments, especially with respect to extremism and splittism.[25] In Central Asia, there are official concerns in Kazakhstan about pollution of rivers flowing west from China, and popular concerns about Chinese immigration, especially in Kazakhstan and the Kyrgyz Republic where numbers are larger.[26]

The speed with which China became a major economic partner for Central Asia between 2000 and 2010 was remarkable. Russia's response has been ambivalent, with creation of the Eurasian Economic Union placing a protectionist wall against Chinese trade in the region. On the other hand, initiation of the rail link from Chongqing to Duisburg required Russian cooperation, which appears to be willingly given, perhaps because with little effort Russia benefits from large transit fees (see section 11.1).

---

zakhstan, the Kyrgyz Republic, Tajikistan, Uzbekistan, Iran, Azerbaijan, and Turkey. The Silk Road Economic Belt was part of the One Belt One Road Initiative, which was rebranded as the Belt and Road Initiative at the formal launch in Beijing in May 2017.

25. China's main concern is separatism in Xinjiang Autonomous Region, where the Turkic-speaking Islamic Uighurs have strong cultural affinities with Kazakhs and Kyrgyz. The implicit agreement with Central Asian governments is that, as long as they do not support Uighur separatism, China has only peaceful intentions.

26. Laruelle and Peyrouse (2009, 56–60) discuss estimates. Violence against Chinese people seems to have been most common in the early 2000s, e.g., in the Kyrgyz Republic nineteen Chinese businessmen were killed on March 27, 2003, and looting during the 2005 Tulip Revolution cost Chinese businesses $35 million (Raballand and Andrésy, 2007, 237).

10.4. The Rise and Fall of US Interest in Central Asia

After the dissolution of the USSR, the USA quickly established embassies in the new independent states. For the USA, a major exercise involved securing and eliminating Soviet-era nuclear and biological weapons materials and facilities in Kazakhstan and, to a lesser extent, Uzbekistan. The USA was also interested in promoting democracy and civil society, and addressing high poverty rates, but actual assistance was limited.[27]

The main US economic interests in the 1990s lay in the energy sector in Kazakhstan, although private firms such as Chevron, Exxon/Mobil, or Haliburton did not require extensive government assistance, and they were largely left to themselves, unless they broke US law as in the Kazakhgate legal cases (chapter 5). The USA engaged with Turkmenistan in the mid-1990s, when Unocal sought US government assistance in its quest to replace the Argentinian company Bridas in constructing a gas pipeline from Turkmenistan through Afghanistan to Pakistan, but the project came to naught following the Clinton administration's withdrawal of any support for Taliban-administered Afghanistan after the massacre of civilians in Mazar-i-Sharif in August 1998. The USA only reengaged in Afghanistan in 2001, after the Taliban government refused to extradite Osama bin-Laden, the alleged mastermind behind the September 11 atrocities in the USA.

After September 11, 2001, Central Asia became more significant for the USA, primarily as "front-line" states for operations in Afghanistan. All five countries offered overflight and other support for coalition antiterrorism operations in Afghanistan. Uzbekistan hosted a major airbase, but after US criticism of the handling of the May 2005 Andijan events, Uzbekistan rescinded the basing agreement. After that, the major US airbase was at the Manas airport in the Kyrgyz Republic, until 2014 when US military involvement in Afghanistan was phased out. After conditions in Pakistan deteriorated in 2009, the Central Asian countries were part of the Northern Distribution Network (NDN) for supplying US forces in Afghanistan with nonlethal supplies.[28] The

27. In the two decades after 1992, Central Asia received about one-seventh of budgeted US foreign aid to the Eurasian region. Out of $5.7 billion aid to Central Asia, Kazakhstan received $2,050 million, Kyrgyzstan $1,222 million, Tajikistan $989 million, Uzbekistan $971 million, and Turkmenistan $352 million, with the remainder allocated to regional projects. In 2011–14 Central Asia was receiving similar amounts to the three much smaller Caucasus countries, and two-thirds to three-quarters of US aid to Central Asia went to the Kyrgyz Republic and Tajikistan (Nichol, 2014, 57 and 76).

28. By late 2011 three-quarters of nonlethal surface shipments to Afghanistan used the NDN and in the first half of 2012 with the halt of shipments through Pakistan the share was effectively 100%. The NDN consisted of several distinct routes (Yuldasheva, 2013). The main rail route ran from the Baltic Sea through Latvia, Russia, Kazakhstan, and Uzbekistan or bypassed Uzbekistan by running from Kazakhstan through the Kyrgyz Republic and Tajikistan by road, while an alter-

countries also participated in the repatriation of US equipment from Afghanistan, driven in part by hopes of receiving vehicles and other equipment that would not be repatriated to the USA.

In the decade after 2001, US relations with Central Asia focused on fighting terrorism and operations in Afghanistan, and to a much lesser extent Iraq.[29] This emphasis was challenged in 2011 by the Arab Spring and vision of similar destabilizing uprisings in Central Asia, and by a sense that space was being left for increasing Russian and Chinese influence in the region. The tempo of meetings between the US and Central Asian governments accelerated, but they were rarely at the highest level (Nichol, 2014, 7).

In 2011 Secretary of State Clinton articulated a "New Silk Road Vision" for Afghanistan and Central Asia, which she explained as "a web of economic and transit connections that will bind together a region too long torn apart by conflict and division." Nine projects were proposed as the most economically beneficial to Central Asia, but these all involved Afghanistan and several have been indefinitely delayed, e.g., the Turkmenistan-Afghanistan-Pakistan-India (TAPI) pipeline or the Central Asia South Asia (CASA) regional electricity trade project.[30] Critics point both to the limited progress and US financial commitment, as well as the limited applicability of the "Silk Road" concept to links through Afghanistan to South Asia. The New Silk Road Initiative seems condemned to irrelevance, while any connections established in running the NDN were allowed to wither during the post-2014 withdrawal from Afghanistan.

Feigenbaum (2011), who had recently been US deputy assistant secretary of state for Central Asia, claims that even after President Obama's much-hyped September 2009 Asian trip the USA "no longer gets Asia" and especially Central Asia, because it is oblivious to the interconnectedness of the continent and still sees bilateral relations in isolation. His criticism is related to the single-minded focus on Afghanistan since 2001. He also bemoans the unwillingness to act with other major powers in this region of limited direct interest to the USA; for example, Chinese and US interests are aligned insofar as Chinese inroads into Central Asian markets and construction of east-west

---

native route via the Georgian Black Sea port of Poti bypassed Russia and connected though Baku and across the Caspian Sea to Aktau Port in Kazakhstan or Turkmenbashi Port in Turkmenistan, and some goods came by air to Navoi in Uzbekistan. Given the harsh terrain of the Kyrgyz-Tajik road routes, most goods passed through Uzbekistan, and entered Afghanistan via Termez. After August 2011, shipments to Mazar-i-Sharif went by rail from Termez/Hairatan.

29. In 2003 Kazakhstan and Uzbekistan endorsed US-led military action in Iraq, and some two-dozen Kazakhstan troops served in Iraq until 2008.

30. The CASA 1000 project to trade 1,000 MW of electricity from the Kyrgyz Republic and Tajikistan through Afghanistan to Pakistan and India had been prepared by the World Bank in 2006 (Feigenbaum, 2011, 47n.), but a decade later was no closer to commencement.

infrastructure reduce the region's dependence on a single partner, Russia, and support the core US objective of strengthening Central Asian sovereignty. For Feigenbaum, other US objectives include promoting free markets, democratization, and human rights, or generally helping the states become "responsible members of the international community rather than degenerate into xenophobic, extremist, and anti-Western regimes that contribute to wider regional conflict and instability."

One reason for apparent inconsistencies and lack of focus in US policy towards Central Asia has been an unresolved tension within the US government between the State Department, whose view of US objectives is described in the previous paragraph, and the Department of Defense whose focus is on strategic and military considerations. In 2005, when the USA and other countries condemned the excessive use of violence in the Andijan incident, the State Department reduced aid to Uzbekistan, but this was offset by increased military assistance from the Department of Defense (Cooley, 2012). In striking continuity over the quarter century after independence, Uzbekistan remained the major US ally in the region due to its strategic location and President Karimov's desire to avoid close formal entanglements with Russia; 2005–8 was only a minor blip in the long-term pattern. In February 2012, the USA elevated relations with Kazakhstan to those of a strategic partnership, i.e. similar to the status of Georgia and Ukraine. The USA has sought little political engagement with the Kyrgyz Republic, despite its lead in bringing democracy to Central Asia and the long US lease on the Manas transit facility until 2014.

10.5. The EU Looks East

The EU's relations with the countries of Eastern Europe and the Soviet Union were dramatically transformed by the collapse of communism between the June 1989 Polish elections and the dissolution of the USSR in December 1991. In the early 1990s, EU economic policymaking was dominated by the consequences of German reunification, transmitted to other EU countries through increased interest rates and the 1992 exchange rate crisis, which would only be (partially) settled by the introduction of the euro in 1999. The EU accession of Austria, Finland, and Sweden in 1995, was relatively simple because they had similar economic and political systems to the twelve existing members. Accession of Eastern European countries in the twenty-first century would be more challenging.

Amidst this turmoil, the EU paid less attention to the twelve CIS countries, apart from Russia, which was too large to be ignored.[31] The EU has since 1992 been undecided whether to treat the twelve non-Baltic Soviet successor states

---

31. The EU generally extends most-favored nation status, and most of the twelve countries receive preferential tariff treatment under the EU's Generalized System of Preferences schemes.

as a group, individually, or in subgroups, and whether to focus on comprehensive agreements or functional arrangements (e.g., on transport, border management, and drugs). Additionally, widely divergent national interests among EU members, especially in the area of oil and gas, have led to bilateral relationships at the national level sometimes dominating EU relations.[32]

Equal treatment of Soviet successor states is made difficult by the huge disparities in size between Russia, Ukraine, and the others, as well as by differing physical proximity to the EU (Ukraine borders four EU member countries, while the Caucasus and Central Asian countries border none). EU policy distinguishes between Russia, six "Eastern Partnership countries" from the western former Soviet Union and the Caucasus, and the five Central Asian countries, although within the last two groups de facto treatment is not uniform.[33] The EU faces the challenge of pursuing foreign policy goals, with nuanced hierarchical relationships and limited, primarily economic, instruments. Nevertheless, Central Asia is clearly at the bottom of the EU's Eastern Europe and former Soviet republics hierarchy.

European Commission funds were provided in the 1990s under the TACIS (Technical Assistance to the Commonwealth of Independent States) and the Transport Corridor Europe-Caucasus-Central Asia (TRACECA) programs. TACIS was launched in 1991 to provide grant-financed technical assistance to the twelve newly independent non-Baltic Soviet successor states.[34] Some useful research projects, especially in agriculture and in rural development, were carried out under the TACIS umbrella, but their impact was minor. TRACECA was set up in 1993 to develop an efficient and integrated transit transport system between Europe, the Caucasus, and Central Asia. The Multilateral Agreement on International Transport for Development of the Europe–Caucasus–Asia Corridor was signed in Baku on September 8, 1998, by twelve countries, and the Office of the Permanent Secretariat was opened in Baku in 2001.

32. This section focuses on EU-level relations. While recognizing that individual EU members' may have differing interests that they pursue individually, it cannot cover all twenty-eight members. The monitoring group EUCAM, which posts working papers and policy briefs on EU relations with Central Asia (at http://www.eucentralasia.eu) runs a national series of policy briefs with reports on individual EU members' relations with and policies towards Central Asia.

33. The Eastern Partnership (EaP) program was launched by the EU member states and six partner countries (Armenia, Azerbaijan, Belarus, Georgia, Moldova, and Ukraine) at a May 2009 summit in Prague. Weaker EU Partnership and Cooperation Agreements signed in 1999 provided a legal framework for cooperation with the Central Asian countries.

34. Mongolia was also included in the TACIS program for part of the period. The INOGATE (Interstate Oil and Gas Transportation to Europe) program, aimed at promoting the regional integration of pipeline systems and facilitating the transport of oil and gas both within the greater Eastern Europe and CIS region and towards the export markets of Europe, was also funded under the TACIS Regional Co-operation Programme. However, during the 1990s, when oil prices were low and production facilities often antiquated, the EU showed little interest in Central Asian energy resources.

Under TRACECA the EU has implemented sixty technical assistance and investment projects to the amount of over €121 million, covering issues such as training freight forwarders, contract supervision for highway rehabilitation, agreements on transport of dangerous goods, and maritime and civil aviation training. In addition, TRACECA has cofinanced projects, e.g., providing the border crossing component of the ADB's loans for upgrading the Bishkek-Almaty road, and identified areas for funding by multilateral institutions, e.g., the EBRD loaned $65 million to Kazakhstan and $40 million to Uzbekistan for railway rehabilitation after TRACECA projects had identified weaknesses in the region's rail system. Despite grand objectives, neither the TRACECA nor the TACIS schemes made a big impact in Central Asia.

The EU became more interested in Central Asia after the turn of the century. The eastern enlargement of the EU in 2004 and Russia's cut-off of energy supplies to Ukraine in 2006 focused policymakers' attention on Central Asia, although in the energy area much wasted effort was expended on the Nabucco pipeline project (eventually abandoned in 2014). The TRACECA route appeared to be fundamentally flawed insofar as by avoiding Russia and Iran it had to involve a Caspian Sea crossing, and few traders liked the multimodal route. In practice, EU assistance to Central Asia became focused on the drugs trade, and after the turn of the century the best-funded initiative of the European Commission was the BOMCA/CADAP program.[35]

The program was initially driven by the drug component, CADAP (Central Asia Drug Action Programme), intended to intercept narcotics being transported from Afghanistan through Central Asia to Western Europe. The accompanying rise in domestic drug abuse in Central Asia had already led all Central Asian governments except Turkmenistan to make opium cultivation illegal and to take steps to combat drug-trafficking, even though in practice many government officials up to high levels were implicated in the drugs trade and interdiction was selective. The national responses to drug-trafficking involved tighter border controls, which led to economic hardship for border communities and small traders, pushing some of those people into the drug trade. The focus of the EU's Border Management in Central Asia (BOMCA) program on upgrading border crossing points (e.g., by providing sniffer dogs, training for customs officials, and equipment) fitted in with these responses, although stricter border controls had the negative side effect of deterring legal trade.

Political relations between the EU and Central Asia deteriorated as the ill-starred 2003 EBRD annual meetings in Tashkent highlighted the lack of

---

35. Security relations were largely at the bilateral level, e.g., Germany maintained a base at Termez in Uzbekistan and France had an airbase in Tajikistan; both were small, with around 163 German troops at Termez and 100 French troops based in Tajikistan.

political leverage that European countries had in authoritarian Central Asian states. The Andijan incident in May 2005 led to a more serious rupture between Uzbekistan and EU members, including the imposition of sanctions by the EU. The shooting of citizens by Uzbek security forces, perhaps armed with equipment provided under the BOMCA program, raised questions about the nature of EU involvement. As part of revising the EU Central Asia Strategy, the BOMCA program was reviewed in 2006–7, and the consequence was a shift from border control to risk assessment and compliance facilitation. BOMCA signaled the importance of behind-the-border trade costs in trade facilitation by embracing the corridor concept, although BOMCA's strength in delivery continued to be at border crossing points. Financial support for the CADAP/BOMCA programs declined in the 2010s, with EU spending on the two programs for 2016–18 a mere €5 million.

Under the German presidency in the first half of 2007, the EU proposed a new strategy for Central Asia. The initiative, which had stalled under the Portuguese presidency, was picked up by the French presidency in the second half of 2008.[36] The Joint Declaration of the EU-Central Asia Forum on Security Issues in Paris on September 18, 2008, defined the main policy areas for joint action as combating illicit trafficking in arms, sensitive material, narcotics, and people; combating terrorism and extremism; and cooperation on energy and the environment. However, the area of energy cooperation has been either negligible or divisive so far. Individual companies' involvement in specific projects has triggered ad hoc political actions, but this has not been part of a consistent EU or national policy; for example, Eni's lead role in Kazakhstan's Kashagan offshore oil field led Italian prime minister Romano Prodi to travel at short notice to Astana in October 2007 and his successor Silvio Berlusconi made a brief unannounced weekend trip to Astana in October 2008.

In 2007–13 EU development assistance to Central Asia amounted to roughly €750 million, one-third to regional programs and two-thirds to bilateral initiatives, and it was planned to increase to €1 billion for 2014–20 (Boonstra, 2015, 4). In addition to EU-funded projects, individual EU member countries have provided development assistance to Central Asian countries; the leading bilateral donors included Germany, France, Sweden, Poland, and the United Kingdom. In total, however, EU financial assistance is dwarfed by the $40 billion pledged by China for the Belt and Road Initiative.

---

36. The rotating six-month chair of the EU Council inhibits a consistent policy position as some member countries have greater interest in Central Asia than others. Abolition of the position of EU special representative for Central Asia in March 2014 further undermined coherence, as well as sending a signal of lack of interest in the region; the position was reactivated and filled in April 2015.

In 2011 the European External Action Service began negotiations with Kazakhstan on an Enhanced Partnership and Cooperation Agreement, suggesting that for the EU Kazakhstan's more developed economy has a special status within Central Asia.[37] The feeling that the EU could not adopt a one-size-fits-all strategy towards the former Soviet republics was exacerbated by the conflict between Russia and Ukraine, and by Kazakhstan's specific situation as an EAEU member that was not bound by the sanctions imposed on and by Russia. Kazakhstan's WTO accession in 2015, following that of Russia and Tajikistan, suggests that trade issues might be resolved through the WTO's dispute settlement mechanism, although some lawyers point to Russia's disregard for legal constraints and preference for presenting a *fait accompli* (Dragneva-Lewers and Wolczuk, 2015).

Despite being Central Asia's largest trade partner, the EU's net economic and political impact in Central Asia has been small. Some individual EU companies have had a high profile in individual countries (e.g., see Garcia (2006) on Bouygues in Turkmenistan) or in energy projects (e.g., Shell, Eni, British Gas), but overall EU companies have lagged behind the higher profile of Russian or US companies and the increasing Chinese economic presence. Nor has the EU been successful in promoting noneconomic goals. Boonstra (2015) concludes that "the overall picture of the EU's engagement in Central Asia is one of limited to no impact. The region has become more unstable; democracy is seen by the regimes as a threat to their survival; and human rights have been backsliding," and in his subsequent submission to the EU Commission (Boonstra and Tsertsvadze, 2016) he was no more optimistic about the 2014–20 strategy.

10.6. Economic Relations with Other Countries

The five Central Asian countries joined Turkey, Iran, and Pakistan in the Economic Cooperation Organization shortly after independence, but ECO quickly experienced internal conflicts and has been ineffective. Individual Turkish companies have traded with or invested in Central Asia and NGOs have run education projects, especially in Turkmenistan, but there has been no concerted Turkish economic involvement in the region. Iran has been a donor of aid, especially to Tajikistan, and some trade has passed through Bandar Abbas, which is the closest ocean port to Central Asia, but UN sanctions

---

37. Kazakhstan was adopting a more proactive stance on engagement with international agencies, assuming the chair of the OCSE in 2010–11, engaging with the OECD on agriculture (OECD, 2013), and playing a lead role in the OECD's annual Eurasia Week, which it hosted in 2017. In 2016, Kazakhstan was elected to a seat on the UN Security Council for 2017–18.

on Iran between 1989 and 2015 dampened economic contacts. In sum, despite cultural ties, Turkey and Iran have remained minor economic partners.

India and Pakistan joined the SCO in 2017, but neither country has strong economic links to Central Asia. The difficulty of transit through Afghanistan inhibits links between Central and South Asia. Proposed trans-Afghan projects such as the TAPI pipeline or the CASA electricity link have languished.

In April 2015, Chinese president Xi Jinping announced plans to invest $46 billion to strengthen the China-Pakistan Economic Corridor, including upgrading the Karakorum Highway, establishing a rail link from Kashgar to Gwadar Port on the Indian Ocean, and providing an electricity transmission line. Although the journey from Central Asia through Kashgar is more geographically challenging than trans-Afghan routes from Central Asia to South Asia, the Chinese investment would open an alternative road and rail corridor in case of deteriorating conditions in Afghanistan. However, Pakistan has not been proactive in encouraging trade or other links with Central Asia.

India had strong political connections with the USSR, but geographic separation inhibits close economic ties with Central Asia. India hopes to play a part in the region, but the idea that a New Great Game was emerging in Central Asia with Russia, China, and India as the major players (Laruelle et al., 2010) proved false. India's 2012 "Connect Central Asia Policy" was effectively trumped by President Xi. When ConocoPhillips announced in November 2012 that it wanted to sell its 8.33% share in Kazakhstan's Kashagan megaoilfield, India's ONGC Videsh, Ltd. thought that it was the preferred buyer, but in July 2013 KazMunaiGas invoked its first-buyer right to preemptively purchase the share and then sell it to the China National Petroleum Corporation. India's long-standing hope for a TAPI (Turkmenistan-Afghanistan-Pakistan-India) pipeline to bring Turkmen gas to South Asia also appeared to be sidelined by Xi's proposal for a Turkmenistan-Afghanistan-Tajikistan-China pipeline (Boulègue, 2013; Tanchum, 2013). India has been investing in Iran's Chabahar Port, which may finally provide a link to Central Asia with the lifting of sanctions on Iran.

Japan and South Korea have both been minor partners. Japan has channeled aid to Central Asian countries through the Japan International Cooperation Agency (JICA) and Japan External Trade Organization (JETRO), but trade with Japan accounts for less than 1% of Central Asian trade (table 10.1). The Korean diaspora in Central Asia, especially in Tashkent and Almaty, stimulated South Korean contact, but the trade flows are little more than Japan's and the largest Korean investment, by Daewoo Motors, is now owned by a US company. Korea has a EurAsia Initiative, centered on (1) the Trans-Eurasia Information Network, which provides dedicated high-capacity internet connectivity for research and education communities across the Asia-Pacific region, i.e. it is not specific to Central Asia, and (2) the Eurasia Express rail service from Korea to the EU. The track is already in place across the rail bridge between North Korea and Russia, which connects to the TransSiberian Railway to Moscow and the EU, but given the situation in North Korea and the time to cross the TransSiberian, the Eurasia Express is unlikely to be a serious alternative to ocean routes or to China-EU rail projects, and the route bypasses Central Asia.[38] In sum, there is really nothing in Korea's EurAsia Initiative for Central Asia. Although it would not be diplomatic to treat any of these initiatives with disrespect, Korea's EurAsia Initiative is in a similar category to Japan's Central Asia and Japan Dialogue, India's Connect Central Asia Policy, the US New Silk Road Initiative, and the EU's (2007) Central Asia Strategy. All involve talk and plans, but little content.

Australia, thinking that economic similarities could lead to close links with Kazakhstan, opened an embassy in Almaty in 1995. Australia's Telstra formed a joint venture, SATEL, with Kazakhstan's state telecommunications company in 1994, but the arrangement broke down in 1997 amid sufficient rancor as to contribute to Australia closing its embassy the following year. Other foreign telecommunications companies struggled to establish operations in Central Asia, but a few companies from Scandinavia and elsewhere succeeded; their experience will be analyzed in section 10.8.

10.7. Private Foreign Direct Investment

Central Asia receives a tiny share of global foreign direct investment (FDI) and totals are dominated by Kazakhstan and Turkmenistan, whose inflows are primarily into the oil and gas sector (table 2.13). However, several features of FDI in CIS countries (such as round-tripping or rerouting of FDI for tax or other reasons) make it likely that the macroeconomic estimates are little more than rough approximations of total FDI. It is extremely difficult to disaggregate the FDI flows by nationality or sector.[39]

An alternative approach to UNCTAD's *World Investment Review* in measuring FDI is a bottom-up method of adding individual projects. This is notori-

38. A sea-rail link between Korea and Uzbekistan via Lianyungang Port, essentially serves a single client, transporting components from Korea to the ex-Daewoo factory.

39. The top five countries holding FDI stock in the "transition economies," whose UNCTAD definition overlaps substantially with the CIS, in 2014 were Cyprus ($125 billion), the USA ($31 billion), Ireland ($27 billion), France ($25 billion), and the Russian Federation ($24 billion). These numbers suggest considerable round-tripping (CIS firms using Cyprus-based affiliates to benefit from "foreign" investment status in the CIS), rerouting from the foreign investors' domicile (using Ireland-based subsidiaries for home-country tax benefits), and intra-CIS FDI by Russia; as will be apparent in the next section, it is sometimes difficult to identify the ownership of "Russian" companies given that many owners were born in the USSR.

ously difficult as omissions are likely due to the difficulty of tracking all foreign-invested projects. At the same time, reliance on announcements of foreign investment may overstate actual flows, as many projects are abandoned or only partially implemented. An advantage of bottom-up approaches is that they can try to separate physical investment, which is often what we want to understand by "FDI," from portfolio capital flows, but it may still be difficult to separate greenfield investments that add to the physical capital stock from mergers and acquisitions that transfer ownership from domestic to foreign sources.

Since 2011 the Eurasian Development Bank Centre for Integration Studies has maintained the *CIS Countries and Georgia Mutual Direct Investments Monitoring Database* (MIM CIS) on mutual FDI stock involving the former Soviet republics except the three Baltic countries.[40] The database relies on corporate statements and other primary information, taking into account investments made through offshore structures, and excluding only projects valued under $1 million. The bottom-up approach highlights the role of a handful of very large investors (table 10.3). The two largest investing companies accounted for almost $16 billion, i.e. over one-third of the total, and their investments were dominated by Gazprom's gas transport subsidiary in Belarus and LUKOIL's oil and gas investments in Uzbekistan and Kazakhstan (led by a 5% share in the Tengiz oil field, valued at $1.8 billion).[41]

Apart from energy-related projects, table 10.3 is dominated by service sectors such as information technology and communications (ITC), finance, and tourism. This is consistent with UNCTAD (*World Investment Review 2016*, 13), which reports that 70% of FDI in "transition economies" was in services, although UNCTAD does not provide a breakdown by country or subsector. While recognizing that the ITC, finance, and infrastructure FDI in table 10.3 are primarily in Russia, Belarus, and Ukraine, such service-sector transnational operations are present in Central Asia, especially the ITC companies and Meridian.[42] The next section examines the experience of MTS and Vim-

---

40. MIM CIS estimates show the stock of mutual FDI increasing to a peak of $57.1 billion in 2012 (up from $36.7 billion in 2009, the earliest year reported), before dropping to $41.8 billion in 2015, and rebounding to $45.1 billion in 2016. Outward FDI is dominated by Russian investors with over three-quarters of the total, followed by Kazakhstan, Azerbaijan, and Belarus in 2016. The leading hosts by FDI stock in 2016 were Belarus 19%, Kazakhstan 18%, Russia 14%, Ukraine 12%, and Uzbekistan 12%. All references to the database are to *Monitoring of Mutual Investments in CIS Countries Report 45* (Eurasian Development Bank Centre for Integration Studies, Saint Petersburg, Russia, 2017). The caveats about the MIM CIS database also apply to other bottom-up approaches such as the World Investment Review's estimates of "announced greenfield FDI projects."

41. The Tengiz investment illustrates a grey area between portfolio and direct investment; LUKOIL is not the lead operator of the project, but clearly has expertise in the industry.

42. Meridian Capital, incorporated in 2002, is an investment and holding company with

TABLE 10.3. Ten Largest CIS Investors in CIS Countries, FDI Stock, December 2016

Investor	Home country	Major sector	FDI stock ($ billion)	Destination countries in CIS		
				number	main destination	share*
Gazprom	Russia	oil & gas	8.34	9	Belarus	62
LUKOIL	Russia	oil & gas	7.59	6	Uzbekistan	50
VimpelCom (VEON)	Russia	ITC	1.82	8	Kazakhstan	43
MTS	Russia	ITC	1.79	5	Belarus	46
Yuras	Belarus	chemicals	1.75	1	Russia	100
SOCAR	Azerbaijan	oil & gas	1.29	2	Georgia	87
Meridian Capital	Kazakhstan	finance	1.19	3	Russia	92
VS Energy	Russia	infrastructure	1.08	1	Ukraine	100
Polymetal	Russia	non-ferrous metals	0.87	2	Kazakhstan	92
Verny Capital	Kazakhstan	tourism/ITC	0.87	2	Russia	81

Source: Monitoring of Mutual Investments in CIS Countries Report 45, page 10.
Notes: * Share of that country in the column 4 total; ITC = information technology and communications. The authors caution about the influence of extra-large deals, such as Yuras purchasing a 20% share in Russia's Uralkali for $1.7 billion in 2016.

pelCom (since 2017 VEON), the two major suppliers of mobile telephone services in Central Asia.

10.8. Mobile Phone Services

External relations of Central Asian countries have often been defined by actions of foreign companies, rather than foreign governments. In the energy sector, most foreign participation has involved large corporations who are used to looking after their interests in challenging circumstances. These companies, and others whose names have come up in earlier chapters (e.g.,

---

worldwide interests in oil and gas, real estate, mining, airports, and more. Its ownership is opaque, but linked to Eugene Feld (as CEO) and Askar Alshinbaev (who named his luxury yacht "Meridian") who were connected to Kazkommertsbank. After the 2017 "Paradise Papers" leak of 6.8 million confidential records from a Bermuda law firm, the Organized Crime and Corruption Reporting Project (Patrucic et al., 2017) compiled some details of Meridian's operations, and established links to Sauat Mynbaev, former minister of finance and chairman of KazMunaiGaz. In the company's earlier years, revenues from Kazakhstan's booming oil industry fueled Meridian's growth, and a 2006 disclosure put its assets at $3 billion. A large portion of Kazkommertsbank's deposits funded Meridian projects; whenever a project failed, the losses were dumped onto the bank's balance sheets, while Meridian kept the successful investments. By 2009, Kazkommertsbank needed government bailouts (section 4.5), and infusions of public funds reached $1.4 billion in 2010; in 2017 the bank was deemed to have failed, the government committed $7.5 billion to resolving bad debts, and ownership passed to Halyk Bank, controlled by the president's daughter and son-in-law.

Bouygues or Polimeks in Turkmenistan, Daewoo in Uzbekistan, or Cameco in the Kyrgyz Republic), have been driven by profits, and have required little or no support from the French, Turkish, Korean, or Canadian governments. One important sector in which foreign firms have been crucial due to their technological advantage has been provision of mobile phone services, and this sector provides a case study for analyzing the profits and pitfalls of investing in service activities in Central Asia.

Mobile phone services have been important in Central Asia. The development of mobile phone technology, coinciding with the independent history of the Central Asian countries, provided the countries' citizens and business-people with a valuable means of leapfrogging one aspect of their low-quality inherited infrastructure, i.e. the poor fixed-line telephone system. Construction and maintenance of mobile phone networks relied on foreign technology, brought into the region by Russian and Scandinavian investors and some independent entrepreneurs with US connections. Although the size of foreign investment flows by sector is difficult to measure, this may be the second-largest area of FDI in Central Asia after oil and gas, and it is the only nonenergy sector where foreign investors have been clearly the dominant players and source of new technology.

The potential profits are clear from the willingness of foreign investors to become involved and to spend money obtaining licenses and constructing a network. To some degree the pitfalls should have also been clear, given the evidence of weak rule of law and protection of property rights in the region. Despite the corruption and summary termination of licenses, the two major companies appear to be there for the long haul. On the other hand, the main Scandinavian investor, TeliaSonera, has decided it is too hard and has withdrawn from Uzbekistan and Tajikistan.[43]

Market penetration (i.e. number of subscriptions divided by population) grew rapidly after the turn of the century, and especially in 2010–14 (Peyrouse, 2016). By 2014, Kazakhstan, the Kyrgyz Republic, and Turkmenistan all had penetration rates well over 100% and Tajikistan was at about 100%.[44] Service provision over these years was dominated by three foreign companies (table 10.4): MTS, Beeline (VimpelCom), and TeliaSonera (sometimes through Megafon, a Russian company part-owned by TeliaSonera). TeliaSonera is a Scandinavian company, and VimpelCom and MTS are controlled by Russian

---

43. Other foreign companies tested CIS markets but withdrew. The 1994 joint venture SATEL between Australia's Telstra and Kazakhstan's state telecommunications company broke down in 1997. Orange (France Telecom) entered the Armenian market in 2009, and had 501,000 subscribers by the end of 2014, but in July 2015 Orange sold out to a local company.

44. The actual number of separate subscribers is unknown. Many people hold multiple subscriptions to take advantage of special offers or features of different plans, which is testimony to the affordability of services in Central Asia.

TABLE 10.4. Major Operators of Mobile Phone Services in Central Asia, c. 2015

Country	1	2	3	Notes
Kazakhstan	KCell (T)	VimpelCom	AlTel/Tele2	
Kyrgyz Republic	Megacom	Sky/Beeline (V)	O! (Nur Telecom)	Megacom being privatized
Tajikistan	Tcell (T)	Babilon	Megafon (t)	VimpelCom 4th
Turkmenistan	Altyn Asyr	MTS		Altyn Asyr state-owned
Uzbekistan	VimpelCom	TeliaSonera	Uzmobile	MTS suspended

Sources: Assembled from company and other websites and from Peyrouse (2016).
Notes: V, M, and T = wholly or majority-owned by VimpelCom, MTS, or TeliaSonera respectively; t = 25% owned by TeliaSonera.

oligarchs, Mikhail Fridman and Vladimir Yevtushenkov. The sector is highly competitive, although network effects mean that national markets tend to become dominated by a small number of firms. Where regulators control the limited number of licenses or access is otherwise restricted, opportunities for corruption are rife and market composition has been unstable.

Providing an overview of national markets is complex, and the following summaries apply to the situation in 2015, approximately. Kazakhstan's market is dominated by Kcell (of which TeliaSonera is majority shareholder) and Beeline (VimpelCom) with 40% and 37% market shares; the third- and fourth-placed, Tele2 (Swedish-owned) and AlTel (state-owned), merged in 2016.[45] The Kyrgyz Republic market is dominated by Megacom and Sky, with a combined market share of 75%. Megacom was owned by ex-president Bakiyev's son, Maxim, and after Bakiyev's overthrow it was acquired by the state and earmarked for privatization, although a scheduled auction in June 2016 was canceled due to lack of bids. Sky operates under the Beeline logo and is owned by Vimpel and Verny. Five firms dominate the Tajikistan market: Tcell (60% owned by TeliaSonera), Babilon, Megafon, Takom (Beeline), and TK mobile. Babilon was originally a US-Tajik joint venture, but Hightronic, a private company of Russian origin registered in the British Virgin Islands, now has 75% ownership of Babilon. In Uzbekistan, Unitel and Ucell have 90% of the market, since former market-leader Uzdunrobita (MTS) lost its license in 2012 and Beeline and TeliaSonera failed to increase market share despite paying bribes to the president's daughter (all of which helps to explain the relatively low penetration rate of 74% in 2014, down from 90% in 2011). In Turkmenistan, MTS acquired the number-one operator in June 2005 and by December 2010 its wholly owned subsidiary BCTI was providing services to more than 2.4

45. Kcell was majority-owned by the state-owned Kazakhtelecom until privatization in 2012. In 2015, TeliaSonera held 62% of the shares, with Turkcell the largest minority shareholder. Turkcell reported to the Securities and Exchange Commission (SEC) allegations of improper payments having been made by Kcell in 2012.

million subscribers, but BCTI's licenses were suspended in December 2010, giving the state-owned Altyn Asyr TM Cell a monopoly until August 2012 when MTS's operations resumed through a wholly owned subsidiary MTS-Turkmenistan.

The next three subsections will examine the three dominant companies: VimpelCom, MTS, and TeliaSonera. They have experienced problems associated with charges of corruption or other unethical behavior; among other cases, all three companies came under external investigation for corruption in Uzbekistan. The lure of a highly profitable sector has kept VimpelCom and MTS in the region despite the institutional problems. TeliaSonera, which often operated in joint ventures as a way of gaining familiarity with local conditions, announced in September 2015 that it was exiting the region.

10.8.1. VIMPELCOM

The black and yellow logo of VimpelCom's Beeline brand of mobile phone service is a familiar sight across much of Central Asia. VimpelCom has over two hundred million mobile phone subscribers worldwide, including fifty-nine million in Russia, ten million in Uzbekistan, and around twenty-four million customers in Armenia, Georgia, Kazakhstan, Kyrgyzstan, and Tajikistan. VimpelCom is one of the three leading mobile phone operators in Russia, the market leader in Uzbekistan, and the second-largest operator in Kazakhstan, Armenia, and Kyrgyzstan. Other major markets are in Italy, Ukraine, Algeria, Pakistan, and Bangladesh.[46]

OJSC VimpelCom was founded in Moscow in 1992 and the Beeline brand was created in 1993. The company was listed on the New York Stock Exchange from 1996 to 2010—the first Russian company to do so. In 2009 the company's major shareholders, Telenor (Norway) and Alfa (Russia), created VimpelCom as the united holding company registered in Bermuda. In 2016 Telenor sold off a large portion of their shares, and as of 2016Q3 the shareholders were Letter One (Luxembourg) 47.9%, Telenor (Norway) 23.7%, and Stichting (Netherlands) 8.3%, with 20.1% in free float; the shares trade on NASDAQ, and the company is headquartered in the Netherlands. Letter One, created in 2013, is controlled by Russian businessman Mikhail Fridman.[47]

---

46. VimpelCom is the number-one mobile phone operator in Ukraine, Algeria, and Pakistan, and number two in Bangladesh. In 2010 VimpelCom acquired Wind, and in 2016 formed a joint venture with the Hutchinson Group to merge Wind and 3 Italia; the joint venture has thirty-one million customers in Italy.

47. Fridman controls Alfa. He was born and raised in Ukraine, but became a Russian citizen. On the *Forbes* Richlist for 2016, he was listed as the second-richest man in Russia. He also has Israeli citizenship. He is resident in London, where he bought a Highgate property (Athlone House) for £65 million (*Sunday Times*, April 17, 2016).

VimpelCom's expansion into Uzbekistan ran into problems with foreign regulators. The company funneled money through Telenor into accounts of Gulnara Karimova in return for the president's daughter using her influence for VimpelCom to obtain operating licenses and a dominant position in Uzbekistan's mobile phone market. The case against VimpelCom was eventually closed in 2016 with a global settlement under the US Foreign Corrupt Practices Act whereby VimpelCom was fined $896 million, of which $498 million went to the USA and $398 million to the Netherlands.

10.8.2. MTS

MTS is the largest mobile and fixed-line operator in the CIS and has the largest mobile phone operations in Eastern Europe. MTS was originally formed in 1993 as a partnership of four Russian and two German (Deutsche Telekom and Siemens) companies. After subsequent stock sales, mergers, and acquisitions, OJSC MTS was created in 2000 and listed on the New York Stock Exchange. In 2016, MTS had over 30% market share in Russia and operations in Armenia, Belarus, Turkmenistan Ukraine, and Uzbekistan in the CIS. MTS shares were 50.44% owned by Sistema JSFC, and the remaining 49.5% were in free float.[48]

In 2005 MTS paid $121 million for a 74% stake in Uzdunrobita, the largest mobile phone operator in Uzbekistan, and in 2007 MTS acquired the remaining shares for $250 million.[49] After MTS had invested a further $1.1 billion in the subsidiary, Uzdunrobita's operating license was suspended in July 2012 for technical violations, and the company was presented with a $1.3 million bill

---

48. Sistema is a Russian investment holding company whose major shareholder with 64% of the company is Vladimir Yevtushenkov. Sistema was an early shareholder in VimpelCom, selling its stake when VimpelCom was listed on the New York Stock Exchange in 1996. Sistema's $1.35 billion IPO in February 2005 was Russia's largest ever at the time. Apart from MTS, other major Sistema assets include children's goods retailer Detsky Mir, pulp and paper holding Segezha Group, and Russia's largest chain of private healthcare clinics MEDSI. In 2014, *Forbes* ranked Yevtushenkov as Russia's fifteenth-richest businessman with an estimated fortune of around $8.3 billion. In September 2014, Russian investigators placed Yevtushenkov under house arrest, accusing him of money laundering in connection with the 2009 acquisition of shares in oil producer Bashneft, and in December 2014 Bashneft was renationalized. In February 2015, the Moscow Arbitration Court awarded Sistema 70.7 billion rubles ($1.1 billion) in damages from the loss of Bashneft, and in January 2016, all accusations related to the acquisition of Bashneft were dismissed as it was found that no crime had been committed ("Russian Oligarch Yevtushenkov Cleared of Charges in Bashneft Case," *Moscow Times*, January 14, 2016). As of May 2016, *Forbes* estimated Yevtushenkov's net worth at $3 billion. Later in 2016 Bashneft was purchased by state-run Rosneft, whose CEO Igor Sechin, a close associate of Vladimir Putin, alleged that Sistema illegally kept Bashneft assets, and sued Yevtushenkov in 2017 for $2.8 billion in damages ("Russian Brawl," *Economist* (London), July 8, 2017).

49. Uzdunrobita was founded on August 1991, as a joint venture between a group of American investors and the Uzbek government. Gulnara Karimova gained control of the firm in the late 1990s or early 2000s.

for unpaid back taxes. Citing repeated regulatory violations, the government of Uzbekistan revoked the company's operating license in August 2012, imposing $900 million in fines and arresting five senior managers.[50] On completion of the case in September 2012, the company's assets were seized, and some of its executives sentenced to prison terms. In April 2013 Uzdunrobita was declared bankrupt and its financial assets seized by the government, and in December 2013 the company's physical assets were transferred to the state telecommunications company, Uzbektelecom.

In June 2005, MTS acquired BCTI, which was by 2010 the largest telecommunications operator in Turkmenistan, providing services to more than 2.4 million subscribers. In December 2010, BCTI's licenses were suspended. In August 2012, operations resumed through MTS's wholly owned subsidiary MTS-Turkmenistan; as of June 30, 2015, MTS was servicing 1.6 million customers, 30% of the market. Although the Turkmenistan check ended up being less severe for MTS than the Uzbekistan debacle, the temporary suspension facilitated loss of market leadership to the state-owned Altyn Asyr TM Cell.

Since 2008 MTS has been diversifying its ITC operations. In October 2009, MTS acquired Comstar-UTS, the leading supplier of integrated telecommunication solutions in Russia and the CIS, providing access to growth markets in commercial and residential broadband. In March 2013, MTS acquired a 25.1% stake in MTS Bank OJSC, increasing its ownership stake in MTS Bank to 26.85%. MTS and MTS Bank have concluded a profit-sharing agreement whereby MTS and MTS Bank would realize 70% and 30% of the proceeds from the MTS Dengi (MTS Money) project. In April 2014, MTS acquired a 10.82% stake in OZON Holdings, the leading Russian e-commerce company, providing exclusive access to OZON's sales channels for MTS's products and services and opportunities to improve MTS's own online store.

In September 2014, MTS took possession of a controlling stake (50.1%) in the Russian-Uzbek entity Universal Mobile Systems. UMS was granted 2G, 3G, and LTE licenses, and the permits required for the launch of operations, and UMS also received investment protection and return on investments guaranties in accordance with the laws of Uzbekistan. In August 2016, MTS sold its UMS stake to the State Unitary Enterprise Centre of Radio Communication, which is part of Uzbekistan's Information Technologies Ministry and already owned the other 50% of UMS. A silver lining to MTS's problems in Uzbekistan was that, although MTS was involved in the same corruption investigation as VimpelCom and TeliaSonera, because fines are related to profits made as a result of corrupt activity, MTS came off relatively lightly due to its absence from the Uzbekistan market in 2012–14.

50. MTS protested the action as a "shakedown," but was unable to effectively oppose it; "RPT-Russia's MTS Fights to Save $1 Bln Uzbek Business," at http://in.reuters.com/article/mts -uzbekistan-licence-idINL6E8JNI6120120824 (posted August 24, 2012).

10.8.3. TELIASONERA

TeliaSonera is the result of a 2002 merger between the Swedish and Finnish telecommunications companies, Telia and Sonera, that followed shortly after Telia's failed merger with Telenor. TeliaSonera is the largest mobile operator in Scandinavia and the Baltic countries.

TeliaSonera operates in Kazakhstan under the brand KCell. TeliaSonera owns 25.2% of Megafon, the second-largest mobile phone operator in Russia and third largest in Tajikistan. In Tajikistan TeliaSonera also owned 60% of mobile phone operator Tcell, which is the result of a merger of Somoncom and Indigo Tajikistan completed in July 2012.

In 2007 TeliaSonera acquired a 3G license in Uzbekistan from Takilant Limited, a company registered in Gibraltar and controlled by Gulnara Karimova. TeliaSonera's Uzbek subsidiary, Ucell, increased the number of its subscribers from four hundred thousand in 2007 to nine million in 2012. TeliaSonera came under investigation by Swedish prosecutors in 2012 for allegations of bribery and money laundering associated with the acquisition of its license in 2007.[51] In 2016 TeliaSonera made a 5.3 billion kronor ($622 million) writedown of its Uzbek operations. TeliaSonera also tried to divest its Tajikistan operations, but ran into delays with the regulatory authorities until in 2017 it sold its Tcell shareholding to the minority partner Indigo, which is owned by the Aga Khan Fund for Economic Development. In February 2016, Turkish company Turkcell submitted a binding offer for TeliaSonera's stake in mobile operations in Kazakhstan, Azerbaijan, Georgia, and Moldova.

10.8.4. ANALYSIS

Mobile phone use has grown rapidly in Central Asia, especially since the turn of the century, and supplying mobile phone services is potentially very profitable. The lead has been taken by foreign companies with the required technical capacity. Initially much of the expertise appears to have come from Scandinavian companies (Telenor, Sonera, and Telia), but by 2016 the dominant players were two Russian oligarchs, Mikhail Fridman and Vladimir Yevtushenkov. All the major players have encountered serious obstacles, especially in Uzbekistan and Turkmenistan.

The difficulties in Uzbekistan were intimately related to the family politics and the close connection between political power and economic power. Gulnara Karimova built up a large financial empire in the 1990s and 2000s,

51. The preliminary investigation followed allegations presented in the Sveriges Television (SVT) program *Uppdrag granskning* ("Commission to Investigate"); reported in "Corruption Probe into TeliaSonera Uzbek Deal," *Gazette of Central Asia*, September 27, 2012, available at http://gca.satrapia.com/corruption-probe-into-teliasonera-uzbek-deal.

part of which was due to her ability to allocate licenses to mobile phone servers. This seems to have involved playing off the three major foreign companies to her own financial benefit. The outcome by 2015 was that all three major companies had been shaken down, and that Uzbekistan had the poorest mobile phone coverage in Central Asia.

The difficulty over licenses in Turkmenistan seems to have been a simpler ploy to help the state-owned provider of mobile services to gain market share. The consequence has been less harmful to the growth of mobile phone use in Turkmenistan than in Uzbekistan, but it is hardly likely to encourage foreign investors.

Despite these setbacks, and other allegations of corruption in what has clearly been a lucrative industry with a few high-profile players, mobile phone use has spread remarkably quickly in Central Asia. Part of the explanation is the lack of embedded regulations and vested interests. Foreign investors played a key role in transferring technology and providing the capital to set up networks, and they encountered little resistance in obtaining operating licenses despite the absence of transparency. Fixed-line telephone services were so bad that they offered no serious alternative. State-owned telecomm enterprises may have played a spoiling game in Turkmenistan and Uzbekistan, but in Kazakhstan the government targeted Kaztelecom's mobile phone division as one of the first acts of its People's IPO privatization program and Megacom, accidentally acquired by the Kyrgyz government, is also targeted for privatization. The net result was a major improvement in this aspect of information and communication technology availability in Central Asian countries.

10.9. Conclusions and Prospects for the Future

The Central Asian leaders have pursued multivector foreign policies, playing balancing acts with foreign powers or sheltered behind "neutrality" in Turkmenistan's case. This has worked because of the absence of a clear hegemon or even a bipolar competition for influence; although Russia and China are both in the SCO and the USA and EU share commitments to democratic development, human rights, and market-based economies, all four act as individual powers rather than allies of another power. The ambivalence is also visible in the Central Asian countries' membership of two UN regional bodies (ECE and ESCAP), hosting of both European and Asian regional meetings, and participation in European and Asian sporting events.[52]

---

52. For the two largest countries, however, choice of continent has been related to prospects of success. Thus, Uzbekistan plays soccer in Asia where it is a powerhouse with serious chances of medals in the Asian Championship and of qualification for the FIFA World Cup, while Kazakh-

The USA will continue to be viewed as a potential counterweight to Russia and China, especially by countries suspicious of Russian designs on the region.[53] From an economic perspective, however, the US role after the 2014 withdrawal from Afghanistan has been minimal with individual US companies participating in mining and energy activities or being competitive suppliers of agricultural and other equipment, but too far away to feature in regional value chains.[54] In striking contrast to the frequent visits of Chinese presidents and prime ministers, no US president has visited Central Asia and the last vice president to do so was Al Gore in 1993, although US presidents have visited Afghanistan.

Trade and investment links with China have grown rapidly in the twenty-first century. China plays a central role in global value chains (so-called "Factory Asia"), and for such networks to flourish trade costs, in both money and time, must be low. This will affect Central Asia as, following adoption of the "Go West" policy, regions such as Sichuan Province and Chongqing Municipality are thriving within global value chains and establishing overland routes through Central Asia along the Eurasian Landbridge rail link. Whether Central Asia will merely be a transit route, or whether the improved communications could provide a springboard for economic diversification within Central Asia is a critical question that will be addressed in the next chapter.

---

stan's weaker soccer team plays in Europe where they have the opportunity of hosting star teams even if their chances of winning are negligible. On the other hand, Kazakhstan has been keen to host Asian events in sports like ice hockey.

53. Uzbekistan fits this role, although relations with the USA are threatened by its human rights record. Indeed, an irony of the region is that the most liberal economies (the Kyrgyz Republic and Kazakhstan) are more closely linked with Russia. Symbolic of this divide was the early decision by Uzbekistan (and Turkmenistan) to adopt a Latin/Turkic alphabet, while Kazakhstan, the Kyrgyz Republic, and Tajikistan have retained the Cyrillic alphabet. However, these patterns are in flux as President Mirziyoyev appears to be taking Uzbekistan in a more open direction and Kazakhstan announced in 2017 that it would adopt a variation of the Latin/Turkic script.

54. Similar comments apply to other second-rank players in the region such as Japan, South Korea, Canada, Australia, or Southeast Asian countries.

11

Central Asia at the Center of Eurasia

FORGING A NEW SILK ROAD

A quarter of a century after independence the Central Asian economies offer many paradoxes. With continued dependence on primary product exports and most of the population in agriculture their economic structure is little changed, but any visitor to the region after a twenty-year absence could not help but be struck by the huge economic transformation, especially in the main cities but also in many small towns and some rural areas. The five countries have pursued different paths to creating national economies, but remain linked by culture, history, and geography. Despite the differences in transition strategies and a gradual shift from state-centric decision making to more decentralized decision making, on region-wide issues such as water management or connectivity for trade or factor flows the predilection to seek top-down solutions is still strong. Water disputes and security and border management issues remain potent although they have been muted.

In key respects, the countries have been fortunate since independence. Although the dissolution of the USSR was an unwelcome surprise in 1991 and in the immediate aftermath the new independent countries faced the triple shocks of the end of central planning, collapse of Soviet demand and supply chains, and hyperinflation, the five countries could focus on nation-building and transition to market-based economies in the 1990s without external threats or, except for Tajikistan, domestic conflicts. Recovery from the transitional recession was accompanied by the commodity boom, which boosted income growth in all five countries. Only after 2014 were governments pushed to seriously consider their long-term development strategy. They all spoke to the need for economic diversification away from the current narrow resource base, but how to achieve this aim? All have signed on to achieving the UN Sustainable Development Goals and meeting commitments under the Paris COP21 climate agreement, but how to succeed?

The answer is surely to develop a modern industrial and service economy. This does not preclude continued specialization in agriculture, pastoralism, energy, and minerals, but it does imply more efficient production of those resources and diversification into new areas, most likely by finding niches in global value chains. This is assuming, of course, that the leaders are willing to change the current economic arrangements.

The external environment is not static, and Central Asia is at the heart of a major change in the Eurasian economy as overland links between China and Europe are being reestablished after a five-century hiatus. The precise nature of this link is still a work in process, and the role of Central Asian countries is difficult to predict. Economically, Central Asia is increasingly seen as a place with dynamic neighbors (three of the four BRICs), rather than as a disadvantaged landlocked region. Changes in the global economy, notably the emergence of more complex global and regional value chains, point to advantages of being in a good neighborhood. The main obstacle to Central Asian participation in global value chains is the high cost of doing business, and in particular of doing business across international borders. The extent to which countries can take advantage of the window of opportunity will depend upon their success in reducing these transactions costs.

11.1. Landlocked or Land-Linked?

After independence, Uzbekistan Airways adopted the slogan of Tashkent as the Crossroads of Asia, and many blueprints aspired to revive historic silk roads. In economic terms, however, the crossroads function had been dormant for centuries. Central Asia became a sleepy backwater after the European voyages of discovery in the fifteenth and sixteenth centuries. From the 1860s until the 1990s, Central Asian economic relations were overwhelmingly northwards to Russia. The EU's TRACECA vision of a route south of Russia from Central Asia to Europe attracted zero commercial interest in the 1990s. Only in the twenty-first century have east-west relations begun to flourish.

Many observers of the new independent countries highlighted the negative role of landlockedness, and the curiosum of Uzbekistan's double-landlocked status, i.e. from Uzbekistan it is necessary to transit at least two other countries to reach an ocean port (a situation shared only with Liechtenstein).[1] How-

---

1. The problems of landlockedness in Central Asia have been analyzed by Raballand (2003); Grafe, Raiser, and Sakatsume (2005); Cadot, Carrère, and Grigoriou (2006); and Grigoriou

ever, it is also possible to see the region as land-linked to a booming neighborhood of emerging economies—a vision set out by Johannes Linn (2004) and subsequently embraced by CAREC. To take advantage of their location, the Central Asian countries need to reduce the high costs of international trade within and beyond the region.

In the 2010s, the concept of a landbridge between China and Europe entered the popular imagination, although there is little precision about the best route. The long-standing link is the TransSiberian railway from Vladivostok through Moscow to Europe, with spurs connecting Mongolia and China to the mainline, but this is not convenient for western China or for the coastal powerhouses of the Yangtze and Pearl River Deltas. China-EU rail connections established since 2010 have mostly gone via Urumqi, Astana, and Minsk to Europe. After President Xi announced China's One Belt One Road Initiative in September 2013, Chinese commentaries on the OBOR were accompanied by maps showing a main line through Tashkent and Tehran. Azerbaijan continues to promote the TransCaspian route espoused by TRACECA; in October 2017 the presidents of Azerbaijan and Turkey and the prime ministers of Kazakhstan, Georgia, and Uzbekistan attended the opening ceremony of the long-delayed Baku-Tbilisi-Kars railway, and on November 5, the first cargo of wheat from Kazakhstan arrived at the Turkish port of Mersin. The common feature of all these routes is that, apart from the TransSiberian, they pass through Central Asia (map 2).

The initial demand for a new Europe-China rail service came from German carmakers supplying their Chinese assembly plant with European components, and some trial runs occurred in 2008–9. Following demand from electronics companies in Chongqing such as Foxconn or HP, freight service to Duisburg began in 2011, and this has been the most successful route, by 2018 operating daily. A Chengdu to Łódź route offered delivery in just over ten days, and in 2013 was the first to offer a guaranteed fixed schedule. By 2014, eight Chinese cities were offering a rail service to Europe (table 11.1). Between Yiwu, a transport hub in Zhejiang Province, and Madrid, the first train had eighty-two wagons; by 2017 it was a regular weekly service. In 2015 Kazakhstan's rail company earned $1 billion in transit fees, and in 2016 it carried forty-two thousand containers en route from China to Europe. In April 2016, the first train from China to France arrived in Lyon. In January 2017, the first train from Yiwu arrived in London.[2]

(2007). In cross-country studies, landlockedness is rarely significantly negatively correlated with growth or level of national income, because some landlocked countries are surrounded by large open markets and benefit from their favorable location (e.g., Switzerland, Austria, Slovakia, and other Central European countries).

2. Pomfret (2018) provides more details on routes and other aspects of the landbridge.

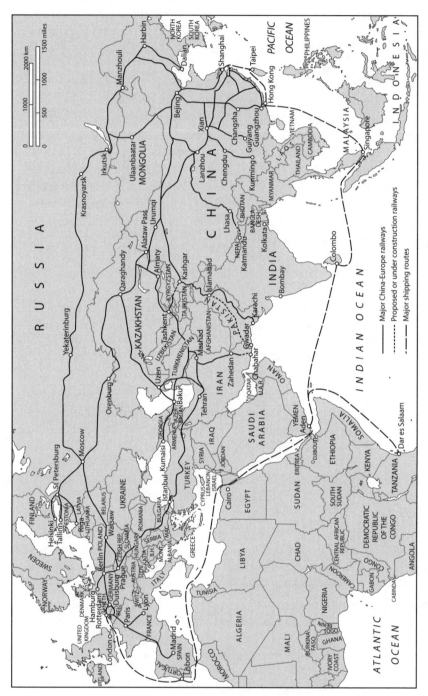

Map 2. China-Europe transport links

TABLE 11.1. Silk Road Railways from China to the EU, to End of 2015

Route	Start	Length Kilometers	Duration Days
Chongqing—Duisburg (DE)	July 2011	11,179	16
Wuhan—Mělnik (CZ)	October 2012	10,863	16
Suzhou—Warsaw (PL)	November 2012	11,200	18
Chengdu—Łódź (PL)	April 2013	9,826	10.5
Zhengzhou—Hamburg (DE)	July 2013	10,124	19–20
Yiwu—Madrid (ES)	November 2014	13,052	21
Hefei—Kazakhstan; Hefei—Hamburg (DE)	June 2014	11,000	15
Changsha—Duisburg/Moscow/Tashkent	October 2014	11,808	18
Harbin—Hamburg (DE)	June 2015	9,820	15

Source: Li, Bolton, and Westphal (2016, 8).

Some of the routes in table 11.1, e.g., Harbin-Hamburg or Suzhou-Warsaw, continue to use the TransSiberian, but most use the Kazakh, Russian, and Belarus rail systems between China and the EU border. Although some trials may prove unsuccessful, the established routes like Chongqing-Duisburg have been market-driven and very profitable for the carriers. The trial-and-error process is a classic market discovery exercise to find on which routes customers are willing to pay for rail service between China and Europe, and it started some years before China announced the One Belt One Road initiative.

Cargos have been mixed. Electronic goods and car components continue to be major freight on the Chongqing-Duisburg-Chongqing route. However, with a regular service, freight forwarders can assemble container loads for anybody willing to pay to ship and wanting a fixed delivery date. Reports of the first trains from France and from the UK to China inevitably invoked cargos of champagne or whisky, but the containers were full of "miscellaneous goods."[3] A rail link between China and Europe offers faster speed and greater reliability than ocean shipping, and it is much cheaper than air freight. As an added benefit, per ton of freight, rail is much more environmentally friendly than road or air.

All the routes are being improved and trying to show their superiority, and there is an incentive for individual Central Asian countries to enhance their

3. Shepard (2016) gives the example of a Chinese ATM manufacturer who needed to send one replacement machine to Europe; sea was too slow and air too expensive, but rail was just right. Although initial services catered to specific firms, the increased involvement of forwarders and couriers offering a variety of services (less-than-full-load shipping, refrigerated containers, etc.) has strengthened the attractiveness of multimodal hubs (Duisburg and Yiwu) as convenient destinations for more customers. Yiwu began exploring options in January 2013, before President Xi's One Belt One Road announcement (Esteban and Li, 2017, 12).

attractiveness for transit so that preferred routes pass through their territory, yielding transit fees and the opportunity to use improved rail services for trade. Travel time on the TransCaspian Aktau-Baku route has been reduced by construction of two new rail sections west of Zhezkazgan in Kazakhstan, which cut the distance to Aktau substantially. However, at a cost of $5,000 per container from Dostyk to Batumi, the route is not competitive with Chongqing-Duisburg for China-EU trade. Meanwhile, DHL and DB-Schenker, a division of the German rail company Deutsche Bahn that focuses on logistics, talk of reducing China-EU travel times to ten days and are exploring new routes via Iran (Shepard, 2016).[4]

Completion in December 2014 of the Uzen-Gorgon railway from Kazakhstan through Turkmenistan to Iran added a further dimension to the regional rail network (map 2). The Caspian coastal line may be most valuable as an outlet for Kazakhstan's grain exports to the Middle East and North Africa, and as a route for Indian trade with Central Asia through Chabahar and the Iranian rail system. In January 2016, the first direct train from China to Tehran used this route, benefitting from the newly completed east-west link in the Kazakh rail system and avoiding transiting Uzbekistan (and sending a message to Uzbekistan about the potential cost of its cumbersome transit regulations).

Other important links in the regional rail network are the second China-Kazakhstan rail line, opened in 2013 and linking Urumqi more directly to Almaty and Tashkent, and construction of rail lines in northern Afghanistan that may eventually connect Tajikistan to Turkmenistan and Iran. These and the above rail developments predate China's One Belt One Road proposal. They are complementary to more recent Chinese plans such as the proposed rail link from Kashgar through Osh to the Fergana Valley. The China-Pakistan Economic Corridor, which involves upgrading the Karakoram Highway and in the future building a rail line south from Kashgar to Pakistan, will offer Central Asian traders an option for trading with Pakistan without transiting Afghanistan.

China appears to be keeping its options open with respect to the preferred route to Europe. It seems likely that an all-land route will dominate over a TransCaspian route, but whether the preferred option runs north or south of the Caspian Sea is still to be determined. The two options have important differences; the former includes Russia as a transit country, while the latter transits Iran and Turkey to Europe and is easily linked to the Arab world. China's

---

4. Times have been shaved, first by avoiding customs stops for the sealed cargoes, and second by speeding up the changeover time at change of gauge points. At the Khorgos Gateway between China and Kazakhstan, two trains are lined up side by side and the containers are transferred from one to the other in forty-seven minutes (Shepard, 2016). By 2017 the Chongqing-Duisburg journey took twelve days (Esteban and Li, 2017, 12).

support for the southern route as a counterbalance to the currently used northern route could be explained by two, not mutually exclusive, motives.

In the current situation, China may be promoting an alternative route in order to reduce the possibility of a country on the northern route using its hold-up power to extort larger transit fees.[5] If the intention is to cut transport times by constructing a high-speed rail line, then the cost is likely to make the two routes mutually exclusive as mainlines between China and Europe and a key issue for the two largest Central Asian countries is whether the route passes through the capital of Kazakhstan, Astana, or the capital of Uzbekistan, Tashkent.[6] Both governments have already shown their eagerness to be on this technological frontier by establishing domestic high-speed passenger services between their two biggest cities (Almaty-Astana and Tashkent-Samarkand).

The important point behind this catalog of transport routes is that, even if only a fraction of them become effectively operational, Central Asia is on the cusp of having greatly improved connectivity to the east, west, and south, to add to traditional links to the north. Financing issues will need to be resolved.[7] In principle, however, the more lines that are open the better it will be for Central Asia, insofar as it will be difficult for any transit country to exploit its hold-up power (in a similar way that multiple pipelines benefited oil and gas exporters) and countries will have a wider choice of destination for their exports.

11.2. Responding to SDGs and COP21

In September 2015, 193 United Nations members adopted the 2030 Agenda for Sustainable Development and its framework of seventeen Sustainable Development Goals (SDGs). Three months later the 21st. Conference of the Parties to the United Nations Framework Convention on Climate Change (COP21, also known as the Paris Climate Conference), reached a global agreement on

5. This could potentially lead to a tragedy of the anti-commons as described in chapter 9.3. It is striking how quickly China reacted to the easing of UN sanctions on Iran in January 2016; President Xi visited Tehran, and the first train left Yiwu for Tehran before the end of the month. In 2017 China established regular rail freight service between Yancheng in Ningxia autonomous region (a Muslim area of China) and Iran. Proposals to build a line connecting Kashgar to Uzbekistan through the Kyrgyz Republic would provide a Central Asian route that does not pass through Kazakhstan.

6. Chinese proposals for a high-speed rail service are not implausible given the speed with which China has constructed its domestic high-speed rail network. For freight trains, the current criteria for "high-speed" is an average of around 200 km per hour.

7. The issue is particularly controversial in the Kyrgyz Republic, and was publicized by Hurley, et al., (2018) who identified eight poor countries, including the Kyrgyz Republic, in danger of becoming debt-dependent as a result of the BRI.

the reduction of climate change; the signatories agreed to reduce their carbon output "as soon as possible" and to do their best to keep global warming "to well below 2 degrees C." The five Central Asian countries were signatories to both the SDG Agenda and to COP21.

With increased concerns about climate change caused by human activities, policymakers will face pressures to reduce their country's energy/GDP ratio and to move from export of fossil fuels to exploitation of renewable energy sources. Decisions about policy will need to shift from promoting oil output and pipelines to facilitating more complex energy choices in response to changing demand and technologies, and evaluating cost-recovery energy-pricing policies. Changes in ownership away from monolithic state-dominated enterprises in the energy sector and elsewhere in the economy would also contribute to greater flexibility of response. Changing policymakers' attitudes is especially important in a sector where key investment decisions' consequences are measured over decades; energy infrastructure constructed today will almost all still be operating in 2050.

The Soviet Union bequeathed an energy system built around providing large volumes of energy to drive industrial production and urban services such as district heating, with only minor regard for energy efficiency or environmental impact. The Karaganda coal and metals complex was the jewel in Kazakhstan's Soviet crown. A quarter century later, much of that legacy has changed, but much remains; although reduced since 1990, the energy intensity of Kazakhstan's economy remains above global norms (Kalyuzhnova and Pomfret, 2018, 268). Indicative of the inefficiency of energy allocation was the limited use of utility meters and haphazard bill collection in centrally planned economies, and this has changed only slowly in Central Asia.

The other side of the legacy concerns the production of primary energy sources and the generation and transmission of electricity. At independence, Kazakhstan was a major Soviet producer of coal and uranium, and Turkmenistan and to a lesser extent Uzbekistan supplied natural gas. In the transitional recession, Kazakhstan's coal exports halved and the integrated Soviet electricity distribution network atrophied; not only did cross-border transmission of electricity drop sharply, but also the efficiency of the system deteriorated and distribution losses increased despite the reduced generation and consumption of electricity. However, after independence Kazakhstan became a major producer of oil and gas.

There is little doubt that energy demand will be transformed in the coming decades. In Europe and North America investment in coal and capacity of coal-fired electricity generating power plants have been shrinking in response to health concerns. Global coal demand is now being affected by the continuing shift in demand of the huge energy-burning Asian countries towards less carbon-emitting primary energy sources. This is especially true for China, which is the world's largest producer and largest consumer of coal.[8] Although coal remains the world's largest primary energy source, there is little doubt that its share in the total will decline over the medium and long term.

In the medium term, oil is especially susceptible to technical change because 60% of global oil demand is for transportation. By 2050 petrol-driven vehicles may be as obsolete as typewriters are today, having been displaced by electric or fuel-cell vehicles.[9] The timing is difficult to predict, but the change could be sudden once the recharging problem has been addressed and it is possible to drive longer distances without fear of not being able to recharge. The demand for oil will not disappear completely, but as a relatively high cost production location Kazakhstan must be concerned about the prospect of an era of low oil prices.

Declining coal and oil demand holds potential opportunities for Central Asia. The shifting energy sources should be to the benefit not just of the region's gas exports, but also of the solar, wind, biomass, and hydropower that Central Asia could potentially supply competitively in large quantities. Such opportunities could be enhanced by geography, given that China and the populous South Asian nations are neighbors, although the infrastructure requirements for transmission lines and so forth will be large.

The pace of technological change in renewables is potentially great, although it is difficult to predict their relative feasibility. Between 2008—the year before the failed COP15 Copenhagen meeting—and 2014, the global solar module price index fell at a far faster rate than anybody predicted in 2008 (Arndt, 2015). The cost of wind power has also fallen rapidly, but not as dramatically as for solar power.[10] Investors in energy production have responded to these changes, and in 2014 newly installed capacity of renewable energy systems surpassed that of fossil-fuel-based systems on a global basis for the first time (REN21, 2015). The dramatic potential of making the right bet on technological change was highlighted by the rapid rise of Qatar from Middle Eastern backwater to energy superpower in the first decade of the twenty-first century (Kalyuzhnova and Pomfret, 2018, 272–73), once the challenge of how

8. China's demand for coal dropped by 1.6% in 2014 despite GDP growth of 7.3%. The price of thermal coal in China fell from almost $150 per ton at the end of 2010 to under $70 in March 2015, while the price of coking coal imported from Australia fell from over $300 per ton to under $150 in the same period. During 2015 and the first part of 2016 five large US coal mining companies, including the world's largest private coal mining company, Peabody, filed for bankruptcy, as did Australia's (former) coal billionaire Nathan Tinkler.

9. As Sheikh Zaki Yamani, the Saudi minister for oil from 1962 to 1986 (OPEC's heyday), famously said: "The Stone Age did not end for lack of stones, and the Oil Age will end long before the world runs out of oil."

10. Moné et al. (2015) provide detailed cost estimates for wind power in the USA, but emphasize the wide geographical variance and that the estimates are sensitive to alternative methods of calculating "cost."

to transport natural gas to overseas markets without massive in-transit losses had been overcome. With solar and wind the big issues are how to convert them into electricity that can be fed into transmission grids, and then how to construct efficient regional grids and delivery to end users.

On the demand side, China is playing a major role in the transition to renewables. China gradually slowed its increasing demand for coal (Cornot-Gandolphe, 2014), and became a major market for Central Asian gas, mostly delivered through the Turkmenistan-Uzbekistan-Kazakhstan-Xinjiang pipeline that opened in 2009. Nevertheless, efforts between 2003 and 2013 to promote environmental goals met with only limited success, as provincial policymakers continued to prioritize economic growth. The situation changed dramatically under President Xi Jinping and Prime Minister Li Keqiang, spurred by the deadly smog that enveloped Beijing in January 2013 and increased popular awareness of the costs of air pollution.[11] The Chinese government announced major energy policy changes in September 2013 and in 2014:

> China reduced its consumption and import of coal for the first time this century, continued to shift to natural gas, reached an ambitious deal with the United States on climate change actions through 2030, was well on track to reducing energy intensity by more than twenty per cent and to increasing its share of renewables and other non-fossil fuels to more than 11 percent of primary energy, and announced construction of a backbone ultra-high voltage electricity grid to create better connectivity between East and West and to integrate renewables more effectively into the national system (Waters, 2015, box 5.1).

Following the deal with the USA, China became more active in the international arena, promoting its carbon reduction targets and contributing to the success of the Paris COP21 meetings in December 2015.

China has been a global leader in developing and installing ultra-high voltage electricity transmission. Construction since 2009 of ultra-high voltage transmission (UHVT) lines has been dramatic, and the improved technology due to learning-by-doing is reflected in the increases in voltage and length of China's transmission circuits (table 11.2). The optimum length is still limited to around 2,000 km, which is a useful distance for Central Asia to emulate.

---

11. The principal villain was hazardous particles, such as PM2.5, rather than CO_2 emissions, but the implications for coal are similar. The State Council's 2013 *Atmospheric Pollution Prevention Action Plan* required the country's more-developed regions, Beijing-Tianjin-Hebei, the Yangtze Delta, and the Pearl River Delta, to cut hazardous particle emissions by 25%, 20%, and 15% respectively, implying absolute reduction in coal consumption (Zhang, 2015a, 4). India has been slower to respond to the challenge of moving from coal, but the smog-stops-play episodes in a December 2017 cricket test match between India and Sri Lanka in Delhi may provide the wake-up call comparable to the 2013 Beijing smog.

TABLE 11.2. China's Operational Ultra-High Voltage Transmission Circuits, Completed or under Construction in 2014

	Voltage KV	Length Kms	Power rating GW	Year completed / to be completed
Jindongnan–Nanyang–Jingmen	1,000	640	5.0	2009
Huainan-Zhejiang–Shanghai	1,000	2 x 649	8.0	2013
North Zhejiang–Fuzhou	1,000	2 x 603	6.8	2014
Yunnan–Guangdong	±800	1,373	5.0	2009
Xiangjiaba–Shanghai	±800	1,907	6.4	2010
Jinping–Sunan	±800	2,059	7.2	2012
Nuozadu–Guangdong	±800	1,413	5.0	2013
Hami–Zhengzhou	±800	2,192	8.0	2014
Xiluodu–Zhejiang West	±800	1,653	8.0	2014
UNDER CONSTRUCTION IN 2014				
Huainan–Nanjing–Shanghai	1,000	2 x 780		2016
Xilingol–Shandong	1,000	2 x 730	9	2016
Inner Mongolia–Tianjin	1,000	2 x 608		2016
Yuheng–Weifang	1,000	2 x 1,049		2017
Ningxia East–Zhejiang	±800	1,720	8	2016
Shanxi North–Jiangsu	±800	1,119	8	2017
Jiuquan–Hunan	±800	2,383	8	2017
Xilingol–Jiangsu	±800	1,620	10	2017
Shanghaimiao–Shandong	±800	1,238	10	2017

Source: Liu, 2014.

Within Central Asia, Kazakhstan has embraced green energy most publicly. In 2013 President Nazarbayev's office pledged to spend 1% of GDP, or an estimated $3–4 billion annually, for "transition to a green economy." A *Strategy Kazakhstan 2050* concept paper stated that "Kazakhstan is facing a situation where its natural resources and environment are seriously deteriorating across all crucial environmental standards. A green economy is instrumental to [a] nation's sustainable development" and that a switch to renewables would free oil and gas for more lucrative exports, rather than subsidized domestic use. Officials talked of weaning Kazakhstan's economy off its hydrocarbon dependence, recognizing that if Kazakhstan is to become an upper-middle-income nation the country must diversify its energy sources. The decision to host EXPO 2017 with the theme *Future Energy* further reaffirmed this commitment. However, there is still far to go. In 2012, the renewable energy share in Kazakhstan's electricity generation was 0.6%. This lags behind neighboring Mongolia—which has similar wind and sun endowments and generates 5% of its electricity from renewables—as well as the 10% achieved by the USA in 2014.

Creating generating capacity is only part of switching to renewables. Since renewables are typically difficult to transport or store, the key to expanding their use is an efficient electricity transmission system. The Soviet grid provided reasonably reliable delivery to electricity users (section 3.6), but the successor states tended to focus on having an integrated national grid rather than maintaining international connectivity. This is unfortunate because effective connectivity over a larger area provides better opportunities for meeting local demand-supply mismatches.

Two major technological advances have improved the potential for electricity trade. The UHVT systems pioneered by China provide a cost-efficient means of transporting electricity from unpopulated areas where the wind blows and the sun shines to population centers within 2,000 km.[12] The other development since 2000 has been improvements in smart grid technology. Even in the richest advanced economies with efficient electricity grids, demand surges have shut down transmission equipment and led to major regional blackouts. All systems incorporate, often substantial, excess capacity to address sudden demand/supply mismatch and in many regions a web of alternative routes is intended to avoid reliance on a single transmission line, but large redundancies are costly. Since the turn of the century the USA, Canada, Japan, and Russia (Veselov and Fedosova, 2015) have led the way in searching for smart technologies that allow monitoring of demand and supply in real time and the option of instant response to any build-up of demand/supply mismatch.[13]

Constructing a modern electricity transmission system involves large upfront fixed costs, and it is important to retain flexibility to adapt installed technology to future innovations. Nevertheless, the development of UHVT and smart-grid technologies offers the opportunity to skip generations and move to frontiers that are well suited to Central Asia—somewhat similar to what happened with telephone technology as mobile phones reduced the pressure to upgrade the poor inherited fixed-line infrastructure (section 10.8).

Central Asia is geographically at a crossroads between the energy-producing regions of Iran, the Gulf, and Russia and the net energy-consuming regions of East and South Asia and Europe. With the demand shifts and technical change that will inevitably occur in coming decades some of these patterns will alter, but Central Asia is likely to remain well situated as long as it devises institutions and policies that can respond flexibly, subject to the con-

12. In 2017 the State Grid Corporation of China built the first UHVT line between Xinjiang and the Kyrgyz Republic (Sejko, 2017).

13. An alternative rapid response system is the Tesla Powerpack (a massive lithium ion battery connected to a wind farm operated by French energy firm Neoen) that Elon Musk installed in South Australia in 2017.

straints that many energy investments are large and long lasting. Even as demand and world prices for coal, oil, and gas lag, Central Asia is likely to have huge potential for producing and exporting gas as well as wind and solar energy. If a Eurasian electricity grid is constructed, Central Asia will be a key region, as envisioned in the CASA 1000 project.

The precise nature of future world energy markets is hard to predict, so governments need to develop institutions and policies that facilitate and reward good decisions; wrong investments could leave a country stranded in a technological backwater. Regional cooperation is also crucial for realizing the benefits of a large network within which demand and supply can be balanced. The collapse of Central Asian electricity trade, especially after 2009, was a critical contributing factor that led to Tajikistan's electricity crisis. Fields et al. (2013, xiv) estimated the potential benefits from rejuvenating electricity trade to be worth more than $2 billion, with limited incremental costs. Trust among neighboring countries may take time to reestablish, although the active diplomacy of Uzbekistan's new president in 2017 suggests that international relations can be improved quickly if the will is there.

Finally, it is important to situate the shift to renewables and associated need for an improved international electricity grid into broader development goals, because they have implications beyond the energy sector. First and foremost, reliable access to energy is a precondition for inclusive growth in the twenty-first century: SDG 7 is to ensure access to affordable, reliable, sustainable, and modern energy for all. Reliable energy access is also a precondition for diversification into a modern industry and service economy; whatever roles the country finds in global value chains, energy is crucial for modern information flows and logistics, and black-outs are fatal for just-in-time delivery schedules. Energy sector policies must also be part of wider regulatory and governance reform to ensure rents are well managed, public procurement includes "green" thinking, and ministries collaborate on the economic/environment balance. In sum, a well-managed energy sector is crucial for realization of the three "i"s of good institutions, interconnectivity, and inclusive growth.

11.3. Is a Window of Opportunity Opening?

A quarter century after independence, the hard infrastructure of roads, airports, border crossing points, and so forth, as described in the individual country chapters and section 11.1, has been steadily improved. The hard infrastructure would be of limited value without substantial improvement in soft infrastructure, which has changed more slowly in Central Asia. However, there is evidence that this is starting to happen.

. Chapter 9 documented the regional economic disintegration in Central Asia during the 1990s and early 2000s. This has been changing since about 2005. The gas pipeline from Turkmenistan through Uzbekistan and Kazakhstan to China was a harbinger of a more cooperative attitude among the three Central Asian governments, and because the project was win-win for all concerned it may have countered the fault-line across Central Asia imposed by the Eurasian Economic Union. Arbitrary and capricious actions against traders appear to be becoming less common, although CAREC's Corridor Performance Measurement and Monitoring project suggests depressingly slow progress in increasing speeds and reducing border delays.

Governments are beginning to undertake measures with the specific goal of trade facilitation. Ge Ju (CAREC, 2014, 32–34) describes how starting from a 2013 initiative, the presidents of China and Kazakhstan signed an agreement in May 2014 to introduce at the Bakhty/Bakhtu BCP a fast-customs clearance green corridor for agricultural goods. The products (jam, beverages, and sunflower seeds from Kazakhstan and apples, grapes, oranges, bell peppers, and cucumbers from China) were passing through the green corridor in less than an hour. Prechecking and risk assessment are important because about two-thirds of all goods carried along the main CAREC corridors were subject to SPS and related measures (Jeff Procak, in CAREC, 2014, 43–46). In 2015, the Kyrgyz Republic and Tajikistan announced that they would introduce green channels at border crossings with China, while across the Caspian Azerbaijan announced similar plans. Although the initial steps are with respect to foodstuffs that may be perishable, the adjective "green" is in the sense of green channels at airports not in the sense of plants. Such rapid clearance for preapproved freight could be used to encourage manufacturers participating in international value chains.

The China-Europe Landbridge could also signal a new opportunity for Central Asia. Connectivity will be improved, especially if there are multiple routes, which may be stimulated by Iran's reintegration into the global economy and Turkey's rail tunnel under the Bosporus. The Eurasian Economic Union offers smoother travel between the China-Kazakhstan border and the Belarus-Poland border and into Schengenland, while China's BRI with promised financing from the Asian Infrastructure Investment Bank could speed up travel along a rail route south of the Caspian Sea and other spurs from and links between the main lines. All Eurasian Landbridge lines between China and Europe, except the TransSiberian, must pass through Central Asia, and the question is whether the domestic environment and soft infrastructure of trade can encourage more small and medium-sized enterprises to follow the example of the Kyrgyz bean farmers by establishing or participating in global value chains.

11.4. At the Center of Eurasia

For centuries, the label Central Asia seemed like an ironic description of a region that was geographically central but economically peripheral. Recalling the Silk Road heritage seemed to hark back to a prehistory without link to the backwater that Central Asia had become since the 1500s. The industrial revolution and globalization largely passed the region by, apart from the introduction of the cotton economy and railways to transport cotton and to support Russian rule. The Soviet Union brought the region into the modern world in many respects, notably through education and social change, but Soviet Central Asia remained isolated from the Eurasian economy beyond the USSR.

A quarter century after independence, this situation in Central Asia appears set to change. The post-1991 domestic agenda has been completed: national economies have been established and market-based economies of various forms have been created. A measure of prosperity was created amidst positive external circumstances of the resource boom and regional peace. The countries are prepared for the next step towards economic diversification including increased international trade, assuming that leaders truly want this outcome. Again, the region is fortunate with respect to external developments, as transport landbridges are built across Eurasia and modern communications and electricity networks are constructed with new technology (smart mobile phones, the internet, ultra-high-voltage electricity transmission within smart grids). Increased connectivity provides a window of opportunity; governments' willingness and ability to create appropriate domestic conditions will determine which countries pass through the window.

The optimistic scenario is of at least parts of Central Asia returning to their pre-1500 role of being at the center of Eurasia.

REFERENCES

Abdullaev, Iskandar, Charlotte de Fraiture, Mark Giordano, Murat Yakubov, and Aziz Rasulov (2009): Agricultural Water Use and Trade in Uzbekistan: Situation and Potential Impacts of Market Liberalization, *Water Resources Development* 25(1), 47–63.

Abdullaev, Iskandar, and Shavkat Rakhmatullaev (2015): Transformation of Water Management in Central Asia: From State-Centric, Hydraulic Mission to Socio-Political Control, *Environmental Earth Science* 73, 849–61.

ADB (2006): *Central Asia: Increasing Gains from Trade through Regional Cooperation in Trade Policy, Transport and Customs Transit,* Asian Development Bank: Manila.

ADB (2014): *Central Asia Regional Economic Cooperation Corridor Performance Measurement and Monitoring: A Forward-Looking Perspective,* Asian Development Bank: Manila.

ADBI (2014): *Connecting Central Asia and Economic Centers; Interim Report,* Asian Development Bank Institute: Tokyo.

Afrasiabi, Kaveh (2000): Three-Part Series on ECO: (1) The Economic Cooperation Organization Aims to Bolster Regional Trade Opportunities, September 14, 2000, (2) ECO Strives to Improve Transportation and Communication Networks, November 1, 2000, (3) Economic Cooperation Organization Presses Energy Initiative, December 5, 2000, http://www.eurasianet.org.

Aitzhanova, Aktoty, Shigeo Katsu, Johannes Linn, and Vlad Yezhov eds. (2014): *Kazakhstan 2050: Toward a Modern Society for All,* Oxford University Press: New York.

Akimov, Alexandr (2001): Reforming the Financial System: The Case of Uzbekistan, *CASE Studies and Analyses 234,* Centrum Analiz Spolaczno-Ekonomicznych: Warsaw.

Alexeev, Michael, and Robert Conrad (2011): The Natural Resource Curse and Economic Transition, *Economic Systems* 35(4), 445–61.

Alimbekov, Aidos, Eldar Madumarov, and Gerald Pech (2017): Sequencing in Customs Union Formation: Theory and Application to the Eurasian Economic Union, *Journal of Economic Integration* 32(1), 65–89.

Allison, Roy (2008): Virtual Regionalism, Regional Structures and Regime Security in Central Asia, *Central Asian Survey* 27(2), 185–202.

Amir, Omair, and Albert Berry (2013): Challenges of Transition Economies: Economic Reforms, Emigration, and Employment in Tajikistan, *Social Protection, Growth and Employment: Evidence from India, Kenya, Malawi, Mexico, and Tajikistan,* United Nations Development Programme: New York, 157–99.

Anceschi, Luca (2008): *Turkmenistan's Foreign Policy: Positive Neutrality and the Consolidation of the Turkmen Regime,* Routledge: London.

Anceschi, Luca (2017): Turkmenistan and the Virtual Politics of Eurasian Energy: The Case of the TAPI Pipeline Project, *Central Asian Survey* 36(4), 409–29.

Anderson, Kathryn, and Richard Pomfret (2000): Living Standards during Transition to a Market Economy: The Kyrgyz Republic in 1993 and 1996, *Journal of Comparative Economics* 26(3), 502–23.

Anderson, Kathryn, and Richard Pomfret (2003): *Creating a Market Economy: Evidence from Household Surveys in Central Asia*, Edward Elgar: Cheltenham, UK.

Arndt, Channing (2015): From CoP15 to CoP21—Three Crucial Changes in the Climate Mitigation Landscape, *WIDER Angle* (UNU Helsinki), November.

Åslund, Anders (2013): *How Capitalism Was Built: The Transformation of Central and Eastern Europe, Russia, and Central Asia*, 2nd edition, Cambridge University Press: London.

Atkinson, Anthony, and John Micklewright (1992): *Economic Transformation in Eastern Europe and the Distribution of Income*, Cambridge University Press: Cambridge, UK.

Auty, Richard (2001): *Resource Abundance and Economic Development*, Oxford University Press, Oxford, UK.

Azevedo, Joao Pedro, Aziz Atamanov, and Alisher Rajabov (2014): Poverty Reduction and Shared Prosperity in Tajikistan, *Policy Research Working Paper 6923*, World Bank: Washington, DC.

Babetski, Jan, and Mathilde Maurel (2002): "Unemployment, Poverty, and Reallocation of the Labour Force in the Kyrgyz Republic," unpublished ms., World Bank: Washington, DC.

Babetskii, Ian, Alexandre Kolev, and Mathilde Maurel (2003): Kyrgyz Labour Market in the Late 1990s: The Challenge of Formal Job Creation, *Comparative Economic Studies* 45(4), 493–519.

Bacchetta, Marc, and Zdenek Drabek (2002): Effects of WTO Accession on Policy-Making in Sovereign States: Preliminary Lessons from the Recent Experience of Transition Countries, *WTO Working Paper DERD-2002–02*, World Trade Organization: Geneva.

Baffes, John (2004): Cotton: Market Setting, Trade Policies, and Issues, *Policy Research Working Paper 3218*, World Bank: Washington, DC.

Barisitz, Stephan, and Mathias Lahnsteiner (2010): From Stormy Expansion to Riding Out the Storm: Banking Development in Kazakhstan, *Finanzmarktstabilitätsbericht 19*, 64–73.

Bauer, Armin, David Green, and Kathleen Kuehnast (1998): *Women and Gender Relations: The Kyrgyz Republic in Transition*, Asian Development Bank: Manila.

Bauer, Armin, Nia Boschmann, and David Green (1997): *Women and Gender Relations in Kazakstan: The Social Cost*, Asian Development Bank: Manila.

Baxter, Eric, and Charles McMillan (2012): All for One and One for All—Foreign Investment in Gold Mining: A Case Study of an Emerging Country, unpublished paper (charlesmcmillansgi@yahoo.ca).

Becker, Charles, Erbolat Musabek, Ai-Gul Seitenova, and Dina Urzhumova (2005): The Migration Response to Economic Shock: Lessons from Kazakhstan, *Journal of Comparative Economics* 33, 107–32.

Beckert, Sven (2014): *Empire of Cotton: A Global History*, Alfred Knopf: New York.

Behar, Alberto (2010): Do Managers and Experts Agree? A Comparison of Alternative Sources of Trade Facilitation Data, *Economics Series Working Papers 503*, Department of Economics, University of Oxford.

Berg, Andrew, Eduardo Borensztein, Ratna Sahay, and Jeromin Zettelmeyer (1999): The Evolution of Output in Transition Economies: Explaining Differences, *IMF Working Paper 99/73*, International Monetary Fund: Washington, DC.

Biddison, J. Michael (2002): The Study on Water and Energy Nexus in Central Asia, *ADB Report ADM/01–576, RSC No.C10732*, Asian Development Bank: Manila.

Birkman, Laura, Maria Kaloshnika, Maliha Khan, Umar Shavurov, and Sarah Smallhouse (2012): *Textile and Apparel Cluster in Kyrgyzstan*, Harvard University Kennedy School and Harvard Business School: Cambridge, MA.

Blackmon, Pamela (2011): *In the Shadow of Russia: Reform in Kazakhstan and Uzbekistan*, Michigan State University Press: East Lansing.

Blanchard, Olivier (1997): *The Economics of Post-Communist Transition*, Clarendon Press: Oxford, UK.

Bland, Stephen (2015): Kazakhstan: Measuring the Northern Aral's Comeback, *Eurasianet*, January 27, http://www.eurasianet.org/node/71781.

Blank, Stephen (2003): Benign Hegemony. Russia's Grand Delusion, *Perspective* 14(1), http://www.bu.edu/iscip/vol14/blank.html.

Blank Stephen (2011): Toward a New Chinese Order in Central Asia: Russia's Failure, *NBR Special Report No. 26*, National Bureau of Asian Research.

Blank Stephen (2017): Russia's Pivot to Asia, *NBR Working Paper*, National Bureau of Asian Research.

Bogolov, Petr (2016): *An Exodus amid Tripled GDP: The Mirage of Uzbekistan's Economic Miracle*, Carnegie Moscow Center, http://carnegie.ru/commentary/63771.

Bohr, Annette (1998): *Uzbekistan: Politics and Foreign Policy*, Royal Institute of International Affairs: London, and the Brookings Institution: Washington, DC.

Bohr, Annette (2016): *Turkmenistan: Power, Politics and Petro-Authoritarianism*, Royal Institute of International Affairs: London.

Boonstra, Jos (2015): Reviewing the EU's Approach to Central Asia, *EUCAM Policy Brief No. 34*, http://www.eucentralasia.eu.

Boonstra, Jos, and Marlène Laruelle (2013): EU-US Cooperation in Central Asia: Parallel Lines Meet in Infinity? *EUCAM Policy Brief No. 31*, http://www.eucentralasia.eu.

Boonstra, Jos, and Tika Tsertsvadze (2016): *Implementation and Review of the European Union-Central Asia Strategy: Recommendations for EU Action*, EU Directorate-General for External Policies, Policy Department, http://www.eucentralasia.eu/fileadmin/user_upload/PDF/Working_Papers/Implementation-EU-Central-Asia-Strategy-Recommendations-2015.pdf.

Boughton, James (2012): *Tearing Down Walls: The International Monetary Fund 1990–1999*, International Monetary Fund: Washington, DC.

Boulègue, Mathieu (2013) Xi Jinping's Grand Tour of Central Asia: Asserting China's Growing Economic Clout, *Central Asia Economic Paper No. 9*, Elliott School of International Affairs, George Washington University: Washington, DC.

Brooks, Douglas, and Myo Thant (1998): *Social Sector Issues in Transitional Economies of Asia*. Oxford University Press, for the Asian Development Bank: Oxford, UK.

Brunnschweiler, Christa (2009): Oil and Growth in Transition Countries, *Center of Economic Research at ETH Zurich Working Paper 09/108*, May, Eidgenössische Technische Hochschule Zürich.

Buchanan, James, and Yong Yoon (2000): Symmetric Tragedies: Commons and Anticommons, *Journal of Law and Economics* 43, 1–13.

Buckley, Cynthia, and Erin Trouth Hofmann (2012): Are Remittances an Effective Mechanism for Development? Evidence from Tajikistan, 1999–2007, *Journal of Development Studies* 48(8), 1121–38.

Buckley, Robert, and Eugene Gurenko (1997): Housing and Income Distribution in Russia: Zhivago's Legacy, *World Bank Research Observer* 12(1), 19–32.

Cadot, Olivier, Céline Carrère, and Christopher Grigoriou (2006): *Landlockedness, Infrastructure and Trade in Central Asia*, two vols., World Bank: Washington, DC.

Calder, Kent (2012): *The New Continentalism—Energy and Twenty-First Century Eurasian Geopolitics*, Yale University Press: New Haven, CT.

Campos, Nauro (2004): What Does WTO Membership Kindle in Transition Economies? An Empirical Investigation, *Journal of Economic Integration*, 19(2), 395–415.

CAREC (2014): *Modernizing Sanitary and Phytosanitary Measures to Expand Trade and Ensure Food Safety*, 2nd edtion, CAREC Trade Facilitation Learning Opportunity, Proceedings, Mongolia, October 6–8, Asian Development Bank: Manila.

Carpantier, Jean-François, and Wessel Vermeulen (2014): Emergence of Sovereign Wealth

Funds, *OxCarre Working Papers 148*, Oxford Centre for the Analysis of Resource Rich Economies, University of Oxford.

Carvalho, Antonio (2015): Reported Utility Service Satisfaction: The Case of Electricity in Transition Economies, *CEERP Working Paper No. 1*, Centre for Energy Economics Research and Policy, Herriot-Watt University: Edinburgh, Scotland.

Center for Preventive Action (1999): Calming the Ferghana Valley: Development and Dialogue in the Geart of Central Asia, *Preventive Action Reports Volume 4*, Century Foundation Press: New York.

Chan-Lau, Jorge (2004): Pension Funds and Emerging Markets, *IMF Working Paper WP/04/181*, International Monetary Fund: Washington, DC.

Chow, Edward, and Leigh Hendrix (2010): Central Asia's Pipelines: Field of Dreams and Reality, *NBR Special Report #23*, National Bureau of Asian Research, 29–42.

CIA (1982): *Uzen Oil Fields: A Case Study of Soviet Mismanagement*, Central Intelligence Agency, USA—released under Freedom of Information at http://www.foia.cia.gov/sites/default/files/document_conversions/89801/DOC_0000498136.pdf.

Cohen, Ariel (2008): *Kazakhstan: The Road to Independence,* Central Asia-Caucasus Institute, Johns Hopkins University: Washington, DC, and Silk Road Studies Program, Institute for Security and Development Policy: Stockholm.

Collins, Kathleen (2006): *Clan Politics and Regime Transition in Central Asia*, Cambridge University Press: New York.

Cooley, Alexander (2012): *Great Games, Local Rules: The New Great Power Contest in Central Asia*, Oxford University Press: New York.

Cooley, Alexander (2017): *Dictators without Borders*, Yale University Press: New Haven, CT.

Cooley, Alexander, and Jason Sharman (2015): Blurring the Line between Licit and Illicit Transnational Corruption Networks in Central Asia and Beyond, *Central Asian Survey* 34(1), 11–28.

Cornia, Giovanni Andrea (2014): Uzbekistan's Development Strategies: Past Record and Long-Term Options, *DISEI Working Paper N.26/2014*, Università degli Studi di Firenze: Florence, Italy.

Cornot-Gandolphe, Sylvie (2014): China's Coal Market: Can Beijing Tame "King Coal?" *Working Paper CL1*, Oxford Institute of Energy Studies, Oxford, UK, http://www.oxfordenergy.org/wpcms/wp-content/uploads/2014/12/CL-1.pdf.

Coudouel, Aline, and Sheila Marnie (1999): From Universal to Targeted Social Assistance: An Assessment of the Uzbek Experience, *MOCT-MOST: Economic Policy in Transitional Economies* 9(4), 443–58.

Coulibaly, Souleymane, and Lotte Thomsen (2016): Connecting to Regional Markets? Transport, Logistics Services and International Transit Challenges for Central Asian Food-Processing Firms, *Central Asian Survey* 35(1), 16–25.

Coutinho, Leonor, Dimitrios Georgiou, Maria Heracleous, Alexander Michaelides, and Stella Tsani (2013): Limiting Fiscal Procyclicality: Evidence from Resource-Rich Countries, *CEPR Discussion Paper No. 9672*, Centre for Economic Policy Research: London.

Cutler, Robert (2003): Turkey and the Geopolitics of Turkmenistan's Natural Gas, *Review of International Affairs* 1(2), 20–33.

Danzer, Alexander, Barbara Dietz, and Ksenia Gatskova (2013): *Tajikistan Household Panel Survey: Migration, Remittances and the Labor Market, Survey Report*, Institute for East and Southeast European Studies: Regensburg, http://www.ios-regensburg.de/fileadmin/doc/VW_Project/Booklet-TJ-web.pdf.

De Broeck, Mark, and Kristina Kostial (1998): Output Decline in Transition: The Case of Kazakhstan, *IMF Working Paper WP/98/45*, International Monetary Fund: Washington, DC.

De Broeck, Mark, and Vincent Koen (2000): The Great Contractions in Russia and the Other

Countries of the Former Soviet Union: A View from the Supply Side, *IMF Working Paper WP/00/32*, International Monetary Fund: Washington, DC.

De Danieli, Filippo (2011): Counter-Narcotics Policies in Tajikistan and Their Impact on State Building, *Central Asian Survey* 30(1), 129–45, reprinted in Heathershaw and Herzig, eds. (2013), 143–59.

Deakin, Roger (2007): *Wildwood: A Journey through Trees*, Hamish Hamilton: London.

Denison, Michael (2012): Game Over? Shifting Energy Geopolitics in Central Asia, *Central Asia Policy Brief No. 5*, Elliott School of International Affairs, George Washington University: Washington, DC.

Djamankulov, Nuritdin (2011): *SPS Regulations and Access of Kyrgyz Goods to the Customs Union*, USAID Regional Trade Liberalization and Customs Project (USAID Contract No.: 176-C-00-07-00011-08), Bishkek.

Djanibekov, Nodir, Kristof van Assche, Ihtiyor Bobojonov, and John Lamers (2012): Farm Restructuring and Land Consolidation in Uzbekistan: New Farms with Old Barriers, *Europe-Asia Studies* 64(6), 1101–26.

Djanibekov, Utkur, Kristof van Assche, Daan Boezeman, and Nodir Djanibekov (2013): Understanding Contracts in Evolving Agro-Economies: Farmers, Dekhqans and Networks in Khorezm, Uzbekistan, *Journal of Rural Studies* 32, 137–47.

Domjan, Paul, and Matt Stone (2010): A Comparative Study of Resource Nationalism in Russia and Kazakhstan, 2004–2008, *Europe-Asia Studies* 62(1), 35–62.

Doolot, Asel, and John Heathershaw (2015): State as Resource, Mediator and Performer: Understanding the Local and Global Politics of Gold Mining in Kyrgyzstan, *Central Asian Survey* 34(1), 93–109.

Dragneva-Lewers, Rilka, and Kataryna Wolczuk (2015): Trade and Geopolitics: Should the EU Engage with the Eurasian Economic Union? *Policy Brief,* April 2, European Policy Centre: Brussels.

Dragneva-Lewers, Rilka, and Kataryna Wolczuk (2017): The Eurasian Economic Union: Deals, Rules and the Exercise of Power, *Chatham House Research Paper*, Royal Institute of International Affairs, London, May.

Driscoll, Jesse (2008): Inside the Leviathan: Coup-Proofing after State Failure, *Stanford University Working Paper*, October 18, 2008 (based on PhD diss.).

EDB (2013a): *Labor Migration and Human Capital of Kyrgyzstan: Impact of the Customs Union*, EDB Centre for Integration Studies, Eurasian Development Bank: Saint Petersburg.

EDB (2013b): *Economic Impact of Tajikistan's Accession to the Customs Union and Single Economic Space*, EDB Centre for Integration Studies, Eurasian Development Bank: Saint Petersburg.

EDB (2017): *Eurasian Economic Integration 2017*, EDB Centre for Integration Studies, Eurasian Development Bank: Saint Petersburg.

Elborgh-Woytek, Katrin (2003): Of Openness and Distance: Trade Developments in the Commonwealth of Independent States, 1993–2002, *IMF Working Paper WP/03/207*, International Monetary Fund: Washington, DC.

Engvall, Johan (2014): Tajikistan: From Drug-Insurgency to Drug-State Nexus, in Svante Cornell and Michael Johnsson, eds., *Conflict, Crime and the State in Postcommunist Eurasia*, University of Pennsylvania Press: Philadelphia, 49–67.

Epkenhans, Tim (2016): *The Origins of the Civil War in Tajikistan: Nationalism, Islamism, and Violent Conflict in Post-Soviet Space*, Lexington Books: Lanham, MD.

Ericson, Richard (1991): The Classical Soviet-Type Economy: Nature of the System and Implications for Reform, *Journal of Economic Perspectives* 5, 11–28.

Esanov, Akram (2009): *Efficiency of Public Spending in Resource-Rich Post-Soviet States*, Revenue Watch Institute at https://resourcegovernance.org/sites/default/files/documents/rwi _esanov_efficiencyofpublicspending.pdf.

Esanov, Akram, and Karlygash Kuralbayeva (2011): Public Prudence and Private Profligacy: Kazakhstan 2000–2008, in Paul Collier and Anthony Venables, eds., *Plundered Nations? Successes and Failures in Natural Resource Extraction*, Palgrave: London.

Esanov, Akram, Martin Raiser, and Willem Buiter (2001): Nature's Blessing or Nature's Curse: The Political Economy of Transition in Resource-Based Economies, *EBRD Working Paper No. 65*, European Bank for Reconstruction and Development: London.

Esenaliev and Steiner (2012); Are Uzbeks Better Off than Kyrgyz? Measuring and Decomposing Horizontal Inequality, *DIW Discussion Papers 1252*, German Institute for Economic Research: Berlin.

Esentugelov, Arystan (2000): The Kazak Regions in the Transition Process, *Kazakstan Economic Trends,* January–March.

Esfandiar, Tamiris (2014): Tajikistan: President's Family Expands Grip with Key Positions, May 27, at www.eurasianet.org/node/68408.

Esteban, Mario, and Yuan Li (2017): Demystifying the Belt and Road Initiative: Scope, Actors and Repercussions for Europe, *Duisburger Arbeitspapiere Ostasienwissenschaften No.117/2017*, University of Duisburg-Essen Institute of East Asian Studies.

Falkingham, Jane (1999): Measuring Household Welfare: Problems and Pitfalls with Household Surveys in Central Asia, *MOCT-MOST: Economic Policy in Transitional Economies* 9(4), 379–93.

Falkingham, Jane (2004): Inequality and Poverty in the CIS-7 Countries, 1989–2002, in Clinton Shiells and Sarosh Sattar eds., *The Low-Income Countries of the Commonwealth of Independent States: Progress and Challenges in Transition*, International Monetary Fund: Washington, DC, 141–69.

Fay, Marianne, Rachel Block, and Jane Ebinger (2009): *Adapting to Climate Change in Eastern Europe and Central Asia*, World Bank: Washington, DC.

Fazendeiro, Bernardo Teles (2015): Uzbekistan's "Spirit" of Self-Reliance and the Logic of Appropriateness: TAPOich and Interaction with Russia, *Central Asian Survey* 34(4), 484–98.

Feigenbaum, Evan (2011): Why America No Longer Gets Asia, *Washington Quarterly* 34(2), 25–43.

Fields, Daryl, Artur Kochnakyan, Takhmina Mukhamedova, Gary Stuggins, and John Besant-Jones (2013): *Tajikistan's Winter Energy Crisis: Electricity Supply and Demand Alternatives*, World Bank: Washington, DC.

Frankel, Jeffrey (2010): The Natural Resource Curse: A Survey, *NBER Working Paper 15836*, National Bureau of Economic Research: Cambridge, MA.

French, Kristen (2014): Kumtor Gold Mine Threatens Central Asian Glaciers and Water, *Glacier Hub,* December 23, http://glacierhub.org/author/kristenfrench/.

Fumagalli, Matteo (2015): The Kumtor Gold Mine and the Rise of Resource Nationalism in Kyrgyzstan, *Central Asia Economic Papers No. 16*, George Washington University: Washington, DC.

Fumagalli, Matteo (2016): *State Violence and Popular Resistance in Uzbekistan*, Routledge: London.

Gang, Ira, Kseniia Gatskova, John Landon-Lane, and Myeong-Su Yun (2017): Vulnerability to Poverty: Tajikistan during and after the Global Financial Crisis, *Inha University IBER Working Paper 2017–12*, Incheon, South Korea.

Ganiev, Bahodir, and Yuliy Yusupov (2012): Uzbekistan: Trade Regime and Recent Trade Developments, *University of Central Asia Institute of Public Policy and Administration, Working Paper No. 4*, Bishkek.

Garcia, David (2006): *Le Pays où Bouygues est Roi*, Éditions Danger Public: Paris.

Gelb, Alan, and Associates (1988): *Oil Windfalls: Blessing or Curse?*, Oxford University Press: New York.

Gemayel, Edward, and David Grigorian (2005): How Tight Is Too Tight? A Look at Welfare Implications of Distortionary Policies in Uzbekistan, *IMF Working Paper 05/239*, International Monetary Fund: Washington, DC.

Gleason, Gregory (1997): *The New Central Asian States*, Westview Press: Boulder, CO.

Gleason, Gregory (2003): *Markets and Politics in Central Asia*. Routledge: London.

Gleason, Gregory (2011): Natural Gas and Authoritarianism in Turkmenistan, in Indra Overland, Heidi Kjaernet, and Andrea Kendall-Taylor, eds., *Caspian Energy Politics: Azerbaijan, Kazakhstan and Turkmenistan*, Routledge: London, 78–90.

Global Witness (2006): *It's a Gas; Funny Business in the Turkmen-Ukraine Gas Trade*, Global Witness: London.

Global Witness (2010): *Risky Business: Kazakhstan, Kazakhmys Plc and the London Stock Exchange*, Global Witness: London.

Goletti, Francesco, and Philippe Chabot (2000): Food Policy Research for Improving the Reform of Agricultural Input and Output Markets in Central Asia, in Suresh Babu and Alisher Tashmatov, eds., *Food Policy Reforms in Central Asia*, International Food Policy Research Institute: Washington, DC, 45–69.

Golub, Stephen, and Stephanie Kestelman (2015): *Uzbekistan's Cotton Value Chain*, report to UNCTAD, available at https://www.swarthmore.edu/sites/default/files/assets/documents/user_profiles/sgolub1/LLDCSUzbekistanCotton-final.pdf.

Gorvett, Zaria (2017): The Deadly Germ Warfare Island Abandoned by the Soviets, *BBC*, September 28, http://www.bbc.com/future/story/20170926-the-deadly-germ-warfare-island-abandoned-by-the-soviets.

Grafe, Clemens, Martin Raiser, and Toshiaki Sakatsume (2005): Beyond Borders: Reconsidering Regional Trade in Central Asia, *EBRD Working Paper 95*, Eurpean Bank for Reconstruction and Development: London.

Gray, Cheryl, Joel Hellman, and Randi Ryterman (2004): *Anticorruption in Transition 2: Corruption in Enterprise—State Interactions in Europe and Central Asia 1999–2002*, World Bank: Washington, DC.

Gray, John (2000): Kazakhstan: A Review of Farm Restructuring, *World Bank Technical Paper No. 458*, World Bank: Washington, DC.

Grigoriou, Christopher (2007): Landlockedness, Infrastructure and Trade: New Estimates for Central Asian Countries, *World Bank Policy Research Working Paper 4335*, World Bank: Washington, DC.

Gullette, David, and Asel Kalybekova (2014): *Agreement under Pressure: Gold Mining and Protests in the Kyrgyz Republic*, Friedrich Ebert Stiftung: Berlin

Heathershaw, John (2013): Tajikistan amidst Globalization: State Failure or State Transformation, in John Heathershaw and Edmund Herzig, eds., *The Transformation of Tajikistan: The Sources of Statehood*, Routledge: London, 177–98.

Hegay, Sergey (2013): Diversity of Beans Grown in Kyrgyzstan and Marker-Aided Breeding for Resistance to Bean Common Mosaic Virus and Anthracnose, *Doctoral Thesis No. 2013:35*, Faculty of Landscape Planning, Horticulture and Agricultural Science, Sveriges lantbruksuniversitet, Alnarp, http://pub.epsilon.slu.se/10425/1/hegay_s_130510.pdf.

Hegland, Mary Elaine (2010): Tajik Male Labour Migration and Women Left Behind: Can They Resist Gender and Generational Hierarchies?, *Anthropology of the Middle East* 5(2), 16–35.

Hoff, Karla, and Joseph Stiglitz (2004): After the Big Bang? Obstacles to the Emergence of the Rule of Law in Post-Communist Societies, *American Economic Review* 94(3), 753–63.

Hofman, Irna, and Oane Visser (2014): Geographies of Transition: The Political and Geographical Factors of Agrarian Change in Tajikistan, *IAMO Discussion Paper 151*, Leibniz Institute of Agricultural Development in Transition Economies: Halle, Germany.

Horák, Slavomir (2013): Educational Reforms in Turkmenistan: Good Framework, Bad Content? *Central Asia Policy Brief No. 11*, Central Asia Program, Elliott School of International Affairs, George Washington University: Washington, DC.

Horton, M., H. Samiei, N. Epstein, and K. Ross (2016): *Exchange Rate Developments and Policies in the Caucasus and Central Asia*, International Monetary Fund: Washington, DC.

Human Rights Watch (2005): "Bullets Were Falling like Rain," The Andijan Massacre, May 13, 2005, *Human Rights Watch Report Vol. 17, No. 5(D)*, https://www.hrw.org/reports/2005/uzbekistan0605/uzbekistan0605.pdf.

Hurley, John, Scott Morris, and Gailyn Portelance (2018): Examining the Debt Implications of the Belt and Road Initiative from a Policy Perspective, *CGD Policy Paper 121*, Center for Global Development, Washington, DC.

ICG (2004): The Failure of Reform in Uzbekistan: Ways Forward for the International Community, *ICG Asia Report No. 76*, International Crisis Group: Osh and Brussels.

ICG (2005): The Curse of Cotton: Central Asia's Destructive Monoculture, *ICG Asia Report No. 93*, International Crisis Group: Bishkek and Brussels.

ICG (2009): Tajikistan: On the Road to Failure, *ICG Asia Report No. 162*, International Crisis Group: Bishkek and Brussels.

ICG (2013): Kazakhstan: Waiting for Change, *ICG Asia Report No. 250*, International Crisis Group: Bishkek and Brussels.

ICG (2014): Kyrgyzstan: An Uncertain Trajectory, *Crisis Group Europe and Central Asia Briefing No. 76*, September, International Crisis Group: Bishkek and Brussels.

ICG (2015): Kyrgyzstan: Widening Ethnic Divisions in the South, *ICG Asia Report No. 222*, International Crisis Group: Bishkek and Brussels.

ICG (2016): Reform or Repeat? *Crisis Group Europe and Central Asia Briefing No. 84*, December, International Crisis Group: Bishkek and Brussels.

ILO (2010): *Migration and Development in Tajikistan—Emigration, Return and Diaspora*, International Labour Organization: Moscow.

IMF (1992): *Common Issues and Interrepublic Relations in the Former USSR*, International Monetary Fund: Washington, DC.

Isakova, Asel, and Alexander Plekhanov (2012): Customs Union and Kazakhstan's Imports, *CASE Research Network Studies and Analyses No. 442*, Center for Social and Economic Research: Warsaw.

Isakova, Asel, Zsoka Koczan, and Alexander Plekhanov (2013): How Much Do Tariffs Matter? Evidence from the Customs Union of Belarus, Kazakhstan, and Russia, *Working Paper No. 154*, European Bank for Reconstruction and Development: London.

Ishankulov, Nozin (2015): Somoni Devaluation: An Assessment of Measures Taken by the National Bank of Tajikistan, *Central Asia Economic Papers No. 15*, Elliott School of International Affairs: George Washington University.

Islamov, Bakhtior (2001): *The Central Asian States Ten Years After: How to Overcome Traps of Development, Transformation and Globalisation?*, Maruzen: Tokyo.

Itoh, Shoichi (2017): Sino-Russian Energy Relations in Northeast Asia and Beyond: Oil, Natural Gas, and Nuclear Power, in *Japan and the Sino-Russian Entente: The Future of Major-Power Relations in Northeast Asia*, *NBR Special Report #64*, National Bureau of Asian Research: Seattle, WA, 29–41.

Ives, Mike (2011): *Saving Ancient Walnut Forests in the Valleys of Central Asia*, http://e360.yale.edu/feature/saving_ancient_walnut_forests_in_the_valleys_of_central_asia/2440/.

Jandosov, Oraz, and Lyaziza Sabyrova (2011): Indicative Tariff Protection Level in Kazakhstan: Before and After the Customs Union (Part 1), *RAKURS Discussion Paper 5.3*, RAKURS Center for Economic Analysis: Almaty.

Jandosov, Oraz, Lyaziza Sabyrova, and Roman Mogilevsky (2010): Effectiveness of the Fiscal Anti-Crisis Package of the Government of Kazakhstan in 2009. Part 1: Object, Amounts, Beneficiaries, *Macroeconomic Notes, N1.6 and N8.2*, RAKURS Center for Economic Analysis: Almaty.

Jenish, Nurbek (2014): Export-Driven SME Development in Kyrgyzstan: The Garment Manufacturing Sector, *Institute of Public Policy and Administration Working Paper No. 26*, University of Central Asia: Bishkek.

Jones Luong, Pauline (2002): *Institutional Change and Political Continuity*, Cambridge University Press: New York.

Jones Luong, Pauline (2003): *The Transformation of Central Asia: States and Societies from Soviet Rule to Independence*, Cornell University Press: Ithaca, NY.

Jones Luong, Pauline, and Erika Weinthal (2001): Prelude to the Resource Curse: Explaining Oil and Gas Development Strategies in the Soviet Successor States and Beyond, *Comparative Political Studies* 34(4), 367–99.

Jones Luong, Pauline, and Erika Weinthal (2010): *Oil Is Not a Curse: Ownership Structure and Institutions in Soviet Successor States*, Cambridge University Press: Cambridge, UK.

Kalyuzhnova, Yelena (1998): *The Kazakstani Economy: Independence and Transition*, Macmillan: Basingstoke, UK.

Kalyuzhnova, Yelena (2008): *Economics of the Caspian Oil and Gas Wealth: Companies, Governments, Policies*, Palgrave Macmillan: Basingstoke, UK.

Kalyuzhnova, Yelena (2011): The National Fund of the Republic of Kazakhstan (NFRK): From Accumulation to Stress-Test to Global Future, *Energy Policy* 39(10), 6650–57.

Kalyuzhnova, Yelena, and Michael Kaser (2006): Prudential Management of Hydrocarbon Revenues in Resource-Rich Transition Economies, *Post-Communist Economies* 18(2), 167–87.

Kalyuzhnova, Yelena, and Christian Nygaard (2009): Resource Nationalism and Credit Growth in FSU Countries, *Energy Policy* 37(11), 4700–10.

Kalyuzhnova, Yelena, and Christian Nygaard (2011): Special Vehicles of State Intervention in Russia and Kazakhstan, *Comparative Economic Studies* 53(1), 57–77.

Kalyuzhnova, Yelena, Christian Nygaard, Yerengaip Omarov, and Abdizhapar Saparbayev (2016): *Local Content Policies in Resource-Rich Countries*, Palgrave Macmillan: London.

Kalyuzhnova, Yelena, and Richard Pomfret, eds. (2018): *Sustainable Energy in Kazakhstan: Moving to Cleaner Energy in a Resource-Rich Country*, Routledge: London.

Kaminski, Bartlomiej, and Gaël Raballand (2009): Entrepôt for Chinese Consumer Goods in Central Asia: Re-Exports through Kyrgyzstan—A Statistical Puzzle, *Eurasian Geography and Economics* 50, 581–90.

Kaminski, Bartlomiej, and Saumya Mitra (2010): *Skeins of Silk: Borderless Bazaars and Border Trade in Central Asia*, Washington, DC: World Bank.

Kaminski, Bartlomiej, and Saumya Mitra (2012): *Borderless Bazaars and Regional Integration in Central Asia: Emerging Patterns of Trade and Cross-Border Cooperation*, Washington, DC: World Bank.

Kandiyoti, Deniz (2009): *Invisible to the World: The Dynamics of Forced Child Labour in the Cotton Sector of Uzbekistan*, School of Oriental and African Studies (SOAS), London.

Kapparov, Kassymkhan (2016): Invisible Pubic Debt: The Case of Kazakhstan, *Central Asia Economic Paper*, Elliott School of International Affairs, George Washington University: Washington, DC.

Kasperson, Jeanne, Roger Kasperson, and B. L. Turner (1995): *The Aral Sea Basin: A Man-Made Environmental Catastrophe*, Kluwer Academic Publishers: Dordrecht.

Kassam, Shinan (2011): One Explanation of Why Farmers Produce Cotton Collectively in Post-Soviet Tajikistan, PhD thesis in Resource Management and Environmental Studies, University of British Columbia: Canada, https://circle.ubc.ca/bitstream/handle/2429/36114/ubc_2011_fall_kassam_shinan.pdf?sequence=7.

Kassenova, Nargis (2009): China as an Emerging Donor in Tajikistan and Kyrgyzstan, *Russie.Nei. Visions No. 36*, Russia/NIS Center, IFRI: Paris.

Keller, Shoshana (2015): The Puzzle of Manual Harvest in Uzbekistan: Economics, Status and Labour in the Khrushchev Era, *Central Asian Survey* 34(3), 296–309.

Kennedy, Ryan, and Adilzhan Nurmakov (2010): Resource Nationalism Trends in Kazakhstan, 2004–2009, *Working Paper of RUSSCASP—Russian and Caspian Energy Developments and Their Implications for Norway and Norwegian Actors*, Fridtjof Nansen Institute, Norwegian Institute of International Affairs and Econ Pöyry.

Kerven, Carol, Sarah Robinson, Roy Behnke, Kanysh Kushenov, and E. J. Milner-Gulland (2016): A Pastoral Frontier: From Chaos to Capitalism and the Re-Colonisation of the Kazakh Rangelands, *Journal of Arid Environments* 127, 106–19.

Khan, Azizur Rahman (2007): The Land System, Agriculture and Poverty in Uzbekistan, in A. Haroon Akram-Lodhi, Saturnino Borras Jr., and Cristobal Kay, eds., *Land, Poverty and Livelihoods in an Era of Globalization*, Routledge: London.

Khasanova, Nariya (2014): Revisiting Water Issues in Central Asia: Shifting from Regional Approach to National Solutions, *The Central Asia Fellowship Papers No. 6*, Central Asia Program, George Washington University: Washington, DC.

Khitakhunov, Azimzhan, Bulat Mukhamediyev, and Richard Pomfret (2017): Eurasian Economic Union: Present and Future Perspectives, *Economic Change and Restructuring* 50(1), 59–77.

Kolstø, Pal (2004): The Price of Stability: Kazakhstani Control Mechanisms under Conditions of Cultural and Demographic Bipolarity, in Yaacov Ro'I, ed., *Democracy and Pluralism in Muslim Eurasia*, Frank Cass: London, 165–85.

Krueger, Anne, Maurice Schiff, and Alberto Valdes (1988): Agricultural Incentives in Developing Countries: Measuring the Effect of Sectoral and Economywide Policies, *World Bank Economic Review* 2(3), 255–71.

Krueger, Anne, Maurice Schiff and Alberto Valdes, eds. (1991–92): *The Political Economy of Agricultural Pricing Policies, 5 Vols.*, Johns Hopkins University Press: Baltimore, MD.

Kucera, Joshua, (2012): The Great Caspian Arms Race, *Foreign Policy*, June 22, http://foreign policy.com/2012/06/22/the-great-caspian-arms-race/.

Kuchins, Andrew, Jeffrey Mankoff, and Oliver Backes (2015): *Central Asia in a Reconnecting Eurasia: Turkmenistan's Evolving Foreign Economic and Security Interests*, Center for Strategic and International Studies, Rowman and Littlefield: Lanham, MD.

Laruelle, Marlène, Jean-François Huchet, Sébastien Peyrouse, and Bayram Balci (2010): *China and India in Central Asia: A New "Great Game?"*, Palgrave Macmillan: New York.

Laruelle, Marlène, and Sébastien Peyrouse (2009): *China as a Neighbor: Central Asian Perspectives and Strategies*, Central Asia-Caucasus Institute Silk Road Studies Program: Washington, DC.

Laruelle, Marlène, and Sébastien Peyrouse (2012): Regional Organisations in Central Asia: Patterns of Interaction, Dilemmas of Efficiency, *University of Central Asia Institute of Public Policy and Administration Working Paper No. 10*.

Lerman, Zvi (2008): Agricultural Development in Central Asia: A Survey of Uzbekistan 2007–2008, *Eurasian Geography and Economics* 49(4), 481–505.

Lerman, Zvi, and Karen Brooks (1998): Land Reform in Turkmenistan, in Stephen K. Wegren, ed., *Land Reform in the Former Soviet Union and Eastern Europe*, Routledge: London, 162–85.

Lerman, Zvi, and David Sedik (2008): The Economic Effects of Land Reform in Tajikistan, *FAO*

Regional Office for Europe and Central Asia Policy Studies on Rural Transition No. 2008-1, Food and Agricultural Organization of the United Nations: Rome.

Lewis, David (2008): *The Temptations of Tyranny in Central Asia*, Columbia University Press: New York.

Lewis, Robert, ed. (1992): *Geographic Perspectives on Soviet Central Asia*, Routledge: London.

Li, Yuan, Kierstin Bolton, and Theo Westphal (2016): The Effect of the New Silk Road Railways on Aggregate Trade Volumes between China and Europe, *Institute of East Asia Studies Working Paper No.109*, Universität Duisburg Essen: Germany.

Libman, Alexander, and Evgeny Vinokurov (2012): *Holding-Together Regionalism: Twenty Years of Post-Soviet Integration*, Palgrave Macmillan: Basingstoke UK.

Libman, Alexander, and Evgeny Vinokurov (2018): Autocracies and Regional Integration: The Eurasian Case, *Post-Communist Economies*, April, 1–31.

Lillis, Joanna (2017): Uzbekistan: Without Forced Labor, Who'll Pick the Cotton? *Eurasianet*, October 31.

Linn, Johannes (2004): *Economic (Dis)Integration Matters: The Soviet Collapse Revisited*, Brookings Institution: Washington, DC.

Lioubimtseva, Elena, and Geoffrey Hennebry (2012): Grain Production Trends in Russia, Ukraine and Kazakhstan: New Opportunities in an Increasingly Unstable World? *Frontiers of Earth Science* 6(2), 157–66, http://dx.doi.org/10.1007/s11707-012-0318-y.

Liu Zhenya (2014): Ultra-High Voltage Transmission Can Break China's Cycle of Energy Dependence, *Forbes*, September 18.

Lubin, Nancy (1999): Calming the Ferghana Valley: Development and Dialogue in the Heart of Central Asia, *Preventive Action Reports. Volume 4*, Century Foundation Press: New York.

MacDonald, Stephen (2012): Economic Policy and Cotton in Uzbekistan, *Report CWS-12h-01*, Economic Research Service, United States Department of Agriculture: Washington, DC.

MacDonald, Stephen, Stephen Golub, Stephanie Kestelman, Mesbah Motamed, and Ralph Seeley (2015): Reforming Uzbekistan's Cotton Sector: Organization, Pricing and Labor Rights, paper presented at the Central Eurasian Studies Society annual meetings, Washington, DC, October 15–18.

Marat, Erica (2015): Global Money Laundering and Its Domestic Political Consequences in Kyrgyzstan, *Central Asian Survey* 34(1), 46–56.

Marat, Erica (2016): Post-Violence Regime Survival and Expansion in Kazakhstan and Tajikistan, *Central Asian Survey* 35(4), 531–48.

Markowitz, Lawrence (2013): *State Erosion: Unlootable Resources and Unruly Elites in Central Asia*, Cornell University Press: Ithaca, NY.

Martius, Christopher, Inna Rudenko, John Lamers, and P.L.G.Viek (2011): *Cotton, Water, Salts, and Soums: Economic and Ecological Restructuring in Khorezm, Uzbekistan*, Springer Verlag: Dordrecht.

McGlinchey, Eric (2011a): *Chaos, Violence, Dynasty: Politics and Islam in Central Asia*, University of Pittsburgh Press: Pittsburgh, PA.

McGlinchey, Eric (2011b): Exploring Regime Instability and Ethnic Violence in Kyrgyzstan, *Asia Policy* 12, 79–98, National Bureau of Asian Research: Seattle, WA.

McMann, Kelly (2014): *Corruption as a Last Resort: Adapting to the Market in Central Asia*, Cornell University Press: Ithaca, NY.

Megoran, Nick, Gaël Raballand, and Jerome Bouyjou (2005): Performance, Representation and the Economics of Border Control in Uzbekistan, *Geopolitics* 10, 712–40.

Menga, Filippo (2015): Building a Nation through a Dam: The Case of Rogun in Tajikistan, *Nationalities Papers* 43(3), 479–94.

Mercer-Blackman, Valerie, and Anna Unigovskaya (2000): Compliance with IMF Program Indicators and Growth in Transition Economies, *IMF Working Paper WP/00/47*, International Monetary Fund: Washington, DC.

Meurs, Hendrik (2015): Staging Legitimacy: Mechanisms for Power Retention in Turkmenistan, in Institut für Friedensforschung und Sicherheitspolitik an der Universität Hamburg, ed., *OSCE Yearbook 2015*, Nomos Verlagsgesellschaft: Baden Baden: Germany, 127–39.

Mihalka, Michael (2008): Should an Unholy Cabal of German Greens and Industrialists Finance a Resurgent Russia? Natural Gas, Central Asia and Europe after the Georgian War, *China and Eurasia Forum Quarterly* 6(3), 129–40.

Milanovic, Branko (1998): *Income, Inequality, and Poverty during the Transition from Planned to Market Economy*, World Bank: Washington, DC.

Mirzoeva, Viloyat (2009): Gender Issues in Land Reform in Tajikistan, *Economics and Rural Development* 5(2), 23–29.

Mogilevskii, Roman (2012a): Trends and Patterns in Foreign Trade of Central Asian Countries, *Institute of Public Policy Working Paper No. 1/2012*, University of Central Asia: Bishkek.

Mogilevskii, Roman (2012b): Re-Export Activities in Kyrgyzstan: Issues and Prospects, *University of Central Asia Institute of Public Policy and Administration, Working Paper No. 9*, Bishkek.

Mogilevskii, Roman (2012c): Customs Union of Belarus, Kazakhstan and Russia: Trade Creation and Trade Diversion in Central Asia in 2010–2011, *University of Central Asia Institute of Public Policy and Administration, Working Paper No. 12*, Bishkek.

Mogilevskii, Roman (2017): Inequality in North and Central Asia, paper presented at UN-ESCAP Expert Group Meeting on Inequality in North and Central Asia, Almaty, October 25.

Mogilevskii, Roman, Nazgul Abdrazakova, Aida Bolotbekova, Saule Chalbasova, Shoola Dzhumaeva, and Kanat Tikeleyev (2015): The Outcomes of 25 Years of Agricultural Reforms in Kyrgyzstan, *IAMO Discussion Paper No. 162*, Leibniz Institute of Agricultural Development in Central and Eastern Europe: Halle, Germany.

Mogilevskii, Roman, Nazgul Abdrazakova, and Saule Chalbasova (2015): The Economic Impact of Kumtor Gold Mine on the Economic and Social Development of the Kyrgyz Republic, *University of Central Asia Institute of Public Policy and Administration, Working Paper No. 32*, Bishkek.

Mogilevsky, Roman, and Rafkat Hasanov (2004): Economic Growth in Kyrgyzstan, in Gur Ofer and Richard Pomfret, eds. (2004): *The Economic Prospects of the CIS—Sources of Long Term Growth since 1991*, Edward Elgar: Cheltenham, UK, 224–48.

Mogilevskii, Roman, James Thurlow, and Adeline Yeh (2018): Kyrgyzstan's Accession to the Eurasian Economic Union: Measuring Economy-Wide Impacts and Uncertainties, *University of Central Asia Institute of Public Policy and Administration, Working Paper No. 44*, Bishkek.

Moné, Christopher, Aaron Smith, Ben Maples, and Maureen Hand (2015): 2013 Cost of Wind Energy Review, *National Renewable Energy Laboratory Technical Report NREL/TP-5000-63267*, http://www.nrel.gov/docs/fy15osti/63267.pdf.

Morrison, Alexander (2014): Introduction: Killing the Cotton Canard and Getting Rid of the Great Game: Rewriting the Russian Conquest of Central Asia, 1814–1895, *Central Asian Survey* 33(2), 131–42.

Mukhamedova, Nozilakhon, and Kai Wegerich (2014): Land Reforms and Feminization of Agricultural Labor in Sughd Province, Tajikistan, *IWMI Research Report 157*, International Water Management Institute: Sri Lanka.

Muradov, Bakhodyr, and Alisher Ilkhamov (2014): Uzbekistan's Cotton Sector: Financial Flows and Distribution of Resources, *Open Society Eurasia Program Working Paper*, New York.

Murzakulova, Asel, and Irène Mestre (2016): Natural Resource Dynamics in Border Communities of Kyrgyzstan and Tajikistan, *Research Report of the Mountain Societies Research Institute*, Graduate School of Development, University of Central Asia: Bishkek.

Najman, Boris, Richard Pomfret, and Gaël Raballand, eds. (2008): *The Economics and Politics of Oil in the Caspian Basin: The Redistribution of Oil Revenues in Azerbaijan and Central Asia*, Routledge: Abingdon, UK.

Nakaya, Sumie (2009): Aid and Transition from a War Economy to an Oligarchy in Post-War Tajikistan, *Central Asian Survey* 28(3), 259–73.

Nazarova, B., S. Saidkarimova, and Sh. Obloqulova (2015): Education Development in Uzbekistan, *Voice of Research* 3(4), 43–44.

Nichol, Jim (2014): Central Asia: Regional Developments and Implications for US Interests, *Congressional Research Service Report 7–5700 RL33458*, https://fas.org/sgp/crs/row/RL33458.pdf.

Nove, Alec (1992): *An Economic History of the USSR, 1917–1991*, Final edition, Penguin.

Novokmet, Filip, Thomas Piketty, and Gabriel Zucman (2017): From Soviets to Oligarchs: Inequality and Property in Russia 1905–2016, *WID.world Working Paper Series No. 2017/09*, World Wealth and Income Database.

Nurmakov, Adil (2010): Resource Nationalism in Kazakhstan's Petroleum Sector: Curse or Blessing?, in Indra Overland, Heidi Kjaernet, and Andrea Kendall-Taylor, eds., *Caspian Energy Politics: Azerbaijan, Kazakhstan and Turkmenistan*. Routledge: London, 20–37.

Nurusheva, Dinara (2017): Improving Governance in Kazakhstan's Mining Towns, *CAP Papers 192*, Central Asia Program, George Washington University: Washington, DC.

Odling-Smee, John, and Gonzalo Pastor (2002): The IMF and the Ruble Zone, *Comparative Economic Studies* 44(4), 3–29.

OECD (2013): *Review of Agricultural Policies, Kazakhstan 2013*, Organisation for Economic Co-operation and Development: Paris.

O'Hara, Sarah (2000): Lessons from the Past: Water Management in Central Asia, *Journal of Water Policy* 2, 365–84.

O'Hara, Sarah, and Tim Hannan (1999): Irrigation and Water Management in Turkmenistan: Past Systems, Present Problems and Future Scenarios, *Europe-Asia Studies* 51(1), 21–41.

Ölcer, Dilan (2009): Extracting the Maximum from the EITI, *OECD Development Centre Working Paper No. 276*, Organisation for Economic Co-operation and Development: Paris.

Olcott, Martha Brill (2002): *Kazakhstan: A Faint-hearted Democracy*. Carnegie Endowment for International Peace: Washington, DC.

Olcott, Martha Brill (2007a): *Kazmunaigaz: Kazakhstan's National Oil and Gas Company*, James Baker III Institute for Public Policy, Rice University: Houston, TX.

Olcott, Martha Brill (2007b): Uzbekistan: A Decaying Dictatorship Withdrawn from the West, in Robert Rotberg, ed., *Worst of the Worst: Dealing with Repressive and Rogue Nations*, Brookings Institution: Washington, DC, 250–68.

Olimov, Ulugbek, and Yadgar Fayzullaev (2011): Assessing Development Strategies to Achieve the MDGs in the Republic of Uzbekistan, United Nations Department for Social and Economic Affairs (DPAD/UN-DESA): New York.

Paoli, Letizia, Irina Rabkov, Victoria A. Greenfield, and Peter Reuter (2007): Tajikistan: The Rise of a Narco-State, *Journal of Drug Issues* 37(4), 951–80.

Pastor, Gonzalo, and Ron van Rooden (2000): Turkmenistan—The Burden of Current Agricultural Policies, *IMF Working Paper WP/00/98*. International Monetary Fund: Washington, DC.

Patrucic, Miranda, Vlad Lavrov, and Ilya Lozovsky (2017): Kazakhstan's Secret Billionaires, Organized Crime and Corruption Reporting Project (OCCRP), posted November 5, https://www.occrp.org/en/paradisepapers/kazakhstans-secret-billionaires.

Petrick, Martin, Duren Oshakbayev, Regina Taitukova, and Nodir Djanibekov (2017): The Return of the Regulator: Kazakhstan's Cotton Reforms since Independence, *Central Asian Survey* 36(4), 430–52.

Petrick, Martin, and Richard Pomfret (2018): Agricultural and Rural Policies in Kazakhstan, in T. Johnson and W. Meyers, eds., *Handbook on International Food and Agricultural Policy Volume I: Policies for Agricultural Markets and Rural Economic Activity*, World Scientific Publishing Company: Singapore, 461–82.

Peyrouse, Sébastien (2009): The Multiple Paradoxes of the Agriculture Issue in Central Asia, *EUCAM Working Paper No. 6*, available at SSRN: https://ssrn.com/abstract=1603907 or http://dx.doi.org/10.2139/ssrn.1603907.

Peyrouse, Sébastien (2010): Berdymukhammedov's Turkmenistan: A Modest Shift in Domestic and Social Policies, *China and Eurasia Forum Quarterly* 8(3), 47–66.

Peyrouse, Sébastien (2012): *Turkmenistan: Strategies of Power, Dilemmas of Development*, M. E. Sharpe: Armonk, NY.

Peyrouse, Sébastien (2016): Stakes and Perspectives of the Portable Telephones Market in Central Asia, *CAP Papers 176*, Central Asia Program, George Washington University: Washington, DC.

Pomfret, Richard (1995): *The Economies of Central Asia*, Princeton University Press: Princeton, NJ.

Pomfret, Richard (1996): *Asian Economies in Transition,* Edward Elgar: Cheltenham, UK.

Pomfret, Richard (1999): Living Standards in Central Asia, *MOCT-MOST Economic Policy in Transitional Economies* 9(4), 395–421.

Pomfret, Richard (2000b): Agrarian Reform in Uzbekistan: Why Has the Chinese Model Failed to Deliver? *Economic Development and Cultural Change* 48(2), 269–84.

Pomfret, Richard (2000c): The Uzbek Model of Economic Development 1991–9, *Economics of Transition* 8(3), 733–48.

Pomfret, Richard (2001a): Turkmenistan: From Communism to Nationalism by Gradual Economic Reform, *MOCT-MOST (Economic Policy in Transitional Economies)* 11(2), 155–66.

Pomfret, Richard (2001b): *The Economics of Regional Trading Arrangements*, Oxford University Press: Oxford.

Pomfret, Richard (2002a): State-Directed Diffusion of Technology: The Mechanization of Cotton-Harvesting in Soviet Central Asia, *Journal of Economic History* 62(1), 170–88.

Pomfret, Richard (2002b): *Constructing a Market Economy: Diverse Paths from Central Planning in Asia and Europe.* Edward Elgar: Cheltenham, UK.

Pomfret, Richard (2002c): The IMF and the Ruble Zone, *Comparative Economic Studies* 44(4), 37–48.

Pomfret, Richard (2003): Economic Performance in Central Asia since 1991: Macro and Micro Evidence, *Comparative Economic Studies* 45 (4), 442–65.

Pomfret, Richard (2004): Structural Reform in the CIS-7 Countries, in Clinton Shiells and Sarosh Sattar, eds., *The Low-Income Countries of the Commonwealth of Independent States: Progress and Challenges in Transition*, IMF: Washington, DC, 75–107.

Pomfret, Richard (2005a): Development Lessons for Central Asia, in K. Fukasaku, M. Kawai, M.G. Plummer, and A. Trzeciak-Duval, eds., *The Impact and Coherence of OECD Country Policies on Asian Developing Economies*, Organisation for Economic Co-operation and Development: Paris.

Pomfret, Richard (2005b): Sequencing Trade and Monetary Integration: Issues and Application to Asia, *Journal of Asian Economics* 16(1), 105–24.

Pomfret, Richard (2006): *The Central Asian Economies since Independence*, Princeton University Press: Princeton, NJ.

Pomfret, Richard (2007): Lessons from Kyrgyzstan's WTO Accession for Kazakhstan, Tajikistan and Uzbekistan, *Asia-Pacific Trade and Investment Review* 3(2), 27–46.

Pomfret, Richard (2008): Kazakhstan, in Kym Anderson and Johan Swinnen, eds., *Distortions to Agricultural Incentives in Europe's Transition Economies*, World Bank: Washington, DC, 219–63.

Pomfret, Richard (2011): Exploiting Energy and Mineral Resources in Central Asia, Azerbaijan and Mongolia, *Comparative Economic Studies* 53 (1), 5–33.

Pomfret, Richard (2012): Resource Management and Transition in Central Asia, Azerbaijan and Mongolia, *Journal of Asian Economics* 23(2), 146–56.

Pomfret, Richard (2013): Kazakhstan's Agriculture after Two Decades of Independence, *Central Asia Economic Paper No. 6*, Elliott School of International Affairs: George Washington University.

Pomfret, Richard (2014): The Economics of the Customs Union and Eurasian Union, in S. Fred Starr and Svante Cornell, eds., *Putin's Grand Strategy: The Eurasian Union and Its Discontents*, Central Asia-Caucasus Institute and Silk Road Studies Program: Washington, DC, 49–58.

Pomfret, Richard (2016): Currency Union and Disunion in Europe and the Former Soviet Union, *CESifo Forum* 17(4), 43–47.

Pomfret, Richard (2018): The Eurasian Landbridge: The Role of Service Providers in Linking the Regional Value Chains in East Asia and the European Union, *ERIA Discussion Paper ERIA-DP-FY2018–01*, Economic Research Institute for ASEAN and East Asia, Jakarta, http://www.eria.org/publications/category/discussion-papers.

Pomfret, Richard, and Kathryn Anderson (1997): *Uzbekistan: Welfare Impact of Slow Transition*, United Nations University World Institute for Development Economics Research (UNU/WIDER WP135): Helsinki.

Popov, Vladimir (2013): Economic Miracle of Post-Soviet Space: Why Uzbekistan Managed to Achieve What No Other Post-Soviet State Achieved, *MPRA Paper No .48723*, http://mpra.ub.uni-muenchen.de/48723/.

Punkari, Mikko, Peter Droogers, Walter Immerzeel, Natalia Korhonen, Arthur Lutz, and Ari Vernäläinen (2014): Climate Change and Sustainable Water Management in Central Asia, *ADB Central and West Asia Working Paper No. 5*, Asian Development Bank: Manila.

Raballand, Gaël (2003): Determinants of the Negative Impact of being Landlocked on Trade: An Empirical Investigation through the Central Asian Case, *Comparative Economic Studies* 45(4), 520–36.

Raballand, Gaël, and Agnès Andrésy (2007): Why Should Trade between Central Asia and China Continue to Expand? *Asia Europe Journal* 5(2), 235–52.

Raballand, Gaël, and Ferhat Esen (2007): Economics and Politics of Cross-Border Oil Pipelines— The Case of the Caspian Basin, *Asia Europe Journal* 5, 133–46.

Rama, Martin, and Kinnon Scott (1999): Labor Earnings in One-Company Towns: Theory and Evidence from Kazakhstan, *World Bank Economic Review* 11(1), 185–209.

Rastogi, Cordula, and Jean-François Arvis (2014): *The Eurasian Connection: Supply-Chain Efficiency along the Modern Silk Route through Central Asia*, World Bank: Washington, DC.

REN21 (2015): *Renewables 2015: Global Status Report*, Renewable Energy Policy Network for the 21st Century (Paris), http://www.ren21.net/wp-content/uploads/2015/07/REN12-GSR2015_Onlinebook_low1.pdf.

Revenue Watch Institute (2011): *Sovereign Wealth Funds: New Challenges for the Caspian Countries*, Revenue Watch Institute: Baku.

Roy, Olivier (2000): *The New Central Asia*, New York University Press: New York.

Rozelle, Scott, and Johan Swinnen (2004): Success and Failure of Reforms: Insights from Transition Agriculture, *Journal of Economic Literature* 42 (2), 404–56.

Rudenko, Inna, and John Lamers (2006): The Comparative Advantages of the Present and Future Payment Structure for Agricultural Producers in Uzbekistan, *Central Asian Journal of Management, Economics and Social Research* 5(1–2), 106–25.

Ruseckas, Laurent (1998): Energy and Politics in Central Asia and the Caucasus, *Access Asia Review* 1(2), 41–84, National Bureau of Asian Research: Seattle, WA.

Ruziev, Kobil, Dipak Ghosh, and Sheila Dow (2007): The Uzbek Puzzle Revisited: An Analysis of Economic Performance in Uzbekistan since 1991, *Central Asian Survey* 26(1), 7–30.

Saalman, Lora, ed. (2017): *China-Russia Relations and Regional Dynamics: From Pivots to Peripheral Diplomacy*, Stockholm International Peace Research Institute: Stockholm.

Saavalainen, Tapio, and Joy ten Berge (2006): Quasi-Fiscal Deficits and Energy Conditionality in Selected CIS Countries, *IMF Working Paper 06/43*, IMF: Washington, DC.

Sachs, Jeffrey, and Andrew Warner (1995): Natural Resource Abundance and Economic Growth, *Harvard Institute of Economic Research Discussion Paper 517*, Cambridge, MA.

Safirova, Elena (2012): The Mineral Industry of Uzbekistan, *2010 Minerals Yearbook Uzbekistan*, US Geological Survey, Department of the Interior: Washington, DC, https://minerals.usgs .gov/minerals/pubs/country/2010/myb3-2010-uz.pdf.

Safranchuk, Ivan (2016): Russia in a Reconnecting Eurasia: Foreign Economic and Security Interests, *A Report of the CSIS Russia and Eurasia Program*, Center for Strategic and International Studies, Washington, DC; Rowman and Littlefield: Lanham, MD.

Sagers, Matthew (1999): Turkmenistan's Gas Trade: The Case of Exports to Ukraine, *Post-Soviet Geography and Economics* 40(2), 142–49.

Said, Akhmed (2014): Uzbekistan at a Crossroads: Main Developments, Business Climate, and Political Risks, *Uzbekistan Initiative Papers No. 10*, Central Asia Program, Elliott School of International Affairs, George Washington University: Washington, DC, and Barcelona Centre for International Affairs.

Sejko, Dini (2017): Financing the Belt and Road Initiative: MDBs, SWFs, SOEs and the Long Wait for Private Investors, *APEC Currents*, November, Australian APEC Studies Centre at RMIT: Melbourne.

Sharsheev, Iskender (2016): Analysis of the Main Outcomes of Kyrgyzstan's Membership in EAEU, Central Asian Bureau for Analytical Reporting, http://cabar.asia/en/iskender -sharsheev-analysis-of-the-main-outcomes-of-kyrgyzstan-s-membership-in-eaeu/.

Shepard, Wade (2016): Why the China-Europe "Silk Road" Rail Network Is Growing Fast, *Forbes*, January 28.

Shepotylo, Oleksandr, and David Tarr (2012): Impact of WTO Accession and the Customs Union on the Bound and Applied Tariff Rates of the Russian Federation, *Policy Research Working Paper 6161*, World Bank.

Shishkin, Philip (2013): *Restless Valley: Revolution, Murder, and Intrigue in the Heart of Central Asia*, Yale University Press: New Haven, CT.

Shtaltovna, Anastasiya, and Anna-Katharina Hornidge (2014): A Comparative Study on Cotton Production in Kazakhstan in Kazakhstan and Uzbekistan, Center for Development Research (ZEF), University of Bonn, Germany (ISSN 1864–6638).

Sievers, Eric (2002): Uzbekistan's Mahalla: From Soviet to Absolutist Residential Community Associations, *Journal of International and Comparative Law at Chicago-Kent* 2, 91–158.

Silitski, Vitali (2012): The 2010 Russia-Belarus-Kazakhstan Customs Union A Classic Case of *PRINUZHDENIE K DRUZHBE* (FRIENDSHIP ENFORCEMENT), PONARS Eurasia Policy Memo No. 110, http://www.gwu.edu/~ieresgwu/assets/docs/pepm_110.pdf.

Slay, Ben (2011): Tajikistan and the Tyranny of Statistics, unpublished paper by the Chief Economist of the Regional Bureau for Europe and the Commonwealth of Independent States (RBEC) of the UNDP, February 9.

SOAS (2010): *What Has Changed? Progress in Eliminating the Use of Forced Child Labour in the Cotton Harvests of Uzbekistan and Tajikistan*, Centre of Contemporary Central Asia and the Caucasus, SOAS: London, https://www.soas.ac.uk/cccac/centres-publications/file 64329.pdf.

Sourdin, Patricia, and Richard Pomfret (2012): *Trade Facilitation: Defining, Measuring, Explaining and Reducing the Cost of International Trade*, Edward Elgar: Cheltenham, UK.

Spechler, Martin (1999): Uzbekistan: The Silk Road to Nowhere?, *Contemporary Economic Policy* 18(3), 295–303.

Spechler, Martin, Joachim Ahrens, and Herman Hoen (2017): *State Capitalism in Eurasia*, World Scientific: Singapore.

Spechler, Martin, Kuatbay Bektemirov, Sergei Chepel, and Farrukh Suvankulov (2004): The Uzbek Paradox: Progress without Neo-Liberal Reform, in Gur Ofer and Richard Pomfret, eds. (2004), *The Economic Prospects of the CIS—Sources of Long Term Growth since 1991*, Edward Elgar: Cheltenham, UK, 177–97.

Starr, Frederick (2008): *In Defense of Greater Central Asia*, Central Asia—Caucasus Institute Silk Road Studies Program Policy Paper, September.

Starr, Frederick, ed. (2011): *The Ferghana Valley: The Heart of Central Asia*, M. E. Sharpe: Armonk, NY.

Stronski, Paul (2017): *Turkmenistan at Twenty-Five: The High Price of Authoritarianism*, Carnegie Carnegie Endowment for International Peace, Washington, DC, http://carnegieendowment. org/2017/01/30/turmenistan-at-twenty-five-high-price-ofauthoritarianism-pub-67839.

Swanström, Niklas (2014): Sino–Russian Relations at the Start of the New Millennium in Central Asia and Beyond, *Journal of Contemporary China* 23(87), 480–97.

Swinkels, Rob (2014): *Assessment of Household Energy Deprivation in Tajikistan: Policy Options for Socially Responsible Reform in the Energy Sector*, World Bank: Washington, DC.

Swinkels, Robertus, Ekaterina Romanova, and Evgeny Kochkin (2016): *Assessing the Social Impact of Cotton Harvest Mechanization in Uzbekistan: Final Report*, World Bank: Washington, DC.

Swinnen, Johan, and Scott Rozelle (2006): *From Marx and Mao to the Market: The Economics and Politics of Agricultural Transition*, Oxford University Press: New York.

Tanchum, Micha'el (2013): India's Central Asia Ambitions Outfoxed by China and Russia, *East Asia Forum*, October 12, http://www.eastasiaforum.org.

Tarr, David (1994): How Moving to World Prices Affects the Terms of Trade of 15 Countries of the Former Soviet Union, *Journal of Comparative Economics* 18(1), 1–24.

Taube, Günther, and Jeromin Zettelmeyer (1998): Output Decline and Recovery in Uzbekistan: Past Performance and Future Prospects, *IMF Working Paper WP/98/132*, International Monetary Fund: Washington, DC.

Tilekeyev, Kanat (2013): Productivity Implications of Participation in Export Activities: The Case of Farmers in Talas Oblast of Kyrgyzstan, *Institute of Public Policy and Administration, Working Paper No. 17*, University of Central Asia: Bishkek.

Tilekeyev, Kanat (2014): Micro-, Small and Medium Enterprises in Tajikistan: Drivers of and Barriers to Growth, *Institute of Public Policy and Administration, Working Paper No. 31*, University of Central Asia: Bishkek.

Tilekeyev, Kanat, Rooman Mogilevskii, Nazgul Abdrazakova, and Shoola Dzhumaeva (2018): Production and Exports of Kidney Beans in the Kyrgyz Republic: Value Chain Analysis, *Institute of Public Policy and Administration, Working Paper No. 43*, University of Central Asia: Bishkek.

Toktomushev, Kemel (2015): Regime Security, Base Politics and Rent-Seeking: The Local and

Global Political Economies of the American Air Base in Kyrgyzstan, 2001–2010, *Central Asian Survey* 34(1), 57–77.

Trend (2003): *Impact of Membership of Azerbaijan into World Trade Organisation on the Lives of Poor People: Final Report*, Analytical-Information Agency "Trend" with support from Oxfam, Baku.

Trilling, David (2013): Centerra Gold and Kyrgyzstan: Time for a Marriage Counselor, *Globe and Mail* [Toronto], April 25.

Tsalik, Svetlana, and Robert Ebel (2003): *Caspian Oil Windfalls*, Caspian Oil Revenues Watch, Open Society Institute: New York.

Tumbarello, Patrizia (2005): Regional Integration and WTO Accession: Which Is the Right Sequencing? An Application to the CIS. *IMF Working Paper*, February, International Monetary Fund: Washington, DC.

Umarov, Khojamahmad, and Alexandre Repkine (2004): Tajikistan's Growth Performance: The First Decade of Transition, in Gur Ofer and Richard Pomfret, eds. (2004), *The Economic Prospects of the CIS—Sources of Long Term Growth since 1991*, Edward Elgar, Cheltenham, UK, 198–223.

UNDP (2005): *Central Asia Human Development Report: Bringing Down Barriers: Regional Cooperation for Human Development and Human Security*, UNDP: Bratislava.

UNECA (2016): *Transformative Industrial Policy for Africa*, United Nations Economic Commission for Africa: Addis Ababa.

UNESCO (2015): *UNESCO Science Report 2015: Towards 2030*, United Nations Educational, Scientific and Cultural Organization: Paris.

van Atta, Don (2009): White Gold or Fool's Gold? The Political Economy of Cotton in Tajikistan, *Problems of Post-Communism* 56(2), 16–35.

van der Ploeg, Frederick (2011): Natural Resources: Curse or Blessing? *Journal of Economic Literature* 49(2), 366–420.

Veldwisch, Gert Jan, and Peter Mollinga (2013): Lost in Transition? The Introduction of Water Users Associations in Uzbekistan, *Water International* 38 (6), 758–73.

Venables, Anthony (2016): Using Natural Resources for Development: Why Has It Proven So Difficult?, *Journal of Economic Perspectives* 30(1), 161–84.

Verme, Paolo (2001): *Transition, Recession and Labour Supply*, Ashgate Publishing: Aldershot, UK.

Verme, Paolo (2006): Macroeconomic Policies and Social Unrest in Uzbekistan, *Post-Soviet Affairs* 22(3), 276–88.

Veselov, Fedor, and Alina Fedosova (2015): Cost-Benefit Estimation of the Smart Grid Development for the Russian Unified Power System, *Working Paper WP BRP 49/STI/2015*, National Research University Higher School of Economics: Moscow.

Vinokurov, Evgeny (2017): Eurasian Economic Union: Current State and Preliminary Results, *Russian Journal of Economics* 3(1), 54–70.

Wandel, Jürgen (2009): Agroholdings and Clusters in Kazakhstan's Agro-food Sector, *IAMO Discussion Paper No.126*, Leibniz Institute of Agricultural Development in Central and Eastern Europe: Halle, Germany.

Wandel, Jürgen (2010): The Cluster-Based Development Strategy in Kazakhstan's Agro-Food Sector: A Critical Assessment from an "Austrian" Perspective, *IAMO Discussion Paper No .128*, Leibniz Institute of Agricultural Development in Central and Eastern Europe: Halle, Germany.

Waters, Jonathan (2015): Managing the Energy Transition, in Rajat Nag, Johannes Linn, and Harinder Kohli, eds., *Central Asia 2050: Unleashing the Region's Potential*. Emerging Markets

Forum, Washington, DC. Published in 2017 by Sage Publications, available at https://www
.amazon.com/Central-Asia-2050-Unleashing-Potential-ebook/dp/B071RXY8W3.

Whitlock, Monica (2002): *Beyond the Oxus: The Central Asians.* John Murray: London.

Wiemer, Calla (2000): *PRC Trade with Central Asia, Paper Prepared for the Project Regional Economic Cooperation in Central Asia* (TA No. 58181-REG), Asian Development Bank: Manila.

Wooden, Amanda (2014): Kyrgyzstan's Dark Ages: Framing and the 2010 Hydroelectric Revolution, *Central Asian Survey* 33(4), 463–81.

Wooden, Amanda, and Christoph Stefes, eds. (2009): *The Politics of Transition in Central Asia and
the Caucasus: Enduring Legacies and Emerging Challenges,* Routledge: London.

World Bank (1992): Measuring the Incomes of Economies of the Former Soviet Union, *Policy
Research Working Paper WPS 1057*, World Bank: Washington, DC.

World Bank (2002): *Irrigation in Central Asia: Where to Rehabilitate and Why*, World Bank: Washington, DC.

World Bank (2009): *Bazaars and Trade Integration in CAREC Countries*, report prepared by Saumya Mitra, Bartlomiej Kaminski and Matin Kholmatov, http://documents.worldbank.org/
curated/en/127141468242390723/pdf/504340ESW0WHIT1BazaarsFinal1P112452.pdf.

World Bank (2012): *Assessment of the Costs and Benefits of the Customs Union for Kazakhstan*
(Report No.659777-KZ), World Bank: Washington, DC.

World Bank (2014): *Kyrgyz Republic—The Garment Sector: Impact of Joining the Customs Union
and Options to Increase Competitiveness*, World Bank: Washington, DC, https://openknowl-
edge.worldbank.org/handle/10986/21103.

World Bank (2016a): Kazakhstan: A Long Road to Recovery, *Kazakhstan Economic Update No.
3*, World Bank: Washington, DC.

World Bank (2016b): *Migration and Remittances Factbook 2016*, World Bank: Washington, DC.

WTO (2013): *Trade Policy Review: The Kyrgyz Republic*, World Trade Organization: Geneva.

Yafimava, Katja (2015): European Energy Security and the Role of Russian Gas: Assessing the
Feasibility and the Rationale of Reducing Dependence, *IAI Working Paper 15/54*, Istituto
Affari Internazionali: Rome.

Yahuda, Michael (2017): Japan and Sino-Russian Strategic Partnership, in "Japan and the Sino-
Russian Entente: The Future of Major-Power Relations in Northeast Asia," *NBR Special Report #64*, National Bureau of Asian Research: Seattle, WA, 1–10.

Yalbulganov, Alexander (2014): Anti-Dumping Procedures in the Eurasec Customs Union, *Law
Working Paper WP BRP 35/LAW/2014*, National Research University Higher School of Economics: Moscow.

Yuldasheva, Guli (2013): The Northern Distribution Network and Central Asia, in Andris Sprūds
and Diāna Potjomkina, eds., *Northern Distribution Network: Redefining Partnerships within
NATO and Beyond*, Latvian Institute of International Affairs: Riga, 93–113.

Zabortseva, Yelena (2009): A Structural Approach to Diversification in the Emerging Economy
of Kazakhstan, *International Journal of Economic Policy in Emerging Economies* 2(1), 23–40.

Zettelmeyer, Jeromin (1998): The Uzbek Growth Puzzle, *IMF Working Paper WP/98/133*. International Monetary Fund: Washington, DC.

Zhalimbetova, Roza, and Gregory Gleason (2001): Bridges and Fences: The Eurasian Economic
Community and Policy Harmonization in Eurasia, unpublished paper, University of New
Mexico—shorter version "Eurasian Economic Community Comes into Being," *Central
Asia—Caucasus Analyst*, June 20, 2001, http://www.cacianalyst.org.

Zhang Zhongxiang (2015a): Making China the Transition to a Low-Carbon Economy: Key Challenges and Responses, *CCEP Working Paper 1511*, Australian National University Centre for
Climate Economics and Policy: Canberra.

Zhang Zhongxiang (2015b): Carbon Emissions Trading in China: The Evolution from Pilots to a Nationwide Scheme, *Nota di Lavoro 38.2015*, Fondazione Eni Enrico Mattei: Milan.

Zimnitskaya, Hanna, and James von Geldern (2011): Is the Caspian Sea a Sea and Why Does It Matter?, *Journal of Eurasia Studies* 2, 1–14.

Zinzani, Andrea (2016): Hydraulic Bureaucracies and Irrigation Management Transfer in Uzbekistan: The Case of Samarkand Province, *International Journal of Water Resources Development* 32(2), 232–46.

INDEX

agriculture, 4, 14, 42, 53–62, 79, 215, 265, 266; in Kazakhstan, 80–86, 90, 91n28, 93, 252n; in Kyrgyz Republic, 164, 180; in Tajikistan, 184, 185; in Turkmenistan, 145; in Uzbekistan, 99, 107, 115

aid. *See* official development assistance

Akayev, Askar, 5n, 6, 156, 162, 167, 171–72, 176, 201, 208

Andijan incident, 106, 124, 162, 227, 235, 251; US reactions, 171, 235, 246, 248

Aral Sea, 3, 53, 55, 56, 64, 136, 169, 223–25

Asian Development Bank (ADB), 133, 161n10, 210

Asian Infrastructure Investment Bank (AIIB), 8, 161, 163, 244

Atambayev, Almazbek, 117, 169n, 176n, 177, 238

Bakiyev, Kurmanbek, 167, 168, 169, 171–72, 176, 177, 178, 258

Baku-Tbilisi-Ceyhan (BTC) pipeline. *See* pipelines

beans, 173–4, 278

Belt and Road Initiative. *See* One Belt One Road

Berdymuhamedov, Gurbanguly, 118, 126, 143–47, 150, 152–53

Caspian Sea, 46n, 47, 76, 130, 139, 146, 150, 152n38, 211n, 233, 250, 278; naval arms race, 138, 150n34, 235–36

Central Asia Cooperation Organization (CACO), 210, 217. *See also* Central Asian Economic Community

Central Asian Economic Community (CAEC), 209–10, 211, 217

Central Asia Regional Economic Cooperation (CAREC), 147–48, 210–11, 214, 217, 220, 222n25, 267, 278

Chabahar port, 8, 253, 270

child labor, 56, 62, 96, 119, 124, 135n9

China, 8, 106, 111n25, 117–18, 147, 152, 212–13, 215, 223n28, 230, 231–32, 235, 240–41, 241–45, 264, 272–76; exports to, 107; gas pipeline from Turkmenistan, 46–47, 48, 77, 107, 110, 126, 138, 143, 147, 148–49, 151, 178, 215, 233, 278; imports from, 83n21, 104, 105 164, 172, 173, 177, 237; oil pipeline from Kazakhstan, 47, 76, 233, 254; rail links to Kazakhstan, 221, 254, 266, 267–71, 278; rail link to Uzbekistan, 124; roadbuilding, 180, 187, 222. *See also* One Belt One Road; Shanghai Cooperation Organization

China-Pakistan Economic Corridor, 8, 222, 253, 270

climate change, 64–65, 272–73. *See also* Paris Agreement on Climate Change

coal, 55, 62, 165n18, 183, 185, 242, 272–74, 277; in Kazakhstan, 7, 23, 39, 48, 62, 272

Collective Security Treaty Organization (CSTO), 207, 208, 213, 217, 227–28

Commonwealth of Independent States (CIS), 72n3, 202, 207–9, 215, 217

Corridor Performance Measurement and Monitoring (CPMM), 220–22, 278

cotton, 4, 7, 11–12, 15, 20, 22, 39, 40, 45, 53, 55–62, 98, 104–5, 125–26, 134, 144, 156, 201, 202, 205, 211, 223–25, 242, 279; and delayed reform, 44; in Kazakhstan, 58–59, 61, 80, 82, 83n20, 84; in Kyrgyz Republic, 58, 156; mechanization of harvesting, 62; rent extraction, 50, 54, 57, 58–59, 152, 195; in Tajikistan, 58, 182, 184–87, 190, 1193, 194; in Turkmenistan, 52, 58, 60, 125–38, 145; in Uzbekistan, 58, 60–61, 95–124

data reliability, 20n, 96n, 110, 128, 131, 133, 136

Doing Business indicators, 35, 37, 219

Dordoi bazaar (Bishkek), 105, 173, 174n33, 177, 179, 180n42

A NOTE ON THE TYPE

This book has been composed in Adobe Text and Gotham.
Adobe Text, designed by Robert Slimbach for Adobe,
bridges the gap between fifteenth- and sixteenth-century
calligraphic and eighteenth-century Modern styles.
Gotham, inspired by New York street signs, was designed
by Tobias Frere-Jones for Hoefler & Co.